MEN
FROM
EARTH

Also By Buzz Aldrin

Return To Earth

Also By Malcolm McConnell

Fiction
Matata
Clinton Is Assigned
Just Causes

Nonfiction
Stepping Over
Into The Mouth Of The Cat
The Essence Of Fiction
Challenger: A Major Malfunction

With Carol McConnell
First Crossing
Middle Sea Autumn
The Mediterranean Diet

With Johnny France
Incident At Big Sky

MEN FROM EARTH

Buzz Aldrin

and
Malcolm McConnell

BANTAM BOOKS
NEW YORK · TORONTO · LONDON · SYDNEY · AUCKLAND

MEN FROM EARTH
A BANTAM BOOK/JULY 1989

Produced by Ink Projects.
Designed by Jeffrey L. Ward.

All photos courtesy of NASA except:
Insert page 14, *top*, and page 15, *bottom*,Wide
World Photos; page 16, *top*, copyright © 1969
The New York Times Company.
Reprinted by permission.
Cover photo courtesy of The National Aeronautics
and Space Administration.

Library of Congress Cataloging-in-Publication Data
Aldrin, Buzz.
    Men from earth / Buzz Aldrin, and Malcolm McConnell.
        p.   cm.
    Includes index.
    ISBN 0-553-05374-4
    1. Project Apollo.   2. Space flight to the moon.   I.
McConnell, Malcolm.   II. Title.
Malcolm.   II. Title.
TL789.8.U6A49   1989   89-323
629.45′4—dc19   CIP

Published simultaneously in the United States and Canada

Bantam Books are published by Bantam Books, a division of
Bantam Doubleday Dell Publishing Group, Inc. Its trademark,
consisting of the words "Bantam Books" and the portrayal of
a rooster, is Registered in U.S. Patent and Trademark Office
and in other countries. Marca Registrada. Bantam Books,
666 Fifth Avenue, New York, New York 10103.

To families, friends, and other folks
   who were, are, and will be touched by men from Earth:
The dedicated pursuit of future dreams comes
   at the expense of present comfort
And exposure to greatness, risks, and
   human vulnerabilities.
So have compassion—and share
   in our rewards.

HERE MEN FROM THE PLANET EARTH
FIRST SET FOOT UPON THE MOON
JULY 1969, A.D.
WE CAME IN PEACE FOR ALL MANKIND

—from the plaque left on lunar
module *Eagle, Apollo 11*

Contents

PROLOGUE: LUNAR MODULE EAGLE   xiii

INTRODUCTION: CAPE CANAVERAL   xix

CHAPTER ONE: THE RACE BEGINS   1

CHAPTER TWO: KHRUSHCHEV'S GAMBIT, AMERICA'S RESPONSE   25

CHAPTER THREE: "LEAD-FOOTED MERCURY"   35

CHAPTER FOUR: KENNEDY'S CHALLENGE   51

CHAPTER FIVE: SKIRMISHES   69

CHAPTER SIX: STRATEGY   89

CHAPTER SEVEN: VOSKHOD VERSUS GEMINI   113

CHAPTER EIGHT: GEMINI TRIUMPHANT   135

CHAPTER NINE: YEAR OF DISASTERS   161

CHAPTER TEN: APOLLO RECOVERS   173

CHAPTER ELEVEN: APOLLO TRIUMPHANT   189

CHAPTER TWELVE: THE LAST LAP   205

CHAPTER THIRTEEN: TRANQUILLITY BASE   225

EPILOGUE: VENTURING OUTWARD   247

ACKNOWLEDGMENTS   261

REFERENCES   263

NOTES   273

INDEX   293

MEN
FROM
EARTH

PROLOGUE

LUNAR MODULE *EAGLE*

JULY 20, 1969

As the spacecraft flew backward, Neil and I watched the green digits blink on the small computer screen. We arched westward along the equator of the moon. Through the triangular windows of the lunar module, we could see a chaotic map of endless gray craters.

At this point, there was no sensation of falling. We glided, our faces parallel to the surface. We were near "perilune"—the lowest point on our coasting orbit—10 miles over the silent craters. Soon the computer would initiate the final 12 minutes of the landing attempt, powered descent.

"*Eagle*, Houston," the capcom, Charlie Duke, called from Mission Control, a quarter million miles away. "If you read, you're go for powered descent."

Charlie's voice was barely distinguishable in my headset. Since coming around the limb of the moon from the far side, our voice and data link with Houston had been shaky. Mike Collins, orbiting 50 miles above us in the command module *Columbia*, heard Houston clearly.

"*Eagle*, this is *Columbia*," Mike called, his voice calm. "They just gave you a go for powered descent."

The green digits flashed, announcing PDI. Beneath our feet,

hypergolic propellants sprayed into the combustion chamber, igniting
on contact with each other, spewing a soundless plume of orange flame
into the sunlit vacuum of space. The lunar module slowed as the
computer throttled up the engine from a 10 percent thrust to full power.
The pocked moonscape rolled closer in my window. Four minutes into
the burn, I began to feel the weight in my arms caused by our first
prolonged sag of deceleration, a subtle imitation of gravity. My pressure
boots flexed and my limbs settled inside my suit.

"*Eagle*, Houston. You are go," Charlie Duke announced, his voice
clearer now through the hissing static. "Take it all at four minutes.
Roger, you are go to continue powered descent...."

The horizon moved across my window and settled at the bottom as
the LM completed its slow rotation on its vertical axis. A gradual pitch-
over would bring the lander to its final descent posture, with our feet
toward the lunar surface. Now we could see Earth, a partial disk of blue,
white, and brown hanging far above the serrated horizon of the moon.

While the engine fired, the pitch-over continued and Earth slipped
past the top of my window. My instrument panel was now alive with
winking data. We passed through 35,000 feet. For the first time we felt
the rapid descent.

At that moment, an alarm we weren't prepared for flashed on the top
row of our computer data screen. "Twelve-oh-two," I called, unable to
control the tension in my voice. "Twelve-oh-two."

Neil and I exchanged quizzical, troubled looks. We were descending
through 33,000 feet, and our primary computer had just signaled
difficulty coping with the cascade of data coming in from the landing
radar. The data screen went blank. All we could do was wait for the
experts in Mission Control to decipher this alarm, but they were more
than two light seconds away, which meant their reaction to the
telemetry data on the alarm would not be immediate. To me the alarm
was ominous. Either the programming was incapable of managing the
landing, or there was a hardware problem. In either case, the potential
for catastrophe was obvious, because our eventual ascent from the
surface in 24 hours and our rendezvous with *Columbia* would place even
greater demands on that computer. Still, we coasted toward the moon.

"Give us the reading on the twelve-oh-two program alarm," Neil
called, voicing the tension we shared.

We both eyed the large red ABORT STAGE button on the panel. Hitting it would instantly blast the LM's bulbous upper stage back toward *Columbia*, ending man's first attempt to reach the moon.

"Roger," Charlie called, the strain in his voice obvious. "We've got...we're go on that alarm." Charlie's transmission shredded with static again.

I felt the immense gulf separating that brightly lit control room in Houston and the dim cabin of the LM. Neil nodded to me through his helmet, his eyes somber in the glow of the panel. Charlie's terse "go" meant the guidance officers at Mission Control had judged the problem an acceptable risk. The time skip in our communications made a discussion of the situation impossible at this critical point. We simply had to trust Houston. Another alarm went off on the data screen. I fought the urge to shout a warning to Neil. Even after years as a fighter pilot and an astronaut, I felt that first hot edge of panic. I knew there had to be something seriously wrong with our guidance computer, and yet we were still descending. Again, Mission Control reassured us with a "go" call. They had dismissed the alarm as noncritical, but they couldn't take the time to explain why. We dropped through 20,000 feet, eating up altitude at 150 feet a second. As the LM continued tilting forward, our triangular windows filled with craters and humped ridges. During this phase we had to be sure we were heading toward a safe landing spot, but all we saw were gray craters and boulder fields. Again the alarms flashed, banishing data from our screen.

"Twelve alarm," Neil called. "Twelve-oh-one."

"Roger," Charlie acknowledged. "Twelve-oh-one alarm."

I licked my dry lips. This was a time for discipline. But the tension had me rigid inside my suit. We *had* to trust Mission Control.

"We're go," Charlie added. "Hang tight, we're go. Two thousand feet...."

The pitch-over maneuver continued, giving us an excellent view of the rills and craters below us. Neil hunched over his hand controller knob, ready to take command if the automatic landing system led us into danger. I began a continuous series of readouts, giving both Neil and Mission Control a detailed description of our final descent.

At 500 feet, Neil was not satisfied with the landing zone. He took over manual control from the computer, slowing our descent from 20 feet per second to only nine, and then at 300 feet, to a descent of only three and a half feet per second. The LM hovered above its cone of flame. Neil did not like what he saw below. He delicately stroked the hand controller like a careful motorist fine-tuning his cruise control. We scooted horizontally across a field of rubbly boulders. Two hundred feet and our hover slid toward a faster descent rate.

"Eleven forward, coming down nicely," I called, my eyes scanning the instruments. "Two hundred feet, four and a half down. Five and a half down. One sixty. . . . Quantity light."

The amber low-fuel quantity light blinked on the master caution-and-warning panel near my face. The lumpy horizon of the moon hung at eye level. We were less than 200 feet from landing on the moon, but Neil again slowed the descent.

Simultaneously, Charlie's voice warned, "Sixty seconds."

The ascent engine fuel tanks were full, but completely separate from the big descent engine. We had a maximum of 60 seconds of fuel remaining in the descent stage before we had to land or abort. But Neil had slowed to a hover again as he searched the ground below.

"Down two and a half," I called. "Forward. Forward. Good. Forty feet. Down two and a half. Picking up some dust. Thirty feet. . . ."

Thirty feet below the LM's gangly legs, dust that had lain undisturbed for a billion years blasted sideways in the plume of our engine.

"Thirty seconds,"Charlie announced solemnly, but still Neil hovered.

The descent engine roared silently, devouring the last of its fuel supply. Again, I eyed the ABORT STAGE button. "Drifting right," I called, watching the shadow of a footpad probe straining to touch the surface. "Contact light." We settled silently onto the moon, with perhaps 20 seconds of fuel remaining in the descent stage. Immediately, I began preparing the LM for a sudden abort ascent, in the event the landing had damaged the *Eagle* or the lunar surface was not strong enough to support our weight.

"Okay, engine stop," I told Neil, reciting from the checklist. "ACA out of detent."

"Got it," Neil answered quietly, disengaging his hand control system.

"Mode controls, both auto," I continued. "Descent engine command override off. Engine arm off. . . ."

"We copy you down, *Eagle*," Charlie Duke interrupted from Houston.

From the window before my face I looked out over the alien rock and shadow of the moon. I breathed inside my helmet, totally absorbed. A mile away, the horizon curved into blackness.

"Houston," Neil called, "Tranquillity Base here. The *Eagle* has landed."

INTRODUCTION

CAPE CANAVERAL

JULY 16, 1988

Project Apollo was the single most audacious endeavor in human history. America's first man in space, Alan Shepard, was launched from Cape Canaveral on May 5, 1961. His flight was merely a suborbital lob that lasted 15 minutes. But only 20 days later, President John F. Kennedy, in a speech before the U.S. Congress, challenged America to send men all the way to the moon and return them safely by the end of the decade. It was a goal we reached eight years later, just six months before the end of the 1960s. We'll probably never know how long the pharaohs' slaves took to build the pyramids. But we do have pretty accurate records of the marathon efforts required to build the Union-Pacific Railroad, the Panama Canal, and the first atomic bomb. The Apollo program was certainly on a par with those undertakings.

This is the story of America's response to a challenge—something we've always been good at.

I was one of the first men to walk on the moon. Nineteen years ago today, Neil Armstrong, Mike Collins, and I rode up 32 stories in an elevator at Launch Pad 39-A and climbed aboard an Apollo spacecraft balanced atop a Saturn V booster, the most powerful rocket ever built. Since that day, an entire generation has come of age that sees the adventure of Apollo as only a colorful sidelight to the bizarre confusions of the 1960s—if they remember it at all. Recently I was in the visitors' building at Johnson Space Center in Houston where there's a lunar module on display. A young couple strolled up with their two kids, a girl around four and a boy a few years older.

"What's that, Dad?" the boy asked, pointing at the strange machine perched like a gold and black cement mixer on four gangly legs.

The father frowned, unsure of himself. They hadn't seen the explanation panel. "I think it goes up on the shuttle, Jason," he finally answered.

I've seen other young people stand before the spacecraft and rockets at the Air and Space Museum in Washington, DC. Their expressions are always interested and respectful, but also tinged with mild confusion. These weird contraptions have about as much relevance to them as dinosaur skeletons at the Museum of Natural History had to me as a kid before the war.

The only tangible artifacts we have left from the Apollo years are buildings and machines. The people, that unique combination of human genius that took mankind to the moon, have dispersed. Many of the key figures are dead. In another 20 or 30 years, the rest of us will be gone.

I decided to tell the story of Apollo so that future generations will have both an understanding of the historical events and the chance to share the experience of what has been called humanity's greatest adventure. I've come to realize that my background gives me a unique perspective on this adventure. My father was one of the pioneers of commercial aviation in this country and an early supporter of Robert Goddard, the founder of American rocketry. As a West Point graduate and Air Force pilot, I flew dogfights against Soviet MiG fighters during the Korean War, the crucible that shaped many of the Apollo astronauts. After the war, I went on to become a pilot-scientist, earning a doctorate in astronautics from MIT before I was selected to be an astronaut. This gave me an understanding of the complex orbital mechanics of spaceflight, a background few other astronauts shared. I was also fortunate to be picked for the *Apollo 11* crew, the first to reach the moon. That put me at the center of the momentous decisions in the final hectic months before the first moon landing flight.

Kennedy's 1961 challenge can only be fully appreciated if we remember that 23 days prior to Shepard's flight the Soviet Union put Yuri

Gagarin in Earth orbit aboard a Vostok spacecraft. The Russians were beating us, hands down. They had huge leads in every element of manned spaceflight: propulsion, life support, and flight control. For Kennedy to dare the Soviets to a moon race in 1961 remains one of the classic examples of chutzpah in modern history.

Eight years was a remarkably short time for America to invent and perfect interplanetary spaceflight. In that brief period, a group of young pilots and scientists were transformed into the most daring explorers in human history. We learned to fly in lumbering propeller planes and practiced our loops and rolls as the slipstream blasted through the open canopies to chill our faces. A few years later, we flew wingless spacecraft at seven miles a second through the interplanetary vacuum and then pitched and rolled the improbable machines among the ridges and craters of the moon.

But this transformation didn't progress as smoothly as it seems it did. My close friend Ed White was one of the three astronauts asphyxiated when their *Apollo 1* spacecraft burned on Launch Pad 34. Five others died in plane crashes before the *Apollo 11* flight. And my mission commander, Neil Armstrong, was almost killed testing the lunar module trainer in Houston. But all test flight programs are dangerous.

What made the Apollo program unique was the complete absence of commercial reward or traditional strategic advantage from the intense struggle. America and the Soviet Union used the race for the moon as a high-technology competition that was an alternative to war. And the struggle was intense. In eight frantic years, 60,000 NASA managers spent $24 billion and coordinated the labor of 400,000 pragmatic engineers and technicians from 20,000 private firms to achieve the most impractical endeavor imaginable: the round-trip journey of men from Earth to the moon's surface.[1]

After our flight, the public accepted the Apollo program as an invincible juggernaut that had easily swept aside the early Soviet competition. It is now fashionable to downplay the notion of a "moon race." The race for the moon was very real, and we now know both sides ran it desperately. Just before our flight in July 1969, that desperation drove the Soviets to test their own giant Saturn-class booster prematurely. The ploy ended in a catastrophe for the Russians that has never been adequately reported.

Following the *Apollo 11* moon landing, Norman Mailer wrote in *Of a*

Fire on the Moon, "The bureaucracy had embarked on a surrealistic adventure."[2] At the time, I dismissed his comment as just another glib 1960s potshot at technology. Now I agree with him. Lunar exploration—the act of departing the safety of Earth and voyaging across a quarter million miles of space to walk on the dusty soil of the moon—was definitely a surreal adventure.

When future generations remember Apollo just as we now recall the voyages of Columbus, they won't be moved by the geopolitical posturing of the Cold War, the back-room politics on Capitol Hill, or the pork-barrel intrigues that throbbed beneath the surface of the program. They will remember, however, that in July 1969, people like themselves first set foot on the moon.

Almost 20 years have passed since Neil and I walked on the Sea of Tranquillity. It's taken that long for me to understand our accomplishment. I am ready to tell the story of Apollo. It's an adventure that began early in this century and, I hope, one that will continue far into the future. It is the story of mankind's ancient dream to fly beyond the sky.

CHAPTER ONE

THE RACE BEGINS
SEPTEMBER 1944 TO OCTOBER 1957

Chiswick-on-Thames, England, September 8, 1944

Early evening September 8, 1944, the West London suburb of Chiswick was shattered by a blast of high explosives followed immediately by another noise that echoed like a giant drumbeat in the empty sky. There had been no air raid siren, nor was there any sign of a German bomber. High overhead a tiny feather of a vapor trail dangled. This section of London had been relatively untouched by the German blitz. The Royal Engineers bomb disposal team initially believed that a large German bomb had somehow gone undetected for several years and had exploded unexpectedly. No one could account for the second blast.

The cause of the explosion in Chiswick was a German ballistic missile, known to its engineers as the Aggregate-4. Soon after the blast, Nazi propaganda minister Joseph Goebbels announced the deployment of the Vergeltungswaffe-2, or V-2, the second in a series of "vengeance weapons." The first was the V-1 buzz bomb, a robot jet plane with a large explosive warhead. Hitler would now rely on these weapons to punish the Allies for their continued saturation bombings of the Third Reich.

The V-2 that struck Chiswick had been launched six minutes earlier from a park on the outskirts of The Hague, over a hundred miles across the Channel from London. It was fueled by alcohol and liquid oxygen

1

(LOX), stood 46 feet high, and weighed 14 tons. The nose was packed with a metric ton of high explosive.

At liftoff the V-2 had climbed slowly, with just enough acceleration to compensate for the force of gravity. But as the missile arched on its trajectory and more fuel was consumed, it began to move faster. Sixty-three seconds later, the V-2 was on the fringe of space, 23 miles high, moving at one mile per second. Automatic timers closed the propellant valves, and the pulsing rocket flame snuffed out. Far above the atmosphere, the V-2 continued climbing to the top of its arched trajectory, 60 miles above the Thames estuary. Then the flight path curved down toward London.[1]

When the V-2 hit it was moving at over 2,000 miles per hour, faster than a rifle bullet and far too fast to be seen overhead. And the missile's speed was too great for accurate radar tracking. The mysterious second blast in the sky reported from Chiswick was a sonic boom. The thirteen people killed and injured by the explosion in Chiswick were the first casualties of a space weapon. Over the next six months, 1,114 more V-2s fell on England, killing almost 3,000 men, women, and children.[2] Even worse was the damage done to the Allies' cross-channel debarkation port at Antwerp: over 2,000 V-2s struck that city, shattering the waterfront. After the war, Supreme Allied Commander General Dwight Eisenhower admitted that D-Day would not have been possible had this rocket bombardment begun earlier and been directed at the Allied invaders on the south coast of England or the Normandy beachhead itself.[3]

The V-2 had been designed by a team of German scientists and engineers under the leadership of a young East Prussian aristocrat named Wernher von Braun. He was to become one of the undisputed giants of spaceflight, a man who combined profound intelligence, startling creativity, and unparalleled managerial skill within a personality that has been described as nothing short of charismatic by those who knew him.

Wernher von Braun was an eighteen-year-old technical school student in 1930 (coincidentally the same year I was born) when he met Professor Hermann Oberth, a German from Rumania who had written widely on the future use of rockets for interplanetary spaceflight. After reading Oberth's work, von Braun was convinced that liquid-fueled rockets could be perfected and that one day they could be made large enough to carry humans to the moon and beyond. Von Braun fell in with a group of like-minded, often eccentric young men who also believed in the possibilities of spaceflight. They formed an amateur rocketry club, the Verein für Raumschiffahrt (VfR), and began testing their tiny missiles in the weedy field of a disused army storage depot outside Berlin. Over the next two years, they slowly developed a crude rocket engine that burned a mixture of LOX and gasoline.[4]

The VfR's labors at the suburban *Raketenflugplatz* were noticed by Colonel Walter Dornberger of the German army's ordnance ballistic section. Dornberger had been ordered by the general staff to develop long-range bombardment weapons that would be in accordance with the stringent disarmament requirements the Allies had imposed on Germany in the Treaty of Versailles. Rockets weren't on that list because, in 1919, they weren't considered serious weapons.

Impressed by the VfR's work, Dornberger became the group's official sponsor. He urged von Braun to complete his education, so that he could better assist the progress of German rocketry. Von Braun received his bachelor's degree in aeronautical engineering in 1932 and his Ph.D. in physics from the University of Berlin only two years later. Dornberger's stewardship is obvious because von Braun's thesis on rocket engines was immediately classified a military secret.

After the Nazis took power in 1933, von Braun's "rocket team" continued their research (though with a relatively small budget compared with the total funds devoted to the massive Nazi rearmament of the 1930s), and under Hermann Goering, the Luftwaffe funded a joint service rocket research center on the Baltic peninsula of Peenemünde. But even after the Germans invaded Poland in 1939, the work of von Braun's rocket team was still neglected by Hitler's general staff.

Von Braun's team continued to grow, however, and was developing larger, longer-range liquid-fueled missiles. Despite repeated failures, the team doggedly overcame the multiple problems of modern rocket engineering: flight stability, fuel management, steady combustion pressure, engine cooling, and guidance. Finally, Field Marshal Walther von Brauchitsch, the Wehrmacht commander, came to the aid of the Peenemünde effort with personnel and funds. Germany's considerable academic talent pool was canvassed for potential rocket experts, who were then sent to work at Peenemünde. The enlarged rocket team's goal was to design a prototype operational missile, the A-4, that would carry a full ton of explosives accurately to a target 180 miles away. By the summer of 1942, von Braun's team had their prototype. They successfully fired it from Peenemünde on October 3, 1942. As the missile roared aloft and climbed on a steady arch to pierce high scattered clouds, Dornberger (now a general) turned to von Braun. "Do you realize what we have accomplished today? Today a spaceship was born!"[5]

Then events moved more quickly. On June 28, 1943, SS Reichsfuhrer Heinrich Himmler visited Peenemünde on Hitler's behalf to assess the potential of long-range rocket weapons. A first demonstration launch of the A-4 was a catastrophic failure, but the second was a near-perfect flight. Himmler was impressed. Von Braun and General Dornberger were brought to Hitler's headquarters in East Prussia where they showed the Führer films of successful A-4 launches. Hitler immediately ordered the rocket into mass production, which meant that the machine Dornberger and von Braun had envisioned as a spaceship was to become the world's first ballistic missile. The night of August 17, 1943, however, almost 600 RAF heavy bombers struck Peenemünde, badly damaging the rocket laboratories and production facilities and killing hundreds of workers and technicians.

After this air raid, Hitler ordered that rocket production be taken out of the hands of the von Braun team and placed under the control of the SS. Von Braun's prototype A-4 was replicated and mass produced as the V-2. The task fell to SS Brigadier Hans Kammler, who used thousands of concentration camp laborers to build an underground production facility in abandoned mine shafts near Nordhausen in the Harz mountains. Kammler was a relentless slave driver; by 1945, the Mittelwerk underground V-2 factory had reached a peak production level of 900 V-2s per month. But the human cost was horrible. In the final weeks of the war, 150 slave laborers a day were dying of starvation in the nearby Dora concentration camp.[6]

By the end of 1943, von Braun's team could concentrate on more advanced projects. Since the VfR days in Berlin, they had been interested in rockets as spaceflight boosters, not as missiles. They also designed enlarged V-2s with greater range and heavier warheads and even larger classes of rockets that were much more than mere offshoots of the single-stage V-2. These larger boosters would have multiple stages to transport winged space-bomber gliders to near-orbital speed. The

A-12 they planned was a true monster, capable of orbiting 30-ton payloads.

This visionary planning soon caught the attention of the SS, and a Gestapo spy denounced von Braun for "sabotage" because he had once mentioned at a cocktail party that the V-2's real purpose was spaceflight, not bombardment. He was arrested with two of his engineers, Klaus Riedel and Helmut Gröttrup. Only the swift intervention of General Dornberger saved them from a firing squad.[7]

By January 1945, it was clear to von Braun and his men that Germany had lost the war and that they should take their expertise to one of the Allied victors. Von Braun called a secret meeting and tried to rally his key personnel. "Let's not forget that it was our team that first succeeded in reaching outer space," he told them. "We have never stopped believing in satellites, voyages to the moon, and interplanetary travel." He directly asked them which Allied power should receive the incredible technical heritage of the rocket team.[8]

They immediately decided that the rocket team would somehow find a way to surrender to the Americans.

With typical organizational skill and energy, von Braun's team packed up the entire Peenemünde technical archives: blueprints, test reports, patents, and enough other essential documents to fill several boxcars. Von Braun created a bogus "Project for Special Dispositions," and with Peenemünde's priority status he commandeered vehicles and fuel to transport the rocket team and their families south and west toward the advancing American forces. In the spring of 1945, he somehow managed to lead 525 people out of the chaos of the collapsing Third Reich, eventually reaching Oberammergau in the Bavarian Alps. Key members of the team took the archives to Dörnten in the Harz mountains, where they buried tons of documents deep in an abandoned mine.

Von Braun and his close associates knew they were still in danger: they had learned of SS plans to liquidate them in order to prevent their capture by the Allies. But on the evening of May 2, 1945, GIs from an antitank company of the 44th Infantry Division were manning a roadblock in a valley beneath the Bavarian ski resort of Oberjoch. A "shabby young German" in a patched leather jacket rode up on a bicycle. "My name is Magnus von Braun," he said. "My brother invented the V-2. We want to surrender."

PFC Fred Schneikert leveled his rifle at the German's chest. "I think you're nuts," the soldier said. In those days, when the war was coming to an end, all kinds of oddball German civilians were trying to climb on the Allied bandwagon. But luckily the GIs did report the incident, and later that night von Braun and Dornberger officially surrendered.[9]

Army Ordnance Colonel Holger Toftoy soon began a secret effort to bring German scientists to America, known as Operation Paper Clip. American ordnance teams rescued the hidden Peenemünde technical archives and assorted parts for 100 V-2 rockets at Nordhausen from the approaching Soviet occupation forces. This material was dispatched to the Army's White Sands Proving Grounds in New Mexico. While waiting for transport to America, von Braun regaled American intelligence officers with details of the rocket team's plans for multistage rockets and space stations.

To the Americans in the summer of 1945, this kind of talk bordered on delusion. But von Braun's enthusiasm was not dampened. On their way west across the Atlantic to the New Mexican desert test ranges, he told his colleagues how fortunate they were to be working for the Americans. This was a country, he stated with conviction, where spaceflight would take root and flourish.[10] But von Braun could not assess the true nature of the American wilderness that awaited them.

West Point, 1947–1951

When I entered West Point in the summer of 1947, spaceflight was still a fantasy to the men who shaped America's military and scientific policy. Postwar America was more enthralled with jet aviation in Earth's atmosphere than with flying above it. Von Braun's team had by this time been relocated to Fort Bliss, Texas, where they conducted unimportant test flights with the captured V-2s in an underfunded and largely neglected program directed by the US Army Ordnance Corps.

Hiroshima and Nagasaki had demonstrated to President Harry Truman's key advisers in the Pentagon that the ability to drop a ton of high explosives on a city was puny compared to the power of the atomic bomb. For that reason they didn't see any immediate practical military application for ballistic missiles. (Atomic weapons then were very cumbersome fission devices, much too heavy to be delivered by any of the missiles of that day.)

But most important, America's postwar priorities just did not include government funding of a grandiose spaceflight program.

We had a lot more serious things to worry about. By now it was clear that the Soviet Union was no longer our ally. Stalin's occupation forces remained in place, installing satellite governments throughout Eastern Europe, and Winston Churchill alerted the world to the situation with his famous "Iron Curtain" speech. The hot war with fascism that my father had fought in was over; the Cold War with communism had begun. Our small nuclear arsenal had become our single most important deterrent to further communist expansion, a counterpoint to the huge conventional forces of the Soviet Union.

Even as a plebe at West Point, it was clear to me that I would end up fighting the Soviets or their surrogates someplace in the world sooner or later, probably sooner. I was just a young man then, learning the mysteries and rituals of military life in a service academy. It was a hard revelation. I decided that if I had to go to war, I wanted to do it as a jet fighter pilot. I didn't have anything particular against the infantry, but I knew my own talents lay more in the field of science and technology, and jet aviation was then the most advanced field around.

The problem was that my dad and I didn't always agree on what direction I should take in my career. Since I was his only son and namesake—"Buzz" is a childhood nickname that stuck—he'd been pleased when I told him I wanted to attend a service academy. Both my parents had military backgrounds. Dad had been an Army Air Corps pilot and an aide to General Billy Mitchell in the Philippines in the 1920s. It was there that he met my mother, Marion Moon, the daughter of a Methodist Army chaplain. But Dad left the Air Corps after Billy Mitchell was court-martialed for his visionary—but outspoken—views on the future of airpower. My father became an executive with Standard Oil of New Jersey and developed their aviation fuel program. He believed that that was the way I should go: first service in the military, leading to a civilian business career.

His years in the Army had given him a definite feeling about that branch of service. That was why he wanted me to attend the Naval Academy at Annapolis, instead of West Point. He said the Navy really prepared a young man for a career in business. As an executive, he'd seen a lot more ex-Navy officers in the boardrooms than Army generals. He also said that Annapolis men took care of their own in a way that the excessively competitive West Pointers didn't. He was probably thinking about what had happened to Billy Mitchell.

But even after I'd made a firm decision for an Air Force career, Dad tried to steer me away from jet fighters. He thought I should become a multiengine bomber or transport pilot. Commanding a crew right away, he reasoned, combined with my academic background, would advance me more quickly and would prepare me for even greater responsibility as an airline executive.

I knew there would be a lot of competition to be an Air Force fighter pilot, so I set out to work as hard as I could at West Point. By the end of my first year, I was number one in my class in both academic and athletic aptitude. I made Star Man, the top five percent academically, five out of the next six semesters. But the competition was intense, and I wasn't the only hard charger at the Point. Among the cadets in classes ahead of and behind me were Frank Borman, Ed White, Mike Collins, and Dave Scott. They all became astronauts and played historic roles in the Apollo program.

Gorodomlya Island, Russia, 1949

As the Cold War intensified, both sides scrambled to develop new military technology. But the Soviet Union was first to recognize the great strategic potential of modern ballistic missiles. The members of von Braun's rocket team were not the only German rocket designers continuing their work. Helmut Gröttrup, who had been arrested by the Gestapo with von Braun in 1944, helped the Soviets, producing improved V-2s at Nordhausen after the war.

While the American generals were absorbed with building bigger manned bombers, the Soviets had other plans. Stalin envisioned a much more powerful derivative of the V-2, a missile with true intercontinental range that could strike the United States from Soviet territory, which would be the world's first intercontinental ballistic missile (ICBM). Such a weapon, he said, "would be an effective straitjacket for that noisy shopkeeper, Harry Truman."[11]

To expedite the development of the ICBM, the Soviets uprooted Gröttrup's team and their families in Germany and moved them to the Soviet Union. There they were broken into two groups, with Gröttrup's design section shuttling between Moscow and the new missile test range at Kapustin Yar, on the empty steppes east of the ruined city of Stalingrad.[12]

Once this test range was operational, Gröttrup's designers joined the other German engineering team in an almost gothic secret enclave on the island of Gorodomlya in Lake Seliger in the empty taiga northwest of Moscow. The living conditions were crude, but the industrial facility was excellent. America may have been ignoring its German rocket team—the cream of the lot—but the Soviets squeezed all they could from their Germans.

The Soviets needed these intercontinental missiles. Unlike the Americans and British, the Russians had not developed long-range bombers during World War II. The Americans were years ahead of them with this technology and had the added strategic advantage of air bases in Europe, North Africa, and the Far East, which virtually ringed the Soviet Union. From these bases, American nuclear bombers would be able to strike at vital targets deep in Soviet territory. The Soviets had no such capability.

But they were developing nuclear weapons. The Soviet Union had begun working on atomic weapons in 1943, one year after the official beginning of America's Manhattan Project, the crash program to build an atom bomb.[13] But the Nazi invasion of the Soviet Union and the lack of adequate uranium supplies delayed their bomb program until after the war. Once the Russians went back to work on their program, however, they quickly caught up. On August 4, 1949, the Soviets exploded an atomic bomb at their Arctic test range. In fact, the 30 months between their first sustained chain reaction in December 1946 and the explosion of the first Soviet bomb in 1949 almost matched the Manhattan Project's speed record.

That achievement should have warned us that the Soviets were far from technologically primitive, as many of our military leaders then viewed them. But we seem destined to be continually shocked by the successes of Soviet technology, even today.

The Russians' closest counterpart to Wernher von Braun was clearly Sergei Korolev, the chief Soviet rocket designer. He came into prominence during the early postwar period. Like von Braun, he combined brilliant theoretical insight, great practical engineering skill, and energetic managerial talent. Also like von Braun, Korolev had served a long apprenticeship in amateur and semiofficial rocketry groups before the war. He was a disciple of Konstantin Tsiolkovsky, who, in his brilliant theoretical book *Exploration of Cosmic Space with Reactive Devices,* written at the turn of the century, envisioned large multistage boosters fueled by liquid hydrogen and oxygen, space stations, lunar bases, and eventually permanent space colonies ringing Earth. Tsiolkovsky was also the first to calculate the velocities and energy levels that later became the routine mathematical language of spaceflight.[14]

Korolev shared Tsiolkovsky's visions of interplanetary travel. But Korolev was obliged to meet Stalin's military requirements while secretly harboring grandiose plans for spaceflight, just as von Braun had been during the war. And the parallel between the two runs deeper. Korolev was arrested along with thousands of other scientists and technicians by the NKVD secret police in the "great terror" of the late 1930s and was imprisoned for seven years as a gulag convict, several months of which he spent at the notorious Kolyma gold mine in the Arctic. For the rest of his captivity during the war he worked as an engineer under aircraft designer A. N. Tupolev in a "special" prison camp. When he was freed after the war, Korolev quickly rose in the new Soviet missile hierarchy. Although he lacked von Braun's charisma, he was every bit as much a wily survivor.

By the late 1940s, Korolev had recognized that the Soviets had learned all they were going to from their captive German scientists. It was time to strike out on his own. He first modified the basic V-2 propulsion technology into a much larger and more powerful engine. Working within the limits of Soviet metallurgy, he solved the overheating problems inherent to high-energy rocket thrust by creating an engine that had four small, thick-walled combustion chambers. Korolev's RD-107 rocket engine was fueled by a mixture of kerosene and LOX and produced an amazing thrust of almost 225,000 pounds.[15]

Even though Korolev now had the principal building block for a huge rocket that could serve as either an intercontinental ballistic missile or a spacecraft booster, he still faced major technical hurdles. The key to a long-distance missile lay in Tsiolkovsky's pioneering concept of multiple vertical stages; the heavy first stage would break the bonds of gravity, allowing the lighter upper stages to accelerate to the speeds needed for an intercontinental warhead trajectory or orbital flight. It would of course be preferable for the engines of these upper stages to be both lighter and more powerful than the first-stage engines—that is, with a better thrust-to-weight ratio, generating more energy to accelerate less weight.

Practically, this concept required engine technology that was beyond the reach of the Soviets at the time. So Korolev's innovative compromise was to design a composite rocket that clustered four strap-on boosters around a central core unit known as the "sustainer." Thus the rocket's stages were parallel rather than vertical. The Soviets used two variants of the original basic engine, the RD-107 and the RD-108, an upgraded version of Korolev's earlier design. The strap-on boosters were tapered, wider at the bottom than at the top, giving the base of the rocket the appearance of a flared skirt. The central core was powered by an RD-107 engine with much larger propellant tanks. At liftoff, all the engines fired simultaneously; the "staging" occurred when the strap-on boosters' fuel was expended. The boosters then fell away, leaving the central core's engine to sustain the flight.[16]

Working with this concept, Korolev's team began designing a large, yet simple missile that would eventually become the most durable spaceflight booster in history. Whenever I see pictures of *new* Soviet space boosters these days, I'm amazed at their flared-skirt strap-on boosters: they are obviously direct descendants of Korolev's first ICBM. The Soviets simply do not throw away useful technology. They improve it. We can learn an important lesson from them.

Huntsville, Alabama, 1950–1953

In the beginning, Wernher von Braun and his rocket team didn't find in America the fertile ground for rocketry that Gröttrup's engineers had found in the Soviet Union. Von Braun's key designers had surrendered Germany's human and technical rocket legacy to the US Army because they thought of America as the world's future leader in spaceflight, the nation, they said, that was "most able to provide the resources required for interplanetary travel."[17] But their early years in America had been a long exercise in frustration.

Colonel Holger Toftoy remained the team's sponsor after they were settled at Fort Bliss in the west Texas desert outside of El Paso in 1945. Toftoy was already committed to the cause of missiles and rocketry, but the Pentagon ignored him. The Germans slowly grew accustomed to the alien culture and climate, but language remained a problem for years. By 1947, they had been joined by their families, and most had become US citizens by 1950.

The rocket team's biggest problem was that they were given low-priority assignments. Their postwar work with V-2s, assembled from the parts Army Ordnance had spirited away from Nordhausen under the noses of the Soviets, was limited to upper-atmosphere probes and minor adaptations of existing German missile technology.

Probably the only excitement the scientists had during this period was the night they accidentally bombed Mexico. Just after 8:45 PM on May 28, 1947, the rocket team fired an unarmed V-2 from the White Sands Proving Ground north of El Paso. The missile veered off course and plunged south toward the Rio Grande, the Mexican border, where it exploded near the Tepeyac cemetery in Ciudad Juárez. When a large Army contingent of engineers arrived in Juárez the next morning, enterprising children tried to sell them twisted shards of the missile.

As someone who can well remember the postwar inflation, I understand why President Harry Truman's priorities were to turn America's economy away from the military and back to civilian production. But this meant American rocketry was eclipsed. Also, the 1947 reorganization of the armed services, which created the Department of Defense, resulted in an interservice rivalry that made Toftoy's German rocket experts even more irrelevant. The newly independent US Air Force made a strong bid for a massive strategic bomber force, and their main competitor for scarce funds, the Navy, wanted "super" aircraft carriers. To enhance its competitive position with the Navy, the Air Force abandoned its tentative preliminary research into a revolutionary intercontinental missile project called the Atlas. This weapon would have used high-pressure rocket engines to boost a huge, heat-shielded nuclear warhead high into space to coast on a ballistic trajectory halfway around the world before reentering the atmosphere. Building the Atlas in the late 1940s would have required an explosion of new technology and a financial investment the Air Force was unwilling to make.

With no American interest in long-range ballistic missiles, von Braun's team simply had no viable work. And they had no sponsor among defense contractors, nor did they have a political patron in Washington. Von Braun learned during these years that such a constituency and patronage would be vital to his future plans, especially because he had not forgotten his dreams of spaceflight.

Von Braun spent his evenings in painstaking research, slowly developing a practical proposal for an international expedition to Mars. By 1948, this became a book manuscript, *Mars Project*, which eighteen US publishers rejected as "too fantastic." Von Braun envisioned a large international interplanetary expedition that would be assembled from a space station in Earth orbit. In essence, von Braun wrote a practical handbook for interplanetary travel, including our Apollo flights of the 1960s.

Von Braun's team was able to advance rocket engine and guidance technology, however, when they were ordered to upgrade the basic V-2 into a tactical nuclear missile for the Army, following the explosion of the first Soviet atomic bomb in 1949. Toftoy, now a general, was dispatched to Huntsville, Alabama, where he acquired and then combined the Redstone and Huntsville arsenals into a single sprawling Army reservation in the red clay hills of the Appalachian Piedmont. He brought von Braun and his team from Texas to the new Redstone Arsenal, home of the Army Ordnance Missile Command. They began work on the long-delayed successor to the V-2, which would become the reliable Redstone missile, the rocket that eventually would put America into space.

Korea, 1952–1953

I was a West Point cadet on a summer study junket in Japan the day the North Korean Army invaded South Korea, June 25, 1950. The Cold War had just turned hot. My trip was cut short. America was at war with a communist army, very well equipped by the Soviet Union. By that December, the Chinese communists had joined the war, and America was bogged down in a bloody stalemate on the Asian mainland.

I graduated from West Point in June 1951, number three in a class of 475 cadets. This academic rating guaranteed that I could enter Air Force flight training, but I still had to face intense competition to earn my wings and win an assignment as a jet fighter pilot. The cadets' code at West Point was "Duty, Honor, Country." Unofficially there was a fourth tenet to the creed: "Work your ass off." And this stood me in good stead during flight training, where the competition for the coveted jet fighter assignments was stiff. By November 1952, I'd managed to stay ahead of the pack, and after completing eighteen months of intense training without "ripping my knickers," as they say at the Point, I was qualified as an F-86 Sabre pilot.

By the time I arrived in Korea in December 1952, the ground war had stabilized. There were still heavy engagements at places like Heartbreak Ridge and Pork Chop Hill, but cease-fire negotiations had begun. It looked as if the Soviet-backed Chinese and North Korean forces had run out of steam fighting the determined resistance of the "United Nations Forces," the politicians' term for America and its allies.

Aerial combat in Korea was unlike anything America had seen in the first two air wars. The Chinese, the North Koreans, and their Soviet advisers had redeployed their fighter bases north of the Yalu River, the frontier between North Korea and China. American planes were forbidden to cross the river, even in hot pursuit.

I was assigned to the 16th Fighter Squadron of the 51st Fighter Interceptor Wing at Suwon Air Base, 20 miles south of Seoul. The better-known American Sabre wing—and our archrival—was the 4th Interceptor Wing, stationed right outside Seoul at Kimpo Field. The 4th had destroyed more enemy MiG fighters than had our outfit; they had more aces and certainly more publicity. American pilots assigned to the Joint Operations Center in Seoul flew combat missions with the 4th. Even though they were "staff weenies," these senior Air Force officers were still fighter pilots, and they wanted to leave Korea with MiG kills to their credit. So when they flew, they made damn sure the 4th got the juiciest missions, up along the Yalu where the hunting was best. They also routinely broke the rules of engagement to fly north of the river, all the way up to the Manchurian air bases, where they could catch the MiGs at low altitude.

My first few trips to "MiG Alley" taught me to respect Soviet aircraft. The MiG-15 was an elusive and dangerous piece of machinery.[18] Most days, we saw nothing but barren mountains below and empty blue sky above. Sometimes we'd see the white chalk lines of MiG exhaust contrails high overhead or the glint of a wing in the sun. Unfortunately, the MiG-15 had definite altitude advantage on us. According to Air Force intelligence, the MiG could fly as high as 51,000 feet, a good 3,000 feet above our maximum altitude. But in reality, the MiG-15s we encountered, flown by Chinese, North Korean, and Soviet pilots, could fly much higher. The reason they could do this was that the standard MiG-15 was lighter than the F-86; it was also stripped down for combat and carried a much smaller fuel load.

In the officers' club, the guys used to sing a song about the MiG's superior ceiling:

> When we get up to fly at noon,
> The MiG-15s take off the moon.
> The fox-eight-six hits forty-four,
> But the boys in blue ain't got no more.... [19]

The "moon" and the "forty-four" referred to the MiG pilots' favorite tactic. They would jump us from above fifty thousand—"the moon"—as we struggled to maintain our true combat ceiling of 44,000 feet.

In an actual dogfight, however, the two planes were closely matched. But one thing was certain: you *never* let a MiG get on your tail, because the Russian fighter carried a 37 mm cannon that could blow your wing off with one hit, and the MiG's two 23 mm automatic cannons could chew up a Sabre pilot in a single burst.

In Korea I developed a respect I still have today for Soviet technology. Their equipment—whether airplanes or spacecraft—isn't as fancy as ours, but it gets the job done. Every time we underestimate them, they surprise us.

I shot down my first MiG on May 14, 1953, up along the Yalu. It was not a heroic engagement. The guy was flying straight and level, probably on a training flight. I don't think he even knew he was south of the river. But the camera attached to my gun got the first graphic footage of an enemy pilot ejecting. Frames from the entire sequence appeared in the next issue of *Life*. That was a real coup over those glory boys of the 4th.

If the first MiG was a piece of cake, the second was the hairiest experience I've had flying machines in this planet's atmosphere. On June 7, 1953, I was flying alone, north of the Yalu. I was trying to catch up with the three Sabres of Tiger Flight, a formation from the 39th Squadron I had been assigned to after my own wingman had aborted the mission earlier with engine trouble. Tiger Flight was commanded by a Marine captain who had the fine military name of Jack Bolt. But the 39th flew the new F-model Sabres that had more thrust and a bigger wing than the F-86-E I flew in the 16th. They also had about a 20-knot airspeed advantage on me. And Captain Bolt wasn't the type to stooge around waiting for me to catch his flight.

Bolt's three planes pitched over into a speed dive, dropping their empty fuel tanks behind them. They were committed for an attack run on the MiG field up in the broad valley to the north. I couldn't abandon them now. I punched off my own drop tanks and joined the dive.

There was no way I could catch up with them. It was obvious their planes were much faster. Even with my airspeed indicator pegged at the top of the clock, they were still walking away from me. The stick got heavy and the plane was buffeting ominously. I was approaching Mach 1—the speed of sound—a forbidden speed for the Sabre. As we descended below 15,000 feet, control of my plane became tenuous. Despite my effort to maintain stability, the aircraft began to wing roll right, gently at first, but steeper as we plunged into the thicker air.

I held her as best I could, practically hanging on to the control stick. The denser air finally dragged off the excess airspeed, and I regained control of the stick and rudder pedals. Captain Bolt's flight was leveling out at 5,000 feet, screaming right across the enemy airfield. I could see MiGs rising from the runway, trailing thick exhaust plumes behind them, and other MiGs racing along the taxi ramps. Dark antiaircraft fire blossomed dead ahead.

"Tiger Three," I called, "I'm behind you. Let me join up."

An airplane banked across my right wing, climbing toward the three Sabres of Tiger Flight. I shook my head to clear my vision. Sharply swept wings, high tail. A MiG-15. If he kept going as he was, he'd fly right into my gunsight. But the MiG pilot saw me just as I chopped my power and dumped my speed brakes to slow down. This guy was no amateur. He increased his bank to turn into me. I was going to overshoot, and then he'd be on my tail.

My only hope was a high-G right turn that would cross his steep left bank. Fighter pilots call this a scissors, the two opposing aircraft crossing like the blades of a broken scissors. Cross and cross again, with each pilot trying to slice the sky more sharply than his enemy.

We slammed through one set of scissors turns with our wing tips tilted almost straight down. The enemy runway and dispersal ramp flashed by. Then pine trees and fields of new green millet.

He broke first, rolling level to clear a ridge. This was my chance. But the goddamn pipper aiming dot of my gunsight was jammed in the lower left corner, knocked ajar by my violent maneuvers. Still rolled over on my left wing, I used my nose as a crude gunsight and snapped off a short burst from my six .50 caliber machine guns. Luck was with me. I saw a spark on his wing as one of the tracers I'd sent his way smacked him. I rolled out and jammed the throttle wide open so I could bounce across the ridge behind him. Now I had a clear shot. He was in a steep right turn. I fired and the bright tracers jumped along his wing from the root to the tip. Smoke shredded back toward me. He rolled out of the turn and pitched over in a shallow dive. I gave him two more bursts. His nose came up and he started to stall out.

His canopy popped, followed instantly by the flash of his ejection charge. I saw a small human being, trailing an implausible red silk scarf. Then he was gone. The empty MiG heeled over and stalled. The pilot had been pretty low to eject, but maybe his chute had opened.

I couldn't wait around gawking, though. There was bound to be a gaggle of angry Russian and Chinese pilots in the area. Since I was low on fuel, I climbed south, hoping to pick up the "Manchurian express" jet stream that blew down the Korean peninsula toward home.

After the mission I couldn't tell anyone where I'd had the dogfight. If headquarters discovered I'd been in off-limits territory, my MiG kill wouldn't be recognized officially. But there was no way to tell from the gun camera film what side of the river I'd been on, so the Air Force gave me an oak leaf cluster to add to the Distinguished Flying Cross I'd gotten for the first MiG. This time I had earned it.

It's interesting to note that some of the best pilots in the astronaut corps got their start flying combat missions in Korea. That experience made a lasting impression on all of us. Gus Grissom put in 100 combat missions in Sabres, and Wally Schirra flew 90. Jim McDivitt flew a total of 145 combat missions in both F-80s and Sabres. And John Glenn was a Marine pilot attached to my Air Force wing. He shot down three MiGs along the Yalu river during the last nine days of the war. My *Apollo 11* crewmate, Neil Armstrong, was a Navy Panther jet attack pilot on the aircraft carrier *Essex*. He flew a total of 78 combat missions. On one low-level raid, he clipped a wing tip on a cable the enemy had stretched across a valley to protect the bridge Neil was bombing. He managed to limp back to American territory before the plane went out of control and he had to eject.

Combat flying requires an intensity and skill far beyond anything in peacetime aviation. Years later those of us who'd served in Korea were prepared for the hazards and uncertainty of spaceflight because we had already come to terms with fear. We'd also been initiated into the East-West conflict that would dominate our lives during the second half of this century.

When I got back from Korea in late 1953 I spent my leave at my parents' home in Montclair, New Jersey. It was great to sleep late and then roll out of bed without worrying about getting shot down over enemy territory later that afternoon. I could savor simple activities that other young men considered perfectly normal, like dating girls.

One of the first things I did was look up Joan Archer, a tall, lithe brunette I'd met before I went to Korea. Joan had a master's degree from Columbia and was starting a career as an actress in New York. She was more sophisticated than most young women in the Jersey suburbs. After a few dates, things got serious. We corresponded while I was a gunnery instructor out at Nellis Air Force Base in Nevada, and we married in December 1954. Our first child, Mike, was born right on schedule in September 1955. Later that fall we arrived in Bitburg, West Germany, where I flew supersonic F-100 "Super Sabre" interceptors with the 36th Fighter Day Wing.

But technology soon overtook us. The F-100 was powerful enough to carry one of the recently miniaturized fission weapons. So the wing was assigned as a nuclear strike force, with our pilots training to deliver atomic bombs deep in Soviet-occupied Eastern Europe, should war break out between NATO and the Russians. The training was hard and the typical German flying weather grim. But I did have the chance to team up with Ed White, a buddy from the West Point track team. Ed was from an Air Force family and was a hell of a pilot. Together we represented our squadron in the NATO gunnery competition, a welcome diversion from the tense monotony of sitting nuclear alert, with our planes fully fueled at the end of the ramp, each with a streamlined nuclear weapon slung beneath its left wing.

The Cold War dragged on. We flew our planes through bad weather and sunshine, and waited for the alert siren we all prayed we would never hear.

Tyuratam, Kazakhstan, 1950–1957

While America was modernizing its nuclear strike force, the Soviet Union matched us move for move, and then jumped far ahead. Just months after the first Soviet atomic bomb test in 1949, Western intelligence agents were again shocked to learn that Soviet nuclear scientists were working to develop a fusion "superbomb," a project America had resisted. This certainly was what spurred Truman to give his approval in early 1950 for the development of our own thermonuclear weapon, or hydrogen bomb. The reasoning was that if the Soviet Union was aggressively expanding, the West would have to match its military capabilities.

From that point on, the military race between East and West really took off. By 1952, Edward Teller's Los Alamos team had produced a 10-megaton thermonuclear weapon, but it was too heavy and cumbersome to be delivered by even our biggest bomber, the lumbering B-36. The next summer, the Soviets jumped ahead of the West by exploding a true H-bomb, which had a smaller yield but was light enough to drop from a bomber. America caught up the next year by vaporizing a test island in Bikini Atoll with a 15-megaton bomb that weighed less than 10,000 pounds. Both countries had now discovered how to build H-bombs that were small enough to be delivered by intercontinental ballistic missiles, ICBMs.

America concentrated on developing its first ICBM, the Atlas missile, while the Soviet Union launched a crash program to produce Korolev's prototype cluster rocket as their own operational ICBM.[20] This weapon was particularly important for the Soviets because it would allow them to leapfrog the American bomber bases that encircled them in Europe and strike directly inside the American heartland. The American weapons designers had an advantage because our sophisticated computers assisted in designing lighter, higher-yielding warheads.[21] As designs were refined, warhead weights were steadily reduced. The Soviet engineers, without such sophisticated computers, were unable to make these leaps, and Soviet weapons remained large and heavy until the late 1960s, although their yields increased to grotesque proportions.

Sergei Korolev's team had now moved to the giant new missile test range at Tyuratam, at the end of a rail line in the empty steppes of Kazakhstan in Soviet Central Asia. By 1955, his design for an ICBM had been approved and prototypes were already in production. Nikita Khrushchev, the new chairman of the Communist Party, was never one to ignore a grandiose gesture. He immediately realized that Korolev's new rocket was an ideal way to demonstrate the superiority of both Soviet missile technology and science—indeed, of socialist civilization itself.

After a visit to Tyuratam, Khrushchev began orchestrating plans for just such a demonstration.[22] The International Geophysical Year (IGY)—the first major postwar scientific collaboration between East and West—would begin during the summer of 1957. The IGY was a program to coordinate efforts by the world's best geologists, oceanographers, and atmospheric scientists, an undertaking of great international importance. Korolev assured Khrushchev and the Soviet Politburo that his prototype ICBM would be flying by then. They also knew that if this missile was capable of carrying a two-ton thermonuclear warhead 4,000 miles to the United States, it was powerful enough to launch an Earth satellite. The Soviet launch of the world's first satellite would be a historic military and propaganda coup for the Soviet Union. Khrushchev authorized an international effort to alert the world to this momentous occasion. Between 1955 and the beginning of the IGY on July 1, 1957, the Soviets took every possible opportunity at international scientific meetings to let the world know about their plans for an Earth satellite. Few in the West took them seriously.

Huntsville, Alabama, 1955–1957

America's own decision to launch an Earth satellite had a convoluted history, well salted with domestic political and Cold War considerations. As early as 1946, American scientists had outlined a practical Earth satellite project. Using German concepts and engineering studies from the Peenemünde archives, the newly created RAND Corporation and the Douglas Aircraft Company set out the practical requirements of a satellite launch in great detail. As prescient as this study was, the cost-conscious Truman Pentagon rejected it as having no practical value.[23]

Given the domination of American postwar rocketry by the US Air Force, it is easy to see why an expensive Earth satellite program was neglected. Postwar Air Force guided missiles were almost exclusively of the winged cruise missile type, such as the Navajo and Matador. They combined liquid-fuel rocket engines with ramjet and conventional turbojet propulsion. They flew through the atmosphere, more robot bombers than rockets. Wartime experiments with solid-fuel rockets had achieved mixed success, as had work on small, liquid-fuel jet-assisted takeoff (JATO) systems, which aided heavily laden bombers using short runways. In the postwar period the Air Force was focused almost entirely on missilery as an extension of conventional aviation.

In essence, America had abandoned the work of its own rocket pioneer, Robert Goddard. Like Tsiolkovsky and Hermann Oberth, Goddard worked in the early decades of the century, slowly perfecting the technology of liquid-fuel rocket propulsion. He was an undisputed genius, but most of his innovations were hidden within scores of patents he obtained in the 1930s. During the war, Goddard applied the talents of his small team of researchers to JATO technology. If Goddard had had the kind of military patronage von Braun's team had enjoyed in Germany, American rocket technology probably would have advanced much more rapidly during World War II. In fact, Goddard's patents were the subject of considerable jingoistic controversy after von Braun's rocket team came to prominence in America. German V-2 designers were said to have actually stolen Goddard's ideas. But as Wernher von Braun later pointed out, all of Goddard's patents were classified as military secrets and never published. Von Braun did concede that they contained the necessary engineering detail for a successful large missile program.[24]

When it became obvious in the mid-1950s that an Earth satellite launch could be the prestigious cornerstone of the upcoming IGY, the Eisenhower administration gave the Pentagon responsibility for the project, with one important caveat: the satellite program could not interfere in any way with the development of ICBMs, particularly the priority Atlas missile project.[25] Because of the obvious conflict of interest with Atlas missile development, the Air Force proposal was not given serious consideration. The real competition was between the Army, with von Braun's rocket team offering their Redstone missile as a satellite booster, and the Navy, which proposed an upgraded version of their small Viking research rocket.

In 1955 von Braun proposed clustering rather old-fashioned Loki solid rockets as upper stages for the well-tested Redstone, converting the battlefield missile into a satellite booster. His Project Orbiter would place an American satellite in orbit, he promised, no later than January 1957. The Navy proposal, Project Vanguard, would take longer, but seemed to offer a more elegant engineering solution than von Braun's scheme, which had "the appearance of a lashed-up job."[26] The Navy's Project Vanguard won the day. The basically nonmilitary role of the Viking rocket made the project appear to be a civilian research effort, but in reality the Navy oversold the program, downplaying the difficulties of designing entirely new upper stages for the Viking.

Eisenhower has been criticized for neglecting American interests during the early years of the space race. It is true that he was opposed to expensive space extravaganzas, but he certainly understood the uses of space exploration from a military perspective. At this time, America needed to penetrate the huge Soviet landmass and to pierce the Russians' compulsive veil of secrecy. We were using U-2 reconnaissance aircraft, but the president knew that the spy planes would not be invulnerable to Soviet air defense forever (as the flight of Gary Powers would later prove). Giving America's planned IGY satellite a civilian scientific coloration helped hide the fact that the Defense Department was secretly conducting research and development for spy satellites. All the time the civilian satellite program was stumbling along underfunded and badly led, the administration had made space reconnaissance a national priority and was moving steadily toward a spy satellite capability.

Although the Navy had gotten the green light, von Braun's team did not give up. By early 1956, they knew that the Viking-based Project Vanguard had little chance of launching a satellite before the end of the IGY—and certainly not before the Soviet competition. Von Braun's years in the desert had not been wasted. He now had a powerful patron—Major General John Medaris, chief of the new Army Ballistic Missile Agency (ABMA)—and von Braun understood the need for bureaucratic trench fighting in the invisible war of interservice rivalry. Rather than abandoning the Army satellite bid, von Braun's rocket team (with Medaris's encouragement) set to work developing a system that could quickly place an American satellite into orbit if Project Vanguard failed.

Von Braun had been authorized to develop a follow-up to the Redstone battlefield missile, the Jupiter, which would have a range of over 2,000 miles. Such a missile would require a nuclear warhead nose cone that could survive the fiery reentry into the atmosphere. In order to test reentry technology, in mid-1956 the rocket team assembled— using Jupiter R&D funds—a composite missile very similar to the proposed satellite booster. This was the Jupiter-C, a bureaucratic ruse to circumvent the decision that had given the satellite program to the Navy. The Jupiter-C had four stages, which combined an upgraded Redstone with clusters of solid-fuel Sergeant rockets that had been developed under Army sponsorship by the Jet Propulsion Laboratory (JPL) in California. Ostensibly, the booster's fourth stage was a reentry test nose cone. But it could equally well have been a 30-pound Earth satellite, which JPL just happened to have on the drawing boards.[27]

Responding to alarm from Navy quarters, the Pentagon began to suspect that von Braun's team planned to launch the world's first artificial satellite "by accident" during test flights of the Jupiter-C. General Medaris was ordered to carry out a personal inspection of the booster's fourth stage on September 20, 1956, the day before its first test flight. The next afternoon, von Braun's Jupiter-C lifted off from Cape Canaveral and delivered its nose cone to a prearranged impact area, 3,000 miles away in the South Atlantic. The fourth stage had attained a velocity of 16,000 miles per hour, just short of satellite injection speed. Von Braun's team now had evidence that they could launch a satellite whenever they wished.[28]

More successful launches of the Jupiter-C during the summer of 1957 led von Braun to declare publicly the booster's satellite capabilities. But the Defense Department saw no reason to switch from the Vanguard program, even though it was clear the Viking booster was experiencing severe development delays. Defense Secretary Charles Wilson had already stripped von Braun's Army rocket team of responsibility for long-range missiles. In a "roles and missions" directive, Wilson had given the Air Force operational control of intercontinental and intermediate-range missiles, including the Jupiter under development by the ABMA. The Army was restricted to battlefield weapons with ranges of 200 miles or less. Thus, the Pentagon saw the Jupiter-C as a temporary anomaly, unworthy of the prominence it would receive as the world's first satellite booster. No doubt the energetic lobbying by the Navy—Vanguard's semiofficial sponsor—contributed to this decision.[29]

Tyuratam, Kazakhstan, 1957

In the Soviet Union during the spring of 1957, Korolev's team assembled his missile, an ICBM that he called the R-7. His cluster concept had grown into a missile with a total of 20 thrust chambers in the sustainer core and four skirtlike strap-on boosters. Also, because this design lacked swiveling engine nozzles, the R-7's flight path through the atmosphere had to be controlled by 12 small steering rockets. Unlike the tall columns of vertically staged boosters later familiar in the West, the R-7 was short and squat, "like a mechanical Cossack in billowing pantaloons," according to historian Walter McDougall.[30]

The first flight tests in the spring of 1957 were disastrous failures. Luckily for Korolev, Soviet doctrine allowed for large production runs, even of prototypes. He had plenty of hardware at his disposal.

The first successful launch of the R-7 took place on August 3 and was soon followed by an equally successful test flight. With all of its clustered engines, the R-7's takeoff was spectacular, combining 32 separate rocket plumes. Liftoff thrust was over a million pounds, making Semyorka ("old number seven") the most powerful booster in the world.[31] After only two successful launches, Khrushchev began bragging to the world that the Soviet Union had an operational ICBM.[32]

Korolev then received his authorization to attempt a satellite launching. Mock warheads on the first two R-7 test flights had achieved near-orbital velocity. Clearly, it would be relatively simple to orbit an experimental Earth satellite that weighed only a fraction of the Semyorka's normal payload. On the night of October 4, 1957, the long-delayed countdown reached the moment of engine ignition. The concrete launch pad was blasted by the plumes of the booster's clustered engines. As the rocket climbed, its glare cast giant shadows from nearby gantries and derricks. The ground shook. Korolev watched the launch through a periscope and then turned to a radar console to verify the booster's flight path to the northeast. His team moved to another section of the launch bunker, where radio receivers were tuned to the satellite's frequency. Within minutes of liftoff, they heard the steady beeping signal from the 83-kilo sphere.[33]

Sputnik was in orbit. The Soviets had won the first important leg of the space race.

CHAPTER TWO

KHRUSHCHEV'S GAMBIT, AMERICA'S RESPONSE

OCTOBER 1957 TO JUNE 1959

When I first heard about *Sputnik*, I was in my squadron dayroom in Bitburg on the morning of Saturday, October 5, 1957. The Armed Forces Radio announcement was subdued, compared to the explosive headlines around the world. My squadron was preoccupied with completing a long alert exercise, so the news of the historic Soviet satellite launch didn't seem to mean that much to me then. That's ironic considering the fact that America's eventual response to the Soviet ICBM and *Sputnik* challenge was Project Apollo.

The New York Times set the tone for America's reaction to the *Sputnik* launch with an unusually massive Saturday edition on October 5, 1957, the day after the Soviet announcement. Most of the front page was devoted to *Sputnik* stories beneath a banner headline and a world map showing the satellite's track. A photo of Konstantin Tsiolkovsky was also prominently displayed. The title of one front-page story—"Device is 8 Times Heavier Than One Planned by U.S."—epitomized American reaction: the Russians had beaten America at its own game, modern technology. And in so doing the Soviet Union had challenged America's self-confidence.

By the next day, journalists around the country were saying that the Soviet Union was not simply America's technical and scientific equal, but its superior. "Soviet Science Far Advanced in Many Fields," was the title of *Times* analyst Harry Schwartz's long feature on October 6. Beating America into space, Schwartz stated, had "profound military and political implications." The Soviet achievement "is a superlative feat of modern science and technology. It could be done only by a nation having top-flight personnel and facilities over a very wide range of scientific and technical fields: mathematics, physics, chemistry, and metallurgy, to name only the most important ones." Soviet personnel and facilities, he stressed, were "often the equals, and sometimes superior to, the best in the rest of the world, including the United States." He emphasized that *Sputnik* was "primarily the achievement of the Soviet scientists and technicians, rather than—as some have believed—the product of German and other scientists brought to the Soviet Union after World War II."

I guess Schwartz must have swallowed the Soviet propaganda line, which categorically denied any contribution by German scientists to Soviet missile development. Concluding his article, Schwartz offered this warning: "The competence in rocketry which that satellite shows is equally applicable to the field of weapons, particularly intercontinental ballistic missiles."[1]

Schwartz's story was illustrated by a large cartoon showing *Sputnik* circling the globe, trailing a pennant emblazoned with "Man's Quest for Knowledge." The cartoon itself was entitled "The New Frontier," which is interesting since John Kennedy would use those same words in his challenge to Soviet space supremacy.

The themes raised by the *Times* echoed and reechoed through American news media over the coming months. During that winter, opinion polls confirmed the media conclusions. Most people thought *Sputnik* was a serious blow to American prestige. It looked like the country was lagging behind the Soviets, not just in missiles, but also in education and overall science and technology. Media pundits painted America as fat, lazy, and complacent, a nation more interested in suburban patios and grotesque tailfins on cars than in the discipline and hard work required of a world leader.

Politicians took a predictably partisan stance. Members of the Eisenhower administration downplayed *Sputnik*, and Democrats— especially potential Democratic presidential candidates—emphasized the urgency of the situation. Senator Jacob Javits of New York, for example, overlooked the already well funded programs for developing the Atlas ICBM, the Thor intermediate-range missile, and the Army's Redstone battlefield nuclear missile, and called for a "Manhattan Project" for missile development.[2] Senate majority leader Lyndon B. Johnson, already an unannounced candidate for the 1960 presidential race, proclaimed *Sputnik* a national emergency that required a full mobilization of America's resources.[3]

President Eisenhower dismissed *Sputnik* as "one small ball in the air, something which does not raise my apprehensions, not one iota." He refused to concede that the tiny ball of the satellite was really a symbolic nuclear warhead, that the missile that had launched *Sputnik* could also deliver an H-bomb. His advisers denied that the United States was in a civil space competition or a missile race with the Soviet Union. America would move at its own pace in space exploration, they said, and would do so for legitimate scientific purposes, not naked propaganda. White House adviser Clarence Randall scornfully described *Sputnik* as "a silly bauble in the sky."[4]

Of course, neither the media's apocalyptic view of *Sputnik's* importance nor the Eisenhower White House's pollyanna-ish dismissal of the event gave a true assessment of what was going on in the US-Soviet competition for scientific and technical strength. *Sputnik* had, in fact, been quite a propaganda gamble for Khrushchev. He had ordered chief designer Sergei Korolev to proceed with the launch of *Sputnik* just days after the first successful test flight of the R-7 missile. So even if the Soviet Union did have an actual orbiting satellite, it would be months, if not years, before they would have a fully operational ICBM. This was the essence of Khrushchev's gambit.

But given the closed nature of Soviet society, the West could not know how advanced Soviet science and technology really were, especially when it came to rocketry. Nor did Western media analysts realize that Korolev had depended heavily on basic German engineering principles to develop his rocket engines. True, the strap-on booster concept was his original contribution, but the multicombustion chamber design of the Semyorka was a compromise stemming from relatively backward metallurgy, not the superior technology proclaimed by the American media. Our mistake was in assuming that the Soviets had followed a rational, Western pattern: that before their civilian scientific project— the *Sputnik*—they had first developed and deployed their missile. If the

Soviets had actually deployed a large arsenal of ICBMs before *Sputnik*, the American reaction would have been justified. But that was not the case. And the West succumbed to what has been aptly called Khrushchev's "missile bluff."[5]

Huntsville, Alabama, 1957–1958

On the day *Sputnik* was launched, Wernher von Braun was given an unusual opportunity to further the cause of his team. On Friday, October 4, 1957, Neil McElroy, Eisenhower's newly appointed defense secretary, was visiting Redstone Arsenal accompanied by top Army brass. Medaris and von Braun had foreseen the visit as an opportunity to present their "frank feelings, backed by facts and figures" about their system's potential as a satellite booster. The drumbeat of announcements from Moscow had finally made it clear that the Soviet Union was serious about attempting a satellite launch, and the Huntsville leaders knew this might be their last chance. That afternoon at a cocktail party, an Arsenal public relations man rushed through the crowd to confront Secretary McElroy, Medaris, and von Braun. The Soviets, he said, "have just put up a successful satellite!"

After a silent moment of shock, von Braun turned to McElroy. The Viking was hopeless, he said, but the Jupiter-C could easily do the job. "For God's sake! Turn us loose and let us do something. We can put up a satellite in sixty days."

Medaris knew that von Braun had made a powerful impression, but even so the JPL team would need more than 60 days to assemble their planned *Explorer I* satellite. "No, Wernher," Medaris cautioned, "ninety days."[6]

A month later, the Soviets orbited a much larger satellite, *Sputnik II*, which carried a small mongrel bitch named Laika. The world's second satellite weighed over 1,000 pounds. During the first seven days in orbit, the Soviets received biotelemetry from the dog's pressurized capsule, until her oxygen supply was exhausted. Many in the West saw the little dog as a precursor to Soviet spacemen, and *Sputnik II* proved that the Russians were serious about spaceflight. The White House and Pentagon could no longer ignore von Braun. On November 8, the Army was given authorization for two satellite attempts.

Over the next three months, while von Braun's team and the scientists at JPL worked feverishly to prepare the mission, America's television screens blossomed with the explosions of seemingly feeble Viking rockets of Project Vanguard collapsing like cardboard on their launch pads. By January 31, 1958, when von Braun's Army team made its first attempt at a satellite launch, von Braun had realized that their future role in American spaceflight depended on a successful Explorer mission. General Medaris insisted that von Braun join him in Washington and wait out the launch in the Pentagon communications room so he could personally brief Army Secretary Wilbur Brucker on the mission.

But if he couldn't be at the Cape, von Braun made sure the Explorer launch was in the hands of his very best people. Willy Mrazek oversaw the Jupiter-C's propulsion system, just as he had the prototype A-4 in Germany. Walter Haeussermann's guidance and control laboratory had perfected the booster's inertial guidance, and Haeussermann was there that day for the final premission tuning. Ernst Stuhlinger, head of the research projects office, did the troubleshooting at the Cape. Overall command of the test launch was under Kurt Debus and his missile firing laboratory. Debus had supervised hundreds of V-2 launches in Germany and New Mexico.

All day, strong winds delayed the launch as the Jupiter-C sat on the concrete platform of Launch Pad 5, supported by a flame-blasted Redstone gantry tower. Von Braun's tone on the telephone showed how anxious he was, but he trusted his colleagues too much to interfere. Then, at 10:48 PM, Debus completed the countdown and issued the ignition command from the firing bunker. The striped cylindrical payload package was "spun up" like a captive toy to stabilize the upper stage in flight. An orange glare ripped out as the Jupiter-C's Redstone first stage roared to life. For several seconds flame blasted sideways from the Jupiter as it stood stationary on the pad.

Then the rocket climbed away into the darkness. Two and a half minutes later, the upper stages were separated by an automatic timer. For the next six minutes the payload coasted higher, to an apex 225 miles above the Atlantic. Walter Haeussermann's guidance package worked perfectly. The second-stage cluster of solid rockets was brought parallel to the Earth's surface by small thruster jets. Stuhlinger transmitted the command to ignite the second stage. After six and a half seconds, he ignited the third stage, comprised of three clustered Sergeants. Finally, he pressed the amber fourth-stage ignition button and the single-Sergeant satellite kicker motor ignited, accelerating *Explorer* to over 18,000 miles per hour, orbital velocity.[7]

Medaris had insisted on a media blackout to prevent embarrassment if the mission failed and to keep down speculation about interservice rivalry. (Despite two Sputniks and the multiple Vanguard failures, the Navy was still in the satellite game.) No reporters were there to watch the delayed countdown and the spectacular launch. Residents of nearby Titusville and Cocoa Beach simply thought another secret missile was being tested. Two hundred and twenty-five miles above West Africa, the tiny *Explorer* satellite glided silently through the day-night terminator line and into brilliant sunlight. The satellite was the size of an overgrown titanium milk bottle and weighed only $10^{1/2}$ pounds. To achieve orbit, *Explorer's* centrifugal energy would have to counter-balance Earth's gravity.

The first American listening station positioned to receive the radio beacon from a properly orbiting Explorer was the Goldstone tracking site in the California desert. Signals should have begun coming in at exactly 12:41 AM. William Pickering of JPL was with von Braun and Brucker at the Pentagon. Pickering was on the phone with his people in California as the deadline passed. There was no signal from *Explorer*.

"Why the hell don't you hear anything?" Pickering yelled.

Secretary Brucker looked up from a table littered with coffee cups and overflowing ashtrays. "Wernher," he asked, "what happened?"

Von Braun watched the sweeping second hand on the wall of the communications room. If they didn't get a signal in 10 minutes, he would have to consider the mission a failure.

At 12:49 AM, Pickering whooped with joy, holding the receiver against his shoulder. Goldstone had *Explorer's* signal. Von Braun beamed, then frowned. "She is eight minutes late," he muttered. "Interesting."

A duty officer telephoned President Eisenhower's vacation retreat in Augusta, Georgia. Ike excused himself from his late-night bridge table to take the call. He then recorded a radio announcement, reading calmly from a single sheet. "The United States has successfully placed a scientific Earth satellite in orbit around the Earth. This is part of our participation in the International Geophysical Year."[8]

Ike intentionally gave the announcement a routine tone so that the public would not come to expect an escalating series of Soviet challenges and dramatic American responses in the fledgling space race. He understood that such a race could undercut his conservative fiscal policy of minimum government involvement in propagandistic space spectaculars designed to win international prestige. The Soviets were good at this type of thing, he knew, and trying to match them would divert scarce resources from the priority task of building a military space system. But Ike's cautious policy was soon overtaken by events. During 1958 it became clear that the Russians intended to fly men, not just dogs, in space. And America would have to face this new Soviet challenge or lose the prestige competition by default.

Bitburg, West Germany, 1958

During my first two years flying F-100s in Germany, Ed White became my closest friend. I met Ed at the Point, where he was a year behind me. We sat together at the track training table, and for a lanky guy without an ounce of extra fat, Ed White could eat a lot of food. He was a sharp pilot and a thoughtful man who made friends easily. Ed had joined the squadron a year ahead of me and would soon be up for reassignment.

One afternoon in late winter 1958, he and I led two flights of younger pilots up to the North Sea for a mock dogfight with a Canadian squadron flying advanced F-86s. It was a jet jockey's fantasy: a whole empty sky to roughhouse in. Macho fighter pilots take a lot more chances in training like this than they do in combat, when there's live ammunition in the cannons. And this day was no exception. We scored several gun-camera "victories" and only lost one of our new guys.

After landing, Ed and I stood together at his plane, waiting for the squadron's last flight to let down through the overcast. Around us the young pilots were laughing, their faces creased with red welts from their oxygen masks, their eyes still excited from the mock dogfights. I looked at Ed and we smiled. Both of us knew we were getting a little old for this.

Ed told me what his next assignment was going to be. He planned to get a master's in aeronautical engineering at the University of Michigan through the Air Force program that sent qualified officers to graduate school. Once he had his degree, he hoped to enter the one-year test-pilot school at Edwards and join the elite group of military pilots who had been through both rigorous academic training and exhaustive cockpit experience. When the Air Force extended their high-altitude rocket plane experimental programs into actual spaceflight, he'd be a good candidate for a seat in the cockpit.

The more we talked the more I realized that the route Ed was taking would suit me a lot better than a career as a line fighter pilot. As much as I liked to fly, my pilot's skills would not last forever. But neither of us knew then what the Air Force's moves into space meant.

"What do you think they're going to call the guys that finally fly up there?" I asked Ed. "Rocket pilots?"

Ed grinned and slung his parachute over his shoulder as we trudged toward the squadron ops office. "No," he laughed. "The Air Force is bound to think up a fancier name than that."

We'd never heard the word "astronaut."

Washington, DC, 1958–1960

Senator Lyndon Johnson was the leading congressional supporter for developing an ambitious American space program. During a highly publicized post-*Sputnik* Senate committee investigation in February 1958, Johnson came to recognize that the "gap" between America's fumbling efforts and Soviet achievements could become a useful political cause in the next year's run up to the 1960 elections.[9]

But President Eisenhower stole some of Johnson's thunder. In April 1958, the White House presented Congress with the National Aeronautics and Space Act. The bill created a new independent government organization, the National Aeronautics and Space Administration (NASA). Ike insisted that NASA be completely separate from the Department of Defense, making it a purely civilian operation. Even so, as historian Walter McDougall has made clear, Eisenhower, his key advisers, and congressional experts realized that "the space program was a paramilitary operation in the Cold War, no matter who ran it."[10]

Eisenhower signed the National Aeronautics and Space Act on July 29, 1958. NASA took over the old National Advisory Council on Aeronautics' (NACA) test centers in Virginia and at Edwards Air Force Base in California, and the small civilian facilities at the Air Force Eastern Test Range at Cape Canaveral. Congress also authorized NASA to construct a new research center completely dedicated to space exploration. It was named the Goddard Space Flight Center and was built in Beltsville, Maryland, near Washington.

What NASA needed most was a separate program to develop research satellites and planetary probes, as well as the boosters to launch them. The new NASA administrator, T. Keith Glennan, formerly president of the Case Institute of Technology, naturally looked to the Jet Propulsion Laboratory and to Wernher von Braun's Development Operations Division at the Redstone Arsenal. If he could acquire these two from the Army, he would have the team that put Explorer in orbit. But the Defense Department, the Army in particular, was not about to give up without a fight. Glennan got his first taste of Washington hardball politics early in his tenure. His bid for the Army's space assets was rebuffed.

In the interim, the von Braun–JPL Explorer team continued to trump the Navy opposition. Although *Explorer II* failed to reach orbit because of an unsuccessful fourth-stage ignition, they orbited *Explorer III* on March 26. These small satellites were marvels of electronic miniaturization, outstripping the heavier Sputniks, which the Soviets were now launching with shocking frequency. The tiny *Vanguard I* satellite was finally put in orbit on March 17, 1958. But the more sophisticated Explorer spacecraft had definitely upstaged their Navy-sponsored rival. Aboard Explorer satellites, geiger counters developed by University of Iowa physicist James van Allen detected energetic radiation belts girdling the planet, trapped by Earth's magnetic field.

In May the Soviets hammered back, using Korolev's big R-7 booster to orbit *Sputnik III*, which weighed over 3,000 pounds. The Soviets called this satellite a "geophysical laboratory," but gave only sketchy details about the onboard equipment. Khrushchev mocked the tiny American satellites, which he said were the size of "oranges."[11]

Over the next several months there was great activity on the launch pads, in design laboratories, and especially in Washington conference rooms. Despite Eisenhower's pronouncements that we were not in a space race with the Soviets, it was clear that continued Soviet success was harming his administration both at home and abroad. So as a propaganda counterattack, Eisenhower secretly authorized the Air Force Atlas ICBM development team to prepare one of the large boosters for an orbital mission that would place a very heavy US "spacecraft" into orbit, thus blunting Khrushchev's mockery of tiny American satellites. But the President was not about to sacrifice sound military doctrine completely for propaganda purposes. He insisted that early Atlas prototypes be launched on normal intercontinental ballistic test flights before the heavy satellite ploy was attempted.

Unlike either the R-7 or the Redstone, which were offshoots of V-2 technology, the Atlas was a composite of innovative American rocket designs, and it owed relatively little to German technology. Begun as an early postwar experimental concept by the Convair company, the missile was scrapped for economy reasons in 1948, only to be resuscitated following the revelation of the Soviet H-bomb in the early fifties. The missile's long body was a huge, thin-skinned, and double-chambered propellant tank. This lightweight "gas bag" was not strong enough to support its own bulk, so it needed internal pressurization to give its metal skin rigidity. The three powerful engines all used this one fuel supply—with the two outboards acting as launch boosters and the central engine being the flight sustainer. Like Korolev's R-7, the outboard Atlas engines fell away toward the end of the initial boost phase of flight. But the Atlas had the advantage of minimal weight with maximum strength—that is, *if* the complex assembly worked as planned. Atlas was elegant engineering when all went well, but overall was dangerously unpredictable.

On December 18, 1958, the Air Force launched the Atlas prototype 10B from Launch Pad 11 at the Cape. Following the secret flight plan, the missile's internal guidance system pitched the Atlas over parallel to the Atlantic at an altitude of 110 miles and the sustainer engine burned up the remaining tons of propellant. Five minutes later, the entire 60-foot, four-ton aluminum shell was in orbit. The Defense Department proudly announced the success of Project SCORE (Signal Communications by Orbiting Relay Equipment). A tiny transmitter inside the empty Atlas shell broadcast tape-recorded Christmas greetings from President Eisenhower to the world below. It was international showmanship worthy of Nikita Khrushchev.[12]

CHAPTER THREE

"LEAD-FOOTED MERCURY"
1959 TO 1960

Washington, DC, 1959

Now that both the Soviet Union and America were orbiting increasingly sophisticated unmanned satellites and were even sending crude robot probes outward into the solar system, the next logical step was manned spaceflights. The Eisenhower administration learned through intelligence reports that the Soviets would try to launch a "new communist man" into space. Ike asked the three armed services to suggest practical manned spaceflight programs that could beat the Soviets. The Air Force's plan was the most ambitious, with an eventual manned base on the moon, but it would cost several billion dollars a year. This was out of the question to Eisenhower. The Navy's scheme for an elaborate winged spacecraft was simply impractical, worse than their botched Vanguard program.

Wernher von Braun's Army rocket team at Huntsville also entered the competition with Project Adam, in which a man would be sent on an arched ballistic suborbital trajectory sealed inside a modified missile warhead, perched atop a Redstone rocket. Such suborbital flight was simply an up-and-down lob above the atmosphere, while an orbital flight meant that the spacecraft would become a satellite of Earth. With a straight face, von Braun's boss, General Medaris, told a House space

35

committee that Project Adam was the first step toward delivering troops to the battlefield by rocket. He reluctantly pointed out that to make the actual delivery von Braun would need a new class of huge, cluster-engine boosters. NASA's Hugh Dryden later testified to the same committee that such a manned ballistic flight had "about the same technical value as the circus stunt of shooting a young lady from a cannon."[1] A Pentagon committee weighed all these different proposals, but Ike—always wary of expensive boondoggles—reserved his prerogative to approve the final plan.

In August 1958, Eisenhower decided that NASA, and not the military, should take the responsibility of launching America's manned space-flights. Administrator T. Keith Glennan met with Robert Gilruth, the deputy director of NASA's center at Langley Field, Virginia (formerly NACA headquarters), and the leaders of Langley's Space Task Group, who had been investigating a design for a manned satellite. After hearing their proposals Glennan said, "All right. Let's get on with it."[2] The group at Langley was in charge of putting Americans into space. Glennan asked Abe Silverstein, NASA's new director of spaceflight development, to find a name for this manned space program. He chose "Mercury," the name of the classic messenger of the gods, a name Americans associated with speed.

The Space Task Group's first priority was to design an orbital vehicle that would protect a human passenger through all phases of a spaceflight "envelope": launch acceleration, weightlessness above the atmosphere, reentry deceleration with its furnacelike heat, and descent to parachute deployment at about 10,000 feet. NASA designers had two basic choices: the first was a winged spaceplane like the rocket-powered X-15 and the futuristic Dyna-Soar space glider the Air Force wanted; the second was a wingless "high-drag, blunt-body" capsule. A capsule was the only design that met the weight limits imposed by the Atlas missile (the sole American booster capable of orbiting a manned spacecraft): approximately 3,000 pounds.

Max Faget, Langley's ablest designer, and his team proposed a variation of the existing conical missile warhead that looked like an upside-down badminton shuttlecock. The blunt bottom was a convex fiberglass heat shield that would point forward and disperse the reentry deceleration heat through a fiery meteor trail—a process known as "ablation." A cluster of small solid retrorockets in the center of the heat shield would brake the capsule from its orbital speed and return it to Earth. The tiny cabin was a lopped-off cone topped by a squat cylinder that held radio antennas and the parachutes. On top of this cylinder was a girdered escape tower powered by solid rockets that would pull the capsule away from a stricken booster (no one really trusted the Atlas), lifting it to a safe altitude for parachute deployment. The whole thing was a far cry from the sleek, winged spacecraft that many popular scientific magazines had imagined.[3]

I remember the guys in my squadron in Germany commenting that the Mercury capsule looked more like a diving bell than an aircraft. The pilot would lie flat on his back on a form-fitting couch. But even if the Mercury spacecraft wasn't as fiercely beautiful as the supersonic fighters we flew, it was designed to "fly" higher and faster than any jet plane, in an entirely new environment, space. There was no need for swept wings to provide lift, or a raked tail for control. The velocity imparted by the booster would lift the Mercury spacecraft far above the atmosphere.

Early in 1959, McDonnell Aircraft Corporation won the prime Mercury development contract, worth $18 million. Given Project Mercury's priority status, McDonnell (which had spent a lot of its own money on preliminary designs) quickly produced a full-scale mock-up of the spacecraft.

About this time, NASA was also deciding what type of Americans would fly the Mercury spacecraft. Some favored "macho seekers of danger," daredevils such as mountaineers, sky divers—even bullfighters.[4] Eventually, President Eisenhower put an end to the debate and decided on military test pilots: he said they combined courage and technical competence, and they were already cleared for classified projects.

In January 1959, Glennan announced that the Pentagon had a list of 110 potential candidates, from which NASA would select six finalists. All met NASA's stringent requirements: a university degree in the physical sciences or engineering, completion of military test-pilot training, a minimum of 1,500 hours of flight time, age of less than 40 years old, height of less than 5 feet 11 inches, optimal physical condition, and "physical and psychological attributes suited for spaceflight."

This new breed of pilots would be called "astronauts."

In February, the Pentagon's original list was shortened to 32 semifinalists who were then subjected to extremely rigorous medical examinations at the Lovelace Clinic in Albuquerque. From there they were flown to the Aero Medical Laboratory at Wright-Patterson Air Force Base in Ohio. Over the next two weeks the candidates were put through "scientific torture." They were shaken, spun in centrifuges, jolted in mock ejection seats, practically frozen or baked in temperature chambers, and driven to exhaustion on treadmills. Air Force medical studies indicated that an astronaut might be subjected to a 20-G deceleration during a launch-emergency abort. NASA wanted to be sure the candidates did not have any flaws in their internal organs that might prove fatal under such extreme stress. Throughout the process they were scrutinized by a team of NASA psychologists who tested them for signs of phobias or other personality flaws.

The candidates had to answer such weird questions as "Who am I?" and such deceptively simple ones as "Whom would you assign to a mission if you could not go yourself?"[5] They were also asked to rank their peers (themselves included) on a series of positive and negative attributes. This kind of psychological probing was popular in the 1950s and eventually became standard practice in the astronaut corps. At the time, however, it seemed like the latest thing in group dynamics, just the right method for picking the "technological man."

Finally, a board made up of senior NASA engineers, flight surgeons, psychologists, and psychiatrists made the selection. In the end, the decision was based on technical competence and flight experience. But the panel was deadlocked, unable to agree on only six, so Bob Gilruth, head of NASA's Space Task Group, intervened: he expanded the astronaut pool from six to seven.

Washington, DC, April 9, 1959

The converted ballroom of the Dolly Madison House on Lafayette Square was jammed with hundreds of reporters. Television and newsreel cameras flanked the conference table facing the audience. At precisely 2:00 PM, NASA administrator Glennan marched in, leading seven young men. All seven had agreed to dress casually in sports jackets, sharply creased slacks, and well-shined shoes. (All of them didn't own good business suits; they were still being paid their military salaries.) The camera lights and flashbulbs glared, but not one of them flinched. They were the kind of guys you'd see on any Air Force or Navy flight line. But here their military pilot's calm self-confidence really stood out. Six had the flattop haircuts then popular with military pilots. The seventh, Marine Lieutenant Colonel John Glenn, didn't even have enough hair to call it a cut. Lined up behind the table facing the massed cameras, they were a handsome, remarkably homogeneous group; it was as if in making the selection the country had merely gone to a secret fraternity of self-assured superpilots.

"Ladies and gentlemen," Glennan proclaimed, "today we are introducing to you and the world these seven men who have been selected to begin training for orbital spaceflight...the nation's Mercury astronauts!" Already they represented the entire country, not just NASA.

Reporters rose to their feet and applauded. This is when the press's love affair with the astronauts began. The seven men grinned and blinked at the flashbulbs. In front of the table stood an elaborate model of the Mercury capsule atop its gleaming Atlas booster. NASA's new logo, Earth ringed by the sweeping red track of an orbiting spacecraft, hung behind the group.[6]

Glennan asked each astronaut to stand and be introduced, and the applause repeatedly swelled. John Glenn was the oldest, 37, and the very essence of a straight-arrow Marine. He was the senior officer and the most experienced pilot, with over 5,000 flight hours and with combat time in both World War II and Korea. I met John during the Korean War when he was a Marine exchange pilot in another squadron in my wing. He was a cool, ambitious professional who worked by the book. In the final week before the ceasefire, when all the pilots were trying to get in their last licks and raise their kill count, he shot down three MiGs along the Yalu.

Astronaut Malcolm Scott Carpenter was a 33-year-old Navy lieutenant and the only multiengine test pilot in the group. Given the widespread disdain fighter pilots had for multiengine "drivers," Carpenter was going to have a hard time with the other guys. At 36, Walter Schirra, a lieutenant commander in the Navy, was the second oldest. Schirra was a talented pilot, but tended to treat everything and everybody as if life were one big joke. Alan Shepard, another Navy lieutenant commander, was a few months younger. He was "gung ho" personified and a rising star in naval aviation. Shepard always scrambled to the top of the heap, no matter what program he was in. He had graduated near the head of his Annapolis class, and he had a knack for making friends with influential people. I suppose he was the kind of officer my dad had had in mind when he'd wanted me to attend the Naval Academy.

The Air Force guys were a rougher cut than the Navy officers. All three had come up the hard way, without the benefit of service academy or ROTC training. Virgil I. (Gus) Grissom was a 33-year-old captain who'd flown 100 combat missions over Korea in addition to over 2,000 hours in jets. He'd earned his wings as an aviation cadet during World War II, graduated from Purdue in mechanical engineering, and then signed up in the Air Force again for Korea. Captain Donald K. (Deke) Slayton, 35, had flown bombers in World War II and had worked for Boeing as an aeronautical engineer. Deke didn't have any of the smooth polish that Glenn and Shepard had, but he knew his way around the real world better than most of them, and his down-to-earth maturity helped keep the others' egos in check. The youngest astronaut, aged 32, was another Air Force captain, Leroy Gordon Cooper. "Gordo" was a scrappy little guy who'd served a hitch in the Marines, earned an Army commission through OCS, and then transferred to the Air Force, where they thought enough of him to put him through engineering school. He was a test pilot in the most advanced fighters out at Edwards. He was passionate about fast cars and flying.

Grissom, Slayton, and Cooper were well outside the network of West Point four stars who ran the Air Force. If those generals had realized that NASA's astronaut program was going to be their only chance of flying men in space, they probably would have encouraged the selection of more sophisticated candidates. But Air Force brass wanted their own Dyna-Soar spaceflight operation and disdained the bush league civilian show.

All seven astronauts were married, fathers, and Protestant. All came from small towns; four were named for their fathers. Schirra and Shepard were Annapolis graduates. There wouldn't be an astronaut from West Point until the second and third selections, when a whole bunch of us came in—Frank Borman, Ed White, Mike Collins, Dave Scott, and me.

Several of America's leading test pilots—including Chuck Yeager—couldn't even apply for the astronaut program because it required a university degree in science or engineering. Education is what marks the difference between aviation and spaceflight. The white-scarf, stick-and-rudder jockey who could hop into the cockpit of anything with wings and "wring the sumbitch out" in the sky over the Mojave Desert didn't really belong in the astronaut corps. I've often thought that Yeager's and his colleagues' bitterness about the "Spam-in-the-can" astronauts was just frustration and envy. Yeager was one hell of a pilot, but I don't believe his sour grapes explanation that he never wanted to fly in space anyway. He said recently that he simply didn't have the education to qualify as an astronaut.[7]

Administrator Glennan outlined the astronaut selection procedure, which gave the media even more excuse to say that the Mercury seven were intrinsically superior to *all* other pilots. They were called the cream of American technological manhood. At the press conference, however, the reporters were less interested in how these seven were chosen than they were in a human peg to hang their stories on. No one cared that there was not much difference between the Mercury seven and the 25 other semifinalists who had made it through the physical and psychological torture tests at Wright-Patterson—that they were actually first among equals.

The country wanted individual heroes, not a team. The reporters bored in on the astronauts' courage, daring, and patriotism and paid little attention to the technical details of Project Mercury. The media treated the astronauts' medical examinations as if the astronauts had overcome some type of arcane ritual ordeal. John Glenn surprisingly provided grist for the sensationalists' mill. "If you figure out how many openings there are in the human body," he said, "and how far you can go into any one of them, you can answer which would be the toughest for you."

NASA's public relations staff had skillfully implied that the astronauts had volunteered out of pure patriotism, and each man at the table was milked for something quotable. "My career has been in service of my country," Gus Grissom sheepishly managed, "and here is another opportunity to serve." There's no doubt that the original seven and all of my colleagues in the astronaut corps were patriotic, but what Gus did not add was that every fighter pilot worth his salt wanted more than anything to fly higher and faster than his peers. *Some* lucky bastard was going to do it, and all of us, from the original seven through the later groups, weren't going to just sit back and let somebody else have all the fun. Nor do we speak easily about this. All astronauts are explorers. We just don't like to talk about it.

John Glenn was the most at ease with the press. He was a PR man's dream: a Sunday-school teacher who had earned five Distinguished Flying Crosses and 19 Air Medals, and was the first pilot to cross North America at supersonic speed. John was also well known from his appearance (dressed in his medal-covered dress blue uniform) on the TV quiz show *Name That Tune*. He charmed the press conference by saying things like: "I'm probably doing this because it is the nearest to heaven I'll ever get."[8] He'd been courting the assignment night and day for months as one of the test pilot advisers to NASA's preliminary spacecraft design team.[9] Glenn knew exactly what he wanted and single-mindedly went after every aspect of the task—including a well-cultivated public image.

One reporter asked the most dramatic question of the press conference: "Can I have a show of hands on how many of you are confident they will come back from outer space?"

All seven men raised their hands. John Glenn raised both of his.

Tom Wolfe must have been thinking about moments like this when he coined the term "the right stuff."

Time magazine said about the press conference that "from a nation of 175 million, they stepped forward last week: Seven men cut of the same stone as Columbus, Magellan, Daniel Boone, Orville and Wilbur Wright."[10] Only the obscure technical journals also covered the Mercury capsule and the project's goals. What was most striking was that many of the reports took it for granted that America's astronauts would also be the *world's* first men in space.

Bitburg, West Germany, Spring 1959

I heard about the Mercury astronaut selection almost simultaneously from Ed White and Armed Forces Radio. At first, the astronaut eligibility requirements and the intense testing seemed absolutely daunting. For a week or so, I went along with the popular myth that the seven really were some kind of superpilots. Then Ed wrote that he'd already sent off his application for test pilot school at Edwards, laying the groundwork for getting into the next astronaut selection, which he was confident was in the offing.

I saw he was right. That spring America and the Soviet Union increased the pace of their satellite launches, making it clear that both countries were in space for keeps. Manned spaceflight was bound to expand beyond Mercury. I had to follow Ed's lead and get more education. Digging through university catalogs at the base education office, I looked for a school that would suit my needs. In the end, there was only one option, the astronautics program at MIT.

Washington, DC, and Huntsville, Alabama, 1959–1960

Even with the successful satellite launches and the Mercury program just starting, NASA was already looking to future projects. Eisenhower, on the other hand, was opposed to expensive space spectaculars in which American assets would be committed to an open-ended space race with the Soviet Union. During Khrushchev's Washington visit in September 1959, Ike got a taste of how extensively Khrushchev intended to use the space race for international propaganda. The Soviet premier boasted of his nation's space achievements, notably the *Luna* probe that had just crashed into the moon bearing a sphere emblazoned with the hammer and sickle. Khrushchev gave Eisenhower a replica of the *Luna*, a gift Ike contemptuously dismissed during a press conference as "...just a little ball...." The actual *Luna*, Ike commented, "probably vaporized" when it hit the moon, making it an empty propaganda gesture, not a real scientific achievement.[11]

Enhancing national prestige through spectacular space achievements—the propaganda use of a country's space program—was not solely the prerogative of the Soviet Union. America also played the game, and it became a dominating passion of the two presidents who succeeded Eisenhower.

George M. Low, a soft-spoken, scholarly research engineer, had joined NASA headquarters with Abe Silverstein to become chief of the Office of Spaceflight Programs. Just a year and a half after *Sputnik I*, Low strongly recommended that NASA's first post-Mercury goal should be to loop a manned spacecraft around the moon (a "circumlunar" mission), eventually leading to the obvious next step—a lunar landing. Low did not make this recommendation lightly; such a goal would represent a horrendously expensive and complex technical challenge. But this became NASA's "long-range plan," the agency's unofficial wish list, even without White House support. The plan called for spacecraft and booster technology that would send men on circumlunar flights by 1968 and possibly a manned lunar landing sometime after 1975. NASA estimated that the first phase of the program would cost around $2 billion. George Low told the press that America stood a chance to "win more gold medals in the space Olympics than any other nation."[12]

NASA realized a circumlunar flight would require a spacecraft that could provide life support for more than one astronaut and be capable of reaching a velocity of 25,000 miles per hour in order to escape from Earth's gravitational field. It would also have to shield the crew from radiation while traveling to the moon and be able to withstand reentry to Earth's atmosphere at this speed, which was much greater than the 17,500-mile-per-hour orbital reentry. The big spacecraft would be far heavier than the booster capacity of any planned military missile.

Von Braun's Huntsville team already had a class of large boosters on the drawing board. Called the Saturn (after Jupiter's neighboring planet in the solar system), the first generation of large boosters incorporated a cluster of Jupiter-type engines as the first stage, to produce 1.5 million pounds of thrust. Von Braun also envisioned a second-generation superbooster he called the Nova, whose first stage would cluster the big F-1 engines that were then being studied by the Defense Department. *Each* F-1 produced a thrust of 1.5 million pounds.

In December 1959, Abe Silverstein and his advanced development group went even further than von Braun's ambitious initial plans for the Saturn class of rockets. Following conventional design philosophy, the first stage of the new boosters would use proven kerosene and LOX propellants. Silverstein, however, knew that the upper stages of any eventual moon booster would require a much higher thrust-to-weight capability than LOX-kerosene technology could provide. His group recommended fueling the upper stages with supercold ("cryogenic") liquid hydrogen and LOX, a high-energy combination whose use was fraught with technical problems. This was the technology that the rocket pioneers Tsiolkovsky, Oberth, and Goddard said offered the most efficient and lightweight conversion of fuel to thrust. Von Braun knew this, of course, but was hesitant to embrace this unconventional propellant technology. His years of trying unsuccessfully to interest America in spaceflight had taught him to be cautious in his recommendations. Now that senior NASA officials were backing this method of fueling the boosters, he was more than happy to follow.[13]

Silverstein's insistence on the high-energy cryogenic upper stages for NASA's eventual Saturn rockets would become the key that would unlock the door to the first moon landing. After the fall of 1959, Wernher von Braun began participating to an even greater extent in both NASA's Project Mercury and ambitious advanced spaceflight plans. Eisenhower, recognizing that if America was going to compete with the Soviets it would need large civilian boosters, finally gave in to Glennan's repeated requests and transferred von Braun's Development Operations Division of the Army Ballistic Missile Agency to NASA, effective July 1, 1960. On that date, Wernher von Braun became director of NASA's new Marshall Space Flight Center (named for Ike's wartime colleague General George C. Marshall) in Huntsville, Alabama. Eisenhower even attended the dedication ceremonies on September 1, 1960. NASA had acquired the Army-funded Jet Propulsion Laboratory (JPL), the nation's preeminent satellite laboratory, the year before. This was part of a White House compromise designed to appease both Glennan and the Pentagon, but actually satisfying neither because NASA didn't get the von Braun team and the Army lost the JPL.

Von Braun's Huntsville center had an in-house industrial capacity unlike anything seen before. His policy, from Peenemünde days, was to have his team actually build their own prototypes, rather than farming out the work to industry. So Marshall was actually a booster factory, not simply an R&D laboratory.[14] JPL had the same type of operation for the construction of prototype satellites and spacecraft systems. NASA now had the ability to begin practical work on a manned lunar landing program. All they lacked was White House approval.

Abe Silverstein again drew on his knowledge of mythology for the name of NASA's post-Mercury manned spaceflight project. "Apollo," the name of the sun god who rode his flaming chariot across the sky, was suitably evocative for this exciting program. Administrator Glennan agreed on the name, but Project Apollo, George Low quickly admitted, had as yet "no official standing." That was probably the understatement of that year.

Eisenhower may have supported unmanned scientific and military reconnaissance satellites, but he only grudgingly approved Project

Mercury and refused to back any post-Mercury plans until an ad hoc panel of science advisers assessed NASA's future goals for cost-effectiveness. The committee concluded that a manned lunar landing would cost almost $40 billion. Ike was outraged and demanded to know why America should undertake such an expense. When a staff man compared the proposed lunar mission to Columbus's voyage to the New World, Eisenhower noted that Queen Isabella of Spain had raided the royal treasury for that adventure, but he was "not about to hock *his* jewels" to put Americans on the moon. When another adviser suggested the lunar flight was actually just the first step toward manned exploration of the planets, the cabinet room rang with scornful laughter.[15] NASA planners realized that they would have to look to the next administration for a more ambitious American space program.

Cape Canaveral, Summer 1960

The first unmanned test flight of the complete Mercury-Atlas system (MA-1) was scheduled for late July. NASA, the Air Force, and McDonnell Aircraft all considered this test critical. This would be the first time an actual prototype capsule would be launched atop an Atlas missile. This flight had been scheduled, delayed, and rescheduled, all with great fanfare. The press was growing impatient with the program, which now seemed on the verge of floundering. A successful flight would show the next administration that Project Mercury deserved support. Politics and science continued to be intertwined.

The morning of Friday, July 29, was squally, with thunderstorms pounding the concrete of Launch Pad 14. In the humid firing room of the nearby blockhouse, Bob Gilruth watched the Convair–Air Force launch team sweat through a series of countdown delays. At 9:10 AM, the clouds lifted high enough and the Navy recovery team 1,300 miles downrange in the Caribbean reported acceptable weather.

At exactly 9:13, the three Atlas engines roared to life and the bulky, shining booster topped by the dull black Mercury spacecraft slowly rose on a cascade of flame. Within seconds it disappeared into the overcast sky, the thunder of its engines pounding the drizzly Cape. The men in the blockhouse hunched over their instruments, closely following the telemetry data. Fifty seconds into the flight everything looked perfect—

"nominal," as we say in missilery jargon. Then, at exactly 58.5 seconds, the screens went blank. All data stopped. Gilruth consulted the test conductors—they only shook their heads.

A radio message from a naval unit reported that debris was splashing down in the ocean seven miles offshore. The Atlas had exploded at 32,000 feet and a velocity of 1,400 feet per second, the point in the flight envelope known as "Max Q"—maximum aerodynamic pressure.[16] Everyone's nightmare had come true. The notoriously dangerous Atlas was incapable of safely launching an unmanned Mercury spacecraft. If an astronaut had been on board, he probably would have been killed. The news media focused on the accident as yet another failure in the trouble-plagued, increasingly expensive program.

The accident had been caused by a structural failure in the interface area between the Atlas booster and the base of the Mercury capsule. But the debris had been so shredded by the explosion that test engineers were unable to determine exactly which component had failed. It would take months of careful analysis before another Mercury-Atlas test flight could be attempted.

The press jumped on this new delay. For the first few months of the Mercury program, the news media had been NASA's uncritical cheerleaders despite the earlier test-flight delays. But as they discovered how technically complex the program was, the press reversed its course and became unfairly scornful. *Time*, which had gushed over the astronauts the year before, now mocked "Lead-Footed Mercury."

Unfortunately, NASA headquarters inadvertently chose the day of the MA-1 failure to announce Project Apollo, their post-Mercury program that would include sustained orbital flights, a circumlunar mission, and one day, perhaps, a manned lunar landing. Given the gap between the MA-1 exploding over the ocean and this ambitious project, it's no wonder Ike's conservative advisers had a belly laugh in the cabinet room when they squashed NASA's grandiose plans.

Throughout the fall election campaign, Democratic presidential nominee John F. Kennedy hammered away at Eisenhower for allowing the Soviet Union to successfully challenge American leadership all over the world—and especially in space. Kennedy portrayed a global struggle in which the uncommitted nations of the Third World would soon choose between the East and the West, and the Soviet Union was winning the global race for hearts and minds. The Soviets had created a "space gap," and if it continued, Kennedy emphasized, it would represent "the most serious defeat the United States has suffered in many, many years."[17]

"What shall we do around the world to reverse the trend of history?" he asked. Then he promised that his administration would see the "American giant" stir once more. Kennedy vowed he would never allow the Soviet Union to dominate and embarrass the United States again.

To make matters worse for the Republicans during the campaign, Sergei Korolev's team launched a series of increasingly heavy Korabl-Sputniks, officially described as manned spacecraft prototypes. Then, in late September, a NASA lunar probe atop an Atlas-Able booster exploded in a widely televised spectacular failure. The contrast of Soviet success and American failure was just the thing John Kennedy needed to underscore his campaign theme of overall American decline.

The Soviets provided NASA's critics with even more ammunition: their "muttniks," Strelka and Belka, flew aboard a Korabl-Sputnik at the end of the summer. American intelligence reported to the White House that the flight was, indeed, the test of a manned spacecraft four times as heavy as the Mercury capsule. And intelligence sources revealed a frantic expansion program at Tyuratam, with a booster assembly line factory under construction. Obviously, the Soviets were building for a long-term space effort.

Tyuratam, Kazakhstan, Fall 1960

In October, Premier Khrushchev held a press conference at the United Nations in New York and announced that the Soviet Union would soon launch a Russian into space. In the past, the Western press had always treated such bravado with scorn, but this time Khrushchev was taken at his word. He even extended his stay, because Soviet scientists were attempting to launch an unmanned space probe to Mars, and the Soviet premier hoped to present the United Nations secretary general, Dag Hammarskjöld, with a model of the Soviet *Mars I* spacecraft, just as he had given Eisenhower the *Luna* replica the year before. The first two attempts to launch the Mars probes, October 10 and 14, 1960, failed when the new fourth stage to Korolev's reliable R-7 booster malfunctioned after reaching Earth orbit. Khrushchev returned to the Soviet Union without having mentioned either of the two failures.

But Soviet scientists at Tyuratam were still trying to launch the Mars probe. Korolev had made a practice of preparing three redundant boosters and spacecraft for every mission, as insurance against failure. There were still a four-stage booster and a Mars probe remaining. The Mars "launch window" (the best planetary alignment for the mission flight path) was rapidly closing, so the final launch attempt was made on the night of October 24, 1960. Marshal Mitrofan Nedelin (Sergei Korolev's superior), commander of the newly organized Strategic Rocket Forces, personally supervised this final launch.

The countdown reached zero and the ignition signal was transmitted. But the clustered booster engines failed to ignite, possibly because of an electronic fault in the massive rocket's first stage. Korolev issued the proper "safing" commands, which disabled the booster's main electrical systems. Under normal circumstances, the rocket would be drained of fuel, tested for malfunctions, and refueled for the next launch attempt: this could take weeks, but Marshal Nedelin could not accept this delay. He desperately needed a success, or he would face Khrushchev's wrath. Nedelin led a team of engineers from the blockhouse to the launch pad to inspect the rocket.

Korolev wisely stayed sheltered within the thick concrete walls of the launch bunker, a safe distance from the pad.

As Khrushchev later recalled in his memoirs, "The rocket reared up and fell, throwing acid and flames all over the place.... Dozens of soldiers, specialists, and technical personnel..." died in the disaster. "Nedelin was sitting nearby watching the test when the missile malfunctioned, and he was killed."[18]

James Oberg, the American expert on the Soviet space program, has subsequently discovered that the rocket engine of the *Mars I* itself had not been disabled by Korolev's "safing" command. Its electronic timer fired the rocket while Nedelin's team stood at the base of the booster, triggering a holocaust that consumed over a million pounds of kerosene and LOX.[19] The deadly fireball was spectacular, visible for miles across the flat steppes of Kazakhstan.

The loss of Nedelin had little effect on the manned Soviet program, but the massacre of Korolev's best launch technicians was a serious blow.

Moreover, the Politburo soon learned that the disaster had been provoked by Khrushchev's demands for space spectaculars. Eventually, such blundering would lead to his downfall.

At the time, Western news media were unaware of the Nedelin catastrophe. That winter NASA continued to work at putting together the Mercury program, all the time tensely waiting for the Soviets to announce another in their apparently unbroken line of space successes.

CHAPTER FOUR

KENNEDY'S CHALLENGE
1960 TO 1961

Cape Canaveral, November 1960

Throughout the 1960 presidential campaign, John Kennedy made good political use of NASA's humiliating failures, but after election day Project Mercury's problems became his. As if to make sure he knew this, that afternoon's test flight of a Mercury capsule failed 16 seconds after it was launched atop a solid-fuel booster called the Little Joe from NASA's Wallops Island range.

Two weeks later, on November 21, the combination of an unmanned Mercury capsule and a Redstone missile was finally ready for its first ballistic test flight. This launch was important because, if successful, the unmanned MR-1 would prove that von Braun's reliable Redstone could safely fly Mercury astronauts on suborbital trajectories into space. Actually launching an American astronaut with a rocket (although not an Atlas) would boost the country's prestige—and maybe even beat the Soviets. Also at stake that day was the reputation of von Braun's Huntsville team as builders of successful rockets. Their competitors in the Air Force's Ballistic Missile Division farmed out much of their booster development work to private contractors such as Convair, but von Braun's Peenemünde group were hands-on perfectionists who personally verified the entire booster assembly and launch.[1] They certainly realized the energetic new president would be watching.

At precisely 9:00 AM, when Kurt Debus's countdown reached zero, bright flame pulsed from the base of the booster. But before the blast of sound even reached the firing room, the rocket plume disappeared. Debus saw the Redstone wobble on the concrete launch stand and rise only a few inches before clanking down on its stabilizing fins. A moment later the escape tower atop the Mercury capsule detached and fired straight up 4,000 feet. The black Mercury spacecraft vibrated atop the Redstone booster, wreathed in thin smoke from the departed escape tower. Then the drogue parachute popped up, dragging out the fluttering canopy of the main parachute. A moment later, the reserve chute spilled down the other side of the capsule and the silent booster.

It looked more like a comic circus stunt than science. But the men in the blockhouse, especially Gilruth and George Low, were not amused. Still, the comedy of errors continued. The Redstone stood there lifeless but fully fueled and dangerous, just like the booster during the Nedelin catastrophe. The pyrotechnic devices designed to separate the capsule and ignite the retrorockets were still armed, and if anyone tried reattaching the launch gantry, the explosives might be triggered. At any moment a strong breeze could fill the 60-foot parachutes and topple the Redstone, triggering a massive explosion. It was hours before the booster's batteries ran down and the German engineers could safely approach the Redstone.[2]

Von Braun's team traced the cause of the fiasco to the electrical umbilical line connecting the booster to the pad. It had been designed for a standard Redstone missile, but the Mercury booster's fuel tanks had been elongated in the Huntsville shops. The umbilical cord was just a bit short and had pulled loose a fraction of a second too early after ignition, causing the engine to shut down prematurely.

The problem was easily correctable, but again the press had a field day. The Eisenhower White House also made the most of this seeming incompetence in its campaign against manned spaceflight. A pattern was emerging in the press: NASA would be rewarded for exciting space successes but unfairly damned for the inevitable failures. The news media still view the science of spaceflight as a public circus and use their own commentators as resident experts.

Finally, in December, the chastised von Braun rocket team successfully completed an unmanned Mercury-Redstone test flight. The capsule—newly christened a "spacecraft" at the astronauts' urging—functioned perfectly throughout the flight envelope, reaching an altitude of 130 miles and a speed of almost 5,000 miles per hour. The escape tower separated normally and the retrorocket pack fired exactly on time. Most importantly, the ablative heat shield held up beautifully against the thermal stress of reentry, and the parachute system functioned flawlessly. At least it was a step in the right direction.

Washington, DC, January–February 1961

Soon after the election, it became obvious that the only cabinet member knowledgeable on space was Vice President Lyndon Johnson. Kennedy decided that LBJ would be his point man on everything related to space policy and that Johnson would chair the National Space Council as an active leader, not just as a figurehead. Kennedy saw this as one way of keeping the dynamic Johnson away from those policy areas he and the East Coast intellectuals the president had chosen as advisers thought were better suited to be the true "New Frontier" successors of Franklin Roosevelt's New Deal.

In any case, despite his focus on the "space gap" during the campaign, space was clearly not one of Kennedy's overriding interests. In fact it was not until late in the transition that the president-elect decided that Johnson would take on the task of choosing a NASA administrator. LBJ asked his friend Senator Robert Kerr to suggest someone as NASA head. Kerr was the Democratic chairman of the Senate Committee on Aeronautical and Space Sciences and a freewheeling oil millionaire from Johnson's neighboring state of Oklahoma. The vice president knew he'd need powerfull allies in both the House and Senate to support the ambitious, expanding space program he envisioned for the new administration. If LBJ understood anything, it was the US Congress, specifically the Senate, where he'd been majority leader before the election. Since Kennedy and his close advisers were obviously not going to give LBJ the power he sought in shaping New Frontier policies, he would have to parlay his expertise on space into a secure private turf.

With typical southwestern gusto, Kerr recommended his business associate James Webb. According to Kerr, Webb possessed "the greatest mental energy for sustained mental and physical effort of anyone I know." Webb also had Washington experience dating back to the New Deal, had served as a Marine Corps aviator, and understood the business side of space, being a member of the board of McDonnell Aircraft. Webb was capable of absorbing and conveying to congressional committees more complex information than any NASA administrator before or since. Equally important, he was deeply loyal to LBJ. Webb also knew that winning the space race demanded that America leapfrog Soviet technical superiority in boosters. And to do this NASA would have to implement the tentative Apollo-Saturn-Nova plans Eisenhower had officially rejected in his final month in office.

Immediately after the inauguration, Kennedy was too preoccupied with pressing foreign policy problems in Cuba and Southeast Asia to listen to Johnson's plans for reshaping America's space policy.

Also, his science adviser, Jerome Wiesner, an MIT physicist, was openly skeptical of the political and scientific value of manned space spectaculars. Before he was made science adviser, Wiesner had headed a Kennedy transition team, which had examined NASA's present and future projects. The Wiesner Report chided NASA for mismanaging Project Mercury and said it was unlikely that America would put a man in space before the Soviets. Wiesner felt NASA had overemphasized manned spaceflight as the major space objective, and he suggested that the White House downplay "space travel" and instead focus on military space programs and unmanned satellites.[3] Wiesner's report clearly drew the battle lines between Johnson's southwestern space enthusiasts and Kennedy's inner circle.

The Johnson-Kerr-Webb space alliance, however, was able to convince Kennedy through Wiesner that large-booster development was vital to whatever space program the president might eventually choose to pursue, because Wiesner favored unmanned space probes, and they, too, would need powerful new boosters. Kennedy requested additional funds for NASA to develop the Saturn booster and the F-1 engine for the Nova. Meanwhile, behind the scenes, Johnson continued to lobby his colleagues in Congress for his informal "Big Space" alliance.

Cape Canaveral, December 1960–January 1961

The first months of Kennedy's New Frontier were an exciting time. In fact, that spirit caught on at NASA, and it looked as if America might launch a man into space before the Soviets. Only six weeks after the successful Mercury-Redstone tests, the von Braun team launched the MR-2 flight with the "monkeynaut" Ham, a 37-pound chimpanzee, riding the spacecraft in his own custom-contour couch. Liftoff went as planned, but unexpectedly high Redstone thrust caused the spacecraft to overaccelerate and climb to a higher altitude, farther downrange than planned. This subjected the chimp to a reentry deceleration of almost 15 Gs. After splashdown he bobbed around in the choppy Atlantic for two hours before a Navy ship picked up the spacecraft. But Ham was uninjured and in good spirits. He happily ate an apple and half an orange while posing for pictures with the sailors.

In principle, America was now ready to launch an astronaut on a Mercury-Redstone suborbital lob. But Wernher von Braun and his close advisers were still not convinced the "old reliable" Redstone was safe enough for manned flight. Instead of scheduling America's first astronaut mission for February or March, von Braun decided he'd play it safe and add a "Mercury-Redstone-booster development flight" for the end of March. The painstaking German rocket team wanted to be absolutely certain that their booster was as reliable as it could be. The delay meant America would not be ready for an actual manned flight until late April at the earliest.

Tyuratam, Kazakhstan, February–April 1961

The Soviets were launching one heavy Korabl spacecraft after another with dogs on board. At MIT it was clear to those of us in the astronautics department—both students and faculty—that there'd soon be a Soviet in space. The Russians seemed to have mastered the business of spaceflight technology development with amazingly few accidents or reversals. Since then we've received considerable inside information from Soviet defectors and Western experts about just how desperate the Soviets were to win.[4]

Like the United States, the Soviet Union was trying to simultaneously develop manned spacecraft and their boosters and new, highly sophisticated ICBMs, including solid-fuel missiles to be launched on a moment's notice from submarines and land-based silos. Both countries experienced rivalry and competition for talent between the civil and military rocket programs. In the USSR, design bureaus named for their

leaders—Korolev, Chelomei, Yangel, and others—combined the functions of NASA or military missile offices and the aerospace companies
that build the hardware. Every chief designer of a bureau wanted to
maintain his support in the Politburo's defense council, just as McDonnell or North American Aviation sought the support of the NASA
administrator or the defense secretary.

Premier Khrushchev had given Sergei Korolev's design bureau the
assignment of building a manned spacecraft—to be proudly named
Vostok ("the East")—in early 1958. Korolev favored the type of spacecraft
the Mercury designers planned—a lightweight titanium "blunt body"
capsule. It would be actively controlled by the astronaut and would
splash down in the ocean. But Khrushchev rejected that design,
insisting that Soviet spacemen would land on the sacred soil of the
Motherland, not in international waters and surrounded by a swarming
flotilla of news media vessels full of spies and saboteurs. (Khrushchev
did have a point: the only practical "ocean" the Soviets could have
splashed down in was the Black Sea, a pretty small target given the
guidance capabilities then.)

This meant Korolev had to build a spacecraft heavy enough to
withstand land impact, but light enough for practical parachute descent.
The Vostok spacecraft would also require redundant automated control
systems; everyone agreed that the delicate business of managing a
complex orbital flight could not be left completely to a human pilot.
According to Soviet air force doctrine, then and now, the pilot doesn't
have much individual initiative. He is steered to the target by a ground
controller, who commands his every action. This command philosophy
spilled over into their manned space program, in the same way that the
individualism of American test pilots influenced ours. In an emergency,
of course, the cosmonaut could intervene with a limited manual
override capacity.

Korolev solved the weight problem with one of his ingenious
compromises. Unlike the Mercury, the Vostok would be a two-part
spacecraft, with a spherical reentry module attached to a heavier
instrument unit. This instrument section, which contained batteries,
retrorockets, and life support supplies, would detach before reentry and
burn up in the atmosphere. Vostok's spherical reentry module was
completely covered by an ablative-resin heat shield, which meant the
angle of reentry trajectory was not as critical as it was with the blunt-

ended Mercury spacecraft. The separated Vostok reentry sphere would plunge like a fiery cannonball until it was 24,000 feet above Earth; then the hatch would automatically blow and the cosmonaut would be catapulted out of the spacecraft by ejection seat for normal parachute descent.

Korolev's team launched the *Korabl-Sputnik 3* mission on December 1, 1960, a dress rehearsal for the first manned Vostok flight. Two dogs, Muchka and Psholka, flew in the reentry module. The launch booster, a modification of the reliable Semyorka (revamped after the Nedelin accident), carried a single RD-107 engine in an upper stage above the central sustainer section. The Vostok spacecraft rode in a protective conical shroud atop the second stage. But disaster struck at the end of the mission. In attempting to descend from orbit after retrofire slowed the Vostok, the reentry angle into the atmosphere was far too steep and the descent module burned up. An even graver calamity, however, occurred later that night when Korolev suffered a heart attack. At the hospital in nearby Leninsk doctors discovered he also had a serious kidney affliction, a common complaint of former gulag inmates.

They urged him to give up his punishing work schedule, but Korolev knew that the future of the Soviet space program depended on delivering Khrushchev a prestigious victory. He left the hospital after only a week and picked up his schedule, driving his team through 18-hour workdays. He was convinced that America's new president would accelerate Project Mercury—a natural assumption given everything John Kennedy had said during the campaign.

In the first months of his administration, Kennedy was caught up in a series of crises that diverted his attention from the space program. The most serious issue was whether to intervene militarily in Laos, where the pro-Western government was on the brink of falling to communist Pathet Lao guerrillas. Kennedy mobilized the American military, but stopped short of direct intervention. Although none of us knew it at the time, he was also involved with the secret plans for the US-sponsored Bay of Pigs invasion. A brigade of anti-Castro Cubans, trained and bankrolled by the CIA, was poised at bases in the Caribbean to strike as soon as the White House gave the green light.

It wasn't long before Khrushchev reminded Kennedy and the world of the Soviets' superiority in space. He ordered Korolev to speed up the launching of the first cosmonaut. In March *Korabl-Sputnik 4* and 5 flights were launched as practice runs for the first manned spaceflight attempt. Again the "cosmonauts" were dogs, and these missions were complete successes, with every piece of equipment functioning perfectly. But there was one more test that needed to be run on the Vostok's parachute ejection system. These parachute tests were originally supposed to be done carefully over an incremental schedule using dummies and larger animals, ending with the first live human jump in May. The news from Cape Canaveral, however, convinced Korolev that Project Mercury would launch an American into space before then, so out of desperation he ordered the ejection system certified for spaceflight by March 1.

Pyotr Dolgov was the chief test subject for the parachute ejection system. He was a dashing, flamboyantly mustachioed parachutist who had over 500 jumps to his credit, including several with ejection seats in new jet fighters. The final test was scheduled in late February. He dressed in a full spacesuit and was strapped into a prototype Vostok ejection seat aboard a mock-up spacecraft that was rolled out the cargo ramp of a high-flying Antonov transport. Dolgov was ejected from the Vostok mock-up, and his parachute opened automatically. When the recovery crew found him lying on the frozen mud of the steppes, his helmet was cracked open. The cheerful parachutist was dead. Only then did Korolev discover his design error. The hatch was too small for the cosmonaut's bulky spacesuit and seat. On ejection, Dolgov had been jammed against the hatch frame and his neck had been broken.

Korolev ordered a priority program to enlarge the hatch and redesign the timing mechanism to blow the hatch free two seconds before the ejection seat was triggered, so that the cosmonaut and hatch would not collide. Finally, he asked his superiors in Moscow to make sure the first cosmonaut was small enough for safe ejection.

The actual selection of the cosmonaut was in the hands of Khrushchev and the Politburo. Out of a group of a dozen young air force pilots training for the first space mission, Khrushchev narrowed the choice to two: Majors Gherman Titov and Yuri Gagarin. Khrushchev understood well that this historic person had to fulfill the special political requirements of the Communist Party of the Soviet Union. Ethnically, the first cosmonaut had to be Russian on both sides of his family back for three generations to ensure that there would be no taint of Asiatic or Jewish blood. And the successful candidate also had to have demonstrable proletarian origins. Both Titov and Gagarin fit these requirements, but Titov's father was a schoolteacher with a suspiciously bourgeois background, whereas Yuri Gagarin's parents were admirable peasants on a collective farm. He was the quintessential "new communist man."

Gagarin was also short enough to fit safely through the enlarged ejection hatch. He received his orders for the flight just two weeks before the April launch attempt.

On April 11, 1961, American intelligence received a confirmation that the Soviets would launch a man before the fifteenth. Kennedy asked Pierre Salinger, his press secretary, to prepare a congratulatory statement for release when the Soviet spaceman was launched. The statement also pledged JFK's continued support for the US space program. That night Wiesner took the latest intelligence estimates to the Kennedy's second-floor quarters and informed the president the Soviet flight would occur within hours.[5]

Moscow, April 12, 1961

Wednesday, April 12, 1961, was a day for the history books. Radio stations across the Soviet Union and Radio Moscow's international service interrupted their morning programming to play a medley of patriotic music, ending with the rousing song "How Spacious Is My Country." Then came the announcement: "The world's first spaceship, *Vostok*, the 'East,' with a man on board, has been launched on April twelfth in the Soviet Union on a round-the-world orbit." The cosmonaut was Air Force Major Yuri Alekseevich Gagarin, age 27. That morning's official Tass statement said *Vostok 1* had been launched from an unidentified location at 9:07 AM Moscow time. For the next hour and a half brief bulletins traced Gagarin's path around the world, his progress relayed by Soviet tracking ships. Over Africa, Gagarin announced, "The flight is normal. I am withstanding well the state of weightlessness." It was not until 12:25 PM that Radio Moscow announced, "At 10:55, Cosmonaut Gagarin safely returned to the sacred soil of our Motherland."[6]

After landing—near Saratov, on the steppes north of Volgograd—Gagarin spoke with Premier Khrushchev in a well-publicized phone conversation.

"You have made yourself immortal because you are the first man to penetrate space," Khrushchev told him.

"Now, let the other countries try to catch us,"Gagarin answered on cue.

"That's right," Khrushchev replied. "Let the capitalists try to catch up with our country, which has blazed the trail into space and launched the world's first cosmonaut."

For the next two days, official Soviet news media were rich with political propaganda and human-interest stories (for example, Gagarin was described as having a handsome Slavic face). But typically, the articles lacked real technical information. The Soviet information ministry had obviously been well prepared for the historic flight. Their gushing patriotism more than matched the American media's jingoistic enthusiasm for the seven Mercury astronauts. Many of the technical details Soviet space experts released were conflicting. First they implied that Gagarin had ridden inside the Vostok to a safe landing, but then confused the issue by saying he had descended by parachute, "landing on his feet, without even tumbling."

Now, of course, we know that Gagarin parachuted from the relatively crude *Vostok 1* spherical reentry capsule when it reached an altitude of about 20,000 feet. But in order not to risk losing the Fédération Aéronautique Internationale spaceflight record, which required the occupant to descend in the spacecraft itself, the Soviets had to keep this as vague as possible. The fact that the five-ton Vostok—almost four times the weight of the Mercury spacecraft—could not support a cosmonaut for landing showed how relatively unsophisticated it was. So did the "automatic flight control system" the Russians boasted about. In fact, Gagarin was much more "Spam in the can" than any Mercury astronaut, because he had strict orders to touch the controls of his spacecraft only in an emergency.

Washington, DC, April–May 1961

President Kennedy was awakened early with a full intelligence briefing on the Soviet Vostok flight. The Soviets had beaten us into space, with a full orbital flight, not just a ballistic lob. If anything, Gagarin's mission was a greater propaganda coup than *Sputnik 1*.

The leading East Coast news media that had backed Kennedy's

election now chided him for ignoring America's space program and
letting the Soviets get away with this monumental victory. The criticism
was also echoed in Congress. Some congressmen became even more
hysterical than they had been at the Sputnik humiliation. James Fulton,
a Pennsylvania Republican, asked deputy NASA administrator Hugh
Dryden in an open hearing if the Russians were capable of sending a
rocket to the moon "which would create a red dust and turn the whole
moon red." Dryden somberly told him that intelligence reports indicated that the Soviets might, indeed, try such an embarrassing
propaganda coup.

"Maybe we should have a project," Congressman Fulton seriously
suggested, "a blue project to scatter blue dust so then the moon is red,
white, and blue."[7]

Kennedy's reaction was noticeably subdued. Salinger's statement
congratulated the Soviets on their "outstanding" technical achievement.
The president cabled congratulations to Premier Khrushchev, stressing
his desire for international cooperation in space. Later that day, in one of
his regular news conferences, he conceded the Vostok flight was a great
personal frustration for him. But, he added, the American space
program would "go into other areas where we can be first...."

Two days later, Kennedy held a meeting with his close advisers and
experts on space. "Is there anyplace we can catch them?" he demanded
impatiently. "What can we do? Can we go around the moon before
them? Can we put a man on the moon before them?" NASA's Dryden
and Webb suggested a crash program, like the Manhattan Project to
build the atomic bomb, that might beat the Soviets to the moon, but
Kennedy's budget director, David Bell, warned of the cost of such an
effort. Wiesner again recommended caution. "Now is not the time to
make mistakes," he pointed out. Kennedy asked the group to prepare
more information on projects that might beat the Soviets in the space
race. "There's nothing more important," he said in closing.[8] He still
hadn't discussed the matter thoroughly with his vice president.

Despite Kennedy's insistence, Wiesner and the president's other key
advisers doubted that chasing the Soviet Union for glory in the manned
space program was a wise thing to do, but JFK knew that if the Soviet
Union continued to score propaganda coups while America was stuck on
the ground, the vigorous New Frontier would appear to be a charade.

Kennedy finally met with Lyndon Johnson at the end of the week and told him to survey America's space effort and propose concrete plans for winning the space race. In his memo confirming this special assignment, Kennedy asked LBJ, "Do we have a chance of beating the Soviets by putting a laboratory in space, or by a trip around the moon, or by a rocket to land on the moon, or by a rocket to go to the moon and back with a man?" He asked Johnson to coordinate his work closely with James Webb, Defense Secretary Robert McNamara, and Wiesner.

Wiesner realized that Johnson's assignment meant the president was leaning toward an accelerated post-Mercury space program even more ambitious than NASA's original concept for Project Apollo. He later said Kennedy had become "convinced that space was the symbol of the twentieth century."[9] In effect, Kennedy was conceding that although his first choice was not to pursue an ambitious, horrendously expensive head-to-head struggle with the Soviet Union in space, the Soviets now controlled the board and could make the rules.

While Kennedy met with Johnson, events in Cuba made a dramatic new American space initiative even more essential. The Bay of Pigs invasion was a bloody debacle. The anti-Castro brigade never made it past the beach. By the night of April 17, the invasion force was pinned down, in desperate need of the American air cover the CIA advisers had promised. But on his brother Bobby's advice, the President refused to commit the American military. The political fallout from this disaster made Kennedy appear both reckless and indecisive—the opposite of the bold confidence he had shown three months before at his inauguration. A cartoon in the London *Daily Mail* epitomized Kennedy's humiliation. It showed the young president with his teeth clenched on an exploding Cuban cigar.

Meanwhile, in a memo to Johnson, Wernher von Braun stated the view of most senior NASA officials. The Soviets had an advantage in boosters that would continue to give them a lead in manned spaceflight for several more years. But if NASA began a priority program to build large boosters and develop the Apollo spacecraft, America would have "an excellent chance of beating the Soviets to the first landing of a crew on the moon...." Von Braun thought this could be accomplished by 1967 or 1968. The intelligence community informed Johnson that the cautious, incremental development pattern of Sergei Korolev's rocket design bureau would probably keep the Soviets from having a large Saturn-class moon booster for several more years. An accelerated

American program employing the full talents of von Braun's team and the US aerospace industry could produce such a booster before the Soviets. In effect, we would be beating them at their own game. That was the kind of competition Lyndon Johnson liked.

The vice president also did not formally consult with Wiesner or any of the science advisers about this. It was the Texas swashbuckler's deliberate snub of the eastern intellectual.

Cape Canaveral, May 5, 1961

On the morning of May 5, 1961, almost a thousand reporters and television crews from around the world gathered at the Cape. NASA was finally ready to launch a Mercury astronaut into space. This was a welcome respite from the Soviet's drumbeat of space successes.

Navy Lieutenant Commander Alan B. Shepard, Jr., had been chosen to ride the first manned Mercury-Redstone suborbital ballistic mission, an important check flight of the full Mercury spacecraft system— including the performance of an actual human pilot. Ham, the chimp who had dutifully completed the earlier flight, could not actually *fly* the Mercury spacecraft, but Shepard could. Out at Edwards Air Force Base in California, Chuck Yeager and his test pilot buddies said Shepard would have to "brush monkey shit" off his seat before climbing aboard his Mercury spacecraft.

The media's anticipation of the flight focused on the mystery of who America's first man in space would actually be. Early in January, Bob Gilruth had assembled the seven astronauts for a confidential meeting at Langley and told them he had picked Al Shepard for the first flight and John Glenn as backup. Gilruth tapped Gus Grissom for the second suborbital mission. He based his decision on overall training perform- ance, peer reviews, and his staff's perception of astronaut competence. Shepard's natural competitiveness and self-confidence had definitely made him stand out from the group. Gilruth had made his choice early so the astronauts could begin intensive training either as flight crew or in specialized ground-support assignments. Gordo Cooper, for example, would be the capsule communicator ("capcom") during liftoff; Wally Schirra would fly the launch chase plane; and Deke Slayton would coordinate flight control communications.

Gilruth had then publicly announced that Shepard, Grissom, and

Glenn were the *candidates* for the first flight, but did not disclose his actual choice. Leading up to the launch the media were speculating about the "inner three" and the "outer four," as though the three first-flight candidates were somehow superior to their colleagues.

Al Shepard, however, didn't seem to have any problems with this. Even a British observer of the space program like Hugo Young of the London *Sunday Times* recognized Shepard's zeal. Young described Shepard as "a tough, prickly character, [who] had the timeless arrogance of the fanatical pioneer."[10] Al and John Glenn were equally gung ho, but Shepard was an intense loner and there wasn't much love lost between the two of them, a natural enough conflict between two aggressive fighter pilots—one in the Navy, the other a Marine. Over the two years since astronaut selection, some of the others had christened Shepard "Professor Al" because of his maddening habit of taking over press conferences with pedantic answers to reporters' questions. As a group, the astronauts fell into mini-cliques: the Air Force guys, Slayton, Grissom, and Cooper, were pretty much from the "I just fly the sonofabitch" fighter pilot school; Scott Carpenter and John Glenn were straight arrows; and Wally Schirra joked his way along, not offending anybody. Shepard burned with a hot intensity that could not be matched. He was determined to be the best in everything he did.

On the morning of launch he ate an early breakfast of bacon-wrapped filet mignon and scrambled eggs. These "cholesterol special" breakfasts became a tradition thereafter, and only recently have the younger, more health-conscious astronauts in the shuttle program modified them. The idea behind the low-residue preflight meal was to postpone defecation, because of the tight-fitting pressure suit.

After breakfast, Shepard, dressed in his gleaming foil-skin suit and lugging a portable suit-ventilator pack, threaded a gauntlet of press photographers, accompanied by NASA technician Joe W. Schmitt. A transfer van carried them to Launch Pad 5, where Shepard took the open-cage elevator to the top of the gantry tower and crossed a swing arm to the tarpaulin "white room" on the open hatch of the Mercury.

Gunter Wendt of McDonnell, chief of the closeout crew, greeted him as he came off the elevator. Gunter would become a fixture at the Cape over the next decade. He was an ex-Luftwaffe flight engineer, who had just as much Germanic thoroughness as von Braun did. Gunter also took care to insert an astronaut properly into a spacecraft. After all, it did sit atop a fully fueled booster. A little after 6:00 AM, Shepard was strapped into his couch and the hatch was bolted. In his suit he was breathing pure oxygen to purge his bloodstream of nitrogen, which could provoke the bends if the cabin explosively decompressed after liftoff.

Shepard had named his Mercury spacecraft *Freedom 7*, partially because it was McDonnell Aircraft's seventh capsule and because he knew that name would go well at the White House. This was the last Mercury that had two small portholes and an awkward periscope for viewing. The year before, the astronauts had proposed certain modifications to the spacecraft, including a wide window and explosive bolts to jettison the hatch after splashdown, but it was too late to make these modifications on *Freedom 7*.

Tom Wolfe correctly described the modifications in *The Right Stuff*, but the movie based on the book made the event into a dramatic confrontation between the outraged astronauts, standing shoulder to shoulder—in spacesuits, no less—and a haughty group of grotesquely Teutonic German designers. This is absolute nonsense. Von Braun's Germans had nothing to do with designing the spacecraft. That was the responsibility of Max Faget (an affable, soft-spoken Cajun) and McDonnell's John Yardley, an easygoing Midwestern engineer.

After almost three hours of last-minute delays, Kurt Debus and his Redstone launch team were ready in the blockhouse. Forty-five million Americans hunched before their television sets, watching the slender black-and-white booster steaming with wisps of supercold LOX. Shepard was so excited he didn't hear the final moments of countdown until Gordo Cooper's exuberant "Ignition!" came through his earphones. The liftoff was much smoother than Al had expected, with no vibration and almost no noise from the engine 70 feet below. He raised his gloved hand to start the mission clock.

"Ahh, Roger," he called. "Liftoff and the clock is started." He gave the fuel and cabin pressure readouts and then said, "*Freedom 7* is go."

For the first minute, the ascent was perfectly smooth. A powerful, invisible piston seemed to slowly squeeze Shepard into his couch. Then the vibrations began, followed by severe up-and-down buffeting. At Max Q, 30 seconds later, the buffeting became so severe his helmet slammed against the headrest despite the web of straps that held him to the couch. The instrument panel went from a blur of lights to a smear of vibrating images. When he got past Mach 1 and Max Q, the ride smoothed out. Then, 2 minutes and 22 seconds into the ascent, the engine shut down on schedule. The Mercury spacecraft was moving at 5,134 miles per hour. The escape tower blasted free right on time and the capsule detached from the booster.

Shepard did not immediately realize he was weightless because restraint straps held him tightly in his seat. The automatic control system fired the thrusters that rotated the spacecraft so that the heat shield faced forward, and a washer floated past his helmet visor and hung eerily in midair before him. America's first astronaut was in space. He couldn't see much from the small portholes—*Freedom 7* was the last capsule without a real window—but he did easily make out a large section of the Florida coast and several islands of the Bahamas group. When *Freedom 7* reached an altitude of almost 117 miles, Shepard exercised the hand controller, using it in both the manual and semi-automatic "fly by wire" modes. The system worked well at both settings, allowing him to "fly" the spacecraft around all three axes of traditional aviation—pitch, roll, and yaw—just as an airplane banks and turns.

Shepard was showing what having a *man* in space really meant. He was controlling the vehicle through the critical parts of the flight envelope, which gave him a margin of safety should the automated control system—which had been provided for the chimpanzee Ham and cosmonaut Yuri Gagarin—fail. Shepard adjusted the pitch for the correct retrofire position at an angle of 34 degrees above the horizon. The retrorockets blasted on schedule, slowing the spacecraft with a slapping thump he heard clearly over the static in his earphones. As the reentry G forces built, Shepard kept the spacecraft properly aligned with the reaction control system thrusters. He later said it gave him a "pleasant feeling of being in full command." Slowly the deceleration Gs mounted, squashing him into his couch at 12 times his normal weight. He waited tensely for his parachute to release. At 10,000 feet, the small drogue parachute pulled away the antenna canister above him, deploying the main chute. The Mercury's skirtlike impact bag was also now in place to cushion his splashdown.[11]

A Marine Corps helicopter was standing by as *Freedom 7* splashed into the Atlantic, 302 miles east of the Cape. Twenty minutes later, aboard the aircraft carrier *Lake Champlain*, Shepard was handed a heavy radiotelephone receiver. It was a congratulatory phone call from the president.

America had put a man in space, and the entire world had seen it. Jack Kennedy was pleased.

Washington, DC, May 1961

The president was not the only person impressed by Shepard's flight. Congressmen were deluged with positive phone calls and telegrams urging them to expand America's space program. And key committee members passed this public support on to Vice President Johnson. "Lead-Footed Mercury" was forgotten.

Johnson gathered a team of space experts, including James Webb, Hugh Dryden, Abe Silverstein, and Robert McNamara, at the Pentagon the day after Shepard's flight. By the end of the day, the group had agreed that a bold, accelerated program aimed at landing American astronauts on the moon was the United States' best chance of beating the Soviet Union. Only a lunar landing initiative could guarantee that the United States would surpass the current Soviet technical lead in boosters and spacecraft. The next day, Johnson personally delivered to Kennedy the group's memo, which read in part: "It is man, not merely machines, in space that captures the imagination of the world.... Dramatic achievements in space therefore symbolize the technological power and organizing capacity of a nation...." It concluded: "The non-military, non-commercial, non-scientific, but 'civilian' projects such as lunar and planetary exploration are, in this sense, part of the battle along the fluid front of the Cold War."[12]

On Wednesday, May 10, 1961, Kennedy met with his closest advisers to discuss the lunar landing project. He listened to Jerome Wiesner's cautious reservations, but abruptly approved the vice president's complete recommendation. Kennedy said he would soon announce that the lunar landing goal was the centerpiece of America's space program. He would request that Congress allocate funds to accelerate the development of advanced spacecraft and boosters as well as research into nuclear-propelled space vehicles and a rapid buildup of communication and weather satellite technology. The moon landing target date was 1967. NASA advised President Kennedy that a landing before the end of the decade was a more practical goal.

Two weeks later, on Thursday, May 25, 1961, Kennedy addressed a joint session of Congress on a subject he called "urgent national needs."

The president spoke passionately about the worldwide struggle between liberty and communist subversion. He addressed difficult social and economic problems of the developing world and the military challenge presented by Soviet expansionism. Two-thirds of the way into his speech, he turned to the space race. "If we are going to win the battle that is going on around the world between freedom and tyranny, if we are going to win the battle for men's minds, the dramatic achievements in space which occurred in recent weeks should have made clear to us all, as did the Sputnik in 1957, the impact of this adventure on the minds of men everywhere who are attempting to make a determination of which road they should take."

In his characteristic ringing tones, Kennedy said it was time "for a great new American enterprise. . . . I believe that this nation should commit itself to achieving the goal, before this decade is out, of landing a man on the moon and returning him safely to Earth. No single space project in this period will be more exciting, or more impressive to mankind, or more important for the long-range exploration of space; and none will be so difficult or expensive to accomplish."

Kennedy made it very clear that the final decision was up to Congress, and behind him Lyndon Johnson, seated in the chair reserved for the president of the Senate, nodded. Speaker of the House Sam Rayburn, another Texan, sat beside Johnson, gazing thoughtfully at Kennedy. Maybe the speaker was thinking how good the expanded space program was going to be for Texas.

Kennedy projected the cost at up to $40 billion for the combined military and civilian space initiative. This figure would have brought an audible gasp from Congress during the Eisenhower administration, but Lyndon Johnson had prepared the audience well. Kennedy's speech was interrupted several times by bipartisan applause. "If we are to go only halfway," Kennedy cautioned, "or reduce our sights in the face of difficulty, in my judgment, it would be better not to go at all."[13]

It was a powerful message. The seven weeks between Yuri Gagarin's flight and this speech had been a crash course on space for Kennedy. He now understood that spaceflight was, in fact, *the* symbol of the New Frontier. For the first hundred days of his administration Jack Kennedy had been struggling to transform his bold inaugural address into reality. A great nation, he now realized, was one that undertook great adventures.

CHAPTER FIVE

SKIRMISHES
1961 TO 1962

Cambridge, Massachusetts, May 1961

Kennedy's speech made it clear that America was moving ahead into space. I watched the president on television and felt the excitement when the congressmen broke into thunderous applause. I'd gotten a letter from Ed White a few days earlier telling me he was applying for the second group astronaut selection and that he'd heard there'd be more if the space program expanded beyond Project Mercury. With Kennedy's backing, NASA was definitely going to need a lot more astronauts.

The country was swept up by the space program, and I wanted to be a part of it. But NASA retained its requirement that astronauts have a diploma from a military test pilot school—not one of my credentials. Since I knew that the moon landing program Kennedy had described would need astronauts with other skills than the ones they drummed into you at test pilot school, I opted for another 18 months of intensive work on a doctorate in astronautics, specializing in manned orbital rendezvous.

MIT had the strongest astronautics department in the world, having consistently produced the best theoretical and practical work in the field. Following Sputnik, Professor Dick Battin, one of my advisers, had helped plan an innovative theoretical Mars probe designed to cross interplanetary space using an automated onboard celestial navigation system. Such conceptual excellence had already drawn the attention of NASA to MIT.

I chose my thesis subject carefully. Hoping to work for either NASA or the Air Force after completing my doctorate, I wanted to make a positive contribution. Manned orbital rendezvous was a vital field, because any way you cut it, if we were going to assemble large interplanetary spacecraft, we'd have to master the techniques of space rendezvous—bringing two or more separately launched spacecraft together in orbit. With computers we could reduce the blizzard of spherical geometry and calculus equations down to automated rendezvous procedures. But I'd seen enough autopilots malfunction during my flying career to realize that the spacecraft NASA planned to use for Earth orbital and lunar spaceflight would need some kind of manual backup.

An astronaut "flying" a spacecraft just isn't the same as throwing a Super Sabre through a dogfight. There's no true up or down in space, nor is there lift in the traditional sense of the term. And orbital rendezvous is very complicated, but can appear deceptively simple. For example, an astronaut in a lower orbit—closer to Earth—might want to catch *up* with his partner in a higher orbit. The fighter pilot's instinct is to fire his engine and increase velocity. But speed and centrifugal energy are intertwined and this maneuver would loop the lower spacecraft above the target, placing him in a still higher orbit. He would also slow down, so that his partner would appear to drop below and speed away. They call this "orbital paradox," and it definitely can be puzzling. In short, the instincts an astronaut had that kept him alive flying jet fighters could easily betray him in space.

The problem becomes much more complex when the astronaut cannot see his rendezvous target or have radar contact with it. There is, however, one important link between standard aviation and manned spaceflight. Through the hand controller, the astronaut can operate the spacecraft reaction control system (RCS) thrusters, which act like the jet fighter's stick and rudder. When a pair of thrusters fires, the spacecraft pitches, rolls, or yaws. Firing a larger thruster propels the spacecraft in one direction—a process known as "translation," which is like opening the throttle of a jet plane. Relative to the direction the spacecraft is pointing, this can change velocity right or left, up or down, forward or aft.

My challenge was figuring out a way of putting these complex orbital mechanics into an exact sequence of maneuvers an astronaut could follow with the spacecraft's attitude and thrust hand controllers. Military flight instructors had done basically the same thing when they transformed theoretical aerodynamics into standard flight maneuvers using a plane's stick and throttle. By December 1962, my graduate work was almost complete and the Mercury program was in full swing. I sweated through my oral and written doctoral exams and emerged with only some finishing touches to put on my thesis. I dedicated it "To the men in the astronaut program, oh, that I were one of them." But I wasn't optimistic. NASA was still requiring that test pilot's diploma.

Cape Canaveral, 1961

NASA's Space Task Group prepared to launch America's second manned Mercury flight. The Soviets weren't saying anything about their future flight plans, but NASA saw the advantage of "openness" in the American space program—or at least the manned civilian side of it.

After Sputnik four years before, the von Braun team's attempt at orbiting an American Earth satellite had been made late at night far away from reporters. Now NASA was staging every flight as though it were a championship sports event.

The Mercury program now had its own public relations staff, led by a salty Air Force pilot, Lieutenant Colonel John (Shorty) Powers. He put the space press corps together with the program experts and astronauts in a series of briefings that made the reporters' task easier and created an atmosphere of frank and honest cooperation never seen before in a government research-and-development project. The press, both foreign and domestic, ate it up, and the resulting international prestige generated solid congressional support and funding.

A whole new language came up during Project Mercury. It was an amalgam of engineering and flight-test terms, Air Force acronyms, and NASA-ese—for example, when a "glitch" developed in a "subsystem," a team of NASA experts would "work the problem" (not *on* the problem) until conditions were back to "nominal," or simply "go." This way of talking seemed to suggest that standard English was too cumbersome for the speed and energy of spaceflight.

America's second man in space, Air Force captain Gus Grissom, wasn't as good with all this press attention as Al Shepard had been. Gus was a fighter jock who'd come up through the Air Force ranks and had gotten his mechanical engineering degree at Purdue on the GI Bill. He and his wife, Betty, were childhood sweethearts; he drank beer from the can and changed his own oil. His favorite pastime was duck hunting with his two sons.

Whether he liked it or not, for two weeks in July 1961, Gus Grissom became one of the most highly visible men in America, if not the world. NASA went out of its way to make Gus—and the astronauts after him— available to every reporter with an inane question about space and every photographer who wanted to justify his trip to Florida. Television crews followed Gus around Cape Canaveral, capturing him in the spartan decor of the crew quarters in NASA's Hangar S, shadowing him when he went out to Launch Pad 5 to inspect the Redstone booster and Mercury spacecraft number 11, which he—obviously uncomfortably— told the eager reporters he'd christened *Liberty Bell 7*.

This spacecraft incorporated the improvements on Shepard's capsule that the astronauts had requested from NASA and McDonnell Aircraft: a wide centerline window instead of tiny portholes, and a side hatch that could be jettisoned instantly by exploding pyrotechnic bolts. The modified hatch would allow the astronaut to get out of the spacecraft quickly if it sprang a leak after splashdown in the ocean. Rescue swimmers could also blow the hatch by pulling a lanyard stowed in an external panel. In short, these changes made the tiny Mercury spacecraft seem more like a jet.[1]

By the morning of Friday, July 21, Grissom had been through two canceled launches because of the weather. He was tired, but he repeated the ritual breakfast and was pushed and prodded by Joe Schmitt's team of suit technicians. In the press grandstand, many of the reporters were nursing hangovers resulting from four days' boredom on the rainy beach. It was raining again out at sea this morning, but was clear above the Cape. Just before Gunter Wendt's closeout team screwed in the hatch's explosive bolts, Air Force psychiatrist George Ruff leaned into the spacecraft and asked Gus how he felt.

"Okay," he muttered. "Fine." What the hell should he have said, that he was scared? Any normal person strapped into that tiny diving bell on top of 25 tons of explosive propellant was bound to be a little worried. Looking back, I guess the whole concept of manned spaceflight was so new that the Air Force figured it had to send one of their psychiatrists to observe poor Gus's reaction to the upcoming flight. I don't know what they intended to do about it.

Liftoff was at exactly 7:20 AM. Like Shepard, Gus Grissom didn't immediately feel the engine ignition. The padding of Gus's couch was thicker, so he wasn't banged around as much as Shepard, and his instruments didn't jump up and down through Max Q. The pale blue horizon of the summer morning turned darker. The escape tower clanged ominously as it was automatically blasted free. Gus watched it sparkle and tumble away in the darkening sky. Exactly 2 minutes, 22 seconds after liftoff came BECO (booster engine cutoff). Gus was in space. He had the unnerving sensation that he was tumbling wildly. Bright sunlight flooded through the window as the spacecraft turned. Gus saw the panorama of the cloud-draped Florida coast and turquoise ovals of sunlit sea more than a hundred miles below. Dust, scraps of insulation, and wiring snippets floated before him in the cabin. He pitched the spacecraft through a complete circle and was awestruck when he saw the curved blue sphere of Earth as it seemed to slide *up* the window.

Gus forced himself to rely on his attitude direction indicator (ADI), the "eight ball" that every kid in basic flight school learns to trust during instrument training. Three minutes later, a light winked on the panel, signaling apogee: an altitude of 118 miles. Other instrument lights flashed: the periscope automatically retracted above his head, and he aligned the spacecraft for the proper retrofire attitude. When the retros fired he felt another rush of disorientation that made it seem like the spacecraft had reversed itself and was somehow plunging face forward toward Florida. Multicolored smoke from the blazing reentry spiraled past the window as the heat shield did its job. Gus's pulse shot up and his breathing grew hoarse. All he could do was wait for the drogue chute to stabilize the spacecraft.

The drogue deployed a little early, at 12,000 feet, and was followed by the main chute. Gus reported that he saw a large L-shaped tear in the orange-and-white canopy, his voice ragged with alarm. But the rip-stop parachute fabric didn't tear any further. Four minutes later the space-craft's inflated landing bag smacked the side of an ocean swell and the *Liberty Bell* pitched over. Grissom stared out through the window into the Atlantic depths for what felt to him like an uncomfortably long time.

The aircraft carrier *Randolph* was only three miles away and its primary and backup recovery helicopters were already orbiting *Liberty Bell*. Gus called Lieutenant Jim Lewis, the primary chopper's com-mander, and told him to delay pickup until he had a chance to record the data from his instrument panel, not an easy thing to do while gripping a grease pencil with pressure gloves the size of sausages. Finally Gus removed the safety pin from the hatch detonator switch, unbuckled his restraint straps and lay back, waiting for confirmation that the chopper had secured its cable hook to the top of the spacecraft.

"I was lying there minding my own business," Gus later reported, "when I heard a dull thud."

The hatch blew off and a warm wave slopped into the spacecraft, flooding the cockpit and turning *Liberty Bell* sharply over. Another wave surged in. The spacecraft was sinking. Gus struggled out the hatch and into the choppy water, directly under the helicopter's blasting rotor wash. The chopper crew mistook Grissom's flailing arms for a signal that he was all right. Instead of rescuing Gus, they bore in on *Liberty Bell* and managed to secure their hoist cable. But by this time it was too heavy and sank beneath the surface, dragging the helicopter down until its wheels were touching the sea.

Grissom was in serious danger. His suit was flooding; as he thrashed his arms, the suit flexed, sucking in more seawater through an inlet valve on his chest he'd forgotten to close. He screamed for help, but his voice disappeared in the noise of the helicopter engine. At the last moment, the backup chopper's copilot tossed Gus a rescue sling, which he dragged backward over his head and arms. He dipped beneath the surface before the cable went taut. But he was then pulled up in bright sunlight, twirling underneath the chopper as he was hoisted aboard like a huge shining fish.

Grissom had been within seconds of drowning. He watched as the primary recovery helicopter was forced to cut the hoist cable. *Liberty Bell* sank almost 3,000 fathoms beneath the surface.

Although Gus always swore he had not touched the hatch detonator, a cloud of shame hung over this incident. Some engineers said it was possible that the external hatch lanyard might have somehow gotten tangled in the swirling nylon skirts of the deflated impact bag, but others claimed the system was foolproof.[2]

Despite *Liberty Bell*'s loss, NASA felt that with the two Mercury-Redstone missions, they had proven the system was "spaceworthy" and that American astronauts could survive the stress of spaceflight.

The next hurdle, of course, would be an orbital flight, during which the spacecraft would become an actual Earth satellite. To do that, NASA would have to use the powerful, unpredictable Atlas booster. "Man rating" the Atlas was still a difficult, frustrating challenge.

Tyuratam, Kazakhstan, Summer 1961

Chief designer Sergei Korolev was given regular briefings on the American space program by the Red Army's GRU intelligence branch. He learned that summer that NASA had overcome the growing pains of the Mercury spacecraft and could now begin an ambitious flight-test schedule. At this rate, it was likely the Mercury would be flying orbital missions within a few months. The most alarming report Korolev received said that NASA had approved an advanced, two-man version of the Mercury, far more advanced than his own Vostok.[3] The program had not been officially announced, but Korolev was told it was called Project Gemini, from the Latin for "twins."

Western news media reported that NASA was both competent and adventurous and that the astronauts now were more than just test pilots in an experimental flight program—they were humanity's, not just America's, representatives on the space frontier. Korolev realized that his own space program would probably never get this kind of international prestige, considering how secretive the Soviet government insisted it be. The Tyuratam space center appeared on no maps. Korolev's name was not known in the United States, or even in the Soviet Union, the country he had brought so much honor. Khrushchev claimed imperialist assassins would kill Korolev if his identity were widely known, and insisted he simply be "the chief designer." Korolev was well aware of how politics had manipulated his space program. During one of the delays in Gus Grissom's Mercury launch, Korolev read a TASS report datelined "Cape Canaveral" that speculated NASA might be hiding serious problems with the Redstone booster.

"Just imagine," Korolev told a colleague, "that there should be a report in one of *our* papers that, say, the flight of *Vostok 2* was due to take place today, but that because of some technical fault we were putting it off until tomorrow!"

His colleague chuckled.

"What the hell are you laughing at?" Korolev shouted. "You ought to be crying!"

Korolev apparently was worried that his American competitors might beat the Soviets at their own game. But he also knew that the people at NASA were smart enough not to undertake anything in front of all those cameras and reporters unless they had first mastered their new technology. He was deeply worried Khrushchev would not be so prudent.[4]

On cue, Khrushchev let Korolev know his feelings about Project Mercury at a meeting at the premier's Black Sea vacation dacha in mid-July 1961. After patiently listening to Khrushchev's predictable tirade that the Soviet Union must accelerate its Vostok flights to upstage the Americans, Korolev told him frankly the problems that would have to be overcome to do this. The Vostok was unsafe to better Mercury, he said, because neither the spacecraft nor the cosmonauts were ready for long orbital missions.

Khrushchev didn't even try to hide his impatience. He ordered Korolev to prepare for a 17-orbit, one-day mission at once. Korolev patiently explained that the Vostok's retrorockets were liquid fueled, and there was no guarantee they would function properly after 24 hours in the weightless vacuum of space. Until they could develop a better retro system, this kind of long orbital mission would risk stranding a Soviet cosmonaut in space.

Again, Khrushchev refused to accept his chief designer's logic and told him the 24-hour *Vostok 2* flight would be launched in early August.[5] Korolev firmly believed this would push the Soviet space program too fast. But he also knew full well that Khrushchev had some overriding political motive for insisting that the mission take place in early August. Korolev could actively defy the premier, but Khrushchev would simply have fired him and probably replace him with his old nemesis, designer general Vladimir N. Chelomei, who had commanded the special gulag where Korolev was held during the war. The future of Soviet manned spaceflight depended on Korolev's obeying the impulsive premier.[6]

On the morning of August 6, 1961, Soviet air force major Gherman Titov fastened his white helmet to the neck of his bright orange spacesuit and climbed through the hatch of the Vostok spacecraft bearing the call sign *Orel* ("eagle"). The Semyorka booster blasted off with the familiar braided flame trail, arching the spacecraft into the blue summer sky of Kazakhstan.

The first five hours of the mission passed uneventfully. Korolev had intentionally kept cosmonaut Titov's flight duties to mere routine communication checks. Titov said he saw the spectacular beauty of orbital sunrise and sunset, and he photographed the eerie incandescent afterglow. During his third orbit, he ate his lunch from tubes: meat spread and liver pâté, bread cubes, and black currant juice.

By the afternoon, however, Titov seemed sluggish and subdued. On his next pass over a ground station, Titov said he was experiencing severe nausea and a clamminess like seasickness. His instrument panel seemed to bob and swim before his eyes, and he couldn't shake the feeling he was flying upside down. When he moved his head the nausea grew worse. He stopped even the few tasks left on his flight schedule. Finally, he dimmed his cabin lights and closed his eyes. "Now I'm going to lie down and sleep," he told the ground controllers. "You can think what you like, but I'm going to sleep."

Korolev realized Titov was too ill to control the spacecraft properly for reentry if the automatic systems failed, but the deorbit braking worked well and *Vostok 2* plummeted into the atmosphere above the grassy steppes north of the Kapustin Yar test range. When the recovery team reached Titov, however, he was still pale and queasy. But the next day he pulled himself together enough to pose with Khrushchev in Moscow before the city's press corps. The premier enthusiastically said that with this flight the peaceful, scientific nature of the Soviet space program had led all of humanity beyond the confines of its parent planet. And, he emphasized, the benevolent, progressive nature of the Soviet socialist system was responsible for this achievement.

Five days later, Red Army engineers and East German border guards rolled prefabricated concrete barricades and barbed wire entanglements into place on the border between East and West Berlin: the Berlin Wall, dividing the former German capital into two parts, had been created. This was why Khrushchev had needed a counterbalancing "progressive" Soviet space achievement and why Korolev had been forced to fly the risky 24-hour mission before the Vostok system was ready. Korolev's carefully engineered space program was a hostage to such events as long as Khrushchev was in power.[8]

Marshall Space Flight Center, Huntsville, Alabama, and Cape Canaveral, 1961

Now that President Kennedy had committed America to a lunar landing, NASA, and especially Wernher von Braun, had to prove they could rapidly outdo the Soviet Union with a booster technology that would take man beyond Earth orbital flights to the moon. By the time of Kennedy's speech, America already had a workable, though untested, booster strategy, which had its origins in the late 1950s. The Pentagon had ordered von Braun's rocket team to design a "large space vehicle booster of approximately 1,500,000-lb. thrust based on a cluster of available rocket engines. . . ."[9] Back then von Braun had had to build on the cheap, using his Huntsville center's in-house industrial capability to enlarge existing Jupiter tank assemblies and upgrade their engines. After NASA took over Huntsville, Abe Silverstein, NASA's director of spaceflight development, accelerated the design of a large booster that would combine von Braun's concept of a multiengine "big cluster" booster with innovative, high-energy liquid oxygen–liquid hydrogen "cryogenic" upper stages. But von Braun worried that, as promising as Silverstein's plans for cryogenic upper stages were, they were fraught with development problems. Von Braun thought it best to pursue incremental growth with the already proven LOX-kerosene propellants. Silverstein had years of theoretical development work with cryogenic engines behind him, however, and he succeeded in convincing the skeptical Germans that the future of high-energy upper stages lay in cryogenics. Von Braun later conceded that Silverstein had overcome the rocket team's "scruples about the risks of the new fuel."[10]

Now von Braun's eight-engine Saturn I became a test-bed for the cluster-engine concept. The new booster was also designed to launch cryogenic upper stages based on the smaller Centaur upper-stage propulsion system that Silverstein's colleagues had developed. Eventually, this interim first stage would be supplanted by some type of "supercluster" of the huge F-1 engines then under development, with a thrust of 1.5 million pounds each.

NASA planners also realized that to break away from Earth's gravitational influence and send a spacecraft weighing as much as 100 tons on an "escape trajectory" to the moon would probably require a truly gargantuan booster. Tentatively called Nova, the rocket would cluster eight big F-1 engines and a total of six powerful cryogenic engines in four separate upper stages. Such a monster booster exceeded even the fertile imagination of Wernher von Braun.

On Friday, October 27, 1961, von Braun was ready to test the Saturn I booster. The Cape Canaveral press corps had never seen anything like it. The booster stood almost 170 feet high from its base on the newly completed Launch Pad 34. The clustered tanks of its first stage were painted alternately black and white, like futuristic temple columns. The two dummy upper stages (filled with water ballast) were gleaming white alloy capped by a pristine Jupiter nose cone. Fully fueled, the Saturn weighed almost a million pounds. NASA was ready to flex its muscles.

No one seemed to care that this Saturn I booster's eventual mission would only be a test of Apollo spacecraft in low Earth orbit and that it was the foundation for cryogenic upper stages that didn't exist even in blueprint form. The Saturn *looked* like a moon rocket.

It certainly sounded like one. The eight F-1 engines ignited perfectly one-tenth of a second apart, beginning with the inner cluster of four and followed by the outside four. Blinding orange flame shot out horizontally from the new pad's flame trench as the booster climbed slowly into the autumn sky. Two miles away, the launch team and reporters were pounded by the rumbling blast of the engines. The ground flexed and trembled. Men who'd seen many missile launches were virtually thunderstruck by the Saturn. The white contrail climbed gracefully over the Atlantic. One hundred seconds after ignition, NASA engineers prematurely cut off one of the Saturn's engines as a demonstration of the cluster concept's safety margin. Even with this reduced thrust the booster reached its planned altitude of 85 miles and a downrange distance of 215 miles. Kurt Debus's launch team analyzed their preliminary data and were amazed that the actual booster performance almost perfectly matched their predicted engineering parameters. The discipline of the Huntsville rocket team had borne fruit yet again.

The next day newspapers around the world carried photographs of NASA's "moon rocket" on its flawless test flight.

Cape Canaveral, Fall 1961–Winter 1962

That fall, while I tested my rendezvous theories on the computers of the instrumentation laboratory at MIT, the lab won the Project Apollo navigation and guidance system contract. I knew my association with MIT would help me when I applied again for astronaut selection. Meanwhile, on the launch pads at Cape Canaveral, NASA was still hammering out the kinks in Project Mercury. The main problem was the temperamental Atlas booster. But by September, a modification of the standard ICBM, a new "thick-skinned" space booster, finally orbited an unmanned Mercury spacecraft.

While all this was going on, NASA's growing public relations staff worked hard to keep the media focused on the moon, and engineers were attending one marathon meeting after another laying the groundwork for Project Apollo. Since the space agency still didn't have a design configuration for the actual Apollo moon vehicle or its booster, the images of lunar landings appearing in newspapers and on television were glamorous but vague.

In early October, NASA administrator Jim Webb announced that the agency would build a new facility, called the Manned Spacecraft Center (MSC), in Harris County, Texas, south of Houston near Clear Lake. This center would be the permanent successor to Langley's Space Task Group. As predicted, a number of northern Republicans in Congress howled in protest, as did certain northern newspapers. It looked like a clear pattern had emerged of southern control over the growing manned spaceflight pork barrel. Florida had Cape Canaveral, Alabama had Marshall, and NASA planned to test its big Saturn boosters at a plant on the Mississippi River near New Orleans. Now Texas had gotten the plum, the space program's vital nerve center, later to become known as Mission Control or, simply, Houston.

It didn't hurt of course that Representative Albert Thomas of Houston was the chairman of the House committee overseeing NASA's budget.

Nor, obviously, did the northern press overlook the influence of the other Texans, House Speaker Sam Rayburn and Olin (Tiger) Teague (who chaired the House Manned Spaceflight Subcommittee). Kennedy's circle of liberal New Englanders, represented by Jerome Wiesner, sneered at the gargantuan vulgarity of Apollo, but the good-old-boy southern congressmen recognized an opportunity when they saw it.

Rice University donated a 1,000-acre tract for the Manned Spacecraft Center—in exchange, some suggested, for a steady stream of future NASA contracts. The ranchland around the center became a real estate bonanza, with the construction of entire neighborhoods, shopping centers, and office complexes. Many journalists have tried to unravel the confusing web of real estate transactions involving this land, but no one has successfully traced the profit line directly back to LBJ or his friends in Congress. It has become widely accepted among political buffs in Houston that these gentlemen's collective net worth increased considerably during this period, but given the thin line between business and politics in Texas in those days, any allegations of impropriety are probably impossible to verify.[11]

To meet official selection rules, the Manned Spacecraft Center had to be near educational institutions and advanced scientific facilities, appropriate housing, and cultural and recreational resources—which could all be found in Houston proper—but Clear Lake, the actual site of the future NASA center, hardly fit the bill. That fall, when the Army Corps of Engineers team was hacking through the scrub oak and brambles, they ran into a grizzled cowboy skinning the carcass of a freshly killed wolf.[12] It hardly seemed possible that in less than eight years this overgrown tidewater wilderness would become the headquarters for man's first voyage to the moon.

At the end of November, NASA launched Mercury-Atlas 5, its first orbital test of a primate. Enos was a 39-pound chimpanzee who flew the mission well, but certainly wasn't clever enough to control the spacecraft manually when one of the RCS thrusters failed. So they brought him down after only two orbits. Shorty Powers quickly pointed out that an astronaut could have easily overcome this difficulty. The same day, Bob Gilruth announced that Marine lieutenant colonel John Glenn was the pilot selected for the first manned orbital flight, with Navy lieutenant Scott Carpenter as his backup. Chuck Yeager and his buddies at Edwards undoubtedly got a kick out of that. A jughead *Marine* was going to brush the monkey shit off the seat before flying the first orbital Mercury mission.

By late January 1962, Glenn had completed all his preflight training, the Atlas booster and the Mercury spacecraft had been successfully checked out, and a record number of over a thousand reporters had been briefed at Cape Canaveral. The weather and technical problems were not as cooperative, and the mission was delayed twice.

John stood by stoically, noting that every aviation test program he'd ever been involved in had had more troubles than Mercury. Bad weather lasted until February 19, when the Gulf Stream squalls finally let up. Air Force forecasters predicted a break in the rain and wind for a few hours early on the morning of February 20. The press was notified and the new global Mercury ground-station tracking network was placed on launch alert. Glenn ate his scrambled eggs and steak and was suited up by 4:00 AM. It was still cloudy, but the wind had dropped. After a temporary break in the overcast, a light rain started, threatening to cancel the launch again. Then another break rolled in from the Atlantic, and Glenn was inserted into his spacecraft, *Friendship* 7.

At 9:47 AM the launch countdown reached T–0, and Glenn was on his way. The Atlas booster's distinctive trident flame plume was dazzling in the hazy sunshine. Glenn reported a smooth ride with almost no vibration. But as the fuel burned away and the Atlas accelerated toward Max Q, the buffeting became severe.

"It's a little bumpy about here," Glenn called, his voice chattering like a truck driver's on a washboard road.

Just over two minutes after liftoff and more than 20 miles high, the outboard boosters shut down and were pushed away, followed a few seconds later by the escape tower. The Atlas obeyed its preprogrammed flight plan and pitched over more steeply as its central sustainer engine continued to blaze.

John described, "...a beautiful sight, looking eastward across the Atlantic."

Soon after, the core booster, almost emptied of fuel now, began to twang and buffet. A moment later the engine cut off, and John realized that the powered ascent was over. He followed the flight surgeon's orders and went through an exact sequence of head and body maneuvers aimed at detecting the onset of the spacesickness that had caused cosmonaut Titov so much trouble. John was neither nauseated nor disoriented. He completed one series of thruster maneuvers and turned the spacecraft so its window pitched forward and he could distinguish landmarks as Earth rolled by below.

John was heard chuckling as the Canary Islands and the tan Sahara coast of Africa crawled over the blue Atlantic horizon. He called the tracking station at Kano, Nigeria, and told the technicians there he could see the dust storm swirling around them. Thirty minutes after launch, he had gone from a North American morning to late afternoon above equatorial Africa. Far below him, John saw towering thunderheads pulse with silent lightning in the twilight. Over the Madagascar tracking station, *Friendship* 7 swept through the day-night terminator line and into starlit darkness.

When the spacecraft crossed the Australian coast near Perth, Glenn contacted Gordon Cooper at the Muchea tracking station. He reported the beautiful twinkling outline of a city on the Indian Ocean coast, which Gordo confirmed was Perth. The spacecraft, Glenn said, was behaving perfectly, although he couldn't quite believe the speed of orbital flight.

"That was about the shortest day I've ever run into," he told Cooper.

The vast, flat interior of Australia and the empty expanse of Oceania ahead were completely dark, so John rotated *Friendship* 7 and studied the unblinking stars. Glenn then got ready for orbital sunrise by adjusting his periscope to capture the first hint of light on the curved horizon ahead. The spacecraft was surrounded by a swarm of what he said were "little specks, brilliant specks floating around outside. . . ." He thought the spacecraft had turned and that he was staring into a field of stars. But then he saw the "fireflies" dancing just outside his window. John Glenn had been in two wars and had thousands of hours of jet time behind him, but for a moment these mysterious particles unnerved him. As the orbital sunrise came through his window, the fireflies disappeared. Glenn reported them to the Pacific tracking stations and then got back to work completing the maneuvers on his flight plan. Almost immediately, one of the RCS thrusters acted up and Glenn had to juggle the system from one mode to another to achieve the desired spacecraft attitude without seriously depleting his hydrogen-peroxide thruster fuel.

That problem he could handle, but in the mission control room at

Cape Canaveral, engineer William Saunders was alerted to a warning on his telemetry console screen. "Segment 51," the sensors monitoring the spacecraft landing system, indicated that *Friendship 7*'s heat shield was no longer locked in place, holding in the compressed landing-impact bag. If this were true, the heat shield had somehow been jarred loose during the violent powered ascent, and it would fly off the tiny spacecraft when Glenn began reentry. *Friendship 7* would be incinerated within seconds, just like the thousands of meteors that burn up each day in Earth's atmosphere.

Flight directors Chris Kraft and Walt Williams gathered their team leaders in Mission Control. Bill Bland, a spacecraft structures expert, telephoned Max Faget, Mercury's chief designer, in Houston to discuss the emergency. Faget patiently explained that it was unlikely the heat shield had actually come loose, because it was held in place by the thick steel strapping of the retrorocket pack. This pack, Faget said, would continue to hold the heat shield in place through reentry after the deorbit retro burn—*provided* all three solid-fuel retrorockets ignited. If they did not burn correctly, they would certainly ignite during reentry, spinning the spacecraft disastrously out of control.

Kraft and his team decided not to alert John. It was better to have a clear course of action before bringing him "into the loop." However, each tracking station John passed ordered him to cycle the landing bag deploy switch from standby to the automatic position. John figured out there was a problem and impatiently demanded to know what it was. Finally, on the third orbit, Glenn was informed of the problem and was told not to jettison the retro pack after the reentry burn, but instead to keep it in place with its steel straps restraining the heat shield. Glenn discussed this thoroughly with Mission Control and agreed with their remedy.[13]

Then, 4 hours and 33 minutes after liftoff, Glenn positioned the spacecraft so the heat shield faced the California coast and followed the automatic retrofire sequence as the three small solid-propellant charges were fired. If any misfired, he had his gloved finger on the override switch to correct the glitch.

"Boy," he called as the braking rockets jolted him, "feels like I'm going halfway back to Hawaii."

As the spacecraft plunged into the atmosphere toward California's High Sierra, Glenn saw orange and black smoke shoot past his window, followed by a stream of molten droplets. He breathed deeply to steady his hand as he used the last of his RCS fuel, keeping the spacecraft in perfect reentry alignment to minimize the stress on the heat shield. The metals and composite materials of the retro pack were white-hot now. A moment later, one of the steel straps burned through. Glenn heard "small things brushing against the capsule." The polychrome flame swelled near his window. "That's a real fireball outside," he called to Mission Control, his voice showing the first signs of anxiety. A red-hot steel strap broke loose from the retro pack and flew by the window, followed by clumps of flaming material.

He was afraid the shield had broken up, but he was in the radio blackout zone generated by the superhot cone of ionized particles that surrounds spacecraft during reentry, so there was no one to tell. To make matters worse, *Friendship 7* began to gyrate wildly—probably because unequal sections of retro pack were still clinging to the spacecraft's underside. When one thruster fuel tank ran dry he switched control modes and used his remaining fuel to hold the craft steady. He was back in the atmosphere now, over the Atlantic Ocean, and just as *Friendship 7* was threatening to tumble out of control, the drogue chute popped and stabilized the spacecraft. Main parachute deployment came right on time.

Less than half an hour later, Glenn was on board the destroyer *Noa*, thirstily gulping lemonade. An officer handed him a radiotelephone and he heard John Kennedy's distinctive voice offering congratulations. Glenn grinned as he talked to the president. John told him the mission had been a "wonderful trip, almost unbelievable."

Across America, 100 million children and adults gazed at their television sets smiling with pride. One of their countrymen had breached the true frontier of space and returned with flying colors.

Tyuratam, Kazakhstan, 1962

Sergei Korolev understood full well what John Glenn's achievement ultimately meant. NASA would now be able to get the congressional funding it needed to meet Kennedy's moon-landing goal. Korolev also realized that the Soviet Union had to begin work immediately on a manned lunar program of its own or forfeit the space race to America. But neither Vostok nor any of several derivative models then in the preliminary design stage could carry a cosmonaut to the moon. To reach that goal, he needed a much more sophisticated spacecraft.

Vostok and Mercury were more or less technological equals—with Mercury being stronger in miniaturized electronics—but the lunar mission required a true spacecraft, not just a barely maneuverable capsule. Korolev and his colleagues had access to the Western press, both popular and technical. And Soviet intelligence supplemented these open sources. So they closely followed American spacecraft development and were able to pick and choose among Western innovations as Korolev pushed his bureau through the initial concept stage of the new lunar spacecraft. Just as Korolev had meshed his own inventive genius with German rocketry to develop the Semyorka booster, he molded existing American spacecraft ideas to his own purposes. In 1962, the American design model that most impressed him was a preliminary study for the Apollo spacecraft completed by General Electric under a NASA development contract.[14]

The proposed GE Apollo vehicle would have three sections joined end to end: the propulsion module, with a maneuvering engine for changing orbit; the beehive-shaped descent module equipped with a heat shield and parachutes, in which three astronauts would ride to and from space; and the pear-shaped mission module that rode on the top of the three-unit cluster. This spacecraft could dock with a larger propulsion rocket for the voyage out to the moon, or it could be used for long-duration missions in Earth orbit. Although the GE design was ultimately rejected by NASA, its innovative concepts proved influential in both America and the Soviet Union.[15]

Korolev set to work refining this concept to meet Soviet needs. Working with his close collaborators Boris Yegorov and L. A. Voskresensky, he embarked on a priority design program for a Soviet spacecraft with advanced capabilities: sustained flight for a two- or three-man crew; orbital maneuver, rendezvous, and docking; and a modular structure, permitting the spacecraft to link into larger, composite assemblies with either manned or unmanned supply-ferry vehicles of similar design.

The spacecraft took shape on the drawing boards as an evolution of Vostok design with separate instrument and reentry modules. But, like the GE Apollo concept, it had a third "orbital module"—in effect, a roomy workshop for long missions that was very close to the American design and size. The reentry module incorporated a convex heat shield with some lift capability so the spacecraft could be precisely steered during atmospheric reentry. The advantage of this design was its flexibility. The spacecraft could fly extended Earth orbit missions or a manned circumlunar flight. With a few adaptations, the new vehicle could be the manned ferry vessel for a larger composite craft carrying a lunar lander.

Landing cosmonauts on the moon was Korolev's ultimate goal. As he pressed ahead with his design in 1962, he knew the Soviet Union stood an even chance of beating America to the moon.

He called this new spacecraft *Soyuz* ("union"). The name was both physically descriptive and ideologically proper. *Soyuz* was the first word in the official name of the motherland. He knew this would please Moscow.[16]

CHAPTER SIX

STRATEGY
1962 TO 1964

NASA Headquarters, Washington, DC, 1962

The week after his flight, John Glenn was given a standing ovation when he addressed a joint session of Congress about America's goal of a lunar landing before 1970. A record four million people lined the streets of Manhattan two days later and showered Glenn with ticker tape. Certainly anyone watching on television (and I was one of millions who did) was moved by John's confidence in the program.

But the senior officials inside NASA and the White House were anything but confident. America had finally orbited a single astronaut aboard a relatively simple spacecraft launched by a comparatively puny booster, but landing men safely on the moon and returning them to Earth within the next eight years would be another matter.

No one at NASA or the White House really had a clear idea of exactly *how* they were going to get to the moon. They knew astronauts would fly in some kind of spacecraft—which for several years had vaguely been called "Apollo"—and that it would be launched by a powerful, equally ill-defined booster or, perhaps, several boosters. By the spring of 1962, the all-important terms "mission modes" and "vehicle configuration" were at the center of a heated struggle within NASA, pitting Wernher von Braun's Huntsville rocket team against Bob Gilruth's new Manned

Spacecraft Center in Houston and Gilruth's former colleagues at NASA's Langley, Virginia, center. Administrator Jim Webb was refereeing this conflict while also fighting his own skirmishes with Jerome Wiesner's White House science advisers. Most of this bureaucratic warfare was hidden from the public, but we now know just how bitter it was.

The conflict focused on the best method of landing Americans on the moon and bringing them back to Earth. There were three basic "modes" for achieving a successful lunar landing. The so-called Direct-Ascent approach would use a single huge Nova booster with a first-stage thrust of 12 million pounds that would propel a powerful spacecraft directly to the moon. There the spacecraft-engine's thrust would brake the vehicle's descent to the lunar surface. The big moon lander would blast off again for the return trip directly to Earth. Initially many people, including Gilruth and Wiesner, were attracted to this approach because of its simplicity.

Von Braun also originally thought direct ascent was the best course. It matched his 30-year-old philosophy: the careful, incremental development of hardware and procedures that improved successful earlier technology. Using one large new booster avoided having to invent new types of spacecraft and procedures. But von Braun soon came to doubt that the Nova booster and its powerful cryogenic upper stages could be built in time to meet Kennedy's deadline. Engineers were also concerned that any lunar lander powerful enough to use thrust to brake its descent and then to ascend from the moon would have to be, in effect, a huge propellant tank, probably a "lighthouselike structure" almost a hundred feet tall.[1]

Even if the lunar lander were to discard its initial braking engine after landing, the amount of propellant needed for a direct ascent back to Earth would still demand an unacceptably massive vehicle. In order to withstand the powerful thrusts involved in such a huge lander, the astronauts would have to lie in contour couches at the top, where they couldn't see well, making landing even more difficult. Couches were acceptable for parachute descent to splashdown in the ocean, but not for a delicate landing among the myriad craters of the moon.

The alternative approach favored by von Braun's rocket team was Earth Orbit Rendezvous (EOR), which would use several smaller, Saturn-class boosters to launch the components of a composite lunar spacecraft that would be assembled in Earth orbit. The spacecraft would then be blasted free of Earth's sphere of gravitational influence toward the moon. The advantages of this method lay in the Saturn. Von Braun was confident his group could develop an upgraded operational Saturn booster within four or five years.

But EOR also presented challenging problems, especially to the launch team at Cape Canaveral. They would have to prepare two complex boosters for almost simultaneous launch, so that the manned spacecraft could rendezvous with the fueled lunar vehicle. However, von Braun was supremely confident that his team could meet this challenge, too, within a few years.

The third and most innovative approach to the moon landing was Lunar Orbit Rendezvous (LOR). Like many others, I initially thought this technique was dangerously complex, even bizarre. The LOR mode called for a lunar spacecraft—composed of a command module (CM) with three astronauts on board; a service module with an engine, fuel, and life-support supplies; and a lunar module (LM), a lander—that would be launched by a single Saturn-class booster. The spacecraft would remain attached to the final booster stage until checkout in Earth orbit. Then the booster would accelerate the three-part spacecraft to escape velocity and be abandoned. Near the moon, the spacecraft would brake into a circular lunar orbit. The small lander would detach from the mother ship and descend carrying two astronauts to the lunar surface. After exploration, the astronauts would launch the lander back to lunar orbit and rendezvous with the combined command and service module (CSM), which would carry the crew home.

The strongest advocate of this concept within NASA was an energetic, prematurely gray Langley engineer named John C. Houbolt, who was chief of the center's theoretical mathematics division. As Houbolt refined the LOR mode, it became elegantly simple. His proposed lunar excursion vehicle (later named the lunar excursion module, and finally just the lunar module, or LM) was a lightweight two-stage spacecraft that used its spent descent section as the launch pad for the upper ascent stage. Once the lunar astronauts had rendezvoused with their mother ship, the lander's ascent stage would be discarded, further reducing the amount of fuel the service module would need to thrust free of lunar orbit and return to Earth. Houbolt understood a fundamental principle of interplanetary flight that took others a long time to grasp: a planet's gravity was like an invisible well shaft, its depth depending on the planet's mass. Any spacecraft descending into the lunar gravitational well would require a considerable amount of energy (fuel) to come back out again. Why, he asked reasonably, should the entire vehicle, including its astronauts, needlessly slide down the lunar gravity well? In effect, the LOR concept solved many of the troubling problems raised by Direct Ascent and EOR.

Houbolt had been working out the basic mathematical soundness of LOR a full year before Kennedy made the moon landing official American policy. When he had first completed his rough, back-of-the-envelope math, he later recalled, "I felt intuitively and at once that this was the answer."[2] Houbolt realized that the composite structure of the LOR lander assembly would keep weight to an absolute minimum for each required phase of the mission. But his initial calculations were overly spartan. The lander he envisioned didn't even have a pressurized ascent stage, so the astronauts would have to soar back up from the lunar surface in a kind of open space scooter, clad in pressure suits. The lander's guidance system was also minimal: a modification of a carpenter's bubble level. Above all, Houbolt's main concern was to ruthlessly minimize weight and thus optimize fuel consumption.

By fall 1961, Houbolt had still not convinced any senior NASA official of the efficacy of LOR. The very idea of astronauts rendezvousing in lunar orbit, a quarter million miles away from their ground control station on Earth, seemed the height of recklessness. And the miniaturized onboard computer capability implicit in this plan sounded more like science fiction than valid engineering projections.

Meanwhile, the Marshall Space Flight Center in Huntsville under von Braun was pushing the dual-Saturn-launch EOR mode energetically. But Gilruth's Space Task Group, now based in Houston, which had overall responsibility for Project Apollo, was also holding onto Direct Ascent as the best answer to the moon-landing problem. "I feel that it is highly desirable to develop a launch vehicle with sufficient performance and reliability to carry out the lunar landing mission using the direct approach," Gilruth reported to NASA headquarters. He considered von Braun's advocacy of EOR a bureaucratic "crutch...to avoid the difficulty of developing a reliable Nova class launch vehicle."[3] The nub of the problem lay in the conflict between Huntsville's Marshall center and Gilruth's people in Houston. Von Braun's team at Marshall was responsible for the booster design and Gilruth's people for the spacecraft. Each side wanted to make its task as simple as possible.[4]

John Houbolt, however, was not a man who quit easily. When he became convinced that his LOR concept had not been considered fairly, he wrote directly to NASA's associate administrator, Robert C. Seamans, Jr., lambasting Direct Ascent's mammoth, unwieldly Nova booster and the complex dual-launch problems of EOR. He was convinced that Lunar Orbit Rendezvous was the logical answer to Kennedy's challenge. "Give us the go-ahead...," Houbolt promised, "and we will put a man on the moon in very short order."[5]

Houbolt's plea arrived at NASA headquarters at just the right moment. George Low, the new director of spacecraft and flight missions, immediately recognized that LOR would break the bureaucratic logjam between Houston and Huntsville. It was also the most practical method of meeting Kennedy's deadline—no matter how bizarre it initially seemed. But still, many officials at NASA headquarters considered LOR a pipe dream. Milton Rosen led a working group charged with choosing among the three conflicting lunar strategies. His group first favored EOR, even though orbital rendezvous techniques were not yet clearly understood. By spring 1962, Gilruth had been forced to abandon Direct Ascent and had become a strong convert to the Lunar Orbit Rendezvous mode. He had been swayed by LOR's lightweight spacecraft concept, which would actually simplify his center's job. Finally, the senior mission planners in both Houston and Washington were forced to accept the stubborn logic of Houbolt's LOR.

Von Braun still favored Earth Orbit Rendezvous—as much for its space-station–building potential as its moon-landing practicality—but he knew Apollo needed a firm mission mode that was accepted throughout NASA without further delay. In June 1962, von Braun officially gave Marshall's stamp of approval to Lunar Orbit Rendezvous. He acknowledged that there had been jealousies about bureaucratic turf on all sides—the "not invented here" syndrome, by which any idea, no matter how valid, was rejected if it came from another center. With a mission as monumental as Project Apollo, von Braun stated, "the issue of 'invented here' versus 'invented there' does not apply."[6] On July 11, 1962, NASA headquarters announced that the Lunar Orbit Rendezvous mode would be used for America's moon-landing missions.

Even after LOR became official NASA policy, Wiesner's Scientific Advisory Committee at the White House was still very skeptical. Their main concern echoed von Braun's earlier qualms. Wiesner and his group thought Earth Orbit Rendezvous was the best mode because it would leave behind hardware that could be used for future civilian and military space stations. The LOR's spacecraft would be ultralightweight and as autonomous from ground control as possible, so it would not leave the same technological legacy. And the White House scientists were troubled by the audacity of LOR's reliance on untested rendezvous and computer guidance techniques. Whereas an EOR mission could always be aborted with no real danger to the astronauts, such failures in lunar orbit could easily result in the tragic loss of the crew.

It's interesting to look back today and note that NASA's pioneering engineers had considerably more faith in computer technology than the President's Science Advisory Committee did. I believe there's a lesson here. America always does best when it accepts a challenging mission. We invent well under pressure. Conversely, we stagnate when caution prevails.

The conflict between NASA and Wiesner reached a boil when President Kennedy visited the Marshall Space Flight Center on September 11, 1962. Wernher von Braun led Kennedy and his entourage, consisting of Lyndon Johnson, Defense Secretary Robert McNamara, NASA administrator Jim Webb, and Wiesner, to a chart mounted beside the gleaming white mass of a Saturn booster. Von Braun explained the key elements of Lunar Orbit Rendezvous to the group, but Kennedy interrupted.

"I understand Dr. Wiesner doesn't agree with this," the president said. He turned, looking for Wiesner, who was strolling around the booster with the VIPs. "Where's Jerry?" Kennedy demanded, his voice echoing in the expanse of the huge Marshall assembly building.

"Yes, sir," Wiesner said, quickly stepping up beside the president. "That's right." He then forcefully listed his committee's many objections to the LOR mode. To hear him tell it, NASA had embarked on an ill-conceived, reckless gamble based on very shaky scientific assumptions.

But Johnson, Webb, and von Braun immediately closed ranks to argue for LOR. Webb emphasized that official requests for proposals for spacecraft designs based on the LOR mode were already out with aerospace contractors. It was too late, he said, to shift now (not true, by the way), and he said a unified front was needed to meet the president's deadline. While nearby reporters strained to eavesdrop, Kennedy listened intently for about two minutes and then nodded brusquely, terminating the discussion. Without explicitly stating his position, he made it clear to all that he was in favor of Lunar Orbit Rendezvous. A major obstacle on the way to the moon had been overcome.[7]

Cape Canaveral, Summer 1962

By mid-May, the space press corps was back at the Eastern Test Range for a manned American spaceflight, Mercury-Atlas 7, Mercury's second orbital flight. Navy lieutenant Scott Carpenter would fly the mission, with Wally Schirra as his backup. On Thursday, May 24, as the rising sun burned through wispy ground fog, the smoothest countdown in the history of America's manned space program was followed by flight director Chris Kraft's announcement that the initial ascent was textbook perfect. Carpenter experienced none of the severe buffeting Glenn had reported, but the jettisoning of the escape tower produced an unexpectedly violent jolt.[8]

Carpenter's *Aurora 7* was in orbit less than six minutes after liftoff. He was not aware of the speed, but for the first time experienced the spherical nature of planet Earth—"an arresting sight." Initially above Africa, and then over the Indian Ocean and Australia, Carpenter rolled the spacecraft repeatedly to better observe interesting landmarks below. During the short night passage above Oceania, Carpenter sampled some experimental space snacks: figs, high-protein date cereal mixes, and raisin-nut squares. He completed his first revolution of Earth with no major problems, but he increasingly became so overcome by the powerful images parading past his window that technicians at ground stations below had to remind him of his schedule of experiments. He wasted considerable fuel trying to perform routine attitude maneuvers John Glenn had easily accomplished. Carpenter even accidentally switched on a thruster backup system, doubling the RCS fuel consumption. He did manage to deploy an experimental towed balloon, but unfortunately, it did not inflate properly.

By the third and final orbit, Carpenter was dangerously low on thruster fuel and was ordered to shut down the RCS system and drift. *Aurora 7* tumbled slowly around Earth for more than an hour, and Carpenter relaxed, photographing the African rain forests, the orbital sunset, and the half moon above him. He also saw the "fireflies" that had so enthralled John Glenn. By now, NASA engineers were certain they were caused by tiny ice crystals fluttering from beneath the rippled Mercury heat shingles. Carpenter said his fireflies seemed more like snowflakes than insects.

On his final pass above the Hawaiian tracking station, Carpenter and ground controllers got into a testy exchange when they urged him to begin his countdown and attitude stabilization for the upcoming retrofire. He told them he'd not yet done so because he was moving at five miles a second and had been preoccupied with the "frostflies" around the spacecraft. Carpenter began his retrofire countdown late and shifted to the automatic thruster mode. But this mode would not keep the spacecraft properly aligned for retrofire, so he hurriedly took control by the semiautomatic fly-by-wire method—negligently forgetting to shut down the manual system. The last of his thruster fuel was bleeding away. But Scott was still more interested in the spectacular view of North America than in correct reentry procedures: "I can make out very, very small farmland, pastureland below. I see individual fields, rivers, lakes, roads, I think. . . . I'll get back to reentry attitude."[9] Carpenter had let his spacecraft drift out of proper yaw alignment. The California ground station sensed trouble in his automatic flight sequencer and ordered him to fire his retros manually, but Carpenter botched this assignment also, igniting his braking rockets three seconds late.

As *Aurora 7* slid into the upper fringes of the atmosphere above California, Carpenter's thruster fuel tanks were empty. The combined effect of being off course and firing his retros late would carry him well past his landing target.

The blazing heat of reentry engulfed *Aurora 7* as it passed through 300,000 feet, east of Cape Canaveral. Carpenter kept reporting what he saw out of his window, even as he was forced deeper into his couch, until finally the sheer weight of the G forces made him unable to speak. The spacecraft oscillated savagely through the lower atmosphere, but Carpenter no longer had thruster fuel to control *Aurora 7*. Finally, the drogue chute dampened the gyrations, followed by the main parachute.

Officially, Carpenter's reentry had been "slightly" off course. But search aircraft were able to pick up his radio beacon. NASA didn't tell the public that *Aurora 7* had landed 250 miles off its target because of the pilot's distraction and inability to control his reentry attitude. Nor did Shorty Powers inform the press that Carpenter's spacecraft had almost been lost during the violent reentry. Several hours later, on the carrier *Intrepid*, Carpenter told President Kennedy by radiotelephone that he was sorry for not "having aimed a little better on reentry."

Even though Shorty Powers's PR crew did a good job of damage control, NASA officials privately vowed that *Aurora 7* was Carpenter's first and last space mission. If a man couldn't overcome his emotions and fly the expensive, carefully designed spacecraft, he had no business representing NASA or his country in space. No one in NASA would officially admit to blackballing Carpenter, but he never flew again.

By the time I became a member of the astronaut corps, it was considered an article of faith that you *never* assigned a multiengine driver like Scott Carpenter to a mission requiring the flying talents of a fighter pilot. Maybe so. But I think the reason Carpenter "screwed the pooch" had more to do with his personal makeup than his professional experience. Later, during the space shuttle program, some of our hottest shuttle pilots were multiengine guys, including Dick Scobee, the commander of *Challenger* on its last mission.

Tyuratam, Kazakhstan, Summer 1962

American intelligence was having a hard time keeping tabs on the Soviet space program during this period. Reconnaissance overflights of Tyuratam by U-2 aircraft had been canceled after Gary Powers's plane was shot down in 1960, and our fledgling reconnaissance satellites simply missed a lot of what was going on below because of overcast and darkness. Given the extreme secrecy of the Soviets about their military and civil space programs and the unswerving loyalty to the motherland of men like Korolev, American intelligence agents were unable to keep our government informed. American leaders had to rely on a combination of Soviet public statements, comments from their scientists at international meetings, and radio intercepts of Soviet spacecraft transmissions by our own ground-tracking stations. In short, we had a pretty murky picture of the Soviets' capabilities and intentions.

Nikita Khrushchev, aware that the Americans weren't up to date on Soviet achievements, orchestrated his space program to take maximum advantage of Western ignorance.[10] Influential Soviet science journalist Leonid Vladimirov, who defected to the West in the 1970s, has called this period Russia's "space bluff." In the summer of 1962, Khrushchev continued pressing Korolev to surpass American achievements. But without a new spacecraft the chief designer was unable to give Khrushchev the type of spectacular he demanded. Finally Korolev reached one of his typically ingenious compromises; since he had only production-line Vostok spacecraft available, he'd fly *two* in a "group flight," arranging their orbital trajectories so that they would appear to be maneuvering to a rendezvous.

This sleight of hand was nothing like a true rendezvous, in which the spacecraft alter their velocities and match the "shape" of their orbits. Korolev simply took advantage of the basic principles of spaceflight: after 17 orbits a Vostok would be directly over the Tyuratam launch pad, exactly 24 hours after liftoff. Given the reliability of his Semyorka booster, Korolev planned to launch a second Vostok precisely one day after the first. This would place the two spacecraft in the same orbit, initially only a few kilometers apart. But that was all Soviet technology was capable of at that time. The cosmonauts couldn't change orbits or actually dock.

On the morning of August 11, 1962, cosmonaut Andrian Nikolayev was launched aboard *Vostok 3*. Exactly 24 hours, 1 minute, and 4 seconds later, *Vostok 4*, with cosmonaut Pavel Popovich on board, lifted off from Tyuratam. The second spacecraft was inserted into orbit within 15 kilometers of *Vostok 3*, a distance that was eventually reduced to five kilometers. This was the closest safe approach, since the spacecraft still lacked onboard orbital maneuvering systems. But Popovich's *Vostok 4* was equipped with an innovative (albeit somewhat crude) TV camera that produced the first television transmissions from space, sending down grainy images of the cosmonaut twirling food tubes and small tools in midair before his open helmet visor. These transmissions were abruptly halted, however, when Popovich experienced the same space-sickness that had plagued Titov. Three days later, the two Vostoks reentered the atmosphere simultaneously, with *Vostok 4* landing less than 200 kilometers from *Vostok 3* and with the two cosmonauts touching down by personal parachute only six minutes apart. Many Western observers now thought the Russians had mastered the techniques of orbital rendezvous, a complex process the Americans still did not completely understand and which NASA would not attempt for another two and a half years.[11]

Cape Canaveral, Fall 1962

NASA's response to both the flawed Carpenter mission in May and the Soviets' August extravaganza was the six-orbit mission of *Sigma 7* on October 3, 1962, piloted by Navy lieutenant commander Wally Schirra. Wally was determined to fly a "textbook" mission, both to uphold the honor of naval aviation and to prove that a disciplined test pilot could function "by the book" in space. And that he proceeded to do. His thruster maneuvers were precise, he didn't waste an ounce of maneuvering fuel, and when his suit overheated he attacked the problem like the diligent test engineer he was. In social situations on the ground (then and now), Wally Schirra often retreated behind a bland, jocular facade. But in space, he was absolutely serious and precisely analytical. As if to compensate for Carpenter's awe at the view from orbit, Wally matter-of-factly ticked off the landmarks.

Like *Vostok 4*, Schirra's spacecraft also had a rudimentary TV camera. Six hours into the mission, as he approached the California coast on his fourth orbit, he "inverted" the spacecraft, with the nose toward Earth so that the planet was *up* from his perspective. During the maneuver, John Glenn told him to say something funny to the 40 million Americans watching on live television. Wally chuckled and told the country he had pitched up *Sigma 7* so that he could see the full moon in the bottom of his window, with the upside-down jumble of the Rocky Mountains above it. He said it reminded him of the old song "Drifting and Dreaming." That was as close as Wally got to his usual nonstop humor.

Alan Shepard was waiting on the Pacific recovery ship to give Schirra the command to fire his retrorockets manually as he came up over the Indian Ocean. As the brilliant chartreuse flame slashed by his window, Wally reported that the reentry was "thrilling." But he didn't give in to his emotions, and he controlled the reentry with amazing precision. Even with a breeze pushing his parachute eastward, he landed within five miles of the planned splashdown site, within sight of the aircraft carrier *Kearsarge* near the Pacific island of Midway.

If Scott Carpenter's flight had raised doubts that a skilled, mature aviator could fly in space, Wally Schirra's *Sigma 7* mission dispelled them.

In the midst of all the euphoria following Schirra's flight, President Kennedy became preoccupied with a grave situation that would carry the world as close to the brink of nuclear holocaust as it had ever been. In August, American intelligence had reported Soviet ships unloading nuclear missiles in Cuban ports. A few weeks later, U-2 reconnaissance planes flying over Cuba had photographed newly constructed missile launch pads. But when Khrushchev was confronted through diplomatic channels, he denied the nuclear buildup. (It's now clear that the "group flight" of *Vostok* 3 and *Vostok* 4—like Titov's one-day Vostok flight launched to divert international attention from the Berlin Wall—was a multipurpose smoke screen designed both to frighten the American military with advanced Soviet space technology and to enhance the USSR's international prestige.)

Kennedy responded with a US naval blockade of Cuba in mid-October—conveniently labeled a "quarantine"—completely calling the Soviet bluff. At the end of October, Khrushchev acknowledged that he had installed offensive nuclear weapons 90 miles from the American mainland and that he was withdrawing them to the Soviet Union and halting work on "weapons construction sites."

America's Strategic Air Command stood down from an unprecedented two-week alert. In the Kremlin, Khrushchev was now seen as a reckless adventurer, willing to gamble the Soviet Union's future in his desperation to one-up the popular young American president. The Cuban missile crisis was the beginning of his decline.

Cape Canaveral, May 1963

At dawn on May 15, Air Force major Leroy Gordon Cooper climbed aboard the spacecraft *Faith* 7 for the longest and final mission of Project Mercury. Gordo wasn't known for being particularly religious and the name *Faith* 7 probably had more to do with his faith in the program's engineering than with spiritual matters. On the other hand, Gordo was an astute poker player, so he might have been simply hedging his bets.

He certainly didn't seem worried about liftoff, as he managed to take a half-hour nap while waiting out a countdown hold. The launch was the prettiest of the entire project. The booster was clearly visible across the cloudless spring sky, like a white pencil line. Once again, the Convair launch team had produced a flawless ascent. Shorty Powers proudly told the large international press corps at the Cape that *Faith* 7's orbital insertion speed of 17,546.6 miles per hour was 99.98 percent "nominal." NASA was continuing its policy of openness, and it was paying off.

Gordo's flight proceeded smoothly, and he too commented on the "frostflies," as well as on the spectacular beauty of planet Earth. Later that afternoon, when he had surpassed Wally Schirra's six-orbit mark, Cooper retired for the "night" and slept well for almost eight hours. (He had to anchor his thumbs under his chest harness to keep his hands from floating free and accidentally tripping switches on his instrument panel.)[12]

At dawn Pacific time the next day, *Faith 7* splashed down less than 7,000 yards from the bow of the aircraft carrier *Kearsarge*, east of Midway. Gordo's flight had been an unqualified success; although a series of minor glitches had cropped up during the second half of the mission, he'd overcome each with a minimum of effort. During his debriefing, he said, "... man is a pretty good backup system...."[13] What Gordo meant by that, I suppose, was that a well-trained and motivated pilot was as capable of operating in space as he was in Earth's atmosphere. The purpose of Project Mercury had been to prove this. NASA was now ready to move on to more ambitious manned missions. Orbital rendezvous and docking were still unsolved problems—as was deep-space navigation and, of course, an actual lunar landing. But the space frontier conquered by the Mercury pilots was now open for the Gemini and Apollo astronauts.

As early as 1960, well before the first Mercury capsule ever flew, the Space Task Group was already studying an advanced type of spacecraft, tentatively called Mercury Mark II. NASA originally hoped to fly an enlarged, two-man version of Mercury on a variety of scientific missions, possibly including a simple circumlunar flyby. Jim Chamberlain, a Canadian-born engineer in Gilruth's group, led the study team that hammered out the basic requirements for the Mark II: a conical spacecraft with a lifting-type heat shield, to be launched by the powerful new Titan II booster. The two astronauts would sit side by side in ejection seats, and each would have his own clamshell-type hatch. A separate instrument section would contain thruster propellant and innovative fuel cells that would produce electricity by combining oxygen and hydrogen.

The new spacecraft would be able to maneuver in orbit and to rendezvous and dock with other spacecraft.

This design study had not yet progressed to a formal project when Kennedy announced the moon landing goal. Now the new spacecraft had another, more immediate purpose than abstract scientific study. It would become the test-bed for the techniques of orbital rendezvous needed for Project Apollo. The rendezvous target for the project would be a modified Agena rocket, launched by an Atlas booster. Using onboard computers and radar, American astronauts would transform the arcane theory of orbital rendezvous that I had struggled with at MIT into a practical, routine skill. The Mark II project was approved in December 1961. In January 1963, NASA officially changed the project's name to Gemini.

It was now understood that the Apollo lunar spacecraft would be several years in design and development. NASA hoped that Project Gemini would fill the gap and be the proving ground for all the innovative maneuvers needed to place Americans on the moon.[14]

Houston, Texas, 1963–1964

After I received my doctorate in astronautics, the Air Force offered me a job in their new Space Systems Division in Los Angeles, working on military experiments for the upcoming two-man Gemini flights. This was what I was trained to do, but I still hadn't given up on becoming an astronaut and sent in my second application, along with my new credentials. I was transferred after a few months to the Air Force–NASA liaison office in Houston, just when the space agency announced that astronaut candidates no longer had to have test pilot qualifications.

The Manned Spacecraft Center, in charge of Gemini and Apollo, had moved from the Langley center in Virginia to Houston, but they weren't yet occupying the new campuslike center at Clear Lake, 25 miles south of the city. Offices were spread among government buildings in downtown Houston, the Rice University campus, and Ellington Air Force Base near Clear Lake. Even though my work didn't put me in direct contact with the astronaut selection officials, I was getting a sense of how the agency did business. It was hot that summer in Houston, but the temperature didn't discourage any of the hard chargers from NASA. They were determined to meet Kennedy's goal. As I went around the temporary NASA offices examining diagrams of the proposed new Saturn booster, the innovative three-part Apollo lunar craft, and the ingenious Gemini hardware, I couldn't help but catch NASA's enthusiasm. All across America academic think tanks and aerospace contractors were gearing up for the push to the moon.

Ed White had been selected as an astronaut in the second group the previous September and was hard at work training. His nine colleagues included Frank Borman, who'd been a year ahead of me at West Point, and one of two civilians, Neil Armstrong, who had been testing the advanced experimental rocket plane, the X-15, for NASA out at Edwards when the group was picked. Ed gave me some good tips on the interview process.

In summer 1963, I made it through the first cut and was eligible for more testing. The physical and psychological examinations were intense, but I passed those hurdles and became one of 34 finalists. The last interviews were deceptively low key, but all the candidates knew that everything we said was being scrutinized, even at parties. And there was a range of social activities in the handsome new suburban developments that had sprung up for NASA personnel among the live oaks and tidal inlets of El Lago, Timber Cove, and Taylor Lake. It certainly helped having Joan with me at these functions. At the end of the week, Deke Slayton—now chief of NASA's expanded Astronaut Office—informed us that only 15 candidates would be selected to continue on to formal astronaut training at the end of the summer.

One hot Tuesday afternoon in early September, my secretary, Bobby Wright, told me Deke Slayton was on the phone. I've faced MiGs and enemy flak, but picking up that phone took more courage than flying in combat. Deke came right to the point in a casual, friendly tone.

"We'd sure like you to become an astronaut," he said. "And I sure hope you'll accept."

My pulse was thudding in my temples. I felt absolutely giddy. "Shoot, Deke," I blurted out, "I'd be delighted to accept."

Shoot? Where the hell had that expression come from? It wasn't one I normally used. But none of this seemed real then. Deke said the selection of the third group of astronauts would be announced in October and that we'd come on board officially on January 2, 1964. I stared out the window at the heat-blasted Bermuda grass, barely hearing Deke Slayton's voice. I'd made it. I was going to be an astronaut.

Huntsville, Alabama, 1963

While NASA was preparing Project Mercury for its first manned flights, the agency was also deeply involved in the design phase of Project Apollo. Unlike the aircraft of an earlier generation that moved from drawing board to prototype in a few months, the complex spacecraft for the lunar mission would take years to design and develop before they were ready for test flight. And complexity certainly was found in all elements of the Apollo program. The command module alone, in which the astronauts would fly to the moon, would eventually contain over a million parts, all jammed into a machine no larger than a good-sized delivery van.

Among Apollo officials and engineers, a process known as "freezing" the design became increasingly critical. No one aerospace contractor could design and build all the countless subcomponents needed for the Saturn boosters and the Apollo spacecraft's three modules. This work had to be farmed out to thousands of subcontractors, who would patiently design, test, and assemble each subsystem, a process of unprecedented difficulty that was bound to take years, despite the urgency of Kennedy's deadline. Freezing the design as quickly as possible was necessary to guarantee that astronauts would be flying Apollo spacecraft before the end of the decade.

As part of this process, von Braun's evolutionary Saturn-class boosters were now given formal names. The single large moon rocket that would launch the Apollo craft would be called the Saturn V. It would be a three-stage vehicle with five huge F-1 engines (then under development by Rocketdyne of North American Aviation) powering the first stage, the "S-IC" that would produce a liftoff thrust of 7.5 million pounds. The two upper stages—the "S-II" and the "S-IVB"—would be powered by the new J-2 liquid-hydrogen–LOX cryogenic engines (also built by Rocketdyne), which Abe Silverstein had pioneered at NASA's Lewis center in Cleveland. This configuration made the big Saturn very flexible; it could carry payloads of 113 tons into Earth orbit or it could dispatch a 41-ton spacecraft at escape velocity toward the moon— "translunar injection" (TLI).[15]

When finally assembled and fueled, the Saturn V stood over 360 feet tall and weighed more than 3,000 tons. Transporting the various parts of this huge booster system was a staggering challenge. Barge canals were cut to move sections from the Mississippi test facility. The tidal creek wilderness of Merritt Island near Cape Canaveral was transformed into a major launch complex dominated by the huge vehicle assembly building (VAB), where the Saturns would be "stacked" for flight. Stretching from Florida to northern California, the new aerospace industrial arc was connected by "super guppy" cargo planes that could transport the massive upper-stage cylinders from the North American and Douglas plants to the Cape. NASA's Huntsville center swelled with new labs and assembly buildings. By 1963, tens of thousands of scientists and engineers were working on Project Apollo, and each month thousands more were coming on board as the big aerospace companies hired subcontractors.

Wernher von Braun's lifelong obsession with spaceflight was finally bearing fruit. The Saturn V rocket was very similar to the gargantuan boosters the Peenemünde scientists had dreamed of during the last days of World War II, when they decided America was the place to be after the war. Now, 18 years later, they had served their apprenticeships in the New Mexico desert, on the sand dunes of Cape Canaveral, and in the treacherous corridors of bureaucratic power. The rocket team would finally have its interplanetary rocket.

The plans for the Apollo spacecraft were equally ambitious. The command module, like both the Mercury and Gemini spacecraft, was conical with an ablative heat shield. But it was much larger than either of the precursor spacecraft and carried its three astronauts in collapsible couches side by side near the large center hatch. The cabin appeared to be as cramped as in the earlier spacecraft, the astronauts jammed cheek by jowl against their instrument panel. But actually, the cone flared out to a wide base, and when the center couch was stowed after liftoff, the crew had plenty of room to stretch out or curl up as they desired. This spacecraft was equipped with communications gear, guidance computers, and navigation equipment that was far more advanced than Mercury's or Gemini's. When the conical command module was coupled to the cylindrical service module, the composite spacecraft looked like a blunt-nosed pistol bullet.

The service module's big engine would both brake the spacecraft into lunar orbit and accelerate it away from the moon again for the return flight to Earth. Therefore, it had to start and stop with *complete* reliability in the weightless vacuum of space. NASA designed the "hypergolic service propulsion engine," which ignited when its hydrazine-based fuel came in contact with a nitrogen tetroxide oxidizer. This same combination powered the spacecraft's attitude thrusters. The fuel was stable, did not have to be refrigerated, and burned well in a vacuum. All of this was fortunate because there was no backup. If that engine didn't fire correctly, the astronauts would not be coming back from the moon. The thick cylinder of the service module was jammed with amazing new hardware. NASA engineers borrowed the concept of fuel cells from Gemini, an ingenious innovation whereby the problem of producing electrical current was solved while converting liquid hydrogen and oxygen to water (which was eventually used for drinking.)

The previous fall, NASA had awarded the lunar module contract to the Grumman Corporation of Bethpage, New York, on Long Island, based on the feasibility study that Grumman had submitted a few months earlier. Both NASA and the company discovered, however, that thousands of knotty technical problems still existed. The Saturn V theoretically could send 41 tons toward the moon, and since the CSM would weigh about 30 tons, that left 11 for the LM. But the lander was certain to weigh more. The solution to this dilemma was that the Saturn booster's upper stages had to be made more powerful over the next six years to accommodate the weight of the LM. Design engineers realized early on that weight restrictions would have a great impact on the LM's fuel supply. But given the moon's gravity, the ascent to Lunar Orbit Rendezvous required a fixed amount of fuel. This meant the descent engine's margin of reserve fuel was the only weight variable, and this affected the landing flight plan by limiting the amount of "hover" time before touchdown.

During this early design phase, the NASA-Grumman team did hammer out some basic concepts for the LM. A report released in 1963 stated that the LM "... will look something like the cab of a two-man helicopter, measuring ten feet in diameter and standing about fifteen feet tall on its skid-type legs."[16] Eventually, the LM became much larger, and the *Eagle*, which Neil Armstrong and I flew to the lunar surface during the *Apollo 11* mission, weighed 16 tons, was almost 23 feet tall, and measured 31 feet between the footpads.

The preliminary design concepts, however, didn't solve the LM's critical propulsion engineering problems. In order to descend to the moon's surface, the LM would have to decelerate, or brake, with the variable thrust of a throttlable rocket motor—a device not yet invented. Normally, rocket engines were ignited, the propellant turbopumps spun up to speed, and the thrust stayed constant until the engine was cut off. But constant thrust would not permit descent or allow hovering above the lunar surface on a cone of flaming exhaust while the crew searched for a smooth landing spot among the tiny craters and boulders. And that wasn't the only problem facing Grumman. Radio signals travel at the speed of light, and there would be more than a two-second "skip" in round-trip communications; so the final phases of descent would occur too far away from the mission control room for ground operators to assist. The LM would have to have a redundant computer guidance capability far beyond the state of the art in the summer of 1963.

Houston, Texas, November 1963

That fall I read whatever technical reports from Projects Gemini and Apollo I could get my hands on. I could see that Gemini was important to the overall moon-landing program because it would be the proving ground for the untested concepts and hardware of orbital rendezvous, docking, and Extra-Vehicular Activity (EVA—NASA-ese for space walks). Before astronauts could walk on the moon, we would need practical spacesuits that would protect us not only in a vacuum, but also from the temperature extremes and the radiation in space. Because of my work on developing rendezvous techniques, I hoped to be assigned to one of the upcoming Gemini flights, and I felt sure that hard work and discipline would eventually get me on an Apollo mission.

That confidence was temporarily shattered on November 22. I was in the middle of an especially obscure technical study in my office at the NASA–Air Force Liaison Division in the VA building when a woman came running down the corridor sobbing that the president had been shot in Dallas. At first I was angry at some idiot's idea of a joke. President and Mrs. Kennedy had been in Houston overnight. I'd seen them on television the night before and wondered if I might pass their motorcade the next morning on the way to work. Now some fool was saying John Kennedy had been shot.

By four that afternoon, the terrible news had been confirmed. Walking numbly to the parking lot, I wondered how to explain this madness to my children. Then it struck me that Kennedy's death might cause the cancellation of Project Apollo, but that was insignificant compared to the horror of the assassination.

Lyndon Johnson, of course, did not cancel Apollo. If anything, he was a stronger supporter of the manned space program than Kennedy. Over the next few months, Johnson showed that his administration would meet *all* the challenges raised by John Kennedy's New Frontier: space, the communist threat in the Third World, civil rights here at home, and all the other unprecedented government programs that became LBJ's "Great Society."

What none of us realized then was that these separate ambitions would interfere with each other and that the eventual entanglement in Vietnam would come perilously close to ripping apart the country's political and social fiber. In many ways, I now understand, that crisp autumn day in Texas was the real beginning of the most turbulent decade in America's history.

Tyuratam, Kazakhstan, 1963–1964

In the summer of 1963, Korolev was again taken away from his work on the development of the Soyuz spacecraft and one of its new boosters—a heavier version of the reliable Semyorka. Khrushchev wanted another international propaganda success, and Korolev had to deliver it. The Cuban missile crisis had revealed to the world how unpredictably aggressive Khrushchev was. No matter what he said about the peaceful, progressive Soviet spirit, Kennedy had forced him to admit publicly that his country had secretly installed offensive nuclear missiles close to the American coast—one of the most globally destabilizing acts since the Soviets had sponsored the invasion of South Korea 12 years before. Khrushchev knew a space spectacular would help bolster his position in the increasingly impatient Politburo, as well as with the nonaligned nations.

Korolev arranged another "group" Vostok flight, but with an interesting twist this time. Cosmonaut Valery Bykovsky was launched aboard *Vostok 5* on the morning of June 14, 1963. Forty-eight hours later, the first woman to fly in space, Valentina V. Tereshkova, joined him in orbit aboard *Vostok 6*. As in the earlier group flight, the two spacecraft were incapable of a rendezvous maneuver, and in fact weren't even as closely aligned as *Vostok 3* and *Vostok 4* had been. At one point they were about three miles from each other. But 24 hours later, they were thousands of miles apart.[17]

Tereshkova was not a pilot or even an engineer. She was a factory worker from Yaroslavl who had joined a sky-diving club at her plant and had soon become quite good in this exciting sport. She was among several women "cosmonauts" who had been hastily selected and put through intensive flight training.[18] She experienced the same nausea as the earlier cosmonauts. Spacesickness is still a mystery, but I'm convinced it is triggered by subtle visual disorientation during weight-lessness. The larger the spacecraft cabin, the more disorientation. So the Russians in their bigger Vostok suffered more than the Mercury astronauts in their tiny cabin. But Tereshkova pulled herself together and made a demanding series of propaganda broadcasts, using her call sign, *Chaika* ("seagull"), to promote the Komsomol, the USSR's communist youth league.

After almost three days in orbit, she made a routine descent to the wheat fields of the southern Urals, although reportedly she was weak when workers on a collective farm found her lying like a beached turtle in her bulky spacesuit. Soon after the flight she addressed an international women's peace conference in Moscow, before heading out on a goodwill tour of the Third World. Within a year, she was married to *Vostok 3* cosmonaut Andrian Nikolayev.

Still this didn't satisfy Khrushchev. He realized that America would have its two-man Gemini spacecraft flying by early 1964, at least a year before Korolev's Soyuz. The final Mercury flights had demonstrated NASA's growing competence. The agency had carefully cultivated the international news media (especially television, which was gaining prominence in the Third World with the advent of communications satellites) and was trumping the Soviets at their own game. Khrushchev again met with Korolev to thrash out an interim project that would divert attention from the impending American successes. Since Gemini would carry two astronauts and Apollo three, Khrushchev ordered Korolev to orbit a Soviet spacecraft with three cosmonauts on board before the November 7 anniversary of the Bolshevik revolution—even if they had to be shoehorned in.[19]

This took Korolev and his design collaborator Konstantin Feoktistov away from their work on the Soyuz. They hastily tried to modify the Vostok spacecraft so that it could carry three men on a brief flight, but their efforts failed. There was no way to adapt the Vostok descent module to carry three ejection seats (with three separate hatches), and the launch system lacked the Mercury-type escape tower. Also, no matter how much equipment was stripped from the Vostok, three men and their life-support systems were going to be too heavy for the regular module parachute.

Finally that summer, Korolev met with Feoktistov, who presented him with a dangerously radical solution. He suggested that the Vostok module be modified to carry three cosmonauts *without* spacesuits, strapped into lightweight honeycomb couches. The descent module would have a braking rocket that would fire just before parachute touchdown, cushioning the craft's impact with Earth.

Korolev studied the design and then shook his head. The braking rocket wasn't a bad idea, he admitted, but there were no ejection seats to save the astronauts during a launch abort, and worst of all, they were unprotected if the hatch seal failed in orbit. "Who on Earth is going to fly without his spacesuit?" Korolev asked.

"I will, for one," Feoktistov answered. He knew how desperate the situation was for Korolev's design bureau. Khrushchev had made it clear that if they did not build the three-man spacecraft, Korolev's rival Chelomei would.[20]

This then led to one of the strangest episodes in the history of spaceflight. On the cold morning of October 12, 1964, Feoktistov (who had no real training in spaceflight), cosmonaut Vladimir Komarov, and flight surgeon Boris Yegorov carefully inserted themselves into the modified Vostok, which had been rechristened *Voskhod* ("sunrise"). Luckily Yegorov was tiny, because his custom-made couch was wedged at a steep angle above the other two and, before liftoff, he had to be held in place until his couch straps were snugged tight. They wore very lightweight coveralls and sneakers, a far-cry from the bulky Vostok spacesuits.

Fortunately, liftoff and ascent to orbit were routine, because the spacecraft had absolutely no provision for an abort.

In his excellent book *Red Star in Orbit*, James Oberg, one of America's leading civilian experts on the Soviet space program, right-fully calls the episode "the Voskhod follies."

That morning, *Pravda* headlined its scornful story "SORRY, APOLLO!" mocking American space technology while praising the "steady advances of Soviet science." However, not everyone in Moscow was satisfied with Khrushchev's brashness. In many ways, the Voskhod gamble was the final straw for the exasperated Politburo. Even while he was speaking by radiotelephone to the three crewmen in space, the officials who would succeed him were acting. Khrushchev joked to the cosmonauts that his colleague Anastas Mikoyan was "pulling the receiver out of my hand." That afternoon, *Voskhod I* landed hard but safely near Kapustin Yar. The next day, Nikita Khrushchev was summoned to Moscow and deposed.[21]

At the sprawling Tyuratam cosmodrome, Korolev was ambivalent about this news. Khrushchev had interfered for the last time, but the months wasted on Voskhod had seriously set back the development efforts for Soyuz. Worse, the uninterrupted work and stress of this period had taken its toll on Korolev and his closest collaborators in the design bureau. They were now in ill health, hardly able to devote the effort needed to complete the Soyuz system before the Americans had their Apollo in space.

Khrushchev had won another meaningless propaganda victory, but in the process he had been stripped of his power and had perhaps lost the moon race.

CHAPTER SEVEN

VOSKHOD VERSUS GEMINI
1964 TO 1965

Clear Lake, Texas, 1964

I joined NASA in January 1964 as part of the third group of astronauts. There were 14 of us, mostly military pilots from the Air Force and the Navy, and a couple of civilians. The Manned Spacecraft Center (MSC) was still being built when we got there, so mud and dust became part of our everyday lives. After several months the center looked like a well-endowed community college, with open lawns and fountains. Beyond the glass-block buildings, though, you found windowless-slab labs cross-hatched with insulated cryogenic plumbing. The place was filled with earnest young engineers who scurried by us on the shaded sidewalks, heading to still more meetings, their holstered slide rules slapping at their belts. They seemed to be speaking pure Fortran. Everyone had a crewcut and wore black-frame glasses, short-sleeved white shirts, and dark, narrow ties. The sixties hadn't hit Clear Lake, Texas, yet.

Outside the gates, shopping centers and fast food outlets had sprouted up along NASA Road 1, where only three years before cowboys had been skinning wolves. Clear Lake was definitely a company town, and the astronauts were its most prestigious citizens.

I soon figured out that there was a definite pecking order in the astronaut corps. According to the public relations guys the original seven were the "Mercury astronauts," the second group of nine were the "Gemini astronauts," and my group of 14 were the "Apollo astronauts." To my amazement, however, there was an utter lack of organizational structure in the Astronaut Office (other than normal bureaucracy). We had entered NASA through a highly structured competition, in which we were ranked and graded quantitatively at every stage. Once we came on board, however, no one ever formally tested us again, nor did anyone give us a clear official explanation of the flight selection criteria. We would simply be trained, assigned mission-support specialty areas, and then "selected for training" for a particular flight. Or maybe *not* selected.

However, we were all obsessed with getting a flight assignment, no matter how much we tried to be good team players. There were going to be 10 manned Gemini flights, each with two men on board, making a total of 20 crew openings. But 27 astronauts were vying for these slots. It was important to be part of Gemini because that experience in spaceflight would give a man entrée to Apollo. Guys like Gus Grissom, Gordo Cooper, and Wally Schirra had a leg up from their Project Mercury missions. John Glenn had retired to enter politics in January 1964. Deke Slayton had been taken off flight status because of a persistent heart murmur, and Al Shepard had been grounded because of Ménière's syndrome, which affected his sense of balance. But neither of these two left the program. NASA wanted to make use of their training and expertise in other ways.

Shepard and Slayton—the two astronauts who couldn't fly—took on jobs that made them the men with the most to say about who flew on Gemini missions. Al was named head of the Astronaut Office, and was commonly known as "chief astronaut," with the responsibility of coordinating our training assignments and overseeing our endlessly bureaucratic lives. Shepard took this job very seriously and was a stern taskmaster who did everything by the book. We even had to check in and out of his office when we traveled on business to the Cape or to the various contractors. Al wanted team players, not individualists, and his style was soon imprinted on the Astronaut Office.

His immediate boss, Deke Slayton, was the chief of flight crew operations, which involved overall supervision of the crew training at the Manned Spacecraft Center. The chain of command ran roughly from

Shepard to Slayton to Chuck Mathews to Bob Gilruth (director of MSC). In theory, all of them had to sign off on a flight assignment, but in reality, Mathews and Gilruth never countermanded any of Deke's or Al's crew recommendations, so we knew it was smart to keep pleasing both of them.

I now realize there was another, less obvious dynamic at work in the Astronaut Office. By 1964, Navy and Marine astronauts (many of them Annapolis graduates) outnumbered the Air Force guys. Of the four civilians, three were ex-Navy officers. So it was hard to deny that there was a certain old-school Annapolis network operating behind the scenes. Being a Navy astronaut sure didn't hurt when it came to crew assignments. Navy leaders stacked the astronaut corps with their own people to assure Navy domination of America's manned space program. (This continues right up to the present day. Every senior astronaut-manager in NASA's space shuttle program is a Navy man, and most are Annapolis graduates. That's no accident.)

The basic reason a West Point mafia never developed in the astronaut corps was that the Air Force leaders didn't give a rat's ass about "civilian" spaceflight. Right up to the end of Project Mercury, the Air Force believed their expensive Dyna-Soar spaceplane project could be salvaged, which would have given the service its own winged space program. By the time I became an astronaut, the Air Force still thought that they'd have their own "Blue Gemini" military spaceflight program eventually, leading to the Air Force's space station, the Manned Orbiting Laboratory. But that program would be squeezed out too, as America became more involved in Vietnam. And the traditional intense competitiveness of West Pointers tended to fragment them within the astronaut corps. Ed White and I were good friends, as were some others, of course, but groups one, two, and three worked and socialized separately, and I saw less of Ed in Houston than I had in Germany.

The space program was expanding fast and becoming more impersonal. The original seven had been idolized and had also been offered a number of tangible benefits, such as a lucrative contract from *Life* for their personal stories. They had also been offered free homes near the center and even long-term "loans" of Corvettes from a patriotic dealer near Cape Canaveral. This had all died down a bit by the time I came on board, but we did share in the ongoing *Life* contract and got good deals on our mortgage rates.

Following NASA practice, the astronauts in my group were given specialty assignments outside our standard training courses. Some of the ex-test pilots concentrated on Gemini spacecraft hardware, such as the life-support and recovery systems or the retrorockets, while others focused on the Gemini's Titan launch booster. I worked on mission planning, specifically on orbital rendezvous flight plans. I finally felt my years at MIT had not been wasted. I was helping develop a concept of space rendezvous eventually known as the "concentric orbit flight plan," in which spacecraft number two (the chaser) would be premaneuvered into an inner matching orbit uniformly below and overtaking spacecraft number one (the target), and then initiate the intercept transfer, maintaining this collision course with small jet corrections to final closure and docking. I knew this approach was the best chance we had for a successful, practical rendezvous and docking for both Project Gemini and the Apollo LOR mission plan, because the concentric orbit concept would give the astronaut crew a second chance at completing the rendezvous if a computer or radar malfunctioned.

It wasn't easy translating these complex orbital mechanics into relatively simple flight plans for my colleagues. After a few months of trying to promote the intricate mechanics of the actual maneuvers at cocktail parties, I saw that most of these guys weren't really interested. Many were hard-core stick-and-rudder fighter jocks who had no appetite for astronautical theory. All they wanted to know was where to point the spacecraft and what thruster to fire to make it maneuver. They started calling me "Dr. Rendezvous"—some out of respect, others sarcastically—when I gave them a hard time for being so intellectually lazy.

The program managers, on the other hand, did appreciate my work in the rendezvous trenches. After I had spent two years in mission planning, Chris Kraft, the assistant director of MSC for flight operations, wrote a memo to Deke Slayton that focused on my contribution to Project Gemini's success and to the planned lunar orbital rendezvous for Apollo. "In the early stages of the development of the Gemini rendezvous mission plan," Kraft wrote, "Major Aldrin almost single-handedly conceived and pressed through certain basic concepts which were incorporated in this operation, without which the probability of mission success would have unquestionably been considerably reduced." Kraft added that I was "... currently exerting a similar influence on the Apollo program in which the rendezvous exercise is not only a primary mission objective but rather a mandatory operation for the safe return of the flight crew from the moon."[1]

Those months in mission planning were among the most demanding and most rewarding of my life. I was enthralled with Gemini. There's no other way to describe my feelings for the program. Gemini was the realization of all the obscure astronautical theory I'd absorbed at MIT. Gemini was also the proving ground for Apollo.

The American public probably thought the Gemini spacecraft looked like a swollen Mercury, and in fact it had the same design pedigree, with Max Faget's original Langley group again teaming up with McDonnell Aircraft to build the spacecraft. Gemini had the same backward-flying shuttlecock appearance, rippled alloy shingles, and convex heat shield as the smaller Mercury. With its two recessed windows and large, side-opening clamshell hatches, however, Gemini was sleeker and more elegant looking than Mercury.

Gemini was also more technically sophisticated. The spacecraft was actually a three-part composite vehicle, made up of the reentry module with the cabin for two crewmen, and the two truncated cones of the adapter modules—stacked like the sections of a wedding cake—holding the retrorockets and the equipment section, where the maneuvering fuel and life-support "consumables" were stored. Among other innovations, Gemini also used a fuel-cell system that combined liquid hydrogen and oxygen to produce electricity and drinking water. The water tasted terrible at first, but later became potable—barely.

The Gemini launch vehicle was an Air Force Titan II second-generation ICBM, a two-stage booster whose twin-engine first stage produced 430,000 pounds of thrust at liftoff. The Titan had made over 100 successful launches when it was adapted to become a manned space booster for Gemini. Basically that meant "man rating" a booster—installing a reliable, automated malfunction-sensor system that would signal an abort to the crew, in case of trouble. Gemini had no escape-tower rocket to extract the spacecraft from an expanding fireball, so the spacecraft was equipped with two ejection seats that could be used up to 60,000 feet during ascent or below that altitude during a reentry emergency—something the Mercury did not have.[2]

The Titan was considered safer than either the Redstone or the Atlas, and it used a powerful hypergolic fuel with the tongue-twisting name of unsymmetrical dimethyl hydrazine (usually called simply "hydrazine"). It was stored at room temperature and ignited on contact with the nitrogen tetroxide oxidizer. If there were a launch pad accident, the Titan's fuel would burn slowly, not explode, as with the Atlas. The Gemini's thruster system also used hydrazine, which meant there was no need for a complicated (and heavy) electrical ignition system—the Achilles heel of many rocket motors.

One of Project Gemini's basic objectives was to prove that a two-man crew could master the long flights necessary for a lunar mission. Serious consideration had even been given to using a Gemini spacecraft for a "free-return" circumlunar flyby, if Project Apollo hit unexpected delays, but NASA administrator James Webb vetoed the concept, saying it offered needless competition to Apollo.[3] Gemini was also vital in testing practical orbital rendezvous and docking. After docking with a smaller Agena target spacecraft (launched separately by an Atlas), the Gemini crew would fire the Agena's powerful rocket engine to change orbit. This would be a vital maneuver for Apollo's composite command and lunar module during LOR. The Gemini spacecraft was equipped with an onboard computer guidance system that controlled rendezvous and the precision of landings from Earth orbit. (The original Gemini design included a steerable, inflated delta-wing "paraglider" that would land the spacecraft, instead of a conventional parachute. But this system was canceled in 1963 when the paraglider experienced repeated test failures.[4]) Gemini could steer back through the atmosphere to a pinpoint ocean splashdown beside the recovery ship—at least when the crew was flying well. In short, Gemini was a true spacecraft, meant to *voyage* in space, not simply to penetrate the new environment like the Mercury capsule.

Project Gemini had another exciting objective: space walks, or "Extra-Vehicular Activity" (EVA). A Gemini crewman would open one of the spacecraft's clamshell hatches and slide up, clad in his pressurized spacesuit; he would then float free of the cockpit and perform a variety of tasks outside the spacecraft, eventually crossing over to the Agena. His only connection to the Gemini spacecraft would be an oxygen-communications umbilical and a nylon tether for strength. The Air Force's Blue Gemini program had contributed a marvelous Astronaut

Maneuvering Unit (AMU) backpack that would allow the EVA crewman to fly free of the spacecraft and become a true human Earth satellite.

The EVAs planned for Project Gemini had more of a purpose than showing the world we could do daredevil stunts in space. We needed to learn how to walk in the vacuum of space before the Apollo crewmen could explore the lunar surface or men could assemble large spacecraft in the weightless environment of Earth orbit.

After two successful tests of the unmanned versions of the spacecraft, NASA announced in April 1964 that *Gemini 3* would be the first manned flight of the new program; it was tentatively scheduled for early spring 1965. Because Gemini carried two astronauts, they would be designated "commander" and "pilot"; Gus Grissom was named *Gemini 3* mission commander, with John Young, a Navy astronaut from the second group, as pilot.

By spring 1964, NASA was also moving ahead full speed with the launching of unmanned weather and communications satellites and working hard to develop the Apollo spacecraft and the Saturn booster. The Gemini-Titan launch complex at pads 19 and 20 was almost finished, and NASA was building the massive Apollo launch and support structures on Merritt Island, just north of the Cape proper. Lyndon Johnson had changed the name of the new 80,000-acre Apollo complex from the Launch Operations Center to the more heroic John F. Kennedy Space Center a week after the president's assassination. The Department of the Interior had followed suit by changing the name of Cape Canaveral to Cape Kennedy. Together, the two adjacent sites became known as "the Cape" and "KSC." Naming the major launch facilities in Florida for John Kennedy was a gesture of respect as well as a wise political act. The Johnson White House wanted to maintain the connection between the energetic young president and the complex and expensive moon landing program. This was especially important as America committed its first combat troops to Vietnam. Congress was beginning to chafe at the fiscal burden of the Asian war, the costly social programs of Lyndon Johnson's recently proclaimed Great Society, and the seemingly bottomless budgetary maw of Project Apollo.

There had been little news of the Soviet manned space program since the spectacular flight of *Voshkod I* the previous year. And it looked to the guys in the Astronaut Office on the third floor of Building 4 at MSC as if we were finally going to beat the Soviets at their own game.

Moscow and Tyuratam, Kazakhstan,
Winter 1964–Spring 1965

During the winter of 1964, chief designer Sergei Korolev hoped the disruptive political manipulation of the Soviet space program had ended with the downfall of Nikita Khrushchev. After all, new party chairman Leonid Brezhnev, Premier Aleksey Kosygin, and their followers in the Politburo had overthrown Khrushchev in part because of his insistence on the propagandistic Voskhod program.[5] Korolev and his close friend Leonid Voskresensky had given Brezhnev and Kosygin a secret report that detailed the negative impact Khrushchev's interference had had on the development of a rational Soviet manned space program. Korolev urged the new leaders to support a well-funded, incremental buildup of Soviet booster and spacecraft capability—independent of any American success. In essence, Korolev was proposing a steady evolution, leading up to two big, new boosters, a permanent orbital station, and eventual circumlunar flights and moon landings using expanded Soyuz-class spacecraft. He recommended that the Soviet Union halt its manned space missions for several years, so that the nation's resources could be concentrated on meaningful, realistic goals, not propaganda.

Although the Brezhnev Politburo was receptive to Korolev's long-range plans, Project Gemini troubled them deeply. The Americans would soon have an advanced, two-man spacecraft flying regular rendezvous and docking missions and giving the hungry Western media spectacular images of astronauts floating freely in space. The Soviet Union couldn't simply relinquish all its international space prestige to NASA without any competition whatsoever. Korolev proposed another of his typically ingenious compromises. The one remaining Voskhod spacecraft could be modified so that Soviet cosmonauts could perform the world's first space walk. He realized that undertaking this mission would definitely disrupt the Soyuz program, but he also understood that winning a propaganda victory for the new leaders would help assure their continued support.[6]

Through the frigid winter months of 1964 and early 1965, Korolev and Voskresensky pushed themselves at a killing pace to get the Voskhod spacecraft ready for an EVA. Week in and week out, 14-hour days, even 18-hour days, were commonplace. But both men's health had been shattered by their years in the gulag (Korolev's heart problem was still severe), and they understood the risks they were taking. Korolev worked at his principal design bureau near Moscow, and Voskresensky traveled aboard drafty, ill-pressurized Antonov transports on many exhausting field-engineering trips to the launch facilities at Tyuratam. Some days, when Korolev's chauffeur dropped him at his apartment in northeast Moscow, he was too tired to climb the stairs and had to sit for a while with his wife before mustering his strength to continue.[7]

The two designers faced a horrendous engineering problem: modifying the spherical Voskhod reentry capsule so that a cosmonaut could exit into the vacuum of space. Many of the cabin's electronics were made with hot, old-fashioned glass tubes that might explode in the chill vacuum of space if the entire cabin were depressurized. Voskresensky's solution was not to depressurize the spacecraft at all; rather, a lightweight, collapsible airlock would be attached to the main hatch. Once in orbit, the airlock tube would be inflated, the hatch would be opened, and the cosmonaut—dressed in a spacesuit with its own oxygen supply—would enter and close the hatch behind him before opening the airlock's outer door. Korolev approved this ingenious compromise, but once again the Voskhod would have to be launched without ejection seats.

The two new Voskhod cosmonauts were trained in great haste. Pavel Belyayev, age 39, a Red Air Force pilot and veteran of World War II, was picked to fly the Voskhod, and Aleksey Leonov was chosen for the space walk. Just to be safe, both men would wear spacesuits throughout the mission, in the already cramped cabin.

In January 1965, Korolev began pressing his engineers even harder because he knew the Americans would orbit their first manned Gemini mission within two months, and continued support from the Politburo depended on beating Gemini. Then Voskresensky was hospitalized with a heart attack, but insisted on working as best he could from his hospital room. His death a few days later devastated Korolev. In his graveside eulogy, the chief designer noted that Voskresensky had been with him since before Sputnik and that without his creative skill and energy, the Soviets would probably not have launched their satellite before the Americans.[8] Korolev's depression deepened following his friend's death, but he forced himself to continue working on the *Voskhod II* mission.

An unmanned test flight (simply called *Cosmos 57*) was launched on February 23, 1965, into a typical Vostok orbit; its radio transmissions were on the same frequencies as those of the first Voskhod flight. In fact, this mission was a full dress rehearsal for the equipment to be used on the manned *Voskhod II*. On the second revolution, however, the spacecraft broke up, and Western air defense radar systems tracked 180 fragments that reentered the atmosphere in small clumps and burned up between February 26 and March 6. It has never been revealed exactly what happened, but Korolev was, apparently, either so depressed or so desperate to upstage Gemini that he did not insist on a second unmanned rehearsal before flying the manned mission.[9] This was yet another time when politics forced Korolev to ignore safety.

Despite the bad late-winter weather at Tyuratam, *Voskhod II* was launched at 10:00 AM on March 18, 1965, the same day NASA's flight readiness review managers confirmed that *Gemini 3* would blast off five days later. Radio Moscow gave the launch considerable fanfare but left out any details about the mission's purpose. From the mission control center near Moscow, Korolev monitored Leonov's space walk preparations during the second revolution. *Voskhod II* would be over Soviet territory for the entire brief EVA, so that ground controllers could follow his movements. He deployed the airlock and completed his required "prebreathing" of pure oxygen to clear his bloodstream of nitrogen and prevent the bends when he reduced the pressure in his spacesuit to six pounds per square inch.

Leonov's suit was simple: his life-support backpack contained an oxygen supply and chemical "scrubbers" to remove carbon dioxide. Since he would be outside the spacecraft for only 20 minutes, the suit's cooling system was rudimentary. Once the main hatch was sealed, Leonov opened the outer door to the vacuum of space and floated free on a short tether. He attached a low-resolution television camera on the airlock lip to record his slow, ghostly pirouettes 300 kilometers above the frigid Siberian cloudscape.

After nine minutes of EVA, the first phase of his task had been accomplished and Korolev personally instructed him by radio to reenter the airlock. Now Leonov ran into trouble. His spacesuit had swollen abnormally during the EVA, because of the so-called football-bladder effect, caused by unequal, motion-induced stresses on the suit's different materials. The suit had become so rigid that he couldn't even bend properly to enter the hatch. He pulled as hard as he could against handholds, but was still unable to get into the hatch. Leonov's limited

oxygen supply was running out. His heart rate and breathing accelerated, further depleting his oxygen. Finally, Leonov risked the bends by
reducing his suit pressure to a dangerous four pounds per square inch.
Korolev heard the cosmonaut's panicked tones: "I *can't*... no, again I
can't get in... I can't...." After eight minutes of extreme effort, Leonov
slid through the hatch and sealed the airlock tube behind him.
"Hurrah!" he called bravely to ground control; under his breath, he
swore bitterly.[10]

The airlock was safely dumped, and the rest of the mission should
have been routine. The two cosmonauts were paying careful attention to
their head movements—a precaution against spacesickness. But on the
seventeenth revolution, trouble struck again: the retrorocket package
did not fire on the radio command from ground control. After three
rapid attempts, Korolev told Belyayev to prepare for a manual retrofire
on the eighteenth revolution. Approximately 80 minutes later, as the
Voskhod crossed north of equatorial Africa, ground controllers gave the
cosmonauts their countdown and Belyayev manually fired the retros.

The cosmonauts were out of danger, but descent from this orbit put
Voskhod II on a trajectory toward the northern Soviet Union. At midday
on March 19, the spacecraft landed by parachute in a snowbound forest
in the western Ural mountains near Perm, almost 1,300 miles from the
planned impact area in Kazakhstan. The descent module was half
buried in snow in an isolated fir forest. All day the two cosmonauts
waited for search aircraft to home in on their emergency radio beacon.
When it got dark they were cold and built a campfire both to warm
themselves and to frighten off a pack of wolves they heard circling in the
darkness. Ski troops rescued them the next morning.

Although the mission had nearly ended in disaster, Korolev had
scored another astounding propaganda victory. News media around the
world were ecstatic over Leonov's space walk. A long cover story in *Time*
the next week echoed the official Soviet account of the flight, even
though *Voskhod II* had landed 2,000 kilometers off course. *Time*
concluded its description of the Soviet space walk with, "Then, as easily
and efficiently as he had emerged from his ship, Leonov climbed back
inside."[11]

Time quoted Kennedy Space Center director Kurt Debus, who
conceded the Soviet's technological "sophistication." The article called
the Voskhod mission simply the latest of the Soviets' many "firsts,"

including the group Vostok missions and the flight of the first woman cosmonaut, Valentina Tereshkova. Comparing American spacecraft with the "spacious, multimanned" Soviet craft, *Time* said the U.S. equipment was inferior. The magazine tipped its hat to the "large Soviet spaceships such as the three-man Voskhod...." *Time* concluded: "Voskhod trailed behind it an embarrassing shadow that seemed to darken the spring sunlight over Florida's Cape Kennedy."

It's safe to assume the Politburo was pleased with this favorable Western press coverage. Over the years, I've met a number of cosmonauts, but I never learned how the *Voskhod II* crewmen enjoyed their night in the woods.

Kennedy Space Center, Cape Kennedy, 1965

There was no sense denying that the Soviets had beaten us again. We were shaken, but our underlying confidence in Gemini made us certain that America would pull ahead in the international space race. George E. Mueller, a former professor of electrical engineering, was NASA's associate administrator for manned space flight. He focused all his technical competence and administrative skill on Gemini. Even though the Apollo program still required a tremendous effort in its early phases, Mueller knew it was essential that Gemini succeed in order to ensure continued support for NASA from an increasingly impatient Congress.

MSC Houston was the lead center for Gemini and Apollo. Administrator Webb gave Robert Gilruth, the center director, responsibility for Gemini, and Chuck Mathews, a veteran of the Space Task Group, took over the day-to-day management of the program. Webb had set up a team he was sure would guarantee the success of Project Gemini. Jim Webb understood Washington politics, and he was hearing rumbles in Congress that the Soviets' *sophisticated* spacecraft seemed destined to beat America to the moon in any event, so it might be better to redirect scarce resources to the problems of poverty at home and the war in Vietnam.

In the years since Project Gemini, some official government historians have noted that the program progressed smoothly and that NASA dealt with unexpected setbacks with decisive vigor and clever improvisation. That may have been true, but there wasn't much choice.

NASA's back was to the wall. Gemini had to work or the whole space program would fall apart.

All of NASA's senior management were in the launch control center at the Cape on the morning of March 23, 1965, when commander Gus Grissom and pilot John Young slid through their twin hatches and were carefully sealed into the cramped cabin of the *Gemini 3* spacecraft by Gunter Wendt's McDonnell closeout crew. The later Gemini missions were officially numbered with Roman numerals and Gus was the last to "name" his spacecraft. He had insisted on calling the spacecraft *Molly Brown*, in honor of the *unsinkable* character in a recent Broadway musical. NASA headquarters thought the name was too undignified, but Gus got his way with *Molly Brown* when he told them his second choice, *Titanic*.[12]

The countdown to the three-orbit mission proceeded smoothly— exactly the routine precision NASA's leaders meant to project. The massive pillar of the Titan II, standing over 130 feet tall with its sturdy black-and-white payload of the Gemini spacecraft, gave the impression of solid strength far beyond Mercury-Redstone's "plumber's nightmare."

The first manned Gemini mission's liftoff and powered ascent were perfect. Two and a half minutes after launch, long-distance television lenses were able to capture the brilliant fireworks of first-stage separation and second-stage ignition. In the spacecraft, John Young gasped as the cabin was surrounded by the dazzling yellow glow of second-stage engine ignition. The two astronauts were jostled from a three-G acceleration to zero G, and then eased back into their couches again as the second-stage thrust increased gradually to an immobilizing seven Gs. Two minutes later, Young heard a thud that sounded like a howitzer shell as the spacecraft blasted free of the spent booster stage. *Gemini 3* was in orbit.

There were a few minor equipment glitches, which the crew quickly overcame during the first revolution, but overall, the spacecraft behaved perfectly. At the beginning of the second revolution Grissom fired the powerful orbit attitude and maneuvering system (OAMS) thrusters to slow the spacecraft and drop it into an almost circular orbit. This was the first true orbital maneuver by any spacecraft, American or Soviet, despite their propaganda about the "maneuvers" of their group Vostok flights. Gus worked hard to complete the task, even though he faced a "really challenging" encounter with his onboard navigational computer.

Grissom next carried out an innovative maneuver that Gilruth and Mathews had insisted become a part of the manned Gemini flights. Called the "fail-safe plan," this burn lowered the orbit even further (closer to Earth), so that atmospheric drag would, eventually, ensure safe reentry should the retrorockets malfunction. In fact, this maneuver had been originally perfected by Korolev.

As the crew began testing the effects of weightlessness and radiation on biological samples, they discovered that the Gemini cockpit, in which they sat elbow to elbow, was just as cramped in weightlessness as it had been on the launch pad. With the clamshell hatch low over the astronauts' heads and small crescent windows in front of them above the crowded instrument panel, the cabin was definitely claustrophobic, especially when they started unwrapping scientific experiments, navigational equipment, or thick, flapping flight manuals. Frank Borman later compared the Gemini cabin to the front seat of a Volkswagen.[13] That's pretty accurate.

One item Gus unwrapped on the second revolution was absolutely not part of the standard equipment. That morning at the suiting station at Launch Pad 16, Wally Schirra—NASA's eternal joker—had slipped Gus a corned beef sandwich on rye from Wolfie's Restaurant in Cocoa Beach. Gus peeled back the waxed paper and took a few nibbles, but quickly shoved the sandwich back in the leg pocket of his spacesuit when some pink crumbs of corned beef floated free.

The mission progressed smoothly until after retrofire, when Gus took over manual control and the spacecraft did not produce as much lift—hence, steering control—as design studies had indicated. According to the computer, Grissom and Young would be splashing down about 50 miles short of their target in the Atlantic. Another surprise came after the main parachute deployed. For splashdown, the parachute harness was designed to flip from a single to a two-point suspension to lower the spacecraft horizontally to the surface. But with *Gemini 3*, when this suspension switchover came, the *Molly Brown* dropped so violently that both astronauts were flung into their windows, breaking Gus's faceplate. Remembering the fiasco with his Mercury capsule, Grissom insisted that the spacecraft's hatches remain sealed until Navy frogmen attached a flotation collar. This took 30 minutes, and Gus finally got seasick in the hot, pitching cabin.

Overall, the mission had successfully proven that the Gemini space-craft could fly and maneuver in Earth orbit. Unfortunately, the practical joke with the corned beef sandwich had unpleasant repercussions when Congress heard about it. Webb, Mueller, and Gilruth were given a fair reaming out at a vital Appropriations Committee hearing. The crew had been assigned to complete an expensive test of the packaging of food samples for long-duration flights, which some congressmen thought was superfluous, but which NASA defended because the packaging prevented crumbs and spills from shorting out vital electronics. One congressman said Grissom's chomping away on his corned beef sand-wich was "digusting."

Webb practically knuckled his forehead and swore to the stern congressmen that "this kind of deviation..." would never happen again.[14] This shows how anxious NASA was about future budget support for the costly moon landing program.

I was at the Cape for the launch of *Gemini IV* on June 3, 1965. Ed White was flying as pilot, with Jim McDivitt as mission commander. This was the first Gemini flight to include a space walk (EVA), so all of the large press contingent gathered again both at the Cape and in Houston. Another first for this flight—the switch from launch control at the Cape to mission control at MSC in Houston—was the inauguration of the elaborate new control room there.

NASA was clearly influenced in its decision to undertake a space walk by Leonov's EVA on the *Voskhod II* mission. Although a space walk had been tentatively planned for *Gemini IV,* it was a real horse race to get the procedure and the equipment ready in time for the flight. And the main Gemini contractor, McDonnell Aircraft, had been resistant to rushing the process. The space walk would have to be simulated in a ground vacuum chamber, a risky procedure in itself. As John Young later described it, NASA was not pleased about "putting guys in vacuums...," a process whose safety seemed to depend too much on a "little old lady" seamstress at the company who sealed their spacesuits with her "glue pot."[15]

The Soviet flight drove NASA to push the ground tests, and Ed White was extremely gung-ho to get on with the job. Deputy admin-istrator Hugh Dryden believed that adding an EVA to the *Gemini IV* flight plan would be an open admission that NASA was reacting to the Soviet propaganda initiative. But Webb overruled him because it was exactly the type of space spectacular NASA needed.

Liftoff came after a brief delay when the launch pad gantry stuck, but the ascent was flawless. Television coverage of the blast-off was broadcast to Europe via Early Bird satellite, another first for NASA (which the Soviets in their determination to be secretive could never do). There were some unpleasant longitudinal "pogo" booster oscilla- tions, which were smoothed out, and *Gemini IV* was in orbit five minutes later. Unfortunately, McDivitt's awkward attempts at an "eye- ball rendezvous" with the spent second stage were an utter failure. He tried to *fly* the spacecraft toward the slowly tumbling Titan booster shell, and naturally, he ran into the predictable paradoxes as the target alternately seemed to speed away and then drop behind. McDivitt had never grasped much rendezvous theory during his Houston training, and after the mission, one of the Gemini engineers, André Meyer, commented that McDivitt "just didn't understand or reason out the orbital mechanics involved."[16] I certainly knew what Andy was saying, having once hoped to interest a bunch of white-scarf astronauts in rendezvous techniques. Unfortunately McDivitt's abortive rendezvous wasted half their thruster propellant.

For his EVA, Ed White had to go through an extremely tiring preparation, attaching his umbilical system and the emergency oxygen chestpack in the tiny cockpit. After resting, Ed opened the hatch while the spacecraft was over the Indian Ocean. He stood in his seat and fired his hand-held "zip gun" maneuvering thruster, which squirted com- pressed gas from the ends of a T-shaped nozzle. He drifted to the end of his tether and was able to maneuver himself using the gun. Ed could see the milky blue vastness of the Pacific slide below him. The sun was bright in his visor, but he had no problem distinguishing details on the spacecraft. He didn't feel at all disoriented, nor did he experience the vertigo that comes when spacesickness begins to set in. After about 15 minutes, Jim McDivitt told Ed to reel himself back in on his umbilical line and prepare to close the hatch.

"It's the saddest moment of my life," Ed said, complying.

Ed had not only become an astronaut—his ambition since our days together in Germany—but he had also been the first American to float free in space. Like Leonov, he had a hard time jamming the legs of his bulky pressure suit into the narrow hatch, and it was even more difficult to work the hatch's torque handle to reseal the spacecraft. But with Jim McDivitt's help, *Gemini IV* was repressurized and they began the nasty task of putting away the awkward EVA equipment.

One of the photographs of Ed's EVA shows him floating freely, the thruster gun in his right hand, the sun reflecting brightly from his visor with the distant ocean cloudscape far below. It's eerie and futuristic. You can clearly see the American flag sewn to his left shoulder—a proud swatch of color. This flight was the first time that the shoulder patch flags were worn. There was certainly no practical reason to slap Old Glory on an astronaut's shoulder. After all, there were no customs posts out there. But showing the flag in space—for both the Soviet Union and the United States—was now increasingly important. That picture of Ed became one of the most famous images of the space age. Years later, Neil Armstrong's photograph of me standing before the American flag on the Sea of Tranquillity became another famous image.

Less than three months later, *Gemini V* was ready to be launched. This was an eight-day mission, and the spacecraft was fully equipped with life-support "consumables" and thruster fuel. Gordo Cooper was commander, with Pete Conrad as pilot. One of *Gemini V*'s objectives was to test our ability to rendezvous with another spacecraft. Since the Agena rocket rendezvous and docking target was not yet ready, the astronauts practiced reaching a point in space the ground controllers called a "phantom Agena." They successfully completed this maneuver, proving the spacecraft could accomplish its end of the rendezvous.

They were also asked to demonstrate precision landing. Here Gordo ran into trouble. After eight days in orbit, the crew fired their retros and steered down through the atmosphere, Cooper flying on instruments as they blazed through the darkness toward orbital sunrise above the Mississippi River. But the instruments said their reentry track was too high, so Gordo rolled a full 90 degrees left to increase drag and to eliminate the risk of overshooting the landing. Deceleration forces shot up to an alarming seven and a half Gs.

When they splashed down, they were 80 miles short of the aircraft carrier *Lake Champlain*. Officials in Houston and at NASA headquarters were not amused, to say the least. The mistake was attributed to pilot error, but Cooper insisted he had only been flying as he'd been trained. Later, it was discovered that the onboard computer had been programmed with an incorrect calculation for the Earth's rate of rotation, which accounted for the problem. Someone had eliminated 98 hundredths of a degree in the so-called "theta sub N" calculation. But program officials still felt Cooper should have done better, and he never flew again.

The implications of the "theta sub N flight" were obvious for the guys in the Astronaut Office. If a national hero like Gordo Cooper could get shafted for screwing the pooch, then it could happen to any of us. An obsession was growing among some astronauts to fly error-free missions, even if it meant passing up good opportunities to further the program.

Houston, Texas, 1965

By the middle of 1965, I still hadn't been named to a crew. Pete Conrad and I sat down and had a drink. Pete was one of the friendliest guys in Houston, and he certainly knew how to get along in the organization. I wanted to pick his brain on how the crew selection process really worked.

"I have no idea how it works," he admitted. "Some day, all of a sudden, somebody comes up behind you and says, 'Hey, how would you like to fly with so and so.'"

That wasn't good enough for me. I was working my tail off in mission planning, thrashing out the details of concentric orbital rendezvous techniques, Project Gemini's prime objective and an absolutely crucial part of Apollo's Lunar Orbital Rendezvous. Even so, I wasn't a good office politician, so I didn't have much chance of flying on a Gemini mission. I went to see Deke Slayton and laid out in detail my work on orbital rendezvous, explaining that I was probably the best-qualified member of the astronaut corps in this area. I wanted to let him know that I felt I was a good candidate for an upcoming flight.

Deke listened and then sat hunched over his desk for a few minutes, considering what I'd said. According to the assignment system, the backup crew for a flight would skip two missions and then become the prime crew. At that time, the first five missions had been decided, but the rest of the roster had not been posted. Finally, Deke looked up, with no expression on his wrinkled, suntanned face. "Buzz," he said, "I'll take this matter under consideration." He nodded. The interview was over.

I'd put Deke in an uncomfortable position. His situation was already awkward; he was one of the original seven who now found himself making decisions far above his normal pay grade.

Three months later, crew assignments for the remainder of the Gemini flights were announced. Standing in the corridor of the Astronaut Office, staring at the mimeographed roster on the bulletin board, I felt a deep stab of sadness. Jim Lovell and I had been assigned as backup crew to *Gemini X* with John Young and Mike Collins flying prime. That meant we were slated for the thirteenth mission, but the program was only funded through *Gemini XII*. By now, it was commonly accepted that NASA would pick the Apollo astronauts from those with spaceflight experience in Gemini. Apparently, petitioning Deke— an arrogant gesture by "Doctor Rendezvous"—had not been well received by the stick-and-rudder guys in the Astronaut Office. By being direct and honest rather than political, I'd shafted myself.

Kennedy Space Center, Cape Kennedy, Fall 1965

One of the first serious mishaps of the program occurred on October 25, 1965. The *Gemini VI* mission was to be the first true orbital rendezvous. Wally Schirra and Tom Stafford were on Launch Pad 19, and half a mile to the south on Launch Pad 14, a gleaming Atlas-Agena roared to life and climbed through the broken clouds above the Cape. The Atlas booster functioned well, but the Agena's engine malfunctioned. The small target vehicle lost stability and broke up: several million dollars transformed into smoking debris in a split second. Flight directors had no choice but to cancel the Gemini-Titan countdown on Launch Pad 19.

Astronaut Frank Borman watched the Atlas launch from a grandstand on Merritt Island. Following the scrub of *Gemini VI*, he rushed to the launch control center to find out what this meant for his own flight, which was scheduled for launch six weeks later. McDonnell Aircraft officials Walter Burke and John Yardley were already discussing using Borman's *Gemini VII* as the rendezvous target for a rescheduled *Gemini VI* flight. Borman liked the concept. *Gemini VI* was going to be the first true long-duration flight, a 14-day marathon that would prove astronauts could survive the weightlessness of a round-trip to the moon. But when Walter Burke began sketching an improvised inflatable docking collar that could be attached to the aft section of Borman's spacecraft, Frank said no way. Gordo Cooper's "theta sub N flight" was still on Frank's mind. He wanted his mission to be as uncomplicated as possible, and he knew that improvised equipment had a way of breaking down in orbit.[17] Undoubtedly, he truly thought the idea wasn't that safe, but I'm sure his main concern was not to screw the pooch.

George Mueller's Gemini officials scurried to salvage as much as they could. They quickly decided to attempt Burke and Yardley's rendezvous concept. Frank Borman and Jim Lovell's Gemini flight was launched on the afternoon of December 4. It was the heaviest spacecraft the United States had ever put in orbit. The spacecraft's adapter section held a record amount of fuel and consumable life-support supplies, and it was also equipped with the new fuel cells.

On December 12, Wally Schirra and Tom Stafford's countdown reached T–0 at 9:54 AM. Schirra's mission, renamed *Gemini VI-A*, would rendezvous with Borman's, which was acting as a passive target in lieu of the Agena. The huge Titan's engines spewed flame, but shut down 1.2 seconds after ignition. Schirra showed his cool fighter pilot's nerve by not pulling the abort ring, which would have blasted both of them in their ejection seats to safety. A small electrical plug had shaken loose in the tail of the Titan, causing premature engine shutdown. That was real discipline—sitting there waiting for the launch crew to reattach the gantry while a fully fueled and armed Titan booster smoked below them.

Three days later, the *Gemini VI-A* mission was finally launched. After six hours of maneuvering, the last three in the automatic, computer-controlled mode, Wally Schirra accomplished America's first true orbital rendezvous. He wasn't exactly sure what he was doing when he fired his thrusters on the computer's orders. About an hour before actual rendezvous, Wally exclaimed, "My gosh, there's a real bright star out there. That must be Sirius." The bright object was *Gemini VII*.

NASA had two spacecraft and four astronauts in orbit, and the news media made the most of the mission. The press was ecstatic when Tom Stafford gleefully said he'd just seen ". . . a satellite going from north to south, probably in a polar orbit. . . . " Then Wally Schirra—ever the prankster—played "Jingle Bells" on his harmonica.

By December 18, when Frank Borman and Jim Lovell splashed down in the Atlantic, America had more than quadrupled the "space hours" racked up by the Soviet Union. Everyone at headquarters—not to mention the NASA supporters in Congress—was pleased.

There could not have been a better time for this success. As Jim Webb had feared, some congressmen had recently called for a serious reassessment and scaling down of the space program and an indefinite postponement of the Apollo moon landing.

America was not the same country it had been when Kennedy issued his moon landing challenge. The civil rights movement had exploded into violent confrontations in towns like Selma, Alabama; the black underclass in the urban ghettos was no longer invisible. That summer, the bloodshed and widespread arson in the Watts section of Los Angeles shocked the nation. America's direct intervention in Vietnam with combat troops had been anything but decisive. The Army's elite First Air Cavalry Division had been battered by regular North Vietnamese Army regiments in the monsoon-shrouded A Shau Valley of the central highlands. Our bombing campaign against North Vietnam was now striking the outskirts of Hanoi, but the enemy continued to send a flood of troops to the south. The antiwar movement was growing on university campuses across the country.

As always, Congress reflected the mood of the country. And the mood regarding the space program was beginning to sour. Increasingly, newspaper editorials were saying that tax dollars were being "wasted" in space, that they could be better spent here on Earth, either fighting the Vietnam War more aggressively or waging a more effective war on poverty at home.

Jim Webb and his subordinates were nervous. Project Gemini had matched the Soviet Voskhod, but the program had still not met its major objectives: routine orbital rendezvous and docking, and EVAs during which an astronaut would accomplish useful work, not simply dangle on his tether, as both Leonov and Ed White had done. Intelligence reports indicated that the Soviets were developing two new classes of large boosters, plus an elaborate, Apollo-type spacecraft.

If Gemini did not meet its objectives in the remaining five flights, Congress and the American people would lose interest in space, and the moon race would be lost.

CHAPTER EIGHT

GEMINI TRIUMPHANT
1966

Moscow, January 1966

During the severe Russian winter of 1966, Sergei Korolev struggled to pull his Soyuz lunar spacecraft program back on track after the disruption of Voskhod. Other Soviet design bureaus were working day and night in a parallel effort to develop two large new boosters, the Proton, similar to our Titan, and the Soviet's own Saturn-class moon rocket, generally known in the West as the G-1.[1] Korolev's design bureau also had the responsibility of upgrading the reliable Vostok booster for Soyuz test missions. But the effort was debilitating the chief designer physically and spiritually.

Korolev still hoped the Proton would launch a Soyuz, carrying one cosmonaut, on a circumlunar flyby (the Gemini mission Jim Webb had rejected earlier) to coincide with the fiftieth anniversary of the Bolshevik revolution in October 1967. The Brezhnev Politburo had persuaded Korolev to undertake the task of developing the Soyuz on a priority basis, despite the government's previous assurance that it would pursue a slower-paced program. To add to his problems, Korolev's domination of the civil space program was now being challenged by his major competitor, military designer general Vladimir N. Chelomei, who ran his own successful ICBM design bureau outside of Moscow, which

135

designed the Proton. It would be Chelomei, not Korolev, who would actually build the boosters that would eventually launch Soyuz on lunar missions.

Chelomei's Proton was similar to the clustered-engine, strap-on booster concept of Korolev's original Vostok rocket. The central sustainer core, however, evolved from the single most horrendous weapon ever conceived, Khrushchev's hypergolic-propellant "City Buster" missile. He had ordered Chelomei to build the missile in 1962 to be capable of delivering an astonishing 100-megaton warhead to the American heartland. But the project was soon abandoned, and the missile was converted to civilian use.[2] This was the Soviets' first attempt at deploying truly complex upper booster stages that could be shut down and restarted in the weightless vacuum of Earth orbit.

The second rocket being developed—the huge moon booster—would be as powerful as NASA's Saturn V. Its eventual mission was an actual lunar landing, using a combined Earth and lunar orbit rendezvous mode.[3]

By the summer of 1965, Chelomei had pushed the staff at his design bureau to the limits of their endurance and had pulled off a successful launch of the first Proton. But this heavy booster would require numerous unmanned test flights before it would be safe enough to launch a crew of cosmonauts.

In January, Korolev was admitted to a special Politburo hospital in Kuntsevo, a Moscow suburb, with the symptoms of bowel obstruction. The Soviet minister of health, Boris Petrovsky, personally operated on Korolev, even though he had not practiced surgery for several years. The surgical team discovered a malignant tumor, and Petrovsky decided to remove it. They weren't prepared for a procedure of this scope. Korolev suffered a severe hemorrhage and his fragile cardiovascular system failed. *Pravda* announced on January 16 that Korolev had died two days earlier of cancer compounded by arteriosclerosis, emphysema, and a "generally disturbed metabolism."[4] He was only 59 years old. Korolev's ashes were interred in the Kremlin wall, an honored resting place for a man who had been kept anonymous for most of his career.

This was a major catastrophe for the Soviet space program.

The Politburo replaced Korolev with Vasily Pavlovich Mishin, an instrumentation and control specialist, not an aerodynamicist like Korolev. Mishin lacked Korolev's innovative energy and ability to inspire his colleagues, and he couldn't easily envision the large integrated spacecraft-booster systems that had been Korolev's hallmark. The Soviet space program had grown to such mammoth proportions by this time that it rivaled even the American effort. But without Korolev the Russians' attempt to beat the Americans to the moon became as risky as any of Khrushchev's earlier space gambles.

Houston, Texas, Winter–Spring 1966

I was finding it hard to concentrate on my assignment to the backup crew of *Gemini X*, knowing how little chance I had of ever flying a Gemini spacecraft. As the months of intense study and travel to training sites passed, I began to question why I'd become an astronaut. I just wasn't an organization man. That was the main reason I'd given up flying fighters and gone to MIT. Now I realized team playing was how you got ahead as an astronaut.

I was really an odd man out in the astronaut corps. My image as "Dr. Rendezvous" alienated me from some of the other astronauts. Most of my group were "right stuff" fighter jocks who'd gotten advanced engineering degrees and had experience as test pilots.

Air Force major Charlie Bassett was probably the best example of these bright, aggressive engineers you were likely to find. Charlie had a BS in electrical engineering from Texas Tech and had been one of the best student test pilots at Edwards. He became a consummate astronaut who could spend hours in the cramped Gemini simulator, "flying" one demanding rendezvous mission after another. Above all, he was gung ho, always rallying the troops during our rigorous survival training in the Arizona desert and the Panama jungle. Most of us had been through similar training as military pilots, but you never really get used to roasting a hunk of iguana tail on a machete blade over a smoky fire while the rain beats down on the banana-leaf roof of your lean-to. But Charlie could make all this seem like a school picnic. My former colleague, astronaut Walt Cunningham, points out that Charlie often went without lunch on field trips—although he always ate his iguana—to show how his self-discipline and will power could overcome such weaknesses as hunger. Charlie was also a genuinely good guy—the kind of hard charger my colleagues respected most.

He was assigned to pilot the *Gemini IX* mission with former Navy test pilot Elliot See as commander. My house in Nassau Bay shared a backyard fence with the Bassetts', and Charlie's wife, Jeannie, and Joan were best friends. Charlie was often away from Houston as his mission training increased, and we saw a lot of Jeannie and their two kids. The astronauts flew by twin-jet T-38 trainers so we could keep our cockpit skills sharp and also maintain the minimum hours we needed for our armed services flight pay.

On the last day of February, Charlie and Elliot See flew up to St. Louis by T-38, with their backup crew, Tom Stafford and Gene Cernan, behind them in a second T-38. The weather was perfect at Ellington Air Force Base near the Manned Spacecraft Center, but the forecast for Lambert Field in St. Louis was for low overcast and poor visibility in rain and fog: what we call instrument flight rules "minimums." Elliot flew the lead plane from the front seat, with Charlie sitting behind. They began their approach to Lambert Field in freezing rain just before nine o'clock that morning. When they finally broke through the ragged overcast, only 600 feet above the ground, with visibility further impaired by snow, Elliot had undershot the landing and was short of the runway.

Tom Stafford in the number-two plane climbed back into the overcast to go around for another attempt. But Elliot stayed below the cloud deck, keeping the field in sight as he banked sharply left to line up again on the runway. It was too late when he realized his sink rate was excessive, and he jammed his throttles full forward to afterburner. Throwing the plane into a steep right turn, Elliot tried to clear the airport buildings looming ahead of him, but his wingtip struck McDonnell Aircraft Building 101—where his spacecraft was in the last stages of assembly—and the plane cartwheeled onto a roadway and exploded.

Charlie Bassett and Elliot See were killed instantly.

After I heard about the accident, around 10 o'clock, I called Joan and then sped back home so we could both console Jeannie. She was out shopping with the kids. A little while later, the minister of our Presbyterian church came and we all stood around Jeannie's kitchen silently drinking coffee and waiting for her to return. An hour later, she came through the kitchen door and saw us. Jeannie Bassett had been married to an Air Force pilot long enough to know instantly why we were there. A shudder passed through her body; she squared her shoulders and swallowed hard, and looked directly at each of us.

I flew the F-86 Sabre in Korea (inset) and the F-100 Super Sabre in Germany (above). "Combat flying requires an intensity and skill far beyond anything in peacetime aviation. Years later those of us who'd served in Korea were prepared for the hazards and uncertainty of space-flight because we had already come to terms with fear."

America's Mercury astronauts, in 1959. (Above, left to right: front) Wally Schirra, Deke Slayton, John Glenn, and Scott Carpenter; (back) Alan Shepard, Gus Grissom, and Gordo Cooper. During the selection process, "They were shaken, spun in centrifuges, jolted in mock ejection seats, practically frozen or baked in temperature chambers, and driven to exhaustion on treadmills." Encouraged by reporters, "The country wanted individual heroes, not a team." But the news media's love affair with the astronauts waxed and waned. By the time Alan Shepard became our first man in space on May 5, 1961 (opposite), the press was already mocking "Lead-Footed Mercury." But ultimately, Mercury was a success.

Giants of the Space Age. Soviet cosmonaut Yuri Gagarin (left), the first human to orbit Earth—aboard *Vostok 1*, on April 12, 1961—and Chief Designer Sergei Korolev, the father of Sputnik, Vostok, and Soyuz. Korolev transformed Germany's V-2 technology into the world's first intercontinental ballistic missile, which became his Semyorka booster, the Soviets' most reliable rocket. Gargarin's flight so alarmed President John F. Kennedy that, in a speech before Congress on May 25, 1961 (opposite), he challenged America to send men to the moon by the end of the decade. Jim Webb, Kennedy's NASA administrator (inset, opposite), the president's point man for Apollo, was capable "of absorbing and conveying to congressional committees more complex information than any NASA administrator before or since."

President John F. Kennedy visited Wernher von Braun in September 1962 at the Marshall Space Flight Center in Huntsville, Alabama (opposite, above), to review the progress of the Saturn V moon booster. Von Braun had evaded capture by the Red Army in 1945, and he and his German "rocket team" (opposite, center) came to America during Operation Paper Clip to work on missiles. But for years they languished in the New Mexico desert before Kennedy's challenge renewed von Braun's faith in America as the "country where spaceflight would take root and flourish." Von Braun became a major supporter of Apollo's daring Lunar Orbit Rendezvous mission concept, championed by NASA scientist John Houbolt (opposite, below). With Project Apollo accelerating, the third group of astronauts (above) reported for duty in Houston in January 1964. I'm in the next-to-last row, on the left, with Mike Collins in front of me. "We were all obsessed with getting a flight assignment, no matter how much we tried to be good team players."

The Soviets' many well-publicized successes with Korolev's Semyorka booster (shown above launching woman cosmonaut Valentina Tereshkova aboard *Vostok 6* in June 1963) brought them great international prestige, which drove NASA to accelerate Project Gemini, the test-bed for the crucial Apollo concepts of orbital rendezvous, docking, and spacewalks. But Soviet propaganda spectaculars hid the fact that their Soyuz moon-landing program was behind schedule. The eventual success of Project Apollo eclipsed the pioneering achievements of Gemini—an essential step on the road to the moon. After months of intense training with Jim Lovell (opposite, above), I prepared for my first spaceflight (opposite, below), the *Gemini XII* mission in November 1966.

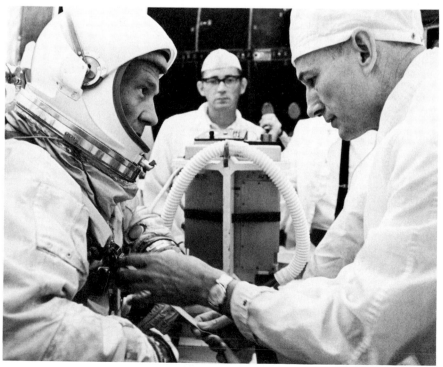

Despite radar and computer problems during *Gemini XII*, we managed to rendezvous and dock with our Agena target vehicle (shown tethered to our spacecraft, top photo), using backup procedures I'd helped NASA develop. I then made world-record spacewalks (above). "Space had a hidden fabric, and the fingers of my pressure gloves were snagging the delicate threads." After a perfect splashdown and recovery, Jim and I (opposite) were honored by President Lyndon Johnson at a White House ceremony (opposite, inset). NASA declared this last flight of the program "an unqualified success."

Frank Borman (left), Jim Lovell, and Bill Anders were trailblazers when *Apollo 11* orbited the moon.

In Houston, Neil Armstrong and I trained hard for the *Apollo 11* moon landing, practicing with experiment packages and the tools needed to scoop up lunar rocks and soil. By July 1969, we had only five months to meet the challenge of President John F. Kennedy's deadline—and to beat the Soviets to the moon. Intense media pressure in the weeks before our flight made us recognize that we represented "all mankind," not just America, on this historic voyage.

A million spectators at Cape Kennedy held their breaths as our Saturn V lifted off (top). (Inset, left to right) Chuck Mathews, Wernher von Braun, George Mueller, and Sam Phillips celebrate. The launch of *Apollo 11* was the culmination of a decade's efforts.

The "magnificent desolation" of the moon. July 20, 1969, *Tranquillity Base*: Neil was reflected in my helmet visor (inset). I planted the solar wind collector in soil that had lain undisturbed for a billion years. The surface where humans "first set foot upon the moon" was soon cross-hatched with boot prints. We were watched on television by the biggest global audience there has ever been. We had a heavy workload during our brief hours on the lunar surface. My EVA "time lines" kept me moving from one task to another. But I found time to gaze out across space at Earth, our home in the infinity of the universe.

We were widely honored, from the traditional ticker-tape parade in Manhattan (above), to a triumphant world tour. America had spent $24 billion and employed 400,000 technicians and workers from 20,000 private firms to ensure our success. "When future generations remember Apollo just as we now recall the voyages of Columbus, they won't be moved by the geopolitical posturing of the Cold War, the back-room politics on Capitol Hill, or the pork-barrel intrigues that throbbed beneath the surface of the program. They will remember, however, that in July 1969, people like themselves first set foot on the moon."

"Thank you for coming to me," she whispered, and then joined the minister.

Charlie's and Elliot's deaths meant that Tom Stafford and Gene Cernan were now the prime crew for *Gemini IX*. In turn, Jim Lovell and I were shifted from the *Gemini X* backup crew to backing up Stafford and Cernan. The ripple effect on crew assignments meant there would be no prime crew for *Gemini XII*, the last scheduled flight. That was how I came to have a mission assignment, but it was a hell of a way to get one. The night I received this news, Joan and I crossed the backyard to Jeannie's house to tell her. I felt terrible, as if I had somehow robbed Charlie Bassett of an honor he deserved.

Jeannie reacted graciously. "Charlie felt you should have been on that flight all along," she said, gripping my hand. "I know he'd be pleased."

I was in the Mission Control room in Houston on March 16, 1966, when Neil Armstrong and Dave Scott accomplished one of Project Gemini's main goals, orbital rendezvous and docking with an Agena target vehicle, during the *Gemini VIII* flight. I didn't know Neil Armstrong that well—he was a civilian astronaut from the second group—but he was highly thought of from his days as a NASA test pilot on the X-15 rocket plane out at Edwards. For almost five hours, Armstrong and Scott maneuvered their spacecraft to match orbits with the Agena and finally rendezvoused above the Caribbean, as Dave Scott called out radar ranges and Neil slowed the spacecraft by "eyeball" judgment.

After about an hour of floating near the Agena ("station keeping"), Mission Control told them, "Go ahead and dock." The spacecraft's cylindrical neck eased into the open throat of the Agena's docking adapter. Mechanical latches sprang out to connect the two vehicles.

"Flight," Neil called to flight director Gene Kranz in Houston, "we are docked! It's really a smoothie."[5]

The Mission Control room was loud with cheers and whistles among the usually quiet flight directors. Gemini had just passed a milestone. Orbital docking brought us one step closer to an LOR mission and a landing on the moon. Because the Agena was built to accept engine commands directly from the Gemini spacecraft, the mission plan next called for Neil and Dave to fire the Agena engine to change their orbit. But the docked Gemini-Agena began rolling, slowly at first, and then with increasingly wilder gyrations.

"Neil," Dave Scott said, "we're in a bank."

Armstrong didn't have to be reminded. He struggled with his hand controllers to keep the cumbersome composite vehicle stable. He had to break away or the roll would become violent enough to damage the neck of the spacecraft—where their parachute was stored. Neil fired the thrusters to undock, but the roll increased. The Gemini's antennas would not stay in alignment, cutting off communication with the Earth station below, the tracking ship *Coastal Sentry Quebec*.

Finally, Scott got through. "We have serious problems here," he announced. "We're tumbling end over end up here...."

One of their RCS thrusters was stuck open, tossing the Gemini in an accelerating spin, which was now one revolution per second. Dave and Neil were having trouble just focusing on the instrument panels; their vision blurred and they became dizzy.

Finally Armstrong broke the spin by completely shutting down the spacecraft's orbital attitude and maneuver system and activating the separate reentry control thrusters. But this meant they would have to descend from orbit quickly because this thruster system could develop leaks once it had been fired.

The Mission Control room was on full alert. Around the country, NASA managers quickly consulted with each other then told Armstrong to go for an emergency retrofire with a descent trajectory into the western Pacific. *Gemini VIII* was above the Congo River when Gene Kranz and his flight controllers ordered the burn. The combined flame of the solid-rocket retros and the control thrusters dazzled the two pilots as they slid through the starry night. For the next 15 minutes they stared anxiously out their windows hoping to see the Pacific Ocean through the bright orbital dawn ahead. They still didn't know if their retrofire had been accurate and whether they would land in the ocean or in some remote jungle—or maybe in enemy territory in Indochina.

As the sun climbed above the Pacific, *Gemini VIII* descended by parachute several hundred miles southeast of Japan. A search aircraft from Okinawa spotted their parachute and dropped rescue frogmen, who struggled to attach a flotation collar to the spacecraft as it rolled in the nasty 15-foot swells. Several hours later, Neil and Dave were aboard the destroyer *Mason*, seasick but otherwise okay. Their flight had lasted less than 12 hours.

Docking meant nothing if the composite vehicle could not be

controlled. Lunar Orbit Rendezvous during an Apollo mission would depend on a perfectly controlled flight of the composite command and service module and the lunar module. But our first attempt at this had failed dangerously. No one was cheering in Mission Control.

Kennedy Space Center, Cape Kennedy, May 25, 1966

Five years to the day after President John Kennedy challenged America to land men on the moon, NASA unveiled its first Saturn V booster. It was an event specifically planned for that anniversary to remind Congress and the nation that Project Apollo was still on track to the moon. The first "roll out" of the Saturn booster was certainly grandiose—as was everything about the new Launch Complex 39. The principal structures were the massive vehicle assembly building (VAB), the launch control center, and the three-mile-long crawlerway that connected the VAB with launch pads 39-A and 39-B on the beach. The VAB was the world's largest structure in terms of volume, enclosing more space than the Pentagon and Chicago's Merchandise Mart combined. It was so far beyond normal human scale that even the launch control center looked small beside it. You could see the VAB from 20 miles away, a windowless cube 525 feet high that dominated the coast like an artificial mountain. Public relations men at the Cape liked to point out that if you mounted the United Nations building on one of the Saturn's mobile launching platforms and picked it up with the monstrous crawler transporter, you could roll the skyscraper in one of the VAB's vertical highbay doors and out the other.

The transporter weighed over 3,000 tons. Its platform was the size of a baseball infield and was mounted between four double sets of gigantic tank tracks with treads that were eight feet wide and 40 long; each link weighed a ton. The transporter rode on a crawlerway that had two 40-foot lanes separated by a 50-foot median. Delivered by barge from the Michoud Test Facility in Mississippi, the Saturn's lower stages were almost as wide as the V-2 was long. The smaller upper stages of the Saturn booster arrived by air aboard a bloated Stratocruiser called the "Super Guppy".

Saturn's two launch pads were squat concrete pyramids hulking above the sea oats and the dunes, slashed by brick-lined flame trenches 40 feet deep and almost 500 feet long.[6]

Launching a Saturn V put all the unique architecture of Launch Complex 39 to good use. The three-stage booster, topped by the Apollo spacecraft, stood over 360 feet high; thus the need for the massive VAB. The mobile launching platform and huge gantry tower had to be moved by the monstrous transporter. And the transporter needed the crawler-way to spread its weight on the thin limestone crust of the barrier island. Each launch pad could support the thousands of tons of the composite booster, gantry, and launching platform. All this engineering was on a scale never before attempted in so short a time. The Hoover Dam and the Panama Canal took much longer to complete. But in three and a half years, NASA had transformed the scrub oak and palmetto wilderness of Merritt Island just north of Cape Kennedy into the assembly of launch facilities for the world's largest rocket.

Traveling to the Cape at that time was very exciting for me. There was something unearthly about Launch Complex 39. As I walked beneath the gray aluminum walls of the VAB and beside the transporter treads, I often felt subdued and unimportant. The Apollo-Saturn vehicle was the size and weight of a World War II destroyer. There was a clenched power in these buildings and machines that had an obvious purpose: to throw the great white spear of Saturn into the sky, and send Apollo to the moon.

Thousands of employees and hundreds of reporters watched that May afternoon as the high bay doors of the VAB were raised by Kurt Debus's launch directorate to reveal the white column of the Saturn V on the mobile launching platform. The transporter clanked and roared, drawing the towering booster and its steel launching platform out of the cavernous VAB into the Florida sun.

It was a great show of what American technology was capable of, but NASA's leaders had a long way to go from this event to a moon landing in less than four years. For one thing, the rocket on the transporter was not an operational booster, just a "500-F test vehicle," assembled to put the VAB and the transporter through their paces. And the gleaming white Apollo spacecraft atop the booster was a "boiler plate" model, never intended for flight.

Both the Apollo spacecraft and the Saturn booster were behind schedule. Widespread organizational and personnel deficiencies at North American Aviation had kept the company from meeting the delivery deadlines of the command and service module (CSM); the

Saturn's S-II second stage was delayed even further. Huntsville and North American's Rocketdyne Division engineers were trying to cluster the five J-2 liquid-oxygen, liquid-hydrogen engines into a practical, relatively compact booster stage, but they continued to run into problems.[7] If these hydrogen-fueled cryogenic engines could not be made reliable, the Saturn V would be worthless as a heavy-launch vehicle.

North American was also struggling to develop two versions of the Apollo command module. One, called Block I, was for simple Earth-orbital missions, a technology test-bed for the CSM's life support and propulsion systems; the Block II Apollo was designed for the actual moon-landing mission. The Block II command module's nose held the docking probe and tunnel that would connect it to the lunar module. Block I spacecraft should have been ready for test flights that summer and the Block II command modules early the next year. These delivery schedules were clearly unrealistic.

General Sam Phillips, NASA's Apollo program director, discovered that AiResearch, North American Aviation's subcontractor for the command module's environmental control unit, was not up to the job. Phillips had successfully directed the Minuteman ICBM development program, and now he was losing his patience with North American and its subcontractors. Phillips and a few other senior NASA managers went directly to the contractors to stress how urgent the situation was, while also emphasizing quality. No one stood up to declare what many felt: deadline pressures and quality control were incompatible.

But it was becoming clear that the traditional piece-by-piece qualification flights for individual components of the booster and spacecraft would drag Apollo far beyond its 1970 deadline. So, early in his tenure, George E. Mueller, associate administrator of NASA for manned spaceflight, told NASA's center directors von Braun, Gilruth, and Debus, "We can now drop this step-by-step procedure."[8] Henceforth, he mandated, all equipment arriving at the Cape would be complete and flight ready, what became known as Mueller's "all up" flight test principle. At the time, no one realized that this decision would be crucial for Project Apollo. In effect, Mueller was demanding that the aerospace industry invent flight-ready equipment on deadline.

The development hurdles that lay before the lunar module (LM) and its prime contractor, Grumman, were on another scale altogether.

NASA's long internal dispute before finally deciding on the Lunar Orbit Rendezvous mission mode had delayed the design, fabrication, and testing of the LM.[9]

Designing of the lander was made complex and difficult by Kennedy's requirement to land men "safely" and return them from the moon. All of the LM's systems were vital to both mission success and astronaut safety. After the LM cast off from the command module in lunar orbit, it would be on its own until it redocked. The astronauts had to be able to throttle their hypergolic descent engine through a thrust range from 10 to 100 percent in order to control their descent. (This wouldn't be a free-fall reentry to parachute deployment as on Earth.) If the engine failed during the final hover before landing, the LM could crash.

And ground testing of the descent engine had uncovered serious problems: rough burning, combustion chamber erosion, even melting of the delicate throttle mechanism. This meant the LM descent engine was at least six months behind schedule in the summer of 1966. No clear solutions were in sight. The lander also had similar problems with its ascent engine, control thrusters, and navigation systems.

But the LM's most serious problem was weight. The vehicle had to be strong enough to land safely on the moon and to be its own launch pad for the ascent stage. But the LM also had to be light enough to carry the propellant needed to meet the inflexible demands of LOR: a smooth ascent to lunar orbit on the first attempt. NASA had placed a 14-ton weight limit on the LM, but that seemed impossible. In official language, the lunar module was Apollo's "pacing item," which politely meant a roadblock.[10] In the summer of 1966, it didn't look as if the LM would be ready for a lunar mission before the end of the decade.

On the next Gemini mission, number nine, Jim Lovell and I were the backup crew to Tom Stafford and Gene Cernan. Their job was to rendezvous and dock with a stand-in spacecraft, the Augmented Target Docking Adapter (ATDA), because they'd lost their Agena target when its Atlas booster had malfunctioned on the first launch attempt.

Launch morning, June 3, 1966, Jim and I checked out the spacecraft before the astronauts were sealed inside. It was great being at the Cape and working on an actual mission with real flight hardware—which had an oily, ozone-tainted smell—rather than with the simulators. The flight lifted off beautifully at 8:39 AM, and once the orbital insertion was accomplished, Jim and I headed back to Houston in our T-38 to support the mission from there.

While we were in the air, however, Tom and Gene ran into the first of several problems. The rendezvous itself went smoothly, with the spacecraft radar coupled perfectly to the onboard computer. But as Tom fired his thrusters to ease up alongside the slowly tumbling ATDA, he exclaimed, "Look at that moose!" The target spacecraft presented a weird spectacle; instead of the circular docking throat at one end, the crew saw the conical white fiberglass launch shroud half open, gaping at them like the jaws of an "angry alligator."

This launch shroud was held in place by a wire that had been improperly stowed before the target vehicle lifted off. It was hard to believe, but a multimillion-dollar mission was now jeopardized by a stainless steel wire worth 50 cents. As soon as Jim and I landed in Houston, we were ordered to an emergency planning meeting with all the flight directors and senior project officials. As backup pilot, I'd spent months training with Gene Cernan for his planned EVA. Gene had told me one day that he thought the way to overcome the problems of space walks was "brute force." He was underestimating the difficulty of an EVA, but I knew he was a resourceful astronaut. I piped up at the meeting and suggested that he begin his EVA early, take along a pair of wire cutters from the spacecraft tool kit, and cut the damned shroud free.

Bob Gilruth and Chris Kraft looked at me like I was crazy. They said Gene could puncture his EVA suit while cutting the wires. No attempt was made to rescue the ATDA, and *Gemini IX* drifted free of its target vehicle. Another opportunity lost. (Deke Slayton later told me that I almost got jerked from my *Gemini XII* assignment for that suggestion. But in my own defense, these impromptu EVA repairs became commonplace on NASA's *Skylab* and the Soviets' *Salyut* space station in the 1970s.)

Two days later, Gene Cernan began his scheduled EVA. The flight plan called for him to leave the cabin, clamber back to the adapter section, and don the bulky AMU backpack, becoming the world's first true human satellite. Unfortunately, none of this worked out. After some tentative grappling around the edge of the hatch, he moved forward to conduct simple hand-tool experiments. But as Gene later said, he "really had no idea how to work in slow motion at orbital speeds."[11]

Any small movement of his fingers sent him tumbling to the limits of the umbilical that kept him attached to the spacecraft. The handholds and Velcro patches on the spacecraft he needed for leverage were either totally inadequate or too clumsy to use; his umbilical "snake" whipped around him, blocking his progress. Everything was harder than he'd thought it would be. He was unable to keep his movements under control. When the spacecraft crossed the terminator line into darkness, all his exertions finally caused his faceplate visor to fog. He was blinded as well as exhausted.

Gene and Tom Stafford decided to cancel the rest of the EVA.

Now the mission's other main objective had also ended in failure.

Watching the *Gemini IX* EVA from Mission Control convinced me that I'd better be well prepared for the space walks I was to perform on the *Gemini XII*. I had a lot of respect for Gene and thought he could have done better had he had different training. In fact, after *Gemini IX*, Gene joined me in a series of underwater training sessions in a pool near Baltimore to prepare for the *Gemini XII* mission. (He was on our backup crew.) I was an experienced scuba diver before beginning this "neutral buoyancy" training. It seemed to me that practicing underwater was better preparation for an astronaut's weightless EVA than with the wire-and-pulley training gadgets that came and went in Houston, but never really worked.

Soon my underwater training became quite elaborate. I wore a carefully ballasted EVA suit to completely neutralize my buoyancy and closely approximate zero G. Eventually I mastered the intricate ballet of weightlessness. Your body simply had to be anchored, because if it wasn't, flexing your pinkie would send you ass-over-teakettle. And you don't want to do that dangling at the end of an umbilical cord 160 miles above Earth.

That July, the four-day *Gemini X* flight went a long way toward putting the program back on track. The Agena and Titan liftoffs were within seconds of "nominal," and commander John Young and pilot Mike Collins's rendezvous and docking went smoothly, though it was relatively expensive in terms of thruster fuel. The Agena worked well, and its engine boosted the composite docked vehicle to a high elliptical orbit, with an apogee of 412 miles. From this point, John and Mike maneuvered to approach the dead Agena from *Gemini VIII* that had been commanded to higher orbit after Armstrong and Scott's emergency reentry.

After completing the back-up technique rendezvous the next day, Mike got off to a good start with his EVA, but he did smack into the derelict Agena after he launched himself through the vacuum from the nose of his spacecraft. *Gemini X* was the first mission that accomplished *all* of the program's objectives that would later be needed on the Apollo lunar missions: orbital rendezvous, docking, orbital maneuvering of the composite vehicle, and controlled work during EVA.

When the spacecraft splashed down in the Atlantic, this time there *were* cheers in Mission Control.

In September, the *Gemini XI* mission flown by Pete Conrad and Dick Gordon was marred by problems during the EVA. Their rendezvous and docking with the Agena went okay and they fired up the composite vehicle into an elliptical orbit with an apogee of almost 740 miles, a manned spaceflight altitude record. They also took some truly spectacular color photographs of Earth.

The next day, however, was another story. The official Gemini flight plan was an exquisitely detailed document of "time lines" and sequences of activities that had been put together by hundreds of engineers and mission planners across the country. For example, the EVA "suiting up" instructions covered six pages, with over a hundred sequential commands, such as

> APPLY WETTING AGENT
> DON HELMET & POSITION MIKES
> DON PRESSURE THERMAL GLOVES.[12]

The two-man crew was supposed to stick their flight plan folder to Velcro on the instrument panel and read it like the Bible. But Conrad and Gordon impatiently skipped around in the formal sequence. As a result, they upset cabin pressurization when they checked out Gordon's oxygen umbilical, and he became overheated long before his EVA began; his suit's cooling system was meant to work in space, not inside the pressurized spacecraft. It took Gordon a long time to fasten his EVA sun visor to the outside of his helmet—a simple enough task on Earth, but exhausting and frustrating in the cramped cabin with an overheated EVA suit and huge gloves on. By the time he was floating in space, his face was flooded with stinging sweat and he was practically blinded.

Pete Conrad told Mission Control that he had "brought Dick back in. . . . He got so hot and sweaty he couldn't see."[13]

Unfortunately this latest snafu directly affected my own space walk. An urgent meeting of senior officials concerned with the *Gemini XII* EVA was held at the end of September, and on the basis of the problems Cernan and Gordon had faced in their space walks, they decided arbitrarily that I stood a poor chance of putting the innovative AMU backpack to good use. They felt the risks outweighed the benefits. The Air Force was tweaking NASA's nose because they believed astronauts should have been better trained, and NASA was returning the favor by implying that military experiments—no matter how interesting—were expendable.

The meeting ended with an agreement that I would carry out a modified space walk, during which I would try the basic tasks that had stymied the astronauts on earlier missions.

I was determined that mine would be a perfect space walk. As the intense preparations for our November flight grew even more demanding, I went to the underwater facility in Maryland and made dozens of flights on NASA's jet transport "vomit comet," which duplicated Zero G with brief roller-coaster swoops from high altitude. I wanted to show NASA, the Air Force, and the entire world just what a well-trained, disciplined American astronaut could do.

Tyuratam, Kazakhstan, Fall 1966

With a background in developing intercontinental military missiles, designer general Vladimir Chelomei was used to managing well-funded priority programs. But he was overwhelmed by the challenge of modifying his Proton for the safe launch of a manned Soyuz on a circumlunar trajectory before the October 1967 fiftieth anniversary of the Bolshevik revolution. This schedule inevitably led to numerous launch failures, most of which involved the delicate hypergolic upper stages. But Chelomei's bureau slogged on because the Proton had the potential of orbiting very large payloads and sending a cosmonaut around the moon. If he succeeded, Chelomei would eclipse the reputation of the legendary Korolev.

Despite what the Soviets said later about never having planned manned lunar missions, historian James Oberg has shown that the

Proton's principal goal was to reach the moon. He points out that after the Proton's first flight, an official Soviet spokesman announced that the booster "opens the road to the moon."[14] This was confirmed by American journalist Nicholas Daniloff in his book *The Kremlin and the Cosmos*. Daniloff cites a 1963 *Izvestia* interview in which Sergei Korolev said, "I'm sure that the time is not far off when the journey of man to the moon will become a reality, although more than one year will be necessary for the practical solution of this problem." Daniloff concludes that Korolev must have been referring to the circumlunar flyby mission (involving, as we now know, a modified Soyuz spacecraft) the chief designer was then planning.[15]

Meanwhile, there were development problems with the even larger G-1 booster, which would nearly equal the thrust of the American Saturn V. Unlike the Proton, the huge G-1 would use proven LOX-kerosene propulsion: clusters of modified Semyorka engines. The rocket would be staged vertically like the Saturn V and would need gargantuan launch support facilities. By the fall of 1966, the Soviets had turned their principal spaceport at Tyuratam into one large construction site, with assembly buildings and launch pads for the new boosters rising out of the dry steppes of Kazakhstan.

According to Charles Vick, an expert on the Soviet space program, as problems increased with the Proton's development, hope faded that a Soyuz circumlunar flyby would be possible for the 1967 anniversary. In Mishin's group, the target date for this mission was "reset for the late spring or early summer, then into the fall of 1968."[16]

Chelomei's design bureau, however, and his superiors in the Kremlin still thought they could beat America to the first manned trip around the moon, even if they did miss the anniversary. And they were sure NASA's priority effort to develop the Saturn V would hit its own setbacks. The Soviets even reasoned that the larger, but less sophisticated, G booster would win the moon race by actually launching a lunar landing mission.

They also had a more immediate goal. Their last manned spaceflight, the *Voskhod 2* EVA mission, had been hastily launched in March 1965 to upstage the first manned Gemini flight. By this time, the Americans had flown nine manned Gemini missions, and my *Gemini XII* booster was stacked on the launch pad, ready to fly. The Soviets still had not launched an unmanned test version of the new Soyuz spacecraft.

Chelomei and Mishin were certainly being reminded by Soviet intelligence services that America planned to fly three astronauts aboard the first Apollo Earth-orbit mission the next winter. The Soviets' international prestige was at stake, so it was essential that Soyuz fly successfully before Apollo.

The moon race had reached a dangerous turn.

In Washington, NASA administrator James Webb had been concerned for over a year about what impact the Soviets' plans to launch a manned lunar mission would have on Project Apollo. He wrote directly to CIA director Vice Admiral William F. Raborn in August 1965, urgently asking him what the Soviets intended to gain by winning the moon race. Webb needed to learn what the Soviets specifically foresaw in this intense competition so he could better judge the resources they might devote to the challenge.[17]

Throughout 1966, the CIA sent Webb mounting evidence that the Soviets had an expanded, ambitious manned space program. Startling photographs taken by America's new generation of reconnaissance satellites, the *Keyhole* 7 and 8, confirmed that the Soviets were building the Proton and G boosters, as well as the spacecraft that could carry cosmonauts to the moon.[18]

During this period, however, Western news media analysts had ironically concluded that the Soviet Union had dropped out of the "moon race." And the chorus of protest about the billions of dollars "wasted" on this dubious competition grew louder both in the press and in Congress.

Webb realized that his most difficult challenge lay not on the launch pads of Cape Kennedy, in the Huntsville laboratories, or in Houston's Mission Control, but in the committee rooms on Capitol Hill.

Cape Kennedy, November 1966

I'd always visited the Kennedy Space Center during the tropical heat of summer, but when Jim Lovell and I arrived for our final premission simulator rehearsals, the crisp fall weather had set in. For two and a half years I'd trained for spaceflight; I'd backed up two other missions and now I was on the actual flight crew.

Joan and I had discussed every aspect of the flight, particularly where

she should be during the dangerous moments of the launch. She wanted
to be with the children for liftoff, and we agreed they were too young to
be dragged all the way to the Cape. So we compromised. She would join
me for the week before the flight and then return to Houston to watch
the launch on television. Since Joan had never seen the spacecraft
simulator near the launch site, she visited the "sim" while we went
through what was probably my thousandth dress rehearsal for the EVA.
I demonstrated a pair of overshoe-type foot restraints, the "golden
slippers" McDonnell Aircraft had given us, which were designed to hold
my legs steady when I did my experiments. They worked perfectly
down here on Earth. I just hoped they'd do as well in orbit.

After my demonstration, Joan commented, "It's a good thing you
won't have any furniture to bump into up there."

Friday, November 11, 1966, was an absolutely gorgeous Florida day.
The launch was scheduled for midafternoon, so Jim and I slept late in
the crew quarters of the manned spacecraft operations building. From
the third-floor window I could see all of Merritt Island. Across the
Banana River stood Cape Kennedy and the launch pads. The new
vehicle assembly building dominated the northern horizon. That was
where Apollo would begin its trip to the moon.

Jim and I had the traditional breakfast of filet mignon and scrambled
eggs, and then we were taken to the suiting-up room. Being launched
into space was like undergoing major surgery. One team after another of
friendly, white-suited specialists cared for us; every step we took was on
a seamless conveyer belt drawing us toward the "white room" atop the
launch gantry.

Jim Lovell is one of the friendliest guys I know, soft-spoken and
easygoing. He'd flown in space before, and to break the tension on this
final Gemini launch, he suggested we wear hand-printed cardboard
signs on the backs of our suits as we rode the elevator at Launch Pad 19.
Jim's said "THE," and mine read "END."

Gunter Wendt was ready for us in the white room, and we made
damn sure we did everything Gunter's *way*. The Atlas booster carrying
our rendezvous target Agena lifted off perfectly from Pad 14 at 2:08 PM.
Our hatches were already securely sealed, but still I could feel the Atlas
launch's rumble a mile to the south. Ninety minutes later as the Agena
approached Florida from the west, we would lift off to begin the
rendezvous sequence. As our own countdown slid by tranquilly, Jim and

I completed our 150-item cabin checklist with the final instruction "Harnesses secure and locked." There wasn't a lot to look at in the cabin; Gemini was made for work, not appearance. All we could do was wait and stare out the almond-shaped windows at the sky. The oxygen we were breathing tasted like warm plastic.

I heard the last seconds of the countdown as if from a great distance through my earphones: ". . . three, two, one, zero. We have ignition. . . ." There was no noise at first, but then a growling rumble began as the spacecraft rolled through its preprogrammed maneuver, twisting to the proper southeast launch trajectory. Jim calmly reported that our spacecraft clock had started and we were undergoing the roll maneuver. From now on we wouldn't be able to distinguish true day or night, just ground elapsed time (GET), measured on our cabin clock.

I was conscious of the D ring ejection handle clutched in my right glove. Then the acceleration slowly increased and the sky became a deeper blue. We pounded toward Mach 1, the speed of sound, and then passed Max Q, maximum dynamic pressure. Our Titan booster sounded like a subway train.

"Mark, fifty seconds," Pete Conrad called from Houston.

"Ready to go," Jim replied, announcing we were prepared for staging.

Above 60,000 feet it was no longer possible to use our ejection seats, so Jim and I stowed the D rings in their elastic pouches, being careful not to tug too hard with our gloves in the cramped, swaying cabin. My first radio call was a routine report that cabin pressure was holding steady at 5.75 psi (pounds per square inch). More calls came quickly as the acceleration built. We were pitching over toward the horizontal now, and the Gs mounted. The engine status light blinked on the instrument panel before me and then went out.

Jim called staging. The second stage engine ignited with a glaring boom. Now the G forces built up, and I could tell my voice was getting deeper as my chin pushed toward my chest. The horizon of the Atlantic bent like a bow. We were passing through 300,000 feet. "Man," I called, "this is a pretty good visual simulation." The sky was still blue, but beyond the thin horizon band ahead it turned black. The pressure of 7 Gs suddenly ended and my limbs rose within the folds of my suit. I felt my right big toe lightly scraping the roof of my boot, as if I were stretching my foot. But I wasn't. I was weightless.

"SECO," Jim announced. We had second stage engine cutoff. We were in orbit.

Jim and I had no chance to relish the silent luxury of orbital flight. We began our long prerendezvous litany, each of us studying the flapping pages of his flight plan like a priest in some solemn ritual. The main computer keyboard of the Gemini cabin instrument panel was on the right side where I sat. Chanting our readouts of speed and altitude, I tapped the data into the computer's memory.

We had rehearsed the procedures for orbital rendezvous hundreds of times, but the real maneuver was still hectic. After stuffing my helmet into a nylon sack between my knees, I jammed my pressure gloves between my right thigh and the edge of the ejection seat. A moment later, as I flipped switches on my instrument panel, I was startled by a gloved hand snaking around behind my head. Of course, it was just my empty glove, which had floated free.

The next hour was extremely busy, working toward the rendezvous with the Agena about 300 miles ahead. With my helmet off, I did manage to look out at the tropical night sky as we passed over Africa on our way toward the Indian Ocean. Orbital sunrise was coming up on Australia. Spears of dawn cut the twilight. One hour after launch, we glided into full day, two-thirds of the way around the planet from the Cape.

Twenty-five minutes later, we made our first attempt at radar contact with the Agena. I have to admit we were both amazed when the computer readout immediately clicked with the desired digits.

"Houston," I called, "be advised, we have a solid lock-on...two hundred thirty-five point fifty nautical miles."

"It looks like the radar meets the specs," Pete Conrad called from Mission Control.

"It sure does," Jim agreed, staring at his instruments.

But our early success was short-lived. As we circularized our orbit to pull behind and below the Agena over North America, the radar malfunctioned. Jim announced this "radar dropout," and it looked like we were heading toward another embarrassing Gemini failure. Now I had to earn my pay. The fallback for this situation was for the crew to consult intricate rendezvous charts—which I had helped develop—

interpret the radar data using the "Mark One Cranium Computer" (the human brain), and then verify all this with the spacecraft computer. It was a demanding task, but it was the only way we could salvage the rendezvous mission. We also had to fly the rendezvous without wasting all our thruster fuel. This was about the best test yet of the Lunar Orbit Rendezvous concept: if astronauts in *Earth* orbit couldn't pull off a contingency rendezvous such as this, LOR was just too risky for Apollo crews.

Jim flew the spacecraft while I verified the radar information and slaved over the charts. I could barely read the data because it was so densely printed. I lost track of time, but I could tell darkness from daylight as we drifted around the Earth, slowly advancing on the Agena. Finally, four hours after liftoff, we pulled up to the long black-and-white cylinder. Jim didn't wait around for permission to dock. He coordinated his two hand controllers and eased the nose of our spacecraft straight into the Agena's docking throat.

"Houston," Jim called, "we are docked."

Below us, the capcom on the tracking ship *Coastal Sentry Quebec* merely replied, "Roger."

I checked the propellant-quantity gauges. We had used less than 280 pounds of fuel, one of the program's most economical and successful rendezvous and dockings.

We practiced docking and undocking several times. The latches hung up once, but Jim shook us loose with no damage (though the grinding noise was a little disturbing). My attempts at docking went easier than they had in the simulators. However, when we began preparations to fire the Agena engine to raise our orbit, Houston told us they had a problem. The Agena had suffered a thrust "decay" after launch, and flight director Glynn Lunney didn't feel right about letting us fire the target vehicle's engine. (It could explode, ruining our day.) So we were stuck here in our original orbital plane for the duration of the mission.

Our food was stored in sealed plastic pouches we called "Christmas packages." All I had to do was tug on the string, and the food pouches would float out like link sausages. Our first food in space was "meal C," a dinner consisting of dehydrated beef pot roast, potato salad, cinnamon toast, chocolate pudding, and brownies. Apparently the life sciences folks thought we would need some kind of sugar fix following the exertion of rendezvous. We snipped off the ends of the pouches and used the water gun to rehydrate the chunks and powder into gritty globs, which we then squirted into our mouths through little accordion throats on the pouches. Unfortunately, since we didn't have hot water, the pot roast didn't quite measure up to my childhood Sunday dinners back in Montclair, New Jersey.

My first EVA came 21 hours into the mission. I was to stand in the open hatch for about two and a half hours—almost two trips around the world. I checked one last time that there was no residual pressure in the cabin before I slid open my clamshell hatch.

We were 160 miles above Ethiopia, traveling southeast toward the terminator line of sunset over the Indian Ocean. The hatch rose easily and I rose with it, floating above my seat, secured to the spacecraft by short oxygen inflow and outflow umbilical hoses.

I had trained for this moment for months, and I was just as determined as the next guy not to screw up. I rose farther until I was clear of the hatch's upper edge, in effect standing upright on my ejection seat, although the spacecraft was rolled right of local vertical and I really couldn't tell what was "up." I certainly did feel the immensity around me. When I'd been peering out of my small oval window, our orbital passage had reminded me of flying very high in a jet fighter, but out here in space I had an entirely different perspective. We—the spacecraft and crew—seemed to be stationary, while a gigantic polychrome sphere turned slowly beneath us. I had no sense of our actual speed: 17,500 miles per hour, or five miles a *second*. But I could feel the curve of Earth. It wasn't the flat, maplike landscape you see from an airplane. Africa's Great Rift Valley snaked through the dry mountains and disappeared into the horizon to the south. Craning my neck I could take in a complete circle. Everywhere I looked there were arcs and curves, nothing straight, nothing perpendicular.

I studied the brown mass of East Africa and saw that the day-night terminator line stroked southeast to northwest, from the Indian Ocean through the Middle East. I felt a mental geometric tumbler fall into place. Earth is tilted 23.5 degrees on its axis, which explains the sloping line between day and night and the short winter days in northern latitudes and short summer nights ahead of us to the south—in other words, the seasons. For the first time, I could actually *see* Earth's relationship to the sun, its parent star.

I did take a moment to exclaim, "Man! Look at that!" when I saw the sparkling wedge of the Red Sea bending over the northern horizon, but I had to get to my EVA duties. First, I dumped a small garbage bag containing empty food pouches. The bag spun away like a top, straight above me toward the washed-out zenith. As I deliberately set to work attaching my cameras to photograph the star fields with ultraviolet film, I happened to glance above and saw a bright, twinkling planet.

"Stars in the daylight?" I asked aloud. "I don't think so." On the early Mercury flights, NASA scientists had predicted the astronauts would see stars in the daylight, but the astronauts, all jet pilots with high-altitude experience, had been skeptical. Soon they figured out that you saw stars in orbit only when you were in Earth's shadow: *night*.

"It's the trash bag, Buzz," Jim told me. Then I realized I was watching a twirling plastic sack that couldn't have been more than half a mile away. Without any frame of reference, however, it looked like a star.

By the time we crossed the coast of western Australia my eyes were fully adjusted to the darkness. Stars, heavy and unblinking, hung in great clumps all around me. Gazing down past the snout of the spacecraft I watched flashing thunderheads in the Timor Sea. The sky cleared over the void of central Australia. I saw a shower of green meteors ahead that disappeared into the black desert below.

As Jim read from the flight plan, I removed and reloaded a fixed ultraviolet camera and retrieved a meteorite collection package. I rested when Jim told me the flight plan called for it, but luckily I wasn't tired. The oxygen flow was cool, now slightly rubber tainted. Breathing deeply through my nose, I allowed my chest to fill within the confines of the suit. I wasn't experiencing vertigo or spacesickness, and I knew Jim was feeling fine—which was good, because if one of us *did* get sick, the other was bound to follow. Our two suits were connected to the same oxygen system, and the stench of vomit would be shared. Worse, a man could choke on his own regurgitated food swirling inside his helmet.

These rest periods gave me a nice chance to sightsee. We had orbital dawn southwest of Honduras and a beautiful sunrise above Cuba. In the day pass over the Atlantic and the yellow wrinkles of the Sahara, I finished the chores of my first EVA.

During the second night EVA pass I saw blue sparks jump between the fingertips of my gloves. Rubbing my thumb on my index finger produced a steady flow of current, miniature lightning. Space clearly was not just an empty void. It was full of invisible energy: magnetism and silent rivers of gravity. Space had a hidden *fabric*, and the fingers of my pressure gloves were snagging the delicate threads.

All the while I worked, I kept an eye on my short umbilical. There wasn't much danger of jamming these hoses in the hatch or surrounding equipment, but my umbilical the next day would be many times as long, and there were plenty of hang-up points around the Agena and the Gemini's adapter section where the wrapped hoses could be jammed. If an EVA astronaut ever got hung up and debilitated outside, there was no way the commander could rescue him. And there was certainly no way the commander could reenter the atmosphere with the hatch open. He'd have to cut loose his stranded colleague.

We had a set of surgical shears with heavy serrated blades for just that purpose. The umbilical could be snipped like a twig. Neither Jim nor I had discussed this, but we knew where the shears were stored.

For my long-umbilical space walk the next day I set up movie cameras so the folks in flight operations could later judge my performance. I then verified my leverage points and groped hand over hand to the nose of the spacecraft and attached a waist restraint strap to the docking adapter. Next, I removed a long tether from a pouch on the Agena and snapped it to the Gemini's docking bar, connecting the two spacecraft for the so-called "gravity gradient" experiment later in the mission.

I thought about every move I made while I was out there, even flexing my fingers or shifting my hips. After reaching through the hatch to exchange cameras with Jim, I worked back to the adapter section and carefully slipped my boots into the golden slipper foot restraints. Anchored at my ankles and by two small waist tethers, I could easily complete the various tool-handling and dexterity tasks at my EVA work station, the so-called busy box.

Back in the buoyancy pool in Maryland, I had torqued bolts and cut metal dozens of times—what I used to call chimpanzee work—and I had no problem with these chores in space. Someone had even put a bright yellow paper Chiquita Banana sticker at my busy box. Much of this work was done on a night pass over the Pacific, and I found myself forgetting I actually was in space. Then I would remember and gaze at the slowly drifting star fields above.

After two hours, I crawled back to the hatch and wiped Jim's window with a cloth. For some reason, command pilots' windows always got dirty on Gemini missions, something to do with the flow of thruster exhaust. As I finished, Jim called, "Hey, would you change the oil, too?" We both were getting comfortable in space.

A few hours later, we undocked and carefully separated the two vehicles so that the tether between them went taut. Then we drifted. Within minutes the two vehicles had stabilized without the aid of thrusters; this was the "gravity gradient." Astrophysicists had long predicted that, of two connected objects, the more massive one (in this case, the Agena) would orbit closer to the Earth than the less massive one (our Gemini). Now we were proving this concept. If tethered composite spacecraft could reach their own orbital equilibrium without burning precious thruster fuel, large space structures would be practical.

We made two complete orbits tethered to the Agena then fired an explosive squib to cut the tether and thrust away from the Agena. The next day, on my final stand-up EVA, I mainly tossed away some equipment we no longer needed and retrieved other gear from outside. I dumped a sack containing my long umbilical and two garbage bags straight over my head so that they would clear any hot thruster plumes from the spacecraft. Eventually the three bags were flying in a perfectly spaced formation like robot bubbles.

On this last long daylight pass northward, I was able to make out the land mass of Indochina below me. There was broken overcast northeast of the Annamite Mountains, bad bombing weather over North Vietnam. I remembered Korea and thought about my friend Sam Johnson. Sam and I had gone through flight training together and flown in the same squadron in Korea. In April, Sam's F-4 had been shot down over the coastal rice paddies of North Vietnam. He was a prisoner of war. My spacecraft drifted silently 160 miles above the steep green ridges where Sam was probably imprisoned in a bamboo cage.

In two days I would be at home on the other side of the planet, but Sam would still be down there in the jungle.

*   *   *

Gemini XII splashed down two and a half miles off the port bow of the aircraft carrier *Wasp*, south of Bermuda, on the afternoon of November 15, 1966. Our flight was the last mission of Project Gemini, and NASA declared it "an unqualified success."[19] We had rendezvoused and docked repeatedly with the Agena target vehicle, using the contingency rendezvous charts I had helped develop, when our computer could not process radar data. My total of five hours and 32 minutes of EVA was a record that would not be passed for a decade. All the tasks I had been assigned to perform during my space walks had gone smoothly, and I had not become overheated or exhausted. In fact, my pulse rate had stayed lower than that of many astronauts simply sitting in the spacecraft cabin.[20]

Project Gemini had finally triumphed. *All* of its objectives had now been met. We were ready to move on to Project Apollo and the conquest of the moon.

Also by this time, space scientists had learned a great deal about the actual nature of the moon from the unmanned American probes Ranger, Surveyor, and Lunar Orbiter. The probes photographed the lunar surface in great detail, revealing craters and boulders as small as one meter across. In the summer of 1966, *Surveyor 1* made the first soft landing on the moon's Ocean of Storms, a rehearsal for an Apollo LM. Not to be outdone, the Soviets put their *Luna 12* in lunar orbit and sent back detailed TV pictures. Mission planning people took all of this as evidence that the lunar surface could definitely support our heavy LM, but some academics, led by Professor Thomas Gold of Cornell University, said that the moon's flat "seas" might be covered by layers of dust thousands of feet deep. Gold believed that any spacecraft landing in such an area would be swallowed up.

Tyuratam, Kazakhstan, November 1966

As an early winter blizzard hit the steppes of Kazakhstan, the Soviets were ready for their first unmanned test flight of the new Soyuz spacecraft. The Proton booster was still months, if not years, from being "man rated." So once again, the Soviets relied on the genius of Sergei Korolev. Mishin had upgraded Korolev's Vostok rocket and would soon present it to the world as the workhorse "Soyuz booster." This launcher was not powerful enough to send a Soyuz to the moon, but it could put the new spacecraft in Earth orbit.

The November test flight of the unmanned Soyuz was announced as *Cosmos 133* and described simply as an automated orbital scientific station. It flew a standard two-day test flight, and the large, cup-shaped reentry module landed in the snowdrifts near Tyuratam 47 hours after launch. When the module was recovered, however, Mishin's engineers discovered that the heat shield had failed during the fiery descent. Ablative plugs had burned through in several places, allowing the superhot reentry plasma to slash the module's metal skin like a giant welding torch. Obviously this was a serious design flaw that would have to be corrected and tested in unmanned flights before a cosmonaut could safely fly aboard the new spacecraft.

But Chelomei was not terribly discouraged. Being senior to Mishin, Chelomei had now been assigned the overall responsibility for the Soyuz program, and he was determined to press ahead. Despite Mishin's objections, Chelomei planned only one more unmanned test of the Earth orbit version of the Soyuz. Then would come a quick progression of manned Earth orbit flights—including an unprecedented docking and crew transfer between two Soyuz on their first manned mission. His new responsibility gave him renewed confidence. He gambled that his bureau could somehow successfully develop the heavy-lift Proton for manned flights by the next summer, possibly leading to a circumlunar spectacular in time for the anniversary of the Bolshevik revolution next autumn.[21] He knew NASA would never have Project Apollo ready for a lunar flight by then.

At a European conference that fall, Soviet space experts joked with their American counterparts, saying that NASA shouldn't worry too much about Congress cutting its budget. "We will help you out with that shortly after the first of the year," they said.[22]

CHAPTER NINE

YEAR OF DISASTERS

1967

Kennedy Space Center, Cape Kennedy, January 27, 1967

By noon on this cool Friday, both workers and NASA officials knew that they weren't going to get the early start on the weekend they had hoped for. The "plugs out" ground test of the Apollo spacecraft on Launch Pad 34 was going to run into the evening. This was a crucial exercise of the spacecraft and booster's internal power systems, during which the electrical and ground umbilical "plugs" would be disconnected toward the end of a mock countdown. Kurt Debus's launch team had mounted the spacecraft atop an operational Saturn IB rocket, and the entire booster-spacecraft assembly was half hidden behind the girders and plumbing of the umbilical tower. Across the Cape a thousand men waited at their stations in control rooms and at the launch bunker for the test to begin. But the astronauts still hadn't entered the command module.

This was the Block I Apollo spacecraft, due to fly in one month. Gus Grissom would be the command pilot, with Ed White and Roger Chaffee as senior pilot and pilot. Just before one o'clock, Gus, Ed, and Roger clomped across the narrow bridge connecting the umbilical tower to the white room, where North American technicians under Donald Babbitt, the pad leader, were waiting for the crew to arrive. The astronauts' boots twanged on the aluminum mesh grating as they lugged their portable spacesuit air conditioners. Getting into the command module in spacesuits was never easy, but the Block I spacecraft had an especially awkward triple-hatch system: there was an inner door sealing the pressure cabin, a second "ablative hatch" that was part of the heat shielding, and an outermost hatch called the boost protective cover (BPC)—a funnel-shaped fiberglass shroud that protected the spacecraft until the launch escape tower was jettisoned above the atmosphere. Ed White, in the center couch, was in charge of sealing the inner hatch, which meant he had to reach behind his shoulders and operate a hand crank, a maneuver requiring both strength and dexterity.

The astronauts were seated by 1:00 PM—Gus Grissom on the left, Ed White in the middle, and Roger Chaffee on the right. They lay on their backs on segmented aluminum-frame couches, their lower legs flexed above and parallel to their chests, with the instrument panels right in front of their faces. Once their suits were connected to the spacecraft's oxygen supply, Gus complained that an unpleasant sour-milk odor was coming out of the environmental control unit. But the smell went away when the cabin was purged of air and filled with pure oxygen at 16.7 psi, slightly greater than normal sea level atmospheric pressure. This was done to test the cabin for leaks during the mock countdown.

The crew had been through this procedure many times in vacuum-chamber trials of the command module and on this very launch pad. But for several years, NASA and North American Aviation managers had been actively debating the pros and cons of this cabin atmosphere. Early in the program, medical experts had feared that breathing pure oxygen for prolonged periods would be harmful to the astronauts, but the long-duration Gemini missions had disproved this. Astronauts could work for weeks in space, breathing pure oxygen at low pressure. Those in favor of the "one-gas environment" stressed its simplicity and reliability. To duplicate the normal Earth atmosphere of approximately 80 percent nitrogen and 20 percent oxygen at standard sea level pressure, we would have had to use complex, heavy equipment (which, by the way, the Soviets employed) and a much stronger spacecraft pressure cabin.

The only serious hazard of the pure-oxygen environment was fire. As every high school chemistry student learns, when a smoldering match is put into a beaker of oxygen, it blazes into a spectacular flame. The Apollo cabin was also an oxygen-rich container, and the spacecraft's many switches, electrical equipment, and over 15 miles of wiring could easily short-circuit, providing the glowing match. But the risk was considered acceptable because, in space, the astronauts could instantly depressurize their cabin while maintaining their own suit oxygen supply.

Gus and his crew had been chosen to fly the first Apollo mission, and they had fully expected some problems both with the new spacecraft and with the complex launch and flight control systems at the Cape and Houston. They hadn't been prepared, however, for the seemingly endless number of glitches they encountered during the weeks leading up to the *Apollo 1* launch.

The spacecraft's trouble-plagued environmental control unit (which General Phillips had been so concerned about) had chronic leaks of corrosive coolant and was replaced twice after the command module arrived at the Cape.[1] Gus's crew had also been through one maddening delay after another with their Apollo spacecraft simulator. Finally, Gus had hung a lemon on the simulator's hatch to show his frustration.[2]

Now delays had again halted work. The spacecraft was connected to the launch control rooms in Pad 34's blockhouse and in the manned spacecraft operations building on Merritt Island by multiple data and voice communication lines and radio channels. But all afternoon, feedback, static, and data "dropouts" filled the lines, and finally there was the nagging problem of an unattended live microphone on the loop, making "comm" between the crew and the flight controllers extremely difficult. After almost an hour, Gus Grissom lost his patience. "How the hell can we get to the moon," he shouted into his microphone, "if we can't even talk between two buildings?"[3]

At four, the test was briefly suspended while one shift of mission controllers and technicians went off duty and another came on. Grissom, White, and Chaffee got no rest during all this. They were strapped on their aching backs to their couches, their necks resting against the ineffectual padding of their helmet connector rings, shoulder to shoulder near the nose of the spacecraft. In the weightlessness of space, the command module was hardly claustrophobic, but on the pad three spacesuited astronauts were definitely cramped.

The sun was setting across the Indian River before the actual "plugs" could be pulled from the spacecraft and booster and the test could begin. But then, after 6:00 PM, another communications glitch cropped

up during the planned hold at T−10 in the mock countdown. Technicians in the operations building noted a sharp voltage fluctuation just
before 6:31 PM, as well as brief cuts in the data channels.

What happened over the next few minutes had that spastic, shocking
quality we remember about all terrible accidents. One moment the
launch pad technicians and crew were in a limbo of tense boredom, and
the next it seemed as if all hell had broken loose.[4]

At four seconds past 6:31 PM, Roger Chaffee shouted, "Hey!" His
shout was followed by a moment of scuffling noise, and then his voice
grew clear again. "We've got a fire in the cockpit." An RCA Communications Company technician, Gary Propst, was watching a television
monitor trained on the one window of the command module not
covered by the boost protective cover. He saw a bright flare inside the
cabin and tongues of flame slashing around the window. The flames
grew brighter and dense smoke billowed. He then saw the silver arms of
Ed White's spacesuit grappling with the awkward hatch system.

"Blow the hatch!" Propst yelled. "Why don't they blow the hatch?"
The command module's awkward hatches had trapped the crew inside.

As the flames spread, Chaffee yelled again, "We've got a bad
fire. . . . Let's get out. We're burning up. . . ." His call ended with a
shriek of pain.[5]

North American pad leader Don Babbitt jumped up from his small
desk in the white room and shouted at his crew, "Get them out of there!"
Babbitt dove for the intercom box to alert the blockhouse. But before he
could reach the switch, flame blasted out of the ruptured side of the
command module, and the explosion threw him to the catwalk door. The
white room was filled with acrid, billowing smoke. The four technicians
scrambled out on the swing arm, convinced that the solid rockets on the
launch escape tower would be detonated by the flames, setting off a
second holocaust that would incinerate the entire white room. Somehow they overcame their fear and scurried to find fire extinguishers and
gas masks on the gantry platform.

Moments later they were back in the white room, using fire
extinguishers to try to douse the flames coming from the command
module. Their gas masks weren't effective against the choking smoke,
so they took turns stumbling out on the catwalk to breathe fresh air. The
clumsy BPC had been distorted by the blast and was too hot to handle.

After several minutes they freed it and began working to open the two inner hatches.

A mile away in the blockhouse, Deke Slayton jumped to his feet and hollered for the two flight surgeons to rush to the pad. Meanwhile, the test director had dispatched a full contingent of Kennedy Space Center fire fighters, but the center's fire station was several miles from Pad 34.

When Babbitt and his men finally unsealed the inner hatch, they were unable to separate it completely from its framework to lower it, so they pushed it to one side on a web of fused plastic and distorted metal. A blast of superheated smoke rushed out, driving them back. The technicians saw that the entire cabin had been swept by flames.

Ed White and Gus Grissom lay in a jumble on the cabin floor just below the hatch frame. Fire had fused the material of their suits with the melted plastic and metal near the hatch. Roger Chaffee still lay on his couch, his restraining straps and oxygen hoses disconnected. All three were dead.

Babbitt went to the catwalk and, using the intercom, announced that they had opened the command module. But he would not describe what he had seen—he wanted to alert the flight controllers that the crew was dead without broadcasting the tragic news on an open channel. Five minutes later the firemen and flight surgeons Fred Kelly and Alan Harter reached the smoky white room. They had difficulty checking the crew for signs of life because their spacesuits had been melted shut with molten nylon from the webbing of the seat harnesses and raschel-knitting storage nets. Finally, the doctors could verify that the men were dead.

At first the doctors and firemen struggled to remove the bodies, but the harder they worked, the clearer it became that the three astronauts were trapped in their melted suit material, fused with the charred nylon from the inside of the spacecraft. The rescue force stopped their efforts when photographers arrived to record the command module before the bodies were removed. A major investigation would follow the tragedy, and it would be essential to have a record of the cabin immediately after the fire.

Ironically, on the day of the accident an Apollo executives' conference was being held in Washington to discuss the lessons learned during

166   MEN FROM EARTH

Gemini and the problems facing Apollo. The conference had just broken its afternoon session when NASA leaders Jim Webb, Robert Seamans, and George Mueller were told about the *Apollo 1* fire at the Cape. Webb, Mueller, Seamans, and General Phillips agreed that Seamans and Phillips would rush to the Cape to take charge of the accident investigation and that Mueller and Webb would continue at the conference. The next morning, Mueller read the report Phillips had planned to deliver—"Apollo Program: Top Ten Problems." Among these problems were "quality assurance and personal errors," polite phrasing for Phillips's normally frank criticism of aerospace contractors, particularly North American. Phillips said that contractors simply were not paying adequate attention to details and the demanding standards of workmanship required to meet NASA's rigorous "zero defects" policy. Sloppiness, he stated, had no place in the program, which was already fraught with huge risks. Prepared weeks before the accident, Phillips's paper was remarkably prescient.[6]

Houston, Texas, January–April 1967

Jim Lovell and I had flown to a contractor's factory the day of the accident and didn't land our T-38 back at Ellington Air Force Base near the NASA center until after dark. We taxied up to the hardstand, shut down the engines, and were writing up our aircraft logbooks when the crew chief crawled up the cockpit ladder, his face strained and pale.

"Sir," he said, shaking his head, "there's been a real bad accident at the Cape. Colonel Grissom and Colonel White are dead. So's Commander Chaffee."

I sat there with my pencil above my clipboard, unable to finish the log entries. Around the NASA hangar, ramp workers carried out their normal tasks on the T-38s. I suddenly remembered that raw afternoon on the aircraft parking ramp at Bitburg 10 years before when Ed and I had first talked about becoming astronauts. He had been so confident then, tall and husky, what everyone thought of as an all-American fighter pilot. Now he was gone. So was Gus. So was Roger. Jim and I gathered up our gear and went to the office to find out what had happened.

NASA's investigation of the *Apollo 1* (officially, the Apollo 204 mission) fire has met with a lot of news media criticism over the years. Some reporters have suggested that there was a cover-up, because the investigators were mainly NASA personnel and they completed their work in only nine weeks. But anyone who knew the members of the AS-204 Review Board realized that they were men of integrity. Frank Borman represented the astronaut corps on the panel. Frank and I don't always see eye to eye on things, but I know he did an honest job, representing his colleagues both living and dead. Floyd Thompson, director of NASA's Langley center, led the group, and Max Faget headed up Houston's contingent. It was an extremely well qualified board.

They presented their report to Jim Webb in early April. It was a highly detailed engineering analysis that pinpointed the probable cause of the fire and the progress of the conflagration through the spacecraft cabin. It also included a review of the management problems that had provoked the tragedy. The board's "Findings, Determinations and Recommendations" severely criticized both NASA management and executives at North American.

The board determined that the "most probable initiator" of the fire was an electrical short circuit in the lower left-hand equipment bay of the command module, where the environmental control unit is connected to an instrument package. That short provoked the momentary power failure technicians had noted just before the astronauts first reported the fire. Sparks from the short ignited "many types and classes of combustible material" in this area, and flames quickly spread in the pure oxygen atmosphere. NASA and North American's collective leadership had forgotten that the Apollo crew sitting on the launch pad with the spacecraft pressurized at 16.7 psi pure oxygen could *not* vent this dangerous gas into the vacuum of space—as they could have after liftoff—should a short circuit ignite flammable material.

Flames jumped from nylon storage netting and along Velcro chafing guards. The heat raised the pressure to such a degree that the inner hatch (which pulled inward) was impossible to open, no matter how hard Ed White struggled with the handle. The crew was trapped in the cabin and died as a result of the poisonous smoke and the terrible burns they suffered.

The board determined that though the "plugs out" test was considered routine, these conditions were in fact "extremely hazardous" because of the pure oxygen atmosphere and the amount of combustible material in the cabin. The organizations responsible for the test had also failed miserably by not adequately training the pad personnel in emergency proceedings and not supplying the white room with rescue equipment. It was inexcusable that emergency medical and fire-fighting teams were not on the scene.

The board recommended that NASA consider a two-gas atmosphere for launch conditions and some alternative to the hazardous triple-hatch system. Finally, the board cited numerous "deficiencies... in design, workmanship, and quality control." They requested a completely new design for the environmental control unit. North American was sharply criticized for delivering a spacecraft with over 100 "open items." The board also came down pretty hard on the technicians at the Kennedy Space Center who had installed additional flammable material in the spacecraft.[7]

This report was followed by congressional hearings in April, which then led to some major changes at NASA and at North American. George Low, the early advocate of the moon landing program, replaced Joe Shea as Houston's Apollo spacecraft program manager; the sloppy work on the spacecraft had occurred on Shea's watch, so he was sacrificed. Harrison Storms, president of North American's space division, was also fired, and he was replaced by William Bergen, a former Martin Company executive. He brought with him two colleagues, Bastian Hello and John Healy, to run North American's operations in Florida and at the Downey, California, assembly plant.[8]

Still, even with these changes and North American's solemn commitment to make design and production changes in the spacecraft, NASA was not content that the company had overcome the "ignorance, sloth, and carelessness" the accident review board had noted in their report.[9] NASA firmly believed that the blame for the *Apollo 1* fire was North American's. Bob Gilruth sent a "tiger team" headed by Frank Borman from Houston to North American's Downey factory, where they virtually took up residence to make sure that the company correctly modified the hatch, wiring, and plumbing and replaced the inflammable netting and wiring bundles with fiberglass and nonflammable spun glass beta cloth. Borman's direct, often abrasive approach to problem solving undoubtedly let them know that the previously cozy relationship between Houston and Downey was over.

One of the things Borman's team uncovered was a shocking level of drunkenness among the Downey plant work force. Borman set them straight. His shoot-from-the-hip managerial style—some called it bullying—worked. The union issued an order that no worker would be allowed to drink until his shift was finished. It's unclear whether the drug abuse that was reported also moderated, although both problems emerged again at the company's plants in later years.[10]

Three months after the accident, NASA had the situation firmly in hand and was working around the clock to modify the Apollo spacecraft. No one wanted to admit it, but the accident had given the Apollo project a respite to work out the remaining problems with the lunar module, the Saturn booster, and other systems.[11]

Once the initial shock and grief had diminished, I was able to look rationally at the details of the accident. No one has said in public just how well the crew behaved during those horrible final moments. Their actions are a monument to the discipline of professional military aviators. Emergency egress procedures called for Gus Grissom to unstrap himself from his couch, for Ed White to remain buckled to the center couch while he worked the difficult hatch crank mechanism, and for Roger Chaffee to maintain the communications link with Mission Control. Despite the flames and the explosion, this is exactly what they did.

It's hard for me to imagine the discipline Ed must have had to keep his hands on that hatch handle, away from the buckles holding him. He is buried where he wanted to be, at West Point. I can't think of a better symbol of courage for future generations of cadets.

Moscow and Tyuratam, Kazakhstan, Winter–Spring 1967

When the Soviets launched their second unmanned test of the Soyuz spacecraft *Cosmos 140* during unprecedented winter conditions that February, they discovered even more serious design problems than those that had been discovered with *Cosmos 133*. What disturbed Vasily Mishin most was the breakdown of the spacecraft's principal reaction control thrusters, located on the instrument module of the three-part spacecraft. Equally alarming was the serious burning of the reentry module's parachute lines. On two more unmanned tests of the lighter

Soyuz circumlunar configuration, *Cosmos 146* and *Cosmos 154*, the thruster malfunctioned again and there were serious malfunctions in the temperature-control equipment, which would be life threatening on a lunar mission.

The Soviet space program didn't then have the sophisticated ground simulators and computerized test equipment NASA used. They had always relied heavily on test flights to find flaws in their equipment—and flaws were showing up in spades. Phillip Clark, Britain's leading observer of the Soviet space program, has recently noted in his book *The Soviet Manned Space Program*: "Clearly, Soyuz was not yet ready to carry men, and it is surprising that the test program was not slowed down as each unmanned test threw up new problems. . . ."[12]

When the Politburo ordered Chelomei and Mishin to prepare for a spectacular dual manned Soyuz mission for that April, Mishin, in an act of real integrity, refused the assignment. But he was eventually pressured into compliance. The Politburo wanted a dramatic mission that would equal all of Project Gemini's achievements in a single stroke: the orbital maneuvering, rendezvous, and docking of two spacecraft, followed by the exciting space walk transfer of two crew members between the docked Soyuz spacecraft. Soviet leaders also demanded that the mission coincide as closely as possible with May Day, so they could celebrate "international solidarity" with Eastern bloc nations.[13]

Test engineers fretted over the obvious design flaws in the new Soyuz, while a four-man crew led by veterans Valery Bykovsky, the pilot of *Vostok 5*, and Vladimir Komarov, the commander of the *Voskhod I* mission, trained for the dual *Soyuz 1* and *2* missions. Komarov would be launched alone aboard the first spacecraft, and Bykovsky and his two crewmates, Yevgeny Khrunov and Aleksey Yeliseyev, orbited the next day aboard *Soyuz 2*. After rendezvous and docking, Khrunov and Yeliseyev would join Komarov aboard *Soyuz 1* via a spectacular space walk, using the docked orbital modules as air locks. This dual flight would not only duplicate Gemini's record of success, it would also demonstrate the Soviets' capability for similar orbital maneuvers on a more ambitious Soyuz lunar flight.

Just before dawn on April 23, 1967, Colonel Komarov climbed aboard the *Soyuz 1* spacecraft, mounted atop a large SL-4 booster. At age 40, Komarov was one of the oldest cosmonauts and certainly the most technically qualified, with years of experience in flight-test engineering. He had been a part of the manned Soviet spacecraft program from its inception and was considered its best-qualified pilot. In addition, his broad shoulders and sharply molded Slavic features made him an ideal representative of this daring new Soviet venture. He had already demonstrated his courage and dedication to duty by commanding the risky *Voskhod I* mission.

The launch itself was normal, the large booster climbing away into the dawn over Kazakhstan. But as soon as the spacecraft was safely in orbit, serious malfunctions arose. The Soyuz spacecraft was equipped with two solor-panel "wings" that would convert sunlight into electricity, but one panel did not deploy, drastically reducing the spacecraft's power supply. Worse, Komarov began experiencing the same type of control-thruster problems that had plagued the earlier unmanned test flights.

Soyuz 1 made no attempt to maneuver in orbit, despite the vehicle's impressive propulsion system. Also, as we now know from Soviet sources, ground control in the Crimea lost the communications link with the spacecraft on several occasions, which indicates that the *Soyuz 1* was tumbling so badly that Komarov couldn't maintain antenna alignment. The original malfunction in the power supply may have affected the spacecraft's guidance computer, its attitude control thrusters, or—most probably—both. Flight controllers scrubbed the *Soyuz 2* countdown as soon as they realized that the first mission was in serious trouble. They had to concentrate on getting their cosmonaut back from space.

Komarov prepared for an emergency reentry with the crippled spacecraft. Mishin became increasingly anxious as Komarov and ground control struggled to align the Soyuz for the braking retrorocket burn as it passed northward across the equator above the Atlantic. On the sixteenth orbit, Komarov prepared for the burn, but it was canceled when he couldn't maintain stability. Ninety minutes later he tried again, but at the last moment the maneuver was stopped because of poor alignment. Komarov was in desperate trouble. He had probably exhausted the fuel not only from the Soyuz's main thrusters on the instrument module, but also from the vital thrusters on the reentry module.

Komarov finally completed his retrorocket burn on the eighteenth orbit, even though he didn't have sufficient fuel to steer the reentry module. Just after 3:00 AM Greenwich time on April 24, *Soyuz 1* plunged back into the atmosphere, spinning wildly; Komarov abandoned all attempts at a controlled reentry path for a normal touchdown near Tyuratam. The cosmonaut imparted a spin to the module that was probably a last-ditch effort to keep the heat shield pointed along the flight path and prevent end-over-end tumbling, which would have incinerated the spacecraft.

The Soyuz module plunged on a ballistic trajectory almost 400 miles short of the designated landing zone, and Komarov was unable to stop the violent spin in the lower atmosphere. When he reached an altitude of about 30,000 feet, he deployed his small drogue parachute, which was quickly followed by the main chute. But the parachute lines fouled around the hot, spinning crown of the module, and his reserve parachute system also tangled.

There have been reports of questionable reliability that Western intelligence overheard Komarov's last radio transmissions as his crippled reentry module plunged toward Earth. He reportedly screamed to his wife: "I love you and I love our baby!" But it's unlikely the Soviets would have allowed a radio connection between the doomed cosmonaut and his wife that we eavesdropping imperialists could hear.[14]

Komarov's death was certainly instantaneous when the Soyuz module plunged into the steppes at several hundred miles an hour. The Soviets' official announcement of the accident stunned the world, especially since they had broadcast just 12 hours before that Komarov's flight was proceeding normally. According to Moscow, Komarov died "...as a result of tangling of parachute cords as the spacecraft fell at a high velocity...."[15]

Whatever the true story of the *Soyuz 1* accident, it now seems obvious that the Soviets were trying to leapfrog the American Gemini achievements by using their advanced new Soyuz for a double mission on its first test flight. And if it had been successful, they would have scored a technological coup. Maybe the tragic loss of Grissom's crew in the pad fire at the Cape, and the inefficiency and hardware problems the accident had revealed, had encouraged the Soviets to try racing ahead of America. They have certainly never admitted this. But the Soviet accident gave them the same pause America felt after *Apollo 1*. Their desperate need for prestige had driven them to ignore the warnings of their best technical experts and to strive for a propaganda victory.

Apollo 1 and *Soyuz 1* taught the world that victories in space would be neither easy nor cheap.

CHAPTER TEN

APOLLO RECOVERS

1967 TO 1968

Washington, DC, and Houston, Texas, Summer 1967

As soon as the dust settled after the fire, NASA's leaders turned their full energies to getting Project Apollo back on its feet. But now relations with Congress had reached the point where NASA began promising the impossible: they would pay more attention to crew safety and hardware reliability, but still not jeopardize America's chances at landing on the moon before 1970.

Many congressmen felt the country could no longer afford the luxury of a manned lunar-landing program. Five hundred thousand American soldiers were fighting a war in Indochina. That summer, more ghetto uprisings exploded with a violence and a disregard for authority that shocked America's leaders.

Project Apollo was beginning to seem irrelevant when compared to the combat in the inner cities and the A Shau Valley. NASA had to beg for the minimum funding it needed to demonstrate its prowess during the next fiscal year. Unless Congress relented, the booster assembly lines would be shut down within months. And without boosters, there would be no program beyond Apollo. Webb spoke bitterly of this situation before the Senate Space Appropriations Subcommittee that July. The Soviets, he said, "... are preparing to launch a booster with an appropriate large payload that will be larger than the Saturn V and that will give them the image and capability for the next several years of being ahead of the U.S. program. So that at the time we are reducing at the rate of 5,000 per month in manpower, they are increasing."[1] Congress was not impressed. They called the big Soviet booster "Webb's Giant."

By late that summer, however, North American Aviation had made great progress on the Block II Apollo spacecraft. Their new point man, Bill Bergen, personally oversaw every detail. North American completed a new hatch in record time, and the new launch-pad cabin atmosphere system provided a safe two-gas mixture on the ground—60 percent oxygen and 40 percent nitrogen—that would automatically "bleed off" to a low-pressure pure oxygen environment when the spacecraft reached orbit.

Apollo's managers met in Washington in September to hammer out the details of a sequence of missions that would place astronauts on the moon. Houston mission planner Owen Maynard, an old Langley hand, had carefully evolved a flight sequence that became known as "A through G." On the unmanned A mission the Saturn V would launch a Block I command module 10,000 miles into space. Then, firing the service module engine would accelerate the spacecraft to the 25,000-mile-per-hour lunar reentry speed. Missions B and C would use Saturn IB boosters to test the unmanned lunar module and Block II command and service module (CSM). On the D and E missions, complete spacecraft would be launched by Saturn Vs for long-duration Earth-orbit flights, with the E flight flown on an elliptical orbit taking the spacecraft far beyond the environs of the Earth to test tracking, navigation, and reentry. The F mission would actually orbit the moon with a crewed Apollo spacecraft. Finally, the G mission would accomplish the first lunar landing.[2]

Maynard's plan didn't leave any room for incompetence or accidents. It was a bold technical gamble. But of course, that was what Project Apollo was all about.

Kennedy Space Center, Cape Kennedy, November 9, 1967

At dawn on this clear Thursday morning, the world's largest rocket stood poised on Launch Pad 39-A, its flanks misted with supercold fumes.

Apollo 4, the A mission, was an "all up" flight of the Apollo-Saturn system. Standing 363 feet high, the composite booster-spacecraft weighed over 3,000 tons, the heaviest object ever to fly. The five F-1 engines in the first stage produced 7.5 million pounds of thrust, making the booster the world's most powerful machine.

Kurt Debus's countdown reached T–0 less than one second after the scheduled launch time of 7:00 AM. The booster erupted in a cataract of red flame, and clouds of exhaust blasted sideways from the flame trenches. At first the thousands of spectators squinted at the glare, and then the noise reached them across the sand dunes—a rolling, crackling barrage that shook the ground and pounded the breath out of their chests. The only noise man had ever made that was louder than the Saturn V was a nuclear blast.

CBS correspondent Walter Cronkite stood clenching his microphone as his image was blurred by the vibrations shaking the cameras. Almost speechless, Cronkite was showered by pieces of insulation and paneling ripped loose from the ceiling of his broadcast booth.[3]

Two minutes and 40 seconds into the flight, the S-IC first stage shut down at an altitude of 38 miles. The five J-2 cryogenic engines of the S-II second stage ignited in perfect sequence. About three minutes later, the S-II shut down normally, and the single J-2 engine of the S-IVB third stage ignited to loft the unmanned Apollo spacecraft into orbit. Huntsville and the KSC had done their jobs.

Nine hours after launch from the Cape, the *Apollo 4* command module descended beneath its three large parachutes and splashed down in the Pacific. It had been a textbook mission. The year that began with tragedy ended in triumph.

Houston, Texas, and Cape Kennedy, Winter–Spring 1968

The next step was to test the Block II CSM on a manned Apollo Earth-orbit flight and to eliminate the remaining flaws in the lunar module.

The ambitious "alphabetical staircase" mission sequence called for the first manned flight, *Apollo 7*, to be flown by Wally Schirra, Walt Cunningham, and Donn Eisele—as soon as the Block II spacecraft was ready—using a Saturn IB booster. After that, another manned flight was planned to test the entire Apollo spacecraft—CSM and LM—in low Earth orbit for 11 days. Mission planners had penciled in Schirra's flight for summer 1968, and early autumn for the complete spacecraft test, the D mission. The E mission, a deep-space test of the entire lunar spacecraft, was planned for sometime in the fall. To keep up with this sequence, NASA had to depend on the availability of hardware: the Saturn V, the Block II CSM, and the lunar module.

The LM, however, was seriously behind schedule. I was unofficially involved in mission planning, and there was a great deal of concern that the LM was becoming the bottleneck of the program. The Apollo fire investigation had shown us that people made mistakes when forced to work under great pressure. And now the screws were tightening on George Low's people responsible for keeping Grumman on the revised LM delivery schedule. The first lunar module (LM-1) was to have been delivered to the Cape in "all up" condition in fall 1966 for an unmanned test mission in spring 1967. But LM-1 didn't reach the Cape until June 1967, and NASA engineers were still trying to work bugs out of the spacecraft when they joined it to a CSM and then mated the two with a Saturn IB booster in November.

The command and service modules had evolved from the Mercury and Gemini spacecraft, but the LM was a new type of vehicle. Since it would operate solely in the weightless vacuum of space and in the one-sixth Earth gravity of the moon, the LM lacked the streamlined curves and heat shield associated with spacecraft that flew through Earth's atmosphere to and from space. The lopsided bulges, jutting struts, and slabs of sheet metal, and the exposed plumbing of its thrusters, made the LM look more like a concrete mixer than a flying machine.

But it wasn't designed to look good; it had to be functional. The LM needed to be light, robust, and dependable. Astronauts landing on the moon would need the LM's ascent stage to thrust back to lunar orbit and rendezvous with the command module. That was the real challenge. If a spacecraft in Earth orbit malfunctioned (as *Soyuz 1* had), it had the option of making an emergency reentry and descent (as *Gemini XIII* had done). But the LM didn't have that luxury. The engine and guidance systems of the LM's ascent stage had to work perfectly: the only "abort" contingency for the crew on the moon was, in fact, powered ascent to lunar orbit rendezvous. If you couldn't do that—and rendezvous with the command module—you would be stranded and die.

For over two years, NASA and Grumman officials had been struggling with endless glitches in the LM's two engines. These engines weren't as complex as the Saturn's because they used standard hypergolic hydrazine-type fuel and oxidizer, which was pressure fed to avoid complex turbopumps. But the descent engine's main requirement was that it be controllable through a computer-assisted throttle to allow the LM to slow down and eventually hover on its rocket plume above the lunar surface. This would give the astronauts time to select a safe landing spot. No one had ever tried to throttle a large manned rocket engine before. And making this innovation reliable wasn't easy. Ground tests of the descent engine revealed rough burning, erosion of the combustion chamber, and serious burn-throughs at the throttle mechanism where the actual mixing of fuel and oxidizer occurred. Synchronized contact between the two propellants in the combustion chamber was vital; if the hydrazine fuel collected there first, contact with the oxidizer could provoke an explosion—which had already happened to an Agena test vehicle during Project Gemini, three years before.[4]

The ascent engine was much simpler, with no throttle and no gimbaled steering. But this engine had to be reliable without the use of redundant parts because of the LM's weight restrictions.[5] And the LM ascent engine had the same type of erosion problems as the descent engine. The thrust chamber had also experienced dangerous gouging. Worse, the welding of the bell-shaped nozzle had been repeatedly plagued with cracks.

Naturally, those of us who were training for a lunar landing flight were very interested in the *Apollo* 5 mission, scheduled for January 22, 1968, which would be the first to fly a lunar module in space. It was an unmanned Earth orbit flight, during which the reliability of the RCS thrusters, the life-support system, and the ascent and descent engines would be tested. There would also be what was called a "fire-in-the-hole" ascent engine burn to simulate an abort either during landing or during ascent from the lunar surface.

The Saturn lifted off from Pad 34 at sunset on January 22. It was the same booster that originally had been planned for Gus Grissom's crew almost a year before. The S-IVB upper stage fired perfectly and placed the CSM and LM-1 in orbit. Three hours later, Gene Kranz's team in Mission Control in Houston gave the commands to put LM-1 through its paces. They fired the descent engine, testing its throttle and its automatic shutdown control. All worked perfectly. For the first time, a throttlable rocket had been fired in the Zero-G conditions of space. Then the mission controllers gave the command for the fire-in-the-hole abort maneuver. The ascent engine blasted the upper stage free of the descent stage, separating the two halves of the LM. Then the ascent engine was shut down and restarted. Despite some minor glitches, this first vital test of a lunar module was a success.

But even as engineers at Houston and the Grumman plant in Long Island were analyzing the test data after *Apollo* 5, new ground tests revealed engine stability and structural problems. Windows blew out or broke under testing, and there were ominous corrosion cracks in the LM's paper-thin aluminum ribs. And as always, each repair and modification seemed to add more weight to what was already a heavy vehicle.[6] I saw a lot more long faces at the mission planning office in Houston. It was looking less and less likely that an "all up" lunar module would be ready for the D mission later that year. The alphabetical mission sequence was scrambled in a complex shuffle that left even NASA insiders confused.

Through all these tests and delays, Wally Schirra, Walt Cunningham, and Donn Eisele had been training intensively for the first manned flight, *Apollo* 7, aboard a Block II command module. They'd been Gus, Ed, and Roger's backup crew and had spent almost a year at North American's Downey plant, shepherding their spacecraft through its final manufacturing stages. Jim Webb told a Senate committee that Schirra's crew would check every detail of the spacecraft's construction on a "day-by-day, month-by-month" basis.[7]

This really wasn't unusual because most of us were still mad that even though Gus Grissom and his crew had *specifically* objected to flammable material before their spacecraft left the plant in California, engineers at the Cape had gone ahead and put that same type of material right back in the command module on the launch pad. We were determined that a foul-up like that would never happen again. And that meant we'd all have to spend a lot more hands-on time with the hardware.

But we didn't have a lot of time. In January 1968 Deke Slayton named the crews for the *Apollo* 8 and 9 flights. Frank Borman, Mike Collins, and Bill Anders were assigned to test the LM—*if* one was available—and then fly the CSM on a so-called high-altitude elliptical orbit that would loop it far out into space before a high-speed reentry. Neil

Armstrong, Jim Lovell, and I were Borman's backup team. I was the lunar module pilot, with Neil as commander and Jim Lovell as command module pilot. Jim McDivitt, Dave Scott, and Rusty Schweickart would fly the complete Apollo spacecraft on a long-duration low-Earth-orbit mission. But Slayton stressed that we all had to be flexible in our plans, given the uncertain status of the LM.

A few weeks after these first two Apollo flight assignments came down, Frank Borman called a meeting of the prime and backup crews. I was still interested in mission planning and spent as much time as my other training duties would allow with my Gemini colleague Bill Tindall's people in MPAD (Mission Planning and Analysis Division). We were investigating improvements in the rendezvous procedures for Borman's mission to better simulate lunar orbit conditions.

I mentioned this to Frank during the meeting, and he immediately snapped back. "Goddamn it, Aldrin," he said, pointing his finger right at my face, "you got a reputation for trying to screw up guys' missions. Well, you're *not* going to screw up mine."

I was flabbergasted. He must have been referring to the Gemini missions when I coached crews on orbital rendezvous and underwater EVA training. In this case all I was trying to do was cue Frank in on what was being said at MPAD about refining some of the goals of his flight. He saw this as unwarranted interference. Frank and I had been very competitive since our days at West Point. He had been one class ahead of me and a senior officer in our battalion. We were both athletes and good scholars, and both of us had joined the Air Force to be jet pilots. But I'd won the more coveted assignment as a Sabre fighter-interceptor pilot, while Frank had flown F-84 fighter-bombers. To make matters worse, he'd ruptured an eardrum in 1952, which grounded him and kept him away from Korea and combat. After the war, he and I had been the principal competitors for honors at the Air Force fighter weapons school. I edged out Frank for the top position, on the basis of my combined cockpit and classroom performance. I don't think he ever forgot this.

Now he was the commander of the prime crew for an important Apollo mission and I was his backup lunar-module pilot. He wasn't going to miss this chance to let me know who was boss. But there was more than just personal rivalry involved here. All of us knew that Project Apollo was entering a critical phase and that *every* mission had to work perfectly in order to continue the program to a lunar landing before our deadline. Borman was determined that his would not be the mission that upset the apple cart. I couldn't blame him for that, and I recognized that his competitiveness had vented itself in aggression at a very stressful time. Each of us handled the pressure in his own way.

Moscow and Tyuratam, Kazakhstan, Spring 1968

The Soviet recovery from the *Soyuz 1* disaster paralleled NASA's efforts after the Apollo fire. Both management and hardware problems were rigorously addressed and everyone was under terrible pressure. Their moon landing program had by now grown into a gargantuan organization with all the major civil and military missile design bureaus participating. Tens of thousands of scientists, engineers, and technicians were involved, representing hundreds of industrial facilities. Even so, the Soviets still kept their lunar program a closely guarded state secret. Officially, the Soviet Union had no plans to land men on the moon. (The Russians have maintained the myth that they never intended to reach the moon for almost 20 years, but today every leading Western expert on the Soviet space program agrees that they were as vigorously involved as we were.[8])

But the Soviet moon program was too large to hide from the West, especially from the electronic eyes of America's Keyhole reconnaissance satellites. Western intelligence reported the construction of new launch pads for large new boosters, as well as a new horizontal booster assembly building at Tyuratam. The mission control complex in Kaliningrad near Moscow with its unmistakable space-tracking dish antennas (which had replaced the primitive ground control station in the Crimea) was the Soviets' equivalent of the Manned Spacecraft Center in Houston. The cosmonaut corps had now grown to over 60 members and could no longer be housed and trained in the original secure center within the GRU military intelligence complex at Khodinka Airfield near the Dynamo soccer stadium in Moscow. So the Soviet air force built a separate cosmonaut residential and training establishment 24 miles northeast of Moscow, dubbed *Zvezdni Gorodok* ("star town"). As cosmonauts told astronauts Mike Collins and Tom Stafford at the Paris Air Show in 1968, they were undergoing the full range of moon mission training, like to their American counterparts, including helicopter instruction, a vital skill for lunar landing.[9] Finally, the Soviets upgraded their limited fleet of space-tracking ships, replacing old trawlers with modern oceangoing vessels that were practically covered with large dish antennas. These ships could stay at sea for months and were obviously intended to serve as relay stations for deep-space operations, not just Earth-orbit missions.

Like the Americans, the Soviets had serious technical problems to solve before cosmonauts could fly aboard the new boosters and spacecraft. They would clearly be taking a step back from *Soyuz 1* before proceeding ahead. But their schedule was still set up to beat America to the moon: first with a successful circumlunar flyby of a single cosmonaut aboard a modified Soyuz and then by an actual lunar landing— tentatively planned for early 1970. Again, with the one-man circumlunar mission, the Soviets were attempting a politically driven space spectacular. This mission, however, also had another objective: it would test the manned module for the larger composite moon landing spacecraft. But even this stripped-down circumlunar Soyuz was too heavy to be launched by the Korolev bureau's Soyuz booster. The spacecraft had to reach escape velocity to achieve the coasting flight path that would loop it around the moon, what Apollo mission planners called "translunar injection" (TLI). This meant that the Soviets had no choice but to man rate their trouble-plagued Proton booster. Working the kinks out of this system became a Soviet priority in early 1968.

In order to camouflage the circumlunar Soyuz missions, the Soviets claimed they were part of the Zond deep-space probe program that had begun in 1964. But the *Zond 4* flight that lifted off from Tyuratam on March 2, 1968, was really the first test of the modified Soyuz and its Proton booster.[10] It was actually launched into empty space directly *away* from the moon, an indication that the Soviets were merely testing their booster, spacecraft, and tracking system and didn't want to draw the West's attention to a manned moon mission rehearsal.[11] The success of *Zond 4* encouraged the Soviets to accelerate the program while also continuing with their ambitious moon landing plans.

To land on the moon would, of course, require a much larger and more sophisticated booster and spacecraft than the Proton–circumlunar Soyuz combination. The Soviets had to make their big Lenin-class booster (generally called the G-1 in the West) fully operational. NASA was committed to the Lunar Orbit Rendezvous mission mode, but the

Soviets' booster capabilities required a more difficult combination Earth orbit and lunar orbit rendezvous mission mode. They would first launch a crew of three cosmonauts aboard a heavy Soyuz atop a Proton, followed by a G-1 booster carrying the remaining parts of the lunar spacecraft—a Soyuz-type mission-support module, a lunar lander, and a lunar braking module. This was a payload of over 20 tons, not counting the booster's third stage. The manned Soyuz would rendezvous and dock with the other lunar spacecraft, which would then be thrust toward the moon. After braking into lunar orbit, the lander, with two cosmonauts, would descend to the surface. The cosmonauts would return to lunar orbit and rendezvous with the Soyuz command module, just as in the Apollo LOR mission mode. On the return to Earth, the heavy Soyuz's descent module would detach for a "skip glide" deceleration from translunar velocity before final reentry into the atmosphere.[12]

This complex mission structure—the two boosters and the rendezvous in both Earth and lunar orbits—was necessary because the G-1 booster didn't have the lifting power to launch an entire moon landing vehicle. Unlike the Saturn V, which used high-energy cryogenic hydrogen-fueled upper stages, the G-1 booster was fueled by conventional LOX-kerosene in all three stages. The Soviets had not yet mastered liquid hydrogen engine technology and therefore were restricted to conventional propellants. This is why even though their lunar booster was huge—the "giant" Jim Webb had warned America about since the mid-1960s—its was slightly less powerful than the Saturn V.

We didn't actually know how big this booster was until our reconnaissance satellites photographed the roll-out of the first test model from the horizontal assembly building at Tyuratam in March 1968. The Soviet engineers moved the first two stages of the booster horizontally on " the world's biggest railroad car," a transport platform 65 feet wide and over 200 feet long, supported on railroad wheels that ran on two sets of widely spaced parallel tracks. The third stage with its long cylindrical payload shroud was transported to the launch pad on a separate single track.[13]

In both scale and design, the G booster's launch pad was unlike anything seen before. Huge concrete spokes—"like the petals of a gigantic flower," according to Soviet-space-program expert Saunders Kramer—pointed toward a circular opening that was 40 feet in diameter above a multichanneled flame trench over 100 feet deep. There was both a standard vertical launch umbilical tower and a massive rotating mobile service structure that made even the gigantic structures at Cape Kennedy look small. When the booster's lower stages were positioned vertically, a hammerhead crane on the mobile service tower delicately placed the third stage and payload on top of the lower stages.

Fully assembled, the G booster stood over 300 feet tall. It was not as tall as the Saturn V, but it was much thicker at the base. Its first stage still had the distinctive flared-skirt design that had originated with Korolev. This stage clustered 21 upgraded Korolev engines, producing a liftoff thrust of over 12 million pounds. The booster may have lacked the Saturn's upper-stage performance, but it certainly made an impressive picture stacked on the Tyuratam launch pad.

Our satellites could determine a lot about what the Soviets were up to, but there was no way for our intelligence analysts to know if the huge white booster on the Tyuratam launch pad was a flight-ready rocket or merely something made of boiler plate.[14] In the past the Russians' flight testing had made ours seem conservative, so NASA's top leadership certainly had reason to worry. After the huge white booster had spent several weeks on the pad, the Soviets rolled it back to the assembly building. Although Jim Webb and his colleagues couldn't judge when this big new booster would be ready for flight, they knew the Soviets were moving aggressively ahead.

That winter, Webb told the House Science and Astronautics Committee he was "quite certain" the Soviets would test their big booster soon. In previous years, congressmen would have been worried, but they now knew that the average American no longer considered the race to the moon an issue of major importance. The January Tet Offensive in Vietnam had shattered the myth that the country had been pacified and that North Vietman was about to withdraw its troops from the south. Even though the offensive had resulted in a crushing military defeat for the Viet Cong and the North Vietnamese army, the coordinated enemy attacks tipped the political balance in America against the war. We were preoccupied with ending that war, not beating the Russians to the moon. NASA leaders had to demonstrate to Congress that a lunar landing was possible in order to maintain government support. In other words, there was room for a few setbacks, but nothing like the Apollo fire.[15]

Cape Kennedy and Huntsville, Alabama, April–May 1968

At dawn on April 4, 1968, NASA launched its second unmanned Saturn V on the *Apollo 6* flight. The purpose of this repeat of the A mission was to demonstrate the Saturn booster's reliability and to test further the Block II Apollo command module in Earth orbit. This launch of the huge Saturn was more impressive than the first, probably because the acoustics were better in the humid early-morning air. Again the ground shook and the five F-1 engines roared as if a giant hand were ripping the sky apart. In the firing room of the new launch control center, von Braun and his project leaders turned from the blast-proof windows to monitor the flight on their telemetry consoles.

As the men from Marshall watched, their splendid booster began to malfunction. First, the entire 360-foot stack bounced like a giant pogo stick. This dangerous "pogo effect" had been seen with smaller boosters but was completely unexpected in the Saturn V. After separation, the five cryogenic J-2 engines of the S-II second stage burned correctly for only a few minutes. Then the number two engine died, and the number three engine beside it signaled a premature shutdown. But Walter Haeussermann's beautifully designed instrument unit correctly analyzed the problem and increased thrust on the remaining three S-II engines for an extended burn. This carried the booster to the proper altitude for separation of the third stage. Even though the S-IVB's single J-2 engine fired correctly and placed the spacecraft in Earth orbit, it couldn't be restarted as planned three hours later. A hundred tons of expensive booster and payload were uselessly drifting through a parking orbit. The engineers tried every trick they knew, but none of the radioed commands worked. Von Braun realized that his team had an exhaustive job of analysis and engineering modifications ahead of them before the Saturn V was ready for a manned flight. "With three engines out," von Braun said, "we just cannot go to the moon."[16]

When von Braun's people flew back to Huntsville that night, they faced the most critical challenge of their long careers in rocketry. They broke into teams and worked around the clock, seven days a week, in a desperate effort to analyze and correct the booster's problems as soon as possible.

First they discovered that the "pogo effect" was due to a resonating harmonic frequency in the F-1 engines that closely matched the natural twanging of the booster stack. They corrected the problem by "de-tuning" the engines' vibration frequencies.

Further analysis also revealed a design flaw in the adapter panels that covered the LM during launch, which allowed condensed humidity to turn into explosive steam pressure. The simple addition of cork insulation and the drilling of ventilation holes corrected this problem.

But it took real detective work to analyze and correct the mysterious flaws in the J-2 engines. After 15 days of intense effort, the Huntsville engineers—assisted by Rocketdyne and university specialists—discovered that the engine's hydrogen fuel line hummed with a destructive vibration in space, an effect that didn't occur during ground tests. This explained the engine failures in both the upper stages. In only 20 days, von Braun's disciplined engineers and scientists had completely overcome these setbacks.

General Sam Phillips called the effort "one of the most aggressive, thorough, and determined engineering test and analysis programs I have ever seen."[17]

Only three weeks after the multiple failures of *Apollo 6*, Huntsville was back on track. That meant the LM could resume its position as the number-one problem.

Houston, Texas, Spring and Summer 1968

No American had been in space since Jim Lovell and I had completed *Gemini XII* 20 months earlier. The *Apollo 1* fire, and the problems with the various pieces of hardware needed to send men into space and to the moon, had kept us grounded. We seemed to be permanently stalled on the ground.

That summer Mike Collins developed a serious bone spur on a neck vertebra that required surgery. He was shifted from the prime crew of Borman's mission to its backup, and Jim Lovell took his place as command module pilot. This shifted me to backup command module pilot, and Fred Haise got my old job as lunar module pilot, backing up Bill Anders. But we still didn't know who would crew the really exciting Apollo flights, including the lunar-orbit F mission and the plum itself—the G mission, lunar landing. You didn't have to be a mathematical genius to figure out that one of the backup crews would follow the standard rotation, leapfrogging two flights, and end up on the moon landing crew. But it was impossible to guess which crew that would be because we didn't really know whether the confusing delays in flight hardware and the equipment failures would affect the mission sequence. So we just got on with our training as best we could.

Part of that training for the Apollo missions included learning to fly a helicopter at the naval air station in Pensacola, Florida, and later at Ellington Air Force Base near the Houston center. Landing the LM on the surface of the moon was very much like flying a chopper, especially when it came to hovering and gradual descent. I guess it did teach us to be humble about the challenge of the actual moon landing. As any airplane pilot who has ever tried can tell you, flying a helicopter is a real challenge. All of us managed to master it, though—some better than others.

In between my training I spent a lot of time working with Bill Tindall's and Morris Jenkins' mission planning people at MPAD, who were trying to hammer out the mechanics of the Lunar Orbit Rendezvous procedures and flight plans. During Gemini their Apollo counterparts had tended to dismiss Gemini, saying it used inferior computers, radars, and other electronics modified from lowly *aircraft*. The Apollo people had a fairly high opinion of themselves. Many had worked at the MIT Instrumentation Lab and had been involved with challenging work on translunar trajectories for several years. Now that they were having to concentrate on the more nuts-and-bolts work of LOR, they were actually kind of lost.

It became pretty clear to me that they were trying to reinvent the wheel. Tindall, Jenkins, and I made a strong case for adapting the "concentric flight plan" orbital rendezvous techniques that had evolved during Gemini. Eventually, the Apollo MPAD people were forced to accept our work. The final rendezvous and docking procedures for Apollo LORs were very similar to those we'd used in Gemini. But there was no direct line of communications between the two programs. We had to go in there and forge one, hammer and tongs. That's just one more indication of how hectic and often disorganized portions of Project Apollo could sometimes be.

Meanwhile, all of us in the Astronaut Office were committed to our training and to meeting our particular responsibilities. Once we'd checked out on helicopters, several of us began training to fly the LM by practicing on a weird machine called the lunar landing research vehicle (LLRV). It took on the nickname "the flying bedstead" because it was a wingless platform—like an old brass bed frame—of struts and spherical propellant tanks built around a small, vertically mounted jet engine. The astronaut sat in an ejection seat, operating a pair of hand controllers like those on the LM. The trainer's jet engine had computerized power settings that balanced Earth's gravity, allowing sets of hydrogen peroxide thrusters to simulate flight in the one-sixth G of the moon.

The LLRV was a dangerous machine to fly. Without wings, it could not glide to a safe landing if the main engine or the thrusters failed. And to train on it properly, an astronaut had to fly at altitudes up to 500 feet. At that height a glitch could be fatal.

On May 6, Neil Armstrong was flying the LLRV during routine training when the machine began to wobble and spin during his descent from 210 feet to the runway. He fought to regain control with the thrusters, but the platform sagged badly to one side and lurched into a spin. He had maybe a second to decide: if the trainer tipped completely over and he fired his ejection seat, the rocket charge would propel him headfirst into the concrete below. But Neil held on as long as he could, not wanting to abandon this expensive piece of hardware.

At the last possible moment, he realized the thruster system had completely malfunctioned, and he pulled his ejection handles. He was blasted up several hundred feet, and his parachute opened just before he struck the grass at the side of the runway. Neil was shaken up pretty badly, and the LLRV exploded on impact. Later it was determined that the thruster system was poorly designed, allowing Neil's propellant to leak out.

This was the second time Neil had ejected from an aircraft. The first had been in Korea, when he had nursed his flak-damaged plane back across American lines to bail out over friendly territory. Apparently Neil had waited to the bitter end, trying to make it to an emergency landing strip. His tendency to hang on to crippled flying machines had shown up again in 1962 when he had a flameout on the X-15 rocket plane out at Edwards. He'd ridden that stubby-wing aircraft almost down to the dry lakebed before getting the engines lit. Neil just didn't like to abort a flight.

Our training in the summer of 1968 made us feel optimistic, but the moon seemed as far away as ever. And we could all tell that the country was losing interest in spaceflight. NASA had to take some bold steps if we were going to make Kennedy's deadline.

CHAPTER ELEVEN

APOLLO TRIUMPHANT

1968

Washington, DC, August 1968

The managers of Project Apollo were beginning to accept the fact that the lunar module was not going to be ready for a manned flight in 1968. The first LM set for a manned flight had arrived at the Cape that summer riddled with defects. George M. Low, manager of Houston's Apollo Spacecraft Program Office, was the first senior official to bite the bullet on the LM issue and look for ways to work around the problem and salvage as much as possible of the so-called alphabetic stairway mission sequence.

Low had been an early advocate of the moon landing mission, soon after NASA was created as an independent agency. Following the *Apollo 1* fire, he had been put in charge of getting the troubled spacecraft development program back on track. On Wednesday, August 7, Low met with Houston's director of flight operations, Chris Kraft, to discuss a daring alternative to the LM bottleneck. *Apollo 7* was scheduled as the first manned command module flight in October. The next flight was supposed to test both the command and lunar modules. But since there was no LM to test, *Apollo 8* wouldn't seem to make any real progress toward the moon. Why not, suggested Low, send this flight, now called the "C-prime mission" (without a lunar module), on a lunar orbit flight and leapfrog the stalled LM? If NASA could fly an actual manned lunar orbit mission during which the CSM would fire its engine to brake out of the safe free-return trajectory and go into orbit around the moon, several major technical obstacles blocking the eventual landing would be hurdled in one daring move. This would also one-up the Soviets, whom NASA managers knew planned a simple circumlunar flyby within a few months.

Kraft was immediately enthusiastic, though he recognized that a lot of work would have to be done very quickly. His flight operations office would have to develop the computer software for the lunar orbit flight path, and they would have to make the tracking and communications network operational many months earlier than they'd anticipated. Still, a lunar orbit mission before the end of the year would push the program well *ahead* of schedule for a change.

On the morning of Friday, August 9, George Low began one of the most hectic days of his life.[1] He met with Houston center director Bob Gilruth, Chris Kraft, and Deke Slayton, who all supported him on the *Apollo* 8 lunar orbit plan. That afternoon they flew to Huntsville to meet with von Braun's team and the leaders of the Kennedy Space Center, as well as General Sam Phillips, the Apollo program director from NASA headquarters. They all agreed that *Apollo* 8 should make the lunar orbit attempt in December, provided the *Apollo* 7 test of the CSM in low Earth orbit was absolutely successful.

Von Braun's people assured the group that the "pogo effect" and J-2 engine problems had been solved and that the big booster was ready for man rating. It was an extremely bold step for the Saturn V's first manned mission to launch an Apollo spacecraft all the way to lunar orbit. But von Braun was well aware of the Soviet pressure and understood that answering the Russian circumlunar flight with a more ambitious— and considerably riskier—lunar orbit mission was necessary. He continued to insist, however, that no technical compromises be made in man rating the Saturn V for the *Apollo* 8 mission.[2] The group agreed to meet the next week in Washington, armed with more data to make their case before deputy administrator Tom Paine.

Deke Slayton called Frank Borman, commander of the mission that had been so often modified since its inception. Borman flew a T-38 back from the North American plant in California on Sunday and met behind closed doors with Deke Slayton. According to Frank, Deke told him,

"We just got word from the CIA that the Russians are planning a lunar flyby before the end of the year." Deke then asked Borman if he would agree to change *Apollo 8* from an Earth orbit to a lunar orbit mission. Frank agreed immediately.[3]

Deke doesn't recall the meeting as vividly as Frank. He agrees that NASA was under "very strong pressure" to fly the lunar orbit mission and says that the knowledge that the Soviets might attempt a circumlunar flyby was *one* of the reasons the *Apollo 8* was changed to a lunar orbit flight, but the need to retain the program's momentum was also a major factor.[4]

George Mueller believes that a possible manned Soviet circumlunar flight certainly helped NASA's managers reach their eventual decision: "It was clear that the Soviets were attempting to beat us to a lunar flyby, if not actually a lunar landing."[5]

Just how large a role the Soviets' competitive pressure played in the *Apollo 8* decision will probably never be fully known. The key participants did not keep written records of classified discussions on this because information gained from American reconnaissance satellites was extremely sensitive. Chris Kraft, one of the key men in the decision process, remembers that everyone involved wanted to "beat the Russians' ass." That's probably an understatement.[6]

NASA's dozen key Apollo officials met in Tom Paine's conference room on August 12. Paine, a metallurgist and former General Electric executive, was considered an excellent manager. He listened to their proposal and then played the devil's advocate by reminding them that only weeks before they had been worried about man rating the Saturn V booster, and now they proposed using it to launch men all the way to lunar orbit.

Von Braun replied, "Once you decide to man AS-503 [that particular Saturn booster's official name], it doesn't matter how far you go."

Bob Gilruth added, "There's always risk, but this is the path of less risk."

George Low concluded, "Assuming *Apollo 7* is a success, there's no other choice."[7]

Paine congratulated them for thinking boldly. He was on their side. But Jim Webb and George Mueller—at a United Nations space conference in Vienna—were less easy to convince. On the telephone, Mueller remained cool to the idea and urged the group in Washington to keep a lid on their plan until Webb returned to study it. The next day, Sam Phillips spoke directly to Webb, who was "shocked and fairly negative."[8] Paine and Phillips got to work immediately, writing a long memorandum supporting the lunar orbit mission proposal, which they sent to Vienna that night by diplomatic courier. George Low's group of "plotters" were busy nailing down the details for the first true inter-planetary voyage. All they needed now was official permission to get on with the job—and, of course, a successful *Apollo 7* mission.

Tyuratam, Kazakhstan, September 1968

At 9:42 PM on September 14, a three-stage Proton booster lifted off from Tyuratam on a blazing trajectory toward the northeast. Its payload bore the distinctive launch shroud and escape tower of the Soyuz spacecraft. But no cosmonauts were on board this *Zond 5* mission, even though the spacecraft was a modified Soyuz with the orbital module removed. The only crew were a collection of tortoises, insects, and plants that scientists had placed there to test the spacecraft's life-support system and radiation screening.

Sixty-seven minutes after launch, while the coupled third stage and modified Soyuz spacecraft were still on their first orbit, the booster engine ignited, thrusting the unmanned spacecraft away from Earth on a translunar trajectory. The spent third stage was then abandoned, and the Soyuz-Zond spacecraft sped on its path to intersect the moon. A midcourse correction two days later bent the flight path slightly, so that *Zond 5* looped around the left-hand "limb" of the moon at an altitude of 1,100 miles. On the return flight path toward Earth, Western tracking stations intercepted tape-recorded messages of a human voice calling out simulated instrument readings that sounded like a well-trained Soviet cosmonaut. Obviously, this was the dress rehearsal for a manned attempt; the tape-recorded voice was part of a tracking and communica-tions exercise. The Soyuz reentry module splashed down in the Indian Ocean on September 21, after a steep, high-speed descent into the atmosphere, during which it was subjected to peak deceleration loads of 16 Gs and a maximum temperature of 13,000 degrees Celsius.[9]

Such conditions would have been intolerable for a human crew. But the major objectives of the test mission had been met. Just as the Americans had predicted, the Soviet Union was rehearsing for the first

circumlunar flyby. Following the doctrine established by Korolev, a
second identical unmanned mission would be required before a cosmonaut flew the mission.

NASA probably had two months, a maximum of three, to send a man
around the moon before the Soviets.

Cape Kennedy, October 1968

Apollo 7, the first manned Block II CSM, lifted off perfectly with the
ignition of the Saturn IB at 11:00 AM on October 11, 1968. This was Wally
Schirra's third flight and the first for Walt Cunningham and Donn
Eisele. Their ride on the Saturn IB booster was bumpy for the first few
minutes, and on ignition the S-IVB second stage gave them a good kick
in the pants. The new, mixed-gas cabin atmosphere in this Block II
command module, composed of 40 percent nitrogen and 60 percent
oxygen, also worked well. After a short time in orbit the nitrogen had
mostly been vented and the crew were breathing pure oxygen at a safe,
low cabin pressure.

The flight's principal objective was to check out the CSM, especially
its big service propulsion system (SPS) engine. The crew worked their
way into the flight plan slowly, trying to avoid the spacesickness that
could ambush an overeager astronaut. As he had on his Mercury and
Gemini flights, Wally Schirra managed to combine the precision of an
experienced flight test engineer with the zaniness of a fraternity boy.
After firing the SPS engine for the first time, Wally shouted,
"Yabadabadoo!" just like Fred Flintstone.

After several more firings to modify their orbit, they made a mock
rendezvous and docking with the S-IVB stage before settling down for a
rigorous orbital test flight of the CSM. Under zero-G conditions, the
command module seemed very roomy. They could float into odd
corners to "sit" or sleep. Unfortunately, several of their many windows
were fogged up with condensation or streaked with soot from the escape
tower's solid rockets. Nobody got spacesick, but they all caught bad
colds, the result of an ill-conceived hunting trip in the Florida marshes
with racing driver and car dealer Jim Rathman. But they had practiced
the mission in simulators so many times over the past months that their
performance was flawless.

Over the next 10 days, Wally and his crew adapted to the spacecraft's quirks, like sweating coolant pipes, banging thrusters, and a rudimentary sanitation system. Walt Cunningham and Schirra even accomplished feats of weightless gymnastics in the spacious lower equipment bay below the crew couches.

Television coverage was a key part of the public relations dividends of this flight. Wally had brusquely vetoed the first planned live TV broadcast because that day's flight plan was overcrowded. (And he later revealed he was mad at Mission Control for launching them into high-altitude winds.) But soon he returned to his jovial self. He and Walt even held up professionally printed placards that quipped to the camera: "Hello From the Lovely Apollo Room High Atop Everything."

For the first time in 23 months, America could see its astronauts in space again. Their competence, their humor, and the Apollo spacecraft's sophistication went a long way to raise the national mood in an extremely troubled year. In the first eight months of 1968 there had been the Tet offensive in Vietnam, the assassinations of Martin Luther King and Bobby Kennedy, the May student revolt in Paris, the riots at the Chicago Democratic Convention, and the Soviet invasion of Czechoslovakia in August. These three grinning astronauts tumbling and pirouetting in their roomy spacecraft were just what the country needed to see.

After splashdown in the Atlantic less than a mile from the aircraft carrier *Essex*, NASA called the mission "101 percent successful."

It was time for a final decision on *Apollo 8*.

Tyuratam, Kazakhstan, October 1968

Early in the afternoon of October. 25, 1968, Western intelligence networks picked up the unmistakable signals of a major space launch under way at Tyuratam. That evening American space trackers confirmed that the Soviets had launched a large Soyuz-class spacecraft into a typical Cosmos-type orbit. But there was no official word from Moscow, not even the familiar cryptic announcement of a scientific probe.

Twenty-four hours later, however, TASS released a priority bulletin that said cosmonaut Colonel Georgy Beregovoi had been orbited aboard the *Soyuz 3* spacecraft that morning and had just completed a successful rendezvous with the unmanned *Soyuz 2*, launched the day before. Over the next 30 hours, Beregovoi maneuvered his spacecraft to complete an additional rendezvous with the unmanned vehicle. Western observers waited for the expected announcement of a successful docking of the two Soyuz, but nothing came. Soviet media said the cosmonaut had gotten his spacecraft within a few meters of the target vehicle. In fact, that rendezvous was transmitted as a fuzzy image on several television broadcasts during the mission. Either the Soviet flight controllers hadn't planned for the two Soyuz actually to dock or the cosmonaut's attempts failed.

The two Soyuz spacecraft, however, worked well. The unmanned *Soyuz 2* was brought down on October 27 on the same type of ballistic reentry trajectory that had killed Komarov the year before. This time the parachute system functioned well.

Meanwhile, Beregovoi continued his flight, putting the Soyuz propulsion system through its paces and giving his Soviet television audience a guided and chatty tour of the roomy spacecraft, which was obviously a page stolen from the Apollo PR book. Four days and 64 revolutions into the flight, Beregovoi began the critical part of the mission. He carefully aligned his spacecraft using an optical horizon scanner, and the automatic sequencer fired his main propulsion engine for a two-minute 25-second burn that braked *Soyuz 3* from orbital velocity. Once the new mission control center in Kaliningrad near Moscow confirmed the success of this maneuver, the cosmonaut separated his reentry module from the orbital and instrument modules and began flying a carefully controlled descent.

Unlike Komarov in the terrifying, uncontrolled reentry of *Soyuz 1*, Beregovoi flew his spacecraft with amazing precision. His parachute deployment was perfect and the touchdown was so close to the target point on the snowy steppes near Karaganda, northwest of Tyuratam, that the recovery crew was actually peering through the steaming reentry module's windows before Georgy Beregovoi could unbuckle his harness and climb out of his seat.[10]

The first successful manned flight of the Soyuz was a great accomplishment. As Phillip Clark, the British expert on the Soviet program has stated, "With *Soyuz 3* the Soviet manned programme regained its confidence, and its success may have encouraged the Soviets to consider a manned flight around the moon in December 1968."[11]

The race for the first circumlunar flight was still on.

Washington, DC, October–November 1968

During the flurry of Apollo operations and the secret planning for the *Apollo 8* lunar orbit mission, NASA administrator Jim Webb suddenly announced that he was resigning, effective on his sixty-second birthday in early October. Managing Apollo, as well as the increasingly bitter budget struggles with Congress, had worn him down. Webb also hoped that by resigning he would ease NASA's transition to the new Nixon administration. Tom Paine became acting administrator, just in time to make the final *Apollo 8* decision.

A series of meetings in October and early November confirmed that both the Saturn V booster and the Block II CSM were capable of making the lunar orbit flight with a safety margin most managers thought was acceptable. General Sam Phillips led an intensive systems analysis that listed the mission's pros and cons. This flight's riskiest component was the spacecraft's SPS engine, specifically its propellant injector and thrust chamber. These engine components simply had to work to thrust the CSM back out of lunar orbit toward Earth. As Phillips noted with an engineer's cool detachment, "The life of the crew depends on the successful operation of the Service Propulsion System during the Trans-Earth Injection Maneuver."[12] This engine was especially critical because the Apollo spacecraft would not be docked to a LM during the mission. Earlier safety reviews of any lunar flight plan had always listed the LM as a potential "lifeboat," whose powerful descent engine could be used in an emergency to kick the spacecraft out of lunar orbit for the return trajectory to Earth, should the SPS fail. But on *Apollo 8*, the service module engine would simply have to work, or Frank Borman and his crew would be stranded.

On November 10, George Mueller called a confidential meeting with NASA manned spaceflight leaders and aerospace contractor executives to discuss the mission. Except for a few disagreements, the majority favored going ahead with the bold lunar orbit flight. Leland Atwood of North American summed up what everyone was thinking: "This is what we came to the party for."[13]

Tyuratam, Kazakhstan, November 10, 1968

The Soviets gave NASA a reason to urgently pursue the *Apollo 8* mission when on November 10 they launched their *Zond 6* flight. It was another unmanned Soyuz circumlunar flyby, very similar to the *Zond 5* mission. Exactly 67 minutes after launch, the Proton third stage blasted the Soyuz-Zond out of Earth orbit on a translunar trajectory.

Western intelligence agencies immediately began tracking the mission. And officials in the Pentagon and at NASA were greatly relieved to learn that there were no cosmonauts on board. However, in an unprecedented move, the Soviets announced while *Zond 6* was in flight that the purpose of the mission was "to perfect the automatic functioning of a manned spacecraft that will be sent to the moon."[14]

If NASA's leaders needed any help making their decision, the Soviets had just given it to them.

Washington, DC, November 12, 1968

NASA called a press conference for acting administrator Tom Paine and General Sam Phillips to officially announce the *Apollo 8* decision. Paine told the reporters, "After a careful and thorough examination of all of the systems and risks involved, we have concluded that we are now ready to fly the most advanced mission for our *Apollo 8* launch in December, the orbit around the moon."

He said that Frank Borman and all of the NASA decision makers were unanimous in their support of the mission and that they had just made the final decision the day before. When a reporter asked if NASA had been influenced by the *Zond 6* flight, Paine replied, "This did not play any part at all in our decision on this flight," adding that he did not know whether the Soviets were planning "a manned circumlunar flyby before December." (It's interesting that Dr. Paine specifically said a Soviet *manned* circumlunar flight, rather than any other type of lunar mission. Obviously, Paine had access to intelligence reports that he had no intention of sharing with the ladies and gentlemen of the press.)

When reporters continued to zero in on the Soviet connection, both Paine and Phillips stuck to denials that Russian pressure had influenced them in any way whatsoever. And Paine defended the manned translunar flight that would not include a functional LM lifeboat by citing the CSM's "redundancy." He did not mention that Sam Phillips had written a memorandum the day before that focused on the *lack* of redundancy in the SPS engine.[15]

Tyuratam, Kazakhstan, November 1968

The Soviet Union dispelled any doubts that it was serious about flying a cosmonaut on a Soyuz-Zond mission when *Zond 6* returned from its lunar flyby on the afternoon of November 17. Unlike the previous Zond's blazing, high-G return, the reentry module of *Zond 6* performed a complex, precise "skip" maneuver. Following a narrow reentry corridor, it skimmed across the top of the atmosphere above the south Pacific, initially decelerating with a relatively moderate G load. Then it skipped back into space so it could reenter the atmosphere at a slower speed, like a spacecraft descending from normal Earth orbit. There were two obvious advantages to this maneuver: cosmonauts returning from the lunar flyby would not be subjected to crushing G forces, and the atmospheric skimming meant the Soyuz reentry module could land on Soviet soil, instead of splashing down in the Indian Ocean (the only aiming point for a pure ballistic return from the moon).[16]

The Soviets had completed the unmanned test flights of the Soyuz-Zond system. But in the United States, they had stiff competition for the race around the moon.

Cape Kennedy, December 1968

More spectators and reporters came to watch the launch of *Apollo 8* than had come for any previous American space mission. Charles Lindbergh was among the celebrities who were at the Cape to see man's first true departure from Earth. At three o'clock on the morning of Saturday, December 21, 1968, Frank Borman, Jim Lovell, and Bill Anders had breakfast in the crew quarters of the manned spacecraft operations building.

They were joined for the traditional steak and eggs by several well-wishers, including Deke Slayton and George Low, two men who'd been very influential in shaping their mission. Out the third-floor windows they could see the floodlit white column of the Saturn V three miles away in the chilly darkness. I don't think anyone had much of an appetite.

Frank hadn't slept well. At many points in the mission, he would have to make "go–no go" decisions, sometimes on the advice of Mission Control, but often alone. His nerves were ragged. The night before, when a priest had given Bill Anders communion in the crew quarters, Frank Borman had snapped, "Are you going to take communion every thirty seconds before the flight?" Bill was hurt by this, and Frank was sorry the moment he said it.[17]

As backup command module pilot, I was involved with preparations for the flight. I was out at the pad by 4:00 AM, setting switches in the spacecraft and helping with the final preflight checkout. It felt odd to be sitting on the left-hand couch, reading from a thick checklist, while the booster below me was being filled with over 2,000 *tons* of dangerous propellants. Gunter Wendt was even more fastidious than usual that morning. He was like a prize-winning brain surgeon conducting his most important operation. There was a lot of tension surrounding this bold mission. It reminded me of flying combat in Korea when my wing had drawn a hot mission up in "MiG Alley."

By the time I left the pad at 6:00 AM, the crew had no more time for nervousness. They were all professionals and had rehearsed the mission so often that the complicated process of suiting up went smoothly. They wore the new fireproof beta cloth spacesuits, an innovation stemming from the launch pad fire. A little after seven, Gunter carefully installed Frank, Jim, and Bill in the command module and sealed the hatch. As the sun rose over the Atlantic, the launch pad spotlights were turned off. Ignition came at 7:51 AM.

In the command module, the crew heard the surging propellants flowing into the engine 300 feet below. Then came a staccato rumble, and they saw the gantry sliding downward past the small side windows.

"The clock is running," Frank called from the commander's seat.

In the grandstands and along the causeways and beaches spectators cheered, gasped, and sobbed as the Saturn climbed on its tail of flame. I had the best seat in the house, the roof of the launch control center. As always, the noise was overpowering and unearthly. The thick concrete roof was bouncing like a trampoline. It was hard to believe that three tiny humans were strapped into the tip of that monster. As the booster climbed past the sunrise, I realized that I might be riding the Saturn on the way to the moon in a few months. That, of course, depended on the success of this mission. The crackling shock waves pounded my chest. Suddenly, all the competition I'd known with Frank Borman over the years fell away.

In the firing room, two floors below, Wernher von Braun and his team tensely studied their telemetry consoles. There didn't seem to be any indication of the "pogo" problem this time. The S-II stage fired flawlessly, as did the S-IVB third stage. Twelve minutes into the flight, *Apollo 8* reached orbit.

The combined spacecraft–S-IVB weighed over 100 tons, making it the heaviest object ever launched into orbit. As this huge payload circled Earth, flight controllers in Houston carefully analyzed data from the booster and spacecraft. Mike Collins was capcom in Mission Control. Two hours and 35 minutes into the flight, as the spacecraft crossed north over the Hawaiian Islands, Mike called, "All right, you are go for TLI [translunar injection]." It was still the middle of the night in Hawaii, but people ran into their yards to watch the spectacular flare of the booster ignition high above in the dark tropical sky.[18]

In Houston, Chris Kraft and flight director Cliff Charlesworth gazed at their consoles, watching the single J-2 engine's performance as the rocket motor devoured 80 tons of supercold propellant, thrusting *Apollo 8* to the fastest speed humans had ever achieved: escape velocity from Earth, 23,226 miles per hour. Frank, Jim, and Bill were pushed back into their couches by the mounting acceleration. Then the engine stopped and the vibrations ceased. They floated again in zero G.

"You're on your way," Chris Kraft told them directly, bypassing the capcom. "You're *really* on your way!"[19]

For the first time in man's history on Earth, people had severed the gravitational connection to their home planet. As the *Apollo 8* crew soared free of Earth, they carried the American flag toward victory in the moon race with the Soviet Union.

The CSM separated now from the spent third-stage booster. Borman had to concentrate on thrusting the spacecraft clear of the booster, which seemed to be catching up to them. Jim Lovell was down in the lower equipment bay with the space sextant, measuring angles on Earth's horizon to establish a preliminary navigational fix. They eventually removed their spacesuits and stowed the center couch. Unfortunately, several of their windows had fogged up, but Frank could see the retreating Earth, more than 25,000 miles behind them. "We see the Earth now," he said, his voice wistful, "almost as a disk."

Over the next few hours, Borman grew quiet. Like Soviet cosmonauts before them, Frank and Jim began to feel nauseous as they moved about the spacecraft. Frank tried to rest, but the spacesickness was relentless. After vomiting and a bout of diarrhea, he was finally able to sleep.

The next day they were over 100,000 miles from Earth. The SPS engine fired perfectly during the planned test burn and course correction. They were on a path to the desired intercept of the moon's eternal track around Earth. However, because their trajectory actually took them *away* from the crescent moon's sunlit face, they couldn't see their target. The moon was a dark presence out there ahead of them, unseen but certainly not forgotten. Borman was over his spacesickness and took a leading role in their first live television broadcast. Even if they couldn't see the moon, they had a good view of Earth, which Frank described as a warm blue sphere with "huge covers of white clouds."

Monday afternoon, the spacecraft had slowed to a fraction of its escape velocity before crossing the invisible boundary that separates Earth's gravitational sphere of influence from the moon's. Then they accelerated toward their rendezvous. After several hours of disciplined work with checklists, verifying the status of dozens of the spacecraft's systems, Borman told Houston they were ready for the lunar orbit insertion (LOI) burn that would brake them into lunar orbit. It was an exciting moment, but they still could not see the moon, though Houston assured them they were less than 1,000 miles from it. When Anders was asked about the view, he muttered, "It's like being on the inside of a submarine."

Borman followed the flight plan to fire the SPS engine in a retrograde mode to slow the spacecraft further. Dressed in their light coveralls, the crew strapped themselves into the couches and prepared to sweep around the back of the moon. Once they crossed the "radio horizon" behind the moon, they would be out of contact with Houston, a condition called "loss of signal" (LOS). There would be a 40-minute period before "acquisition of signal" (AOS), during which they would have to fire the service module engine for lunar orbit insertion.

The countdown toward this critical burn clicked off with silent green digits on their computer display-keyboard (DSKY) screen. When the computer demanded a go–no go decision, Borman punched PROCEED, committing them to lunar orbit. They were moving head down toward the unseen lunar surface. As the SPS engine twanged and throbbed, dropping the spacecraft into an elliptical orbit, the crew waited tensely. They knew they would be able to see the sun rise above the moon's horizon almost immediately if the LOI burn had been on time. And there it was, a dazzling glare above the gray horizon of the moon. Suddenly, they could see the entire sphere beneath them, a jumbled ash-colored *presence*.

After verifying their instruments, they unstrapped themselves and drifted to the clearest windows to study the moonscape drifting 70 miles below. Their orbital flight above the moon seemed almost leisurely. Because the moon is so much less massive than Earth, orbital velocity around it is also slower. They seemed to float above the gray chaos of craters, with ample time to gaze in awe.

In Mission Control, the flight controllers sat tensely at their consoles, and Chris Kraft paced behind the back row, smoking one of his strong little cigars. Thirty-six minutes and nine seconds after the burn, the data screens came alive with AOS. *Apollo 8* was in lunar orbit. On Earth, it was Christmas Eve.

The day wore on, and the spacecraft continued to glide through its lunar orbit. Jim Lovell said, "The moon is essentially gray, no color. Looks like plaster of Paris...." Bill Anders described it as "a very whitish gray, like dirty beach sand with lots of footprints in it."

They were very busy for the next several hours, photographing landmarks for the future lunar landing and practicing navigational fixes. But before turning in for the night they had a special presentation for those of us listening across a quarter million miles of space. It was a biblical reading Frank had prepared. Bill Anders said the crew had a message "for all the people back on Earth." In turn, each crew member read from the book of Genesis, with Anders leading: "'In the beginning God created the heavens and the earth....'" Frank Borman ended the reading: "'...and God called the dry land Earth and the gathering together of the waters he called Seas: and God saw that it was good.'"

Borman stared out at the lifeless moon drifting beneath them, then across space at the moist blue disk of Earth. From this distance there was no sign of human existence, no evidence of city or farmland, no ruins of war. "And from the crew of Apollo," Frank said, "we close with a good night, good luck, a Merry Christmas and God bless all of you... all of you on the good Earth."

After a fitful rest and more preparations, the *Apollo 8* crew again fired their SPS engine on the back side of the moon, 20 hours and nine minutes after beginning their 10 orbits of the moon. The burn was good, increasing their velocity by about 3,000 feet per second. At AOS half an hour later, Jim Lovell told the tense, chain-smoking men in Mission Control, "Houston, please be informed there *is* a Santa Claus."[20]

It was Christmas Day, 1968. *Apollo 8* was now triumphant. The first men from Earth were homeward bound.

CHAPTER TWELVE

THE LAST LAP
JANUARY TO JULY 1969

Washington, DC, and Houston, Texas, January 1969

Chris Kraft and his flight controllers finally gave themselves a belated Christmas when the *Apollo 8* spacecraft and crew were safely aboard the aircraft carrier *Yorktown*. The mission had definitely achieved one of its unofficial objectives—to "restore the morale of the troops" who had worked so hard on Apollo's recovery following the launch-pad fire.[1]

On the morning of Monday, January 6, 1969, Deke Slayton called Mike Collins (who was back on our crew following his surgery), Neil Armstrong, and me to his office. Deke wasn't the type to close doors, but this time he did. He filled us in on NASA's latest changes to the planned mission sequence leading to the moon landing. The next mission, *Apollo 9*, commanded by Jim McDivitt, would be an "all up" test of the combined CSM and LM in Earth orbit. McDivitt and Rusty Schweickart would fly the LM over 100 miles away from the command module, which Dave Scott would pilot. Jim and Rusty would "exercise the full system," the first manned checkout of the lunar module. Next, *Apollo 10*, commanded by Tom Stafford, with Gene Cernan and John Young on board, would orbit the moon for three days. Tom and Gene would fly the LM to within 50,000 feet of the lunar surface in a test of the descent systems before igniting their ascent engine and climbing back to rendezvous with John Young in the CSM.

Deke said that if those two missions were successful, *Apollo 11* would be the first moon landing attempt. It was tentatively scheduled for July. Deke tried very hard to remain low-key and to stay at a distance from us. He had been a combat bomber pilot during the war in both Europe and the Pacific, and he knew it wasn't a good idea to be close buddies with the men you sent on risky missions. But that morning, even stone-faced Deke Slayton was excited.

I was absolutely twanging with adrenaline, but tried to remain the unflappable astronaut I was supposed to be, as did both Neil and Mike. (This wasn't easy for Mike, given his grin. The musical chairs that resulted from Mike's bone-spur operation had moved me, first from pilot of the lunar module to command module pilot and now back to LM pilot on the *Apollo 11* mission.) Deke was saying that Neil and I were going to be the first humans to land on the moon—if, of course, all went well with the earlier missions and with our own flight. Some very large ifs.

NASA planned to release the news officially at a press conference on Thursday, January 9, which gave us a couple of days to get used to the idea. The first thing we had to do was tell our families, but I didn't want to break the news over the phone and I couldn't get home for lunch.

At five that afternoon, Joan drove up in the station wagon outside Building 4. The car was jammed with laundry baskets because our washing machine had broken down that morning. I told her about the mission at a laundromat off NASA Road 1. I guess that was an unusual place to tell her I was going to the moon, but then again, is there a *normal* place to break that kind of news? Joan was a good fighter pilot's wife and had taught herself to remain calm about these things—testing a new aircraft, earning an important combat command, and so on. It was the same in the spaceflight business. The really plum missions were dangerous. That night she wrote in her diary, "So it is really happening, and I am scared."

I wouldn't say I was scared, but I certainly was uneasy about the enormity of the whole event. There was bound to be intense media attention and public relations pressure involved with the first landing. Dealing with these things was not my long suit: I was really uncomfortable with publicity. And Neil Armstrong, one of the quietest, most private guys I'd ever met, has often been described as taciturn, but that's an understatement. Neil was a man from rural Ohio who'd worked his way through a career in aviation and spaceflight, carefully watching everything he did and said. His family was his social life. He was *not* the hard-drinking, fast-driving "right stuff-er" the public seemed to think all the astronauts were. Mike Collins was not quite as quiet, but he was hardly what you'd call flashy. None of us was going to have an easy time with the public relations part of our mission.

That Thursday, Tom Paine held a press conference in Washington and announced that *Apollo 11* was scheduled for either mid-July or mid-August and that it was "currently considered as the earliest possible mission to attempt the landing on the moon." About 10 minutes later in Houston, the phones started ringing in our offices. Local TV and newspaper reporters were hungry for a scoop from Neil, Mike, or me: "How does it feel to be...." When I walked in the door that night, Joan handed me a stack of phone messages from reporters around the world. Luckily, the PR people at NASA took this over from us. But our lives were already changed, and we didn't even have a firm launch date yet.

Tyuratam, Kazakhstan, January 14–18, 1969

NASA's *Apollo 8* mission had leapfrogged the Soviets in orbiting a man around the moon, but we now know that the Soviet Union had been prepared for a manned Zond circumlunar flight in mid-December 1968. They had, however, chosen a more cautious route: flying a third unmanned Zond mission to repeat the unique "skip" reentry flight path pioneered by *Zond 6*.[2] The chairman of the State Civil Space Commission, General Kerim Kerimov, had duplicated the caution Wernher von Braun had shown in 1961 when he'd insisted on another unmanned Mercury-Redstone flight before Alan Shepard's mission. But the preparations for this Zond mission dragged on past *Apollo 8*, and when it was finally launched in January 1969, the Proton's second stage exploded.

Western experts on the Soviet space program now believe that flying a single cosmonaut on the free-return circumlunar flyby was merely an option available to the Soviets to beat the Americans at this intermediate stage of the moon race. The Zond missions' most important goal was testing the crew reentry module of their manned lunar landing program.[3]

The Soviets now had to accelerate their moon landing program. They understood full well the deadline America faced, and they knew that at any point in the next two or three missions, the Americans could suffer a setback as bad as, or worse than, the *Apollo 1* fire. The Soviets had to be ready to take advantage of such an opportunity.[4] Their priority now was to test their lunar spacecraft, their Proton and G-1 boosters, and the complex flight plans that would land cosmonauts on the moon.

The Americans were clearly ahead, and the moon race was entering the final lap. According to Nicholas Johnson, a respected American expert on the Soviet space program, "The Americans had raised the ante. It was now up to the Soviets to call or fold."[5] But the Soviets' own moon landing program was really not that far behind NASA's, considering the problems that still existed with the LM and the potential propulsion malfunctions in the Saturn V.

Since the hectic days of the moon race in the late 1960s, official Soviet sources have denied that their country even had a moon landing program. But that's nonsense. Experts like Phillip Clark, Nicholas Johnson, James Oberg, and Charles Vick have put together enough evidence from the Soviets' own public announcements to prove that they had an active manned lunar program. In the sixties, Soviet cosmonauts spoke openly about these plans. We know that the lunar cosmonaut group practiced sea recovery (in Zond-like Soyuz reentry modules) and trained in helicopters (just like our LM crews) as early as 1967.[6]

The Soviets are so guarded about this subject that we can't be absolutely certain what their landing mission profile was, but Western experts have, for the most part, done an excellent detective job in figuring out their plans.[7]

Korolev's reliable Semyorka booster had been modified to launch the heavy Soyuz spacecraft. The Proton was almost ready for man rating. And the big G-1 booster—although built on a mammoth scale—was actually an amalgam of Semyorka-type and Proton-type hardware. *Apollo 8* had taught the Soviets a lesson: there was a time for cautious, incremental test flights and a time for daring improvisation. And 1969 was a time for boldness.

The most probable Soviet lunar mission configuration would have used their Proton and G-1 boosters and a composite spacecraft made up of a heavily fueled Soyuz (possibly with a separate propulsion module), a mission support module (similar to our service module), a two-stage lunar landing module (incorporating a modified Soyuz orbital module), and a lunar braking module.[8] The heavy Soyuz would be launched by a Proton into a circular orbit, and a crew of three would wait for the rest of the lunar vehicle to be launched the next day by the big G-1. Following the G-1 booster launch, the Soyuz would dock with the three-part lunar payload, and the crew would prepare for translunar injection. When they neared the moon, the lunar braking module would be fired, putting the big spacecraft into lunar orbit. Two of the cosmonauts would then transfer to the lunar module by a risky but technically simple process: a space walk. The lander with the cosmonauts on board would descend to the surface. After the cosmonauts had explored the surface, they would return to the lunar module's modified Soyuz ascent stage, which would lift them back to orbit for rendezvous with the heavy Soyuz and another EVA transfer. Then they would burn for trans-Earth injection and the coasting flight back to Earth. Finally, the reentry module would separate for the "skip" atmospheric descent pioneered in the Zond program.[9]

This might seem overly complex, but our Apollo mission planners actually used the same kind of incremental, "go–no go" decision sequence. The Soviets had a number of abort possibilities that would have brought the crew home safely. The space walk provision for crew transfer does seem a little spectacular, but again it had a built-in safety factor: there was no need for the complicated, and vulnerable, internal docking tunnels we used on Apollo. Western experts also now believe the Soviet lunar module's side hatch would have allowed the two cosmonauts to crawl onto the "porch" of their descent stage and then climb down the ladder to the surface.

These technical details indicate the Soviets were moving toward their goal, prodded by pressure from the Americans. By this time, their cosmonauts were so well educated and well trained they simply would not have tolerated any risky Voskhod-type space spectaculars. That's probably why the Soviets didn't try a manned Zond flyby during the December launch window before *Apollo 8*. But according to Tom Paine, the Russians still had hopes of safely developing their lunar spacecraft technology before the Americans.

On the morning of January 14, 1969, Radio Moscow announced that *Soyuz 4*, with a single cosmonaut, Vladimir A. Shatalov, had been launched from the "Baikonur Cosmodrome" (Tyuratam). The announcement was delayed until Shatalov had maneuvered the Soyuz into a nearly circular 150-mile orbit. Almost exactly 24 hours later, the Soviets announced the launch of *Soyuz 5* with three cosmonauts on board: Boris Volynov, the commander; Aleksey S. Yeliseyev, the flight engineer; and "research engineer" Yevgeny Khrunov. For the next 18 hours the two spacecraft maneuvered in similar orbits and the crews rested. Then *Soyuz 4* was given the active rendezvous role by ground controllers. By midday Moscow time, Shatalov's automatic rendezvous guidance system had brought his spacecraft within 100 meters of *Soyuz 5*.

Volynov kept the target spacecraft stable while Shatalov performed the docking. Shatalov eased the probe of his orbital module into the drogue on *Soyuz 5*. The two spacecraft were now linked, and an electrical latch mechanism was engaged to strengthen the attachment.

While Volynov fired his thrusters to test the maneuverability of the linked spacecraft, Yeliseyev and Khrunov entered their orbital module and sealed the hatch between them and the reentry module. They put on their bulky white EVA suits with oxygen life-support systems in narrow packs strapped to their legs. After prebreathing oxygen to prevent the bends, they depressurized the orbital module and opened the hatch to space. Khrunov was the first to cross over to the open orbital module hatch of *Soyuz 4*, using handrails on both spacecraft. His only connection was a short nylon tether with a snap clip. Once he was safely inside, Yeliseyev did the same. The first EVA transfer of men in space was successful.

What Moscow never announced about this mission, however, was that the two cosmonauts had been in training for their space walks for almost three years. They were the crew originally intended to complete the EVA on the *Soyuz 1* and *2* mission that had killed Vladimir Komarov.[10]

When the two orbital modules were repressurized, the commanders could open their internal hatches. Khrunov and Yeliseyev gave Shatalov a copy of *Pravda* that headlined his launch two days before and a note from his wife. A greatly improved onboard television system transmitted the ceremonies. Less than five hours later, Shatalov backed *Soyuz 4* away, breaking free of the docking link. *Soyuz 4* reentered the atmosphere for a perfect landing near Tyuratam on the morning of January 17, and Volynov brought down his *Soyuz 5* reentry module for an equally safe and accurate landing 25 hours later.[11]

The mission had been a complete success. According to Charles Vick, "The Soviets achieved the equivalent of the entire Gemini program in one flight. They were now ready to test their procedures with actual lunar landing hardware."[12]

Cape Kennedy, March 1969

Eight years after Wernher von Braun's Redstone booster launched Alan Shepard on a brief, suborbital lob into space, a fully fueled Saturn V stood on Launch Pad 39-A with an Apollo spacecraft perched on top. This rocket was five times taller than the Redstone and 100 times heavier. The Saturn's first stage alone produced a liftoff thrust of 7.5 million pounds, a force 100 times more powerful than the Redstone's. NASA had transformed manned spaceflight into bold exploration on a truly heroic scale.

At exactly 11:00 AM on March 3, *Apollo 9* lifted off with Jim McDivitt commanding, Dave Scott as command module pilot, and Rusty Schweickart sitting in the center couch as lunar module pilot. This would be the first manned test of the lunar module. Once again the huge crowd assembled at the Cape was physically and emotionally overpowered by the thunder of the booster.

For the crew, however, the first stage S-IC burn was very smooth—"an old lady's ride," McDivitt called it. But staging to the S-II was a real bumper-car jolt. Violent pogo oscillations developed seven minutes into the second-stage burn. The jolting continued through the third-stage ignition, but less than 12 minutes after liftoff the linked S-IVB and Apollo spacecraft became the heaviest object ever placed in orbit.

McDivitt's crew wanted to prevent the spacesickness Frank Borman's crew had had, so they tried to control their head movements and took Dramamine. These precautions helped, but they still felt dizzy and nauseous as they moved about the spacecraft.

A couple of hours later they were feeling better and had separated the CSM from the S-IVB third stage. Scott then deployed his command module's docking probe and thrust the spacecraft neatly around to line up with the conical drogue that was nestled at the top of the lunar module. The latches all snapped properly into place. Just over three hours into the mission, they were hard-docked with the LM. Dave Scott then backed the two docked spacecraft away from the third stage and thrust well clear of the slowly tumbling white booster.

As they worked through their long flight plan, dizziness came in waves. But they had plenty of work to keep them occupied. They had to equalize the pressure between the CSM and LM cabins and prepare the connecting tunnel that would allow McDivitt and Schweickart to move from the CSM into the lander. At one point on the night side of their third orbit, Rusty glanced out and shouted, "Oh, my God, I just looked out the window and the LM wasn't there."

Dave Scott began laughing and kidding his crewmate. Dave reminded Rusty that Jim McDivitt was already up in the tunnel and the missing LM was simply hidden by the absolute darkness of orbital night. When Scott fired the SPS engine to boost the combined spacecraft to a higher orbit, he commented, "The LM is still there, by God!"[13]

They were all surprised at how slowly the spacecraft accelerated, but that was understandable because it was carrying almost 16 more tons of mass—the fully fueled LM. Over the next several hours, they repeatedly fired the engine, moving the docked spacecraft through the complex orbital maneuvers that would be needed for the LOR.

The crew was so confident in their spacecraft that they all slept during the same "night" period. On waking, however, Rusty Schweickart was hit by a sudden bout of nausea. He and Jim McDivitt were putting on their spacesuits for the transfer over to the LM. Luckily, Rusty found a nearby barf bag. Pulling on the bulky pressure suit was no fun in the weightless cabin, and Jim McDivitt also went through some dizzy spells as he tugged at all the tubes and Velcro tabs.

Rusty then experienced brief vertigo as he floated *up* through the tunnel into the LM and ended up staring *down* at the lander's flight deck. When he recovered he began flipping switches to power up the lander, preparing it for free flight. Jim McDivitt joined him soon after. The LM was noisy with chattering fans and strange, gonglike rumbles. Unlike the command module, the lander was ultralightweight. Jim McDivitt later said it felt like tissue paper.

With no warning, Rusty Schweickart vomited again. McDivitt became alarmed because Rusty was due for an EVA on the porch of the LM later that day. If he got spacesick while wearing a bubble helmet, he could choke on his own vomit. Jim did the right thing and called for a private medical consultation on a "discreet" radio channel to Houston.

The hundreds of reporters at the center had a field day making up sensational rumors when they were cut out of the loop.

Now that McDivitt and Schweickart were aboard the LM, the lander began to feel like a separate spacecraft, not just an impersonal hunk of hardware. They referred to it by the name they'd chosen for this mission, *Spider*; the command module became *Gumdrop*, an evocative description of its shape.

The crew spent almost two days, while the two spacecraft were still linked, checking out the LM's many redundant systems and making sure the thrusters were in working order. Then Rusty and Jim crossed over to the lander once more and connected both their portable life support system (PLSS—pronounced "pliss") backpacks and the LM's oxygen hoses to their suits, before depressurizing their spacecraft. Jim McDivitt opened up the waist-high forward door—which took a lot of muscle—and Rusty crawled out onto the porch on the edge of the descent stage. From that porch he could see almost a quarter of Earth's blue-and-white surface—quite a view.

The crew now had three radio call signs: Scott in *Spider*, Jim in *Gumdrop*, and Schweickart, the EVA man, now known as "Red Rover." Rusty used the same golden slipper foot restraints I had used on *Gemini XII*. With these and the handrails on the outside of the LM, he had no trouble moving around.

The next day the crew put the LM through its most crucial task: fully testing the LM's two engines and the spacecraft's rendezvous radar, guidance computers, and docking system. Despite the playroom names they bantered with during the mission, there were real hazards involved in free-flying *Spider* up to 90 miles away from *Gumdrop*. If any of the LM's components failed, McDivitt and Schweickart could be marooned in the LM. *Spider* had no heat shield, so they could not reenter Earth's atmosphere.

In the CSM, Dave Scott flipped a switch to release the latches gripping the LM, but they hung up. It wasn't a good start. He flipped the button back and forth—"recycling" in NASA-ese—and finally the LM broke free. Now came the test of the descent engine. Jim McDivitt stood on the left side of the flight deck, and Rusty Schweickart occupied the similar place on the right. Ignition and the throttle-up to 10 percent were smooth. But suddenly there was a harsh chugging at 20 percent. After several loud thumps, Jim released the throttle hand grip and the noise stopped. When he opened the throttle again, the problem had gone away.

Now they were completely on their own. The spacecraft's four dangling legs, braced by shorter angular struts, actually did make the LM look like a spider.

I was at Mission Control, standing behind the flight directors as they bent over their consoles, monitoring this critical maneuver. *Gumdrop* changed orbit to simulate its position during an actual lunar rendezvous. Many of these maneuvers were near repeats of the rendezvous exercises I'd helped develop during Gemini. Next, Jim and Rusty "staged," breaking the *Spider* into two separate sections. Now the part of the spacecraft they were in was only the bulbous cabin of the LM ascent stage, perched atop its squat engine nozzle. When they ignited that engine, they felt the sudden sagging weight of their limbs as they left Zero G.

Approaching *Gumdrop* in the darkness, McDivitt fired his thrusters to maneuver, illuminating the LM cabin "like the Fourth of July." Dave Scott watched the fireworks, carefully matching what he saw with the radar data on his computer display. The final approach and docking went smoothly. *Spider* and *Gumdrop* were joined again, and the two men in the LM had completed their most critical maneuver. The lunar module, which had been the program's bottleneck for years, had just performed flawlessly in space.

In Mission Control, there were cheers. The *Apollo 9* crew still had five days left in their mission, but they'd accomplished all their major tasks. I could hear Kennedy's words—". . . landing a man on the moon and returning him safely to Earth . . ."—as I walked down the corridors of the Mission Control building.

Houston, Texas, Spring 1969

That spring, NASA could no longer ignore the question of who would be the first man to walk on the moon. A tradition had developed from Gemini days in which the commander remained in the spacecraft while the number two man performed the EVA. Since Neil was the commander of *Apollo 11* and I was the LM pilot, I figured I'd be the first one out. The media had even begun quoting unnamed "NASA officials" who said that I was going to be the first man on the moon. Then I began hearing rumors that NASA had decided that Neil should be the first out because he was a civilian. That disturbed me, not so much because they'd picked Neil, but because I didn't think it was a very good reason. Most of the astronauts were career military officers, and Neil was a former naval aviator. And though I was an Air Force colonel, I hadn't served in a regular unit for almost 10 years.

This was all happening at the height of the Vietnam War, though, and the military wasn't exactly popular. I thought the best thing to do was to go to Neil and discuss this touchy question. We'd both seen the earlier mission plans that had the LM pilot exiting first, but we'd also seen the more recent draft procedures that left the issue unresolved. I asked him directly, "Neil, you probably know I don't care very much one way or another about this. But we've got some tough training ahead of us and I think we have to settle this matter before it gets blown out of proportion."

Neil Armstrong was a no-frills kind of guy who didn't talk a whole lot, but usually said what he meant. But there was also a more complex side to Neil, and I think at this point we were both beginning to realize just how important being the first man to set foot on the moon was. Neil hemmed and hawed for a moment and then looked away, breaking eye contact with a coolness I'd never seen in him before. "Buzz," he said, "I realize the historical significance of all this, and I just don't want to rule anything out right now."

I was amazed. We'd become quite friendly during the weeks of our intensified training, but now Neil was distancing himself. I didn't think the decision was his to make. And I sure hoped that business about choosing a civilian over a military officer was not true.

I let this nag at me for a few days before I went to see George Low, head of the Apollo program office in Houston. I told him that I thought it would be best for morale if NASA made its decision quickly so that we could get on with our training. Within a week, Deke Slayton came by and we went next door to Neil's office. Neil would be the first man out of the LM, he said, and then gave us the reasons. First, Neil was senior, being from the second group of astronauts selected. Equally important, though, Deke said, were more mundane considerations. NASA executives were concerned that our work load on the moon would be very stressful. The final descent, landing, preparation of the LM flight deck for any postlanding abort, and actual EVA on the lunar surface were all very demanding. But the most critical challenge would be our ascent and LOR maneuver to link back up with Mike Collins in the CSM.

Therefore, they wanted our entire stay on the lunar surface to proceed with as few difficulties as possible. Deke said that when he'd reexamined the old EVA procedures, he'd realized that it would be hard for the LM pilot, clad in a bulky pressure suit and wearing a large, awkward life-support backpack (the PLSS) to slide past the commander, kneel down, and back out the hatch to the LM porch. The position of that hatch was the key here. The guy on the left almost had to be the one to open and close it.

The lander simply wasn't big enough for the kind of moving around we'd have to do to get the LM pilot in position to exit first. Neil would have to go out first and come back last. I would remain at my station on the right side of the flight deck to guide him off the porch and down the ladder to the footpad at the bottom of the leg. Then I could follow Neil out of the narrow LM cabin, without banging into delicate instrument panels with my equally delicate PLSS backpack. When the EVA was finished, we'd run this process backward, with me climbing back in first, followed by Neil. As Deke patiently outlined the procedure, I felt a flood of relief. He wasn't giving us any nonsense about a civilian versus an Air Force officer.

The decision marked the end of a long debate within NASA about what our work load would be on the lunar surface. George Low's engineers thought that there should be a minimum of activity, to prevent straining the astronauts, but some scientists wanted us to collect as many lunar samples and erect as many experiments as possible. There was a compromise. Our "early Apollo scientific experiments package" was designed to be scientifically meaningful, but easy to set up. There would be two subpackages stored in a compartment in the side of the LM. They would contain a passive seismic experiment to measure "moonquakes" and an angled array of 100 small specialized mirrors to reflect a laser beam from Earth—and help measure continental drift.[14]

The training for the first landing, surface exploration, ascent, and LOR should have taken months, but we didn't have that kind of time. That meant that between March and July our work weeks would be considerably longer than normal. But while Neil, Mike, and I dug into the trenches of the simulator rooms, Tom Stafford, Gene Cernan, and John Young were preparing for the next critical milestone mission.

Cape Kennedy and Houston, Texas, May 1969

Eleven minutes before one o'clock on the afternoon of May 18, a glaring orange flame blasted from the Saturn V on Launch Pad 39-A.

"Ignition and liftoff. We have liftoff of *Apollo 10*." The dress-rehearsal mission for the first moon landing had begun. The flight plan called for the crew to orbit the moon above the lunar equator and for Stafford and Cernan to swoop the LM to within 50,000 feet of the surface near our prime landing area on the Sea of Tranquillity. Their mission had to be a complete success for Tom Paine to approve the first landing attempt in July.

Three hundred thirty feet above the blazing first-stage engines, Tom Stafford, John Young, and Gene Cernan lay on their couches gazing at their instruments as the huge rocket ponderously cleared the tower.

"Roger," Stafford, the commander, calmly reported, as if the liftoff of the heaviest booster ever to fly was something that happened every day. "The clock has started."

Once more, the Saturn V launch stunned the thousands of people standing in the hot Florida sunshine. As the shock waves cascaded across the tidal inlets of the Banana River, the people on the ground shielded their eyes to watch. It looked like another perfect launch.

But suddenly the ascent became violent, and the crew was slammed back and forth, even though they had their restraint straps securely fastened. Like the Mercury astronauts seven years before, they were unable to read the vibrating instrument panel. The "pogo effect" that von Braun was sure his team had conquered was back with a vengeance. Stafford was so battered by the vibrations that he had trouble confirming the staging of the S-IC. And this "growling, rumbling, and vibrating" flight continued through the burns of the next two stages.[15] Tom, Gene, and John exchanged alarmed glances as the booster stack rattled and snapped like the tin roof of a barn during a windstorm. They were worried that the violent motion would damage the LM tucked in its aluminum shroud beneath them.

Once *Apollo 10* was in orbit, however, Glynn Lunney's flight controllers discovered that nothing had been damaged during the rough ride up. The capcom gave them the go-ahead for translunar injection (TLI). Two and a half hours after liftoff, a computer aboard the S-IVB fired the third-stage engine again and accelerated *Apollo 10* to escape velocity: just over 25,000 miles per hour. As they climbed away from Earth above the Pacific, the spacecraft began shaking. But when the burn finished, things quieted down nicely. John Young, the command module pilot, turned the CSM end for end and docked with their lunar module. The two spacecraft—the CSM was called *Charlie Brown*, and the LM was called *Snoopy*—were now linked top to top, like shunt engines in a railroad switching yard.[16]

As Earth slowly receded in their windows, the crew calmly worked with Mission Control to verify their onboard systems. Three hours later, they were convinced they had a "good bird" for the lunar flight, and they could relax. Luckily they had so far been spared any signs of spacesickness.

For the next two days, Earth became smaller and smaller, until it looked like a flat disk about the size of a quarter. But unlike the *Apollo 8* crew, they could see the moon quite well on this flight path. The night before launch, the moon had been only a waxing crescent above the Florida coast, but now that they were 150,000 miles closer, the face of the moon began to take on the definition and depth of a true sphere.

Stafford's crew prepared for lunar orbit insertion. Their trajectory had been so good that they'd needed to make only one midcourse correction. As they looped around the left-hand limb of the moon, only 75 miles above the jumbled craters, they were ready for the vital SPS burn that would place them in lunar orbit. Just before loss of signal (LOS), Tom Stafford told Houston they were riding above a huge "plaster of Paris cast" and that he couldn't believe they were really orbiting the moon.

The next day's vital LM descent rehearsal and rendezvous began badly. Tom Stafford and Gene Cernan were suited up and about to seal the LM's docking hatch connecting it with the command module when they discovered that the lander had twisted out of line on the latching points. If the docking mechanism had been damaged, the pins might shear off when they separated the two spacecraft, and it would then be impossible to redock.

In Mission Control, George Low, quiet and thoughtful as ever, bent over flight director Glynn Lunney's console and told him that the docking mechanism hadn't been twisted badly enough to harm it. The crew could safely undock. This was a calculated risk on Low's part, but he trusted the redundancy of the safety mechanisms built into the system. I was watching all of this from the row of seats reserved for official observers, and I slowly focused on each flight controller hunched at his illuminated console screen. They were about to put LOR to the acid test. This was the moment when we would learn whether John Houbolt or Jerome Wiesner had been right.

Once John Young had pulled *Charlie Brown* well clear of the LM, Tom Stafford punched a command into his computer's display-keyboard (DSKY), and the descent engine ignited at minimum thrust. They began the descent orbit insertion, dropping their orbit to take them near the lunar equator above the Sea of Tranquillity. As the computer slowly throttled up thrust, the engine continued to burn silently and smoothly. Gene Cernan said the descent was a "pleasant pace" compared with the rough booster engine burns leaving Earth.

The glaring sun was behind Tom and Gene as they flew backward (landing legs first) above the lunar equator toward the west. With their windows parallel to the surface, they could photograph landmarks along "US 1," the name for the approach to the Sea of Tranquillity landing site. The sun was 15 degrees above the horizon and swept the surface like a floodlight, casting harsh shadows that exposed each ridge and crater. The rockscape reminded Tom of California's high desert near Edwards Air Force Base.

Fifty miles overhead, John Young followed their descent through the magnified optics of *Charlie Brown*'s sextant. John wedged himself in a corner of the lower equipment bay, his face to the eyepiece, tracking the tiny LM below as it seemed to skitter across the fields of craters like a water bug on a rippled pond.

Tom and Gene peered ahead, looking 50,000 feet below at the flat Sea of Tranquillity, searching for site number 2, *Apollo 11*'s planned landing spot. Gene watched the digits blink on the DSKY screen. The landing radar was giving them perfect altitude and speed information.

Fifty-seven minutes after beginning their descent, they reached "perilune," their point of closest approach to the moon. Tom turned

Snoopy around and throttled up the engine to 100 percent. They climbed back toward rendezvous with John Young in the command module. Tom and Gene stood shoulder to shoulder at the controls, reading carefully from their checklist to get the LM in correct alignment for the critical separation of the ascent and descent stages.

Back in Mission Control, we heard them speaking softly to each other. Suddenly, Gene shouted to Tom: "Son of a bitch!"

The LM had thrown itself into a violent corkscrew bank. For several seconds, they yelled commands back and forth, struggling to regain control. Tom dumped the descent stage and took command away from the computer. But both men were badly shaken.

The flight dynamics officer (FIDO) down in the first row of the control room reported that the crew had accidentally switched the compter to the abort guidance mode and that the system had begun swinging the LM through the lunar sky, its rendezvous radar vainly seeking the command module. The two astronauts thanked Houston for the information and said they were ready—no doubt eager—to fire the ascent engine. This burn went well, though the LM corkscrewed again, and the LM (minus its octagonal descent stage) docked with *Charlie Brown.*

The whole operation took just over eight hours. Tom and Gene had flown within 47,000 feet of the surface. They had tested both the landing and rendezvous radars, as well as the computers that made these instruments function. They had also completed the first lunar orbit rendezvous.

The door was open wide for *Apollo 11.*

Houston, Texas, and Cape Kennedy, June–July 1969

After the *Apollo 10* crew's splashdown on May 26, NASA confirmed that on its next manned space mission, astronauts would attempt to land on the moon. By mid-June, Neil, Mike, and I were on a training treadmill that seemed to have no end. When Tom Stafford's crew had been training for *Apollo 10*, we had always stepped aside and given them first priority use of the spacecraft simulators at Houston and the Cape. But now that we were "number one on the runway," the pressure was on us to fine-tune our performance.

Mike Collins was probably the best-trained command module pilot NASA had. If it hadn't been for his neck injury he would have been part of the *Apollo* 8 mission. He spent more than 400 hours working in the CSM simulator—most of it on his own, but often "docked" to Neil and me in the LM simulator.[17] On other days, Neil and I put on our hot suits and rehearsed our moon walk beside an LM mock-up on a pulverized lava "sandbox" in the MSC's Building 9. Engineers and NASA officials sat on rows of folding chairs, studying every move we made.

NASA had tried to create a lunar module simulator that was as accurate as possible. Neil and I could stand at our stations in the simulator wearing our full spacesuits (even tethered to the deck with elastic cords, the way we'd be on landing). A television camera linked by computer to our LM controls projected images of the "descent" on our windows. But the visual effects were crude because no one knew what the last few thousand feet would look like through the triangular windows of the LM. Disneyland it was not, but the combination of images and instrument readouts gave us a fairly good idea of what would happen.

One day in the middle of an especially frustrating landing rehearsal, we completed the final descent for what must have been the tenth time that afternoon. When we looked up from our instruments at the blurred gray image of the moon rising toward us, we saw a huge, bug-eyed space monster waiting on the surface. One of training officer John Van Bockel's technicians had stuck a dead horsefly on a pin in front of the camera projecting the moon images. The laughter echoed all the way from the simulator room at the Cape to Mission Control in Houston.

We commuted constantly between Houston and the Cape. I can remember being alone at dawn in a T-38—punchy with fatigue, flying the aircraft on instinct—and having to check my compass to see whether I was heading southeast to the Cape or northwest to another meeting in Houston.

Meanwhile, the flight controllers, the dozens of spacecraft and booster systems task forces and teams, Van Bockel's training specialists (the "zookeepers," who kept watch over our training for hours on end in the simulators), and all the NASA executives right up to Tom Paine were just as busy as we were. *Apollo 10* had looked like a great success on television, but there'd been a number of glitches. All the raw engineering data and the hundreds of landing-site pictures from the flight had to be analyzed before *Apollo 11*'s flight readiness review would formally give us the green light to proceed with the July 16 launch.[18]

Thankfully, NASA's engineers put an end to Thomas Gold's doomsday prediction that the LM might be swallowed up by deep moon dust. Gold and his supporters were still getting considerable media attention by saying that the lunar surface was covered by dust deposits or a fragile "fairy castle" crust that the LM's footpads might pierce, toppling the lander. NASA had already checked this out. The unmanned Surveyor and Lunar Orbiter space probes had brought back data that gave us confidence the lunar surface would support the LM.

Unfortunately, not all our problems were technical. The media were going wild over the *Apollo 11* moon landing mission. The press, which previously had been engrossed with Vietnam, assassinations, the sexual revolution, and all the other political and social distractions of the 1960s, realized they were dealing with one of the most historic events of this century. Sometimes, the magnitude of the mission seemed to over-whelm them.

During the final preflight press briefings early in July, NASA's public relations chief, Julian Scheer, told reporters that immediately after splashdown the *Apollo 11* crew and its cargo of moon rocks would be quarantined for 21 days and put through an elaborate process of biological isolation in the sealed Lunar Receiving Laboratory at MSC in Houston. It was quite possible that the lunar rocks and soil we would bring back to Earth could harbor extraterrestrial microbes just as deadly as the bubonic plague bacteria that reached Europe with the rats aboard trading vessels. This was patiently explained to the reporters, but a few maintained cynically that NASA was grandstanding and trying to withhold information from them.

At our final press conference in Houston, NASA made us wear ugly rubber filter masks as we marched on stage and then sat in an air-conditioned enclosure, because there was a bad summer flu bug around and we couldn't risk getting sick this close to the flight. Again some reporters didn't believe this and saw it as a NASA ploy to hype the mission. The media also questioned the more nationalistic aspects of the mission. For instance, they accused NASA of staging events when they heard we would be planting an American flag on the moon that had an internal telescoping support arm to extend it because there was no lunar atmosphere. But other reporters were very moved when they learned we planned to leave on the moon a mission patch to honor the dead *Apollo 1* crew and medals commemorating the dead Soviet cosmonauts.

The press, however, was not the most serious worry for NASA executives in Washington. The latest spy satellite photographs revealed that the Soviets had again rolled out their huge booster to the Tyuratam launch pad. And this time the rocket was the real thing, not just a test model.

Tyuratam, Kazakhstan, July 4, 1969

For two days photo analysts at CIA headquarters in Langley, Virginia, watched with increasing alarm as the Soviets once more stacked their huge white G-1 booster on the launch pad. Nine kilometers from the G-1 pad a heavy Proton was also now stacked, capped with the unmistakable white shroud and escape tower of a Soyuz spacecraft. American electronic intelligence listening posts in Pakistan and Turkey eavesdropped on the communications traffic of a double countdown at Tyuratam.[19]

Building on the successful *Soyuz 4* and *5* mission, the Soviets were preparing the first test flight of their fully manned lunar landing system. The huge G-1 booster would launch a 50-ton unmanned composite lunar spacecraft into orbit; 24 hours later, the Proton booster (on its first manned mission) would launch a heavy Soyuz carrying cosmonauts Anatoly Filipchenko, Georgy Shonin, and Valery Kubasov. Their mission was to rendezvous and dock with the lunar payload and then put the entire spacecraft through a rigorous workout: a flight similar to our *Apollo 9*.

Soviet space officials had accepted the fact that America would probably be the first to land men on the moon, but they were determined that their long years of struggle would also bear fruit. If this mission were successful, they could land cosmonauts on the moon at least before America achieved a second lunar landing mission. And of course, America's first landing attempt might still fail.

On launch morning for the G booster the rocket was carefully filled with thousands of tons of propellant, beginning with the LOX and kerosene tanks of its massive first stage. By 10:00 AM, the fueling was almost complete. Liftoff was scheduled for midday, the optimal Tyuratam summer launch window for EOR missions. The American Keyhole spy satellite passed overhead that morning and photographed this fueling.

Our satellite was out of range an hour later when an electrical short—probably in a propellant line—ignited fuel in the third stage, more than 200 feet above the concrete pad. Flames jumped to the second stage, where LOX lines ruptured in a blazing flood. As Soviet launch directors watched in horror from their bunker several kilometers to the east, their booster collapsed into a mushrooming fireball. In a moment the solid structures of the booster system became an angry orange-and-black sphere of smoke and flame. Almost 3,000 tons of explosive propellant fed the holocaust. The cosmonauts scheduled for the next day's Soyuz launch were still in their quarters, and though shaken by the blast, they were unharmed. Naturally, their mission was canceled.

When the American spy satellite passed overhead late that afternoon, its cameras recorded a scene of utter devastation. The white pillar of the booster was gone; the launch pad's multiple towers and gantries were gone; the distinctive concrete petals of the launch pedestal flame trench were blackened and twisted. The flat expanse of wild rye and steppe grasses was now a huge blackened scar, "shaped like an artist's palette," several miles in diameter.[20]

The Soviet Union's hard-fought struggle to pull even with its American rival in the moon race was over.

Cape Kennedy, July 1969

By the afternoon of Friday, July 10, 1969, everything was finally "go" for *Apollo 11*. Tom Paine completed the last formal flight readiness reviews with his Apollo team and then gave a long interview to John Reistrup of *The Washington Post*. They talked about America's eight-year race with the Soviet Union to land on the moon. On the basis of "sketchy" information, Paine said he would be "very surprised" if the Russians succeeded in landing a man on the moon before April 1970. He made no reference to the spy satellite photos the week before. But Paine added that he would also be surprised if the Soviets didn't succeed sometime in the next 18 months.[21]

At that moment, *Apollo 11*'s Saturn V was shimmering in the Florida sun across the steamy Banana River.

CHAPTER THIRTEEN

TRANQUILLITY BASE
JULY 1969

Kennedy Space Center, Cape Kennedy, July 16, 1969

Campfires twinkled on the beaches and along the causeways near the Cape. Over a million people had come to watch the launch of *Apollo 11*. Even at 3:00 AM on this muggy Wednesday morning, the headlights of over 200,000 cars cut through the darkness, intensifying the excitement. There were tents and campers along the roads, and thousands of boats were anchored on the Indian and Banana rivers. For most of the night before, people had sweated in bumper-to-bumper traffic on the highways from Cocoa Beach and Titusville. This was an event no one was about to miss.

At 4:15 AM Deke Slayton woke us. "It's a beautiful morning," he said. "You're go."

Deke and Bill Anders ate a steak-and-eggs breakfast with us. They were friendly and talkative, but they were also somewhat distant. We were going and they were staying.

Joe Schmitt and his crew had our equipment laid out in the suiting room. The place looked like an anatomy lab for robots. I was hooked up to my portable ventilator and Joe snugged down the brown and white "Snoopy cap" with my earphones and microphone. When Joe snapped my clear bubble helmet in place, I couldn't hear anything anymore.

It was almost dawn when the van stopped at the base of the gray mobile launching platform. The pad was deserted because Rocco Petrone's launch team had already loaded the Saturn with more than 2,000 tons of supercold LOX and liquid hydrogen propellant. The booster had the explosive power of an atomic bomb. Gunter Wendt, gray-haired now, his shoulders slightly stooped, greeted us at the 320-foot level with a quick smile and a pat on the back.

We were to enter the command module according to our seat assignments for liftoff. Neil would be in the left couch because the abort handle was there. Mike would take the right until after translunar injection (TLI), our actual departure toward the moon. That left the center couch for me, which meant I was responsible for sealing the hatch. I'd be the last man to enter. Gunter led Neil and Mike out the swing-arm bridge to the white room, leaving me standing on the platform, holding my portable suit ventilator like a commuter carrying a briefcase.

The only sound I could hear was the whirring ventilator fan. When I walked I could feel my soft pressure boots twang on the grating. The sun was just rising. Surf rolled soundlessly onto the beach, half a mile away. Across the Banana River thousands of cars were parked around the VAB. Millions of people lined the roads and beaches around the Cape, all gazing at this launch pad. Across America and Europe, millions more were watching on television. But here I was completely alone, breathing cool oxygen inside the sterile cocoon of my suit. A feeling of calm confidence rose inside me.

The marathon training was over. We were actually going. Two nights before, NASA administrator Tom Paine had joined us for dinner in the crew quarters. He'd ordered us not to take any chances on this mission. "If you have to abort," he'd said, "I'll see that you fly the next moon landing flight. Just don't get killed."

Sheets of frost drifted off the booster beside me. The Apollo spacecraft, all 50 tons of the command, service, and lunar modules— over a million separate parts—was hidden beneath the launch shroud. When we reached the moon, the command module would be called *Columbia* and LM Number 5 would become *Eagle*. They were American names that showed the pride we took in our country's greatest adventure.

I looked south down the coast and saw the older launch pads of the

Cape. First were the rusty Redstone and Atlas gantries and then the taller girders and assembly buildings of the Titan complex. I stared for a moment at Launch Pad 34, where Gus, Ed, and Roger had died 30 months before. In a special pocket of my spacesuit I had an *Apollo 1* mission patch and Soviet medals honoring cosmonauts Vladimir Komarov—killed on *Soyuz 1*—and Yuri Gagarin, the first man in space, who had died in a plane crash the year before. I was taking them to leave on the moon.

Joe Schmitt appeared on the platform. They were ready for me in the white room.

Sixty seconds before ignition, Firing Room 1 grew quiet. Rocco Petrone was on a raised dais so he could watch the engineers and technicians seated at their ranks of consoles. Each man and woman had the same tense expression as the electronic countdown clock swept past T–50 seconds.

In the glass enclosure reserved for visiting officials, Wernher von Braun stood beside George Mueller and General Sam Phillips. They held their binoculars and stared out the tall blast-proof windows at Launch Pad 39-A. The launch sequence computer was now in full control. We would have ignition in 20 seconds unless Petrone canceled the launch. He sat motionless at his console listening to the final seconds of the countdown. Wernher von Braun lowered his binoculars and smiled. "So," he said softly and began to pray silently, *Our Father, who art in heaven....*

"T minus ten, nine..." The voice from the firing room sounded calm. I looked to my left at Neil and then turned right to grin at Mike. "*..* four, three, two, one, zero, all engines running." Amber lights blinked on the instrument panel. There was a rumble, like a freight train, far away on a summer night. "Liftoff! We have a liftoff."

It was 9:32 AM.

Instead of the sudden G forces I remembered from the Titan that launched *Gemini XII*, there was an unexpected wobbly sway. The blue sky outside the hatch window seemed to move slightly as the huge booster began its preprogrammed turn after clearing the tower. The rumbling grew louder, but was still distant.

All five F-1 engines were at full thrust, devouring tons of propellant each second. Twelve seconds into the flight, the Houston capcom, astronaut Bruce McCandless, announced that Mission Control had taken over from the firing room at the Cape. We were approaching Max Q, one minute and 20 seconds after liftoff. It felt like we were at the top of a long swaying pole and the Saturn was searching the sky to find the right trajectory into orbit.

"You are go for staging," Bruce called.[1]

Neil nodded, gazing at the booster instruments on his panel. He had a tuft of hair sticking out from the front of his Snoopy cap that made him look like a little kid on a toboggan ride. "Staging and ignition," he called. The gigantic S-IC burnt out and dropped away toward the ocean, 45 miles below us.

Oddly enough the S-II's five cryogenic engines made very little noise, and the Gs built gently. Three minutes into the flight, the escape tower automatically blasted free, dragging the boost protection cover with it.

Now that the cover was gone, we could look out and see the curved Atlantic horizon recede. Six minutes later, we could clearly make out the division between the arched blue band of Earth's atmosphere and the black sky of space. The S-II dropped away and the single J-2 engine of our S-IVB third stage burned for two and a half minutes before shutting down. A Velcro tab on the leg of my suit fluttered in the zero G. *Apollo 11* was in orbit.

Above Madagascar we crossed the terminator into night. While Neil and I continued our equipment checks, Mike removed his helmet and gloves and carefully floated down to the lower equipment bay to check our navigation system by taking star fixes with the sextant. We had to be sure our linked gyroscopes—the "inertial platform"—were working well *before* we left Earth orbit.

Two hours and 45 minutes after liftoff we were into our second orbit, just past orbital dawn near Hawaii. We were strapped tightly to our couches, with our gloves and helmets back on. Restarting the third-stage cryogenic engine in space was risky. The temperature of liquid hydrogen was near absolute zero, but the engine's plume was hot enough to melt steel. It was possible that the damn thing could explode and riddle our spacecraft with shrapnel.

The TLI burn began silently. But as the acceleration load went from zero to 1.5 Gs, our cabin began to shake. The Pacific tilted beneath us.

Six minutes later, the burn stopped as abruptly as it had started, and my limbs began to rise once more in weightlessness. McCandless said the TLI burn had been excellent. We were traveling at a speed of 35,570 feet per second and were passing through 177 nautical miles above Earth. "It looks like you are well on your way now," he added.

Next Mike had to carry out the "transposition and docking" maneuver he'd practiced hundreds of times in simulators. With the flick of a switch, Mike blew the explosive bolts and separated the CSM from the skirt holding us to the Saturn's third stage, which contained the LM. At this point the CSM and LM were free of each other. Mike thrust ahead at slow speed and then used his hand controller to rotate us a complete 180 degrees. The big booster stage topped by the awkward-looking LM froze in place against the Pacific backdrop. Mike didn't hesitate at all or gawk at the view. A few moments later, he moved our conical command module until the triangular probe at its apex was nestled firmly in the doughnut-ring drogue on the roof of the LM. We heard a reassuring clank and a whirring bump as the 12 capture latches snapped into place, forming an airtight tunnel between the two spacecraft.

We were kind of bizarre looking now, with the bulletlike CSM wedged into the cement-mixer LM. Also, the bulky white tube of the S-IVB was still firmly attached to the LM, and we couldn't separate until we'd completed a long checklist. Finally, I was able to call, "Houston, *Apollo 11*, all twelve latches are locked."

I looked out my window and could make out the cloud-covered mouth of the Amazon. Even at this speed, there was no way to actually sense Earth receding, but if I glanced away from the window, then looked back, more of the planet was revealed. The next time I stared out, I was startled to see a complete bright disk. We were 19,000 miles above Earth, our speed slowly dropping as Earth's gravity tugged at us and the distance grew.

Flying steadily this way may have given us a nice view of Earth, but it also meant that one side of the spacecraft was constantly in sunshine, while the other was in darkness. You can't do this for very long because in space the sun's heat will literally broil delicate equipment and burst propellant tanks on the hot side, while on the shaded side the gear will freeze in the deep cold. We had to begin the "barbecue roll," turning slowly on our long axis so that we would distribute the sun's heat evenly.

Mike fired the thrusters and tilted the spacecraft, making us perpendicular to the plane of the ecliptic, that invisible disk of Earth's orbit about the sun. Most people probably thought *Apollo 11* was shooting toward the moon like a bullet, with its pointed end toward the target. But actually we were moving more like a child's top, spinning on the nozzle of our SPS engine.

This movement meant that every two minutes Earth disappeared, then reappeared from left to right, moving from one window to another, followed by the hot searchlight of the sun. We could see the crescent moon out a couple of our windows, though the view was obscured by the LM's many bulges. By this point we had entered the limbo of so-called cislunar space, the void between Earth and the moon. We didn't have any sense of moving up or down, but in fact we were climbing out of the deep gravity well of Earth. And as we coasted upward, our speed dropped. In 20-some hours, we would be over halfway to the moon, but moving at only a fraction of our original 25,000-mile-per-hour escape velocity. A little later, when we would reach the crest of the hill and come under the moon's gravitational influence, we'd speed up again.

After five hours in space, we removed our bulky suits, and the cabin seemed more spacious. We could curl up in any corner we chose, and each of us soon picked a favorite spot. I settled in the lower equipment bay, and Neil seemed to like the couches. Mike moved back and forth between the two areas, spending as much time at the navigation station down below as with the hundreds of spacecraft system instruments grouped around the couches.

Our first Apollo meal went better than we expected. None of us was spacesick—we'd been careful with head movements—so we were actually quite hungry for the gritty chicken salad and sweet applesauce. The freeze-dried shrimp cocktail tasted almost as good as the kind you get on Earth. We rehydrated food with a hot-water gun, and it was nice to eat something with a spoon, instead of squirting it through tubes the way we'd done on Gemini.

The deep-space tracking station at Goldstone in southern California (there were two others, one outside Madrid and another near Canberra, Australia) wanted us to test our television system. Neil was the narrator, and he gave the weather report for Central and South America. I got some good shots of Mike floating from one window to another, and then he held the camera while I took the TV audience on a little tour of the navigation station below.

When this impromptu TV show was over, I realized I was very tired. It had been a full day, and we needed sleep. When I curled up in my lightweight sleeping bag, I couldn't help thinking how adaptable humans are. There we were, three air-breathing creatures bedding down for the night in this tiny bubble of oxygen. Our spacecraft was like a miniature planet, built by humans like us. We were able to live inside it comfortably, though only an inch or two of alloy and plastic separated my face from the vacuum outside.

Somehow I still felt secure. Ventilators whirred softly and thrusters thumped at odd times. The radio was turned low; Houston would call us only in an emergency. We shaded our windows and dimmed the cabin. I hooked up my sleeping bag beneath the couch and stretched, floating in the luxury of weightlessness. It was time to rest.

When we'd finished our TV broadcast the next day, Charlie Duke, the capcom on duty, gave us some good news about the Soviet unmanned moon probe *Luna 15*. Three days before our mission lifted off, the Soviets launched this robot spacecraft in an attempt to beat America in returning the first sample of lunar material. But it now looked like their mission wouldn't succeed. The Soviet probe was definitely in a lunar orbit, but it would not interfere with our flight path in any way. Charlie also told us that *Pravda* was calling Neil the "czar of the ship." Mike and I had a good time with that. It was pretty funny to think of Neil, the pride of Wapakoneta, Ohio, as a czar.

At a ground elapsed time (GET) of 26 hours and 34 minutes, Mike fired the SPS engine for just under three seconds to begin our midcourse correction maneuver. Houston said the burn was "absolutely nominal" and that, so far, our flight path had been perfect. We were halfway to the moon.

After two full days into the mission we were 150,000 miles from Earth and our speed was less than 3,000 miles an hour. The moon was approximately 30 hours and 90,000 miles ahead of us.

We broke out the TV camera again. This would be our first time up into the LM, and Mission Control wanted to inspect it along with us. To give us room to pass through the connecting tunnel, Mike removed the probe and drogue assembly we'd used to dock the command module with the LM. We were immediately given a shock when we smelled the unmistakable stench of burned wiring that every astronaut dreads. But nothing seemed to be amiss and the electrical panel gave us good voltage readings for the circuits of the docking mechanism. Mike handed Neil the triangular spearpoint of the probe. This vital piece of equipment was in perfect condition.

"Mike must have done a smooth job on that docking," Neil told Houston. "There isn't a dent or mark on the probe."

I floated up through the tunnel, dragging the portable TV camera with me. Because the command module and the LM were docked head to head, I expected a jolt of disorientation when *up* and *down* reversed themselves as I crossed into the LM cabin, but the transition seemed perfectly natural.

The LM flight deck was about as charming as the cab of a diesel locomotive. Weight restrictions prevented the use of paneling, so all the wiring bundles and plumbing were exposed. Everywhere I looked there were rivets and circuit breakers. The hull had been sprayed with a dull gray fire-resistant coating. Some people had said the first moon landing would be the culmination of the Industrial Revolution; well, the lunar module certainly looked industrial enough to prove it.

But the *Eagle* was a featherweight locomotive. It could accelerate from zero to 3,000 miles per hour in two minutes during the ascent. The walls of the pressure cabin were so thin I could have jabbed a screwdriver through them without a lot of effort. Everything had been stripped down to the extreme. Even the safety covers had been removed from the circuit breakers and switches.

After lunch that day I asked Neil if he knew what he was going to say when he stepped onto the lunar surface. He took a sip of fruit juice and shook his head. "Not yet," he said, "I'm still thinking it over."

On our second day outbound, *Apollo 11* flew into the shadow of the moon, which was now less than 40,000 miles away. From where we were the moon eclipsed the sun, but was lit from the back by a brilliant halo of refracted sunlight. There was also a milky glow of Earthshine highlighting the biggest ridges and craters. This bizarre lighting transformed the moon into a shadowy sphere that was three-dimensional but without definition.

"The view of the moon that we've been having recently is really spectacular," Neil reported. "It's a view worth the price of the trip."

We strapped ourselves to the couches again the next day to get ready to swing around the left-hand edge of the moon. Hidden around the far side, we would experience loss of signal and would be out of touch with Houston for 48 minutes; that would be when Mike would punch the PROCEED button that would fire the SPS engine for lunar orbit insertion. I gazed to my right out the small window. All I saw was the corrugated, grayish-tan moonscape. The back side of the moon was much more rugged than the face we saw from Earth. This side had been bombarded by meteors since the beginning of the solar system millions of centuries ago. Mike read off the digits from his DSKY screen. The burn began exactly on time. My hand settled on my chest, and the calves of my legs flexed. This had to go right. For six minutes the SPS engine burned silently, slowing the spacecraft to just over 3,600 miles per hour, the speed necessary for us to be "captured" by lunar gravity. When the engine finally stopped, we rose again, weightless against our couch straps. Mike was beaming. We had slipped over the rim of the moon's gravity well. Tomorrow, Neil and I would board the LM and slide all the way down to the surface.

Thirty minutes later, we passed around the front of the moon and our earphones crackled with the static of Houston's radio signal.

"...*Apollo 11*, this is Houston. How do you read?" I could hear in Bruce McCandless's voice the strain they'd endured waiting for us. For over 40 minutes no one had known if the LOI burn had gone safely.

"Read you loud and clear, Houston," Mike answered.

"Could you repeat your burn status report?" In my mind I could see the rows of anxious faces at the consoles in Mission Control.

Mike was grinning his famous grin. "It was like . . . it was like *perfect*."

Before the second burn, which would circularize our lunar orbit, we had to align our navigation platform's gyroscopes using star sightings. Mike was down at the navigation station, his face against the eyepiece, his legs floating free. He used the code numbers of the stars from our charts, but we double-checked them with their proper names . . . Rigel, Altair, Fomalhaut. . . . These exotic names had been given to the stars by the ancient Sumerians, the world's first navigators. The names had been carried forward by the Greeks and Romans, through the Arab mariners to the Age of Exploration. When Columbus took a star sight, he too pronounced those names. Now Mike Collins, command module pilot of *Apollo 11*, was using them in our voyage to the moon.

Neil and I had moved into the LM in preparation for undocking from *Columbia*. Mike told us to be patient while he worked through his preseparation checklist. Mike had to replace the drogue and probe carefully before sealing off the command module and separating from the LM. We were all conscious of the fragile docking mechanism. In 24 hours, we would be needing that tunnel again. When Mike finally finished we were on the far side of the moon again, in the middle of our thirteenth orbit.

Back on the moon's near side, we contacted Houston, so that Mission Control could monitor the stream of data from the LM and CSM. The hatches were sealed; now the LM was truly the *Eagle* and the command module was *Columbia*. "How's the czar over there?" Mike asked Neil.

Neil watched the numbers blinking on our DSKY, counting down for the separation maneuver. "Just hanging on and punching buttons," Neil answered. We exchanged long blocks of data with Mike and with Houston. The numbers seemed endless.

Houston rewarded us with a terse, "You are go for separation, *Columbia*."

Mike backed the command module away with a snapping thump. Then the moonscape seemed to rotate slowly past my window as the LM turned, until it hung above my head. "The *Eagle* has wings," Neil called.

Neil and I stood almost shoulder to shoulder in our full pressure suits and bubble helmets, tethered to the deck of the LM by elastic cords. Now we were the ones who were engrossed with long checklists. But I felt a sharp urgency as I flipped each switch and tapped the data updates into the DSKY. When Mike thrust away from us in *Columbia*, he simply said, "Okay, *Eagle*, you guys take care."

"See you later," was all Neil replied. It sounded as if they were heading home after an easy afternoon in the simulator room.

Just before Neil and I looped around the back of the moon for the second time in the LM, Charlie Duke, who was now capcom, told us, "*Eagle*, Houston. You are go for DOI."

"Descent orbit insertion" was a 29.8-second burn of our descent engine that would drop the perilune, the lowest point in our orbit, to eight miles above the surface. If everything still looked good at that point, Houston would approve powered descent initiation (PDI). Twelve minutes later, Neil and I would either be on the moon or would have aborted the landing attempt.

The LM flew backward, with our two cabin windows parallel to the gray surface of the moon. The DOI burn was so smooth that I didn't even feel a vibration through my boots, only a slow sagging in my knees as the deceleration mounted when we throttled up from 10 percent to 100 percent thrust. Before the throttle-up was finished, I could tell from the landing radar data that our orbit was already bending. Neil turned a page in the flight plan and grinned at me through his helmet.

The moon rolled by silently outside my window. The craters were slowly becoming more distinct as we descended. There wasn't much to do except monitor the instruments and wait for AOS (acquisition of signal). As we got closer, the moon's color changed from beige to bleached gray. The hissing crackle of Houston's signal returned to our earphones. "*Eagle*, Houston," Charlie Duke called through the static. "If you read, you're go for powered descent. Over."

Neil nodded, his tired eyes warm with anticipation. I was grinning like a kid. We were going to land on the moon.

Manned Spacecraft Center, Houston, Texas, July 20, 1969

Mission Control was quiet. The terracelike rows of consoles descended to the front rank, the "trench." Plaques from all of NASA's manned missions were hung along the walls. Wide data-projection screens covering the front wall "scribed" the *Eagle*'s descent trajectory toward the surface of the moon.

Flight director Gene Kranz hunched over his console in the second row, listening to his team's callouts. Their acronyms had become nicknames: FIDO (flight dynamics officer) and GUIDO (guidance officer), and this shift's capcom was Charlie Duke. *Eagle* was descending through 42,000 feet and had just yawed around to its pre-programmed attitude. GUIDO, a 26-year-old engineer named Steve Bales sitting at the middle console in the trench, gave Kranz the intermediate "go."

"Capcom," Kranz told Charlie, "they are go."

"*Eagle*, Houston," Charlie Duke called. "You are go. Take it all at four minutes.... You are go to continue powered descent."

The data on the consoles showed that the LM's pitchover was correct. But when the digits 12 02 suddenly appeared on Bales's screen, he knew the same alarm was flashing on *Eagle*'s DSKY.

"Twelve-oh-two," I called. "Twelve-oh-two."

The 12 01 and 12 02 codes were called "executive overflow," meaning that the LM's onboard computer was overloaded with data. We didn't necessarily have to abort on this signal—not yet, at least. Bales saw that *Eagle*'s computer was recycling, so the hardware was probably still in good condition. But with the LM a quarter million miles away, dropping toward the moon's surface, he couldn't be 100 percent certain this wasn't an indication that something else was wrong.

"Give us the reading on the twelve-oh-two program alarm," Neil Armstrong called, his voice strained.

"GUIDO?" Kranz asked.

Bales again scanned his data, and then replied, "Go."

Charlie Duke frowned. "We've got...we're go on that alarm."

In the back row, Bob Gilruth, Chris Kraft, George Low, and Sam Phillips stared at their consoles. Kraft was the only one who knew anything about the program alarms. A man with close-cropped white hair sat alone at the far end of the row. It was John Houbolt, the Langley mathematician who had successfully backed Lunar Orbit Rendezvous.

Eagle was approaching 4,000 feet. Gene Kranz leaned forward to speak into his microphone. He had a crewcut and wore narrow black ties that made him look like he'd successfully avoided the 1960s altogether. "All flight controllers, coming up on go–no go for landing," he told his officers. "FIDO?"

"Go!"

"GUIDO," Kranz asked, "you happy?"

Bales had to either fish or cut bait. The program alarms were popping up again, though they weren't signaling an obvious problem with the hardware. But he just couldn't be certain *Eagle* would have a good computer for ascent the next day. "Go!" he answered.

"*Eagle*," Charlie Duke called, "you're go for landing."

Twenty seconds later, *Eagle* passed through 2,000 feet and another program alarm flashed.

"Twelve alarm," Neil called. "Twelve-oh-one."

"Roger," Charlie acknowledged. "Twelve-oh-one alarm."

"GUIDO?" Kranz asked. Even his voice was strained.

Deke Slayton was sitting next to Kranz, and he was almost doubled over with tension, dragging deeply on a cigarillo.

Bales looked at the data on his screen. "Go."

"We're go," Charlie Duke told *Eagle*. "Hang tight, we're go...."[2]

Lunar Module *Eagle,* July 20, 1969

We were just 700 feet above the surface when Charlie gave us the final "go," just as another 12 02 alarm flashed. Neil and I confirmed with each other that the landing radar was giving us good data, and he punched PROCEED into the keyboard. All these alarms had kept us from studying our landing zone. If this had been a simulation back at the Cape, we probably would have aborted. Neil finally looked away from the DSKY screen and out his triangular window. He was definitely not satisfied with the ground beneath us. We were too low to identify the landmark craters we'd studied from the *Apollo 10* photographs. We just had to find a smooth place to land. The computer, however, was taking us to a boulder field surrounding a 40-foot-wide crater.

Neil rocked his hand controller in his fist, changing over to manual command. He slowed our descent from 20 feet per second to only nine. Then, at 300 feet, we were descending at only three and a half feet per second. As *Eagle* slowly dropped, we continued skimming forward.

Neil still wasn't satisfied with the terrain. All I could do was give him the altimeter callouts and our horizontal speed. He stroked the hand controller and descent-rate switch like a motorist fine-tuning his cruise control. We scooted across the boulders. At two hundred feet our hover slid toward a faster descent rate.

"Eleven forward, coming down nicely," I called, my eyes scanning the instruments. "Two hundred feet, four and a half down. Five and a half down. One sixty...." The low-fuel light blinked on the caution-and-warning panel, "...quantity light."

At 200 feet, Neil slowed the descent again. The horizon of the moon was at eye level. We were almost out of fuel.

"Sixty seconds," Charlie warned.

The ascent engine fuel tanks were full, but completely separate from the descent engine. We had 60 seconds of fuel remaining in the descent stage before we had to land or abort. Neil searched the ground below.

"Down two and a half," I called. The LM moved forward like a helicopter flaring out for landing. We were in the so-called dead man's zone, and we couldn't remain there long. If we ran out of fuel at this altitude, we would crash into the surface before the ascent engine could lift us back toward orbit. "Forward. Forward. Good. Forty feet. Down two and a half. Picking up some dust. Thirty feet...."

Thirty feet below the LM's gangly legs, dust that had lain undisturbed for a billion years blasted sideways in the plume of our engine.

"Thirty seconds," Charlie announced solemnly, but still Neil slowed our rate.

The descent engine roared silently, sucking up the last of its fuel supply. I turned my eye to the ABORT STAGE button. "Drifting right," I called, watching the shadow of a footpad probe lightly touching the surface. "Contact light." The horizon seemed to rock gently and then steadied. Our altimeter stopped blinking. We were on the moon. We had about 20 seconds of fuel remaining in the descent stage. Immediately I prepared for a sudden abort, in case the landing had damaged the *Eagle* or the surface was not strong enough to support our weight.

"Okay, engine stop," I told Neil, reciting from the checklist. "ACA out of detent."

"Got it," Neil answered, disengaging the hand control system. Both of us were still tingling with the excitement of the final moments before touchdown.

"Mode controls, both auto," I continued, aware that I was chanting the readouts. "Descent engine command override, off. Engine arm, off...."

"We copy you down, *Eagle*," Charlie Duke interrupted from Houston.

I stared out at the rocks and shadows of the moon. It was as stark as I'd ever imagined it. A mile away, the horizon curved into blackness.

"Houston," Neil called, "Tranquillity Base here. The *Eagle* has landed."

It was strange to be suddenly stationary. Spaceflight had always meant movement to me, but here we were rock-solid still, as if the LM had been standing here since the beginning of time. We'd been told to expect the remaining fuel in the descent stage to slosh back and forth after we touched down, but there simply wasn't enough reserve fuel remaining to do this. Neil had flown the landing to the very edge.

"Roger, Tranquillity," Charlie said, "we copy you on the ground. You've got a bunch of guys about to turn blue. We're breathing again. Thanks a lot."

I reached across and shook Neil's hand, hard. We had pulled it off. Five months and 10 days before the end of the decade, two Americans had landed on the moon.

"It looks like a collection of just every variety of shapes, angularities, granularities, every variety of rock you could find...," I told Houston. Everyone wanted to know what the moon looked like. The glaring sunrise was directly behind us like a huge searchlight. It bleached out the color, but the grays swam in from the sides of my window.

Charlie said there were "lots of smiling faces in this room, and all over the world."

Neil grinned at me, the strain leaving his tired eyes. I smiled back. "There are two of them up here," I told Charlie.

Mike's voice cut in much louder and clearer than Mission Control. "And don't forget the one in the command module."

Charlie told Mike to speak directly to us. "Roger, Tranquillity Base," Mike said. "It sounded great from up here. You guys did a fantastic job."

That was a real compliment coming from a pilot as skilled as Mike Collins.

"Thank you," Neil said. "Just keep that orbiting base ready for us up there now."

We were supposed to do a little housekeeping in the LM, eat a meal, and then try to sleep for seven hours before getting ready to explore the surface. But whoever signed off on that plan didn't know much psychology—or physiology, for that matter. We'd just landed on the moon and there was a lot of adrenaline still zinging through our bodies. Telling us to try to sleep *before* the EVA was like telling kids on Christmas morning they had to stay in bed until noon.

I decided to begin a ceremony I'd planned with Dean Woodruff, my pastor at Webster Presbyterian Church. He'd given me a tiny Communion kit that had a silver chalice and wine vial about the size of the tip of my little finger. I asked "every person listening in, whoever and wherever they may be, to pause for a moment and contemplate the events of the past few hours, and to give thanks in his or her own way." The plastic note-taking shelf in front of our DSKY became the altar. I read silently from Dean's Communion service—*I am the wine and you are the branches...*—as I poured the wine into the chalice. The wine looked liked syrup as it swirled around the sides of the cup in the light gravity before it finally settled at the bottom.

Eagle's metal body creaked. I ate the tiny Host and swallowed the wine. I gave thanks for the intelligence and spirit that had brought two young pilots to the Sea of Tranquillity.

Suiting up for the moon walk took us several hours. Our PLSS backpacks looked simple, but they were hard to put on and tricky to operate. They were truly our life-support systems, with enough oxygen, cooling water, electrical power, and radio equipment to keep us alive on the moon and in constant contact with Houston (via a relay in the LM) for four hours. On Earth, the PLSS and spacesuit combination weighed 190 pounds, but here it was only 30. Combined with my own body weight, that brought me to a total lunar-gravity weight of around 60 pounds.

Seven hours after we touched down on the moon, we depressurized the LM, and Neil opened the hatch. My job was to guide him as he backed out on his hands and knees onto the small porch. He worked slowly, trying not to jam his backpack on the hatch frame. When he reached the ladder attached to the forward landing leg, he moved down carefully.

The new capcom, Bruce McCandless, verified that we were doing everything correctly. Once Neil reached over and pulled a line to deploy the LM's television camera, Bruce said, "We're getting a picture on the TV."

"I'm at the foot of the ladder," Neil said, his voice slow and precise. "The LM footpads are only depressed in the surface about one or two inches." The surface was a very fine-grain powder. "I'm going to step off the LM now...."

From my window I watched Neil move his blue lunar overshoe from the metal dish of the footpad to the powdery gray surface.

"That's one small step for... man, one giant leap for mankind."

*   *   *

Lunar gravity was so springy that coming down the ladder was both pleasant and tricky. I took a practice run at getting back up to that high first step, and then I hopped down beside Neil.

"Isn't that something?" Neil asked. "Magnificent sight out here."

I turned around and looked out at a horizon that dropped steeply away in all directions. We were looking "down sun," so there was only a black void beyond the edge of the moon. For as far as I could see, pebbles, rock fragments, and small craters covered the surface. Off to the left, I could make out the rim of a larger crater. I breathed deeply, goose flesh covering my neck and face. "Beautiful, beautiful," I said. "Magnificent desolation."

Stepping out of the LM's shadow was a shock. One moment I was in total darkness, the next in the sun's hot floodlight. From the ladder I had seen all the sunlit moonscape beyond our shadow, but with no atmosphere, there was absolutely no refracted light around me. I stuck my hand out past the shadow's edge into the sun, and it was like punching through a barrier into another dimension. I moved around the legs of the LM to check for damage.

"Looks like the secondary strut has a little thermal effect on it right here, Neil," I said, pointing to some engine burn on the leg.

"Yeah," Neil said, coming over beside me. "I noticed that."

We were both in the sun again, our helmets close together. Neil leaned toward me and clapped his gloved hand on my shoulder. "Isn't it fun?" he said.

I was grinning ear to ear, even though the gold visor hid my face. Neil and I were standing together on the *moon*.

As we moved about getting ready to set up our experiments, I watched the toe of my boot strike the surface. The gray dust shot out with machinelike precision, the grains landing nearly equidistant from my toe. I was fascinated by this, and for the first time *felt* what it was like to walk on the airless moon.

One of my tests was to jog away from the LM to see how maneuverable an astronaut was on the surface. I remembered what Isaac Newton had taught us two centuries before: mass and weight are not the same. I weighed only 60 pounds, but my *mass* was the same as it was on Earth. Inertia was a problem. I had to plan ahead several steps to bring myself to a stop or to turn, without falling.

But after a few jogging turns, I figured out how to move quite easily. Time was going by quickly, I realized, when Neil signaled me over to unveil the plaque. We stood beside the LM leg and Neil read the words:

"HERE MEN FROM THE PLANET EARTH

FIRST SET FOOT UPON THE MOON

JULY 1969, A.D.

WE CAME IN PEACE FOR ALL MANKIND."

One of the first things Neil did on the surface was take a sample of the lunar soil in case we had to terminate our moon walk early. Now he started working with his scoop and collection box while I set up the metal foil "window shade" of the solar wind collector. The moon was like a giant sponge that absorbed the constant "wind" of charged particles streaming outward from the sun. Scientists back on Earth would examine the collector to learn more about this phenomenon and, through it, the history of the solar system.

As we removed the flag from the equipment compartment at the base of the LM, I suddenly felt stage fright. Since childhood I'd been fascinated by explorers planting flags on strange shores. Now I was about to do the same thing, but on the most exotic shore mankind had ever reached.

Of all the jobs I had to do on the moon, the one I wanted to go the smoothest was the flag raising. Bruce had told us we were being watched by the largest television audience in history, over a billion people. Just beneath the powdery surface, the subsoil was very dense. We succeeded in pushing the flagpole in only a couple of inches. It didn't look very sturdy. But I did snap off a crisp West Point salute once we got the banner upright.

I noticed that the legs of my spacesuit were smeared with sooty dust, probably from the LM footpad. When we removed our helmets back inside *Eagle*, there would be no way we would be able to keep from breathing some of that dust. If strange microbes *were* in this soil, Neil and I would be the first guinea pigs to test their effects.

Bruce told us that President Richard Nixon wanted to speak to us. More stage fright. The president said, "For one priceless moment, in the whole history of man, all the people on this Earth are truly one."

I looked high above the dome of the LM. Earth hung in the black sky, a disk cut in half by the day-night terminator. It was mostly blue, with swirling white clouds, and I could make out a brown landmass, North Africa and the Middle East. Glancing down at my boots, I realized that the soil Neil and I had stomped through had been here longer than any of those brown continents. Earth was a dynamic planet of tectonic plates, churning oceans, and a changing atmosphere. The moon was dead, a relic of the early solar system.

Time was moving in spasms. We still had many tasks to accomplish. Some seemed quite easy and others dragged on. It took me a long time to erect the passive seismometer (the "moonquake" detector). We were supposed to level it by using a BB-type device centered in a little cup. But the BB just swirled around and around in the light gravity. I spent a long time with that, but it still wouldn't go level. Then I looked back, and the ball was right where it should be.

"You have approximately three minutes until you must commence your EVA termination activities," Bruce told us. Our time walking on the moon was almost over.

I was already on the ladder when Neil reminded me about the mementos we had planned to leave on the moon. From a shoulder pocket I removed a small packet that held the two Soviet medals and the *Apollo 1* patch, as well as a small gold olive branch, one of four we'd bought. We'd given the other three to our wives as a way of joining them to our mission. The packet also contained the tiny silicone disk marked "From Planet Earth" and etched with goodwill messages from the leaders of 73 nations, including the Soviet Union. I tossed the pouch onto the soil among our jumbled footprints. Once more I thought of Ed White. Only 10 years before we had talked about becoming rocket pilots. In a way, Ed had come with me to the moon.

Inside the LM, we still had to stow 40 pounds of moon rocks in two aluminum boxes. Houston needed endless exchanges of data so we could align our navigation computer. Then we had to discard our PLSS backpacks, our overshoes, and all the other refuse of our brief stay to cut down on our weight for the ascent. Mission Control told us that our moonquake seismometer had recorded the impact of our gear being tossed out the hatch.

Finally it was time to eat and sleep. After we snacked on cocktail sausages and fruit punch, I stretched out on the deck beneath the instrument panel, and Neil propped himself across the ascent engine cover, with his boots wedged into a sling under the DSKY. With the windows shaded, the LM grew cold. Neil was having trouble getting to sleep because of the glare of Earth reflected through our telescope on his face. We had moon dust smeared on our suit legs and on the deck. It was like gritty charcoal and smelled like gunpowder from the fireworks I'd launched so many years before on the New Jersey shore.

Seven hours later we prepared for ascent. There was an almost constantly active three-way loop of radio traffic connecting *Columbia*, *Eagle*, and Mission Control. We discovered during a long checklist recitation that the ascent engine's arming circuit breaker was broken off on the panel. The little plastic pin simply wasn't there. This circuit would send electrical power to the engine that would lift us off the moon. Finally I realized my backpack must have struck it when I'd been getting ready for my EVA.

Neil and I looked at each other. Our fatigue had reached the point where our thoughts had become plodding. But this got our attention. We looked around for something to punch in this circuit breaker. Luckily, a felt-tipped pen fit into the slot.

At 123 hours and 58 minutes GET, Houston told us, "You're cleared for takeoff."

"Roger," I answered. "Understand we're number one on the runway."

I watched the DSKY numbers and chanted the countdown: "Four, three, two, one...*proceed*."

Our liftoff was powerful. Nothing we'd done in the simulators had prepared us for this amazing swoop upward in the weak lunar gravity. Within seconds we had pitched forward a sharp 45 degrees and were soaring above the crater fields.

"Very smooth," I called, "very quiet ride." It wasn't at all like flying through Earth's atmosphere. Climbing fast, we finally spotted the landmark craters we'd missed during the descent. Two minutes into the ascent, we were batting along at half a mile per second.

Columbia was above and behind us. Our radar and the computers on the two spacecraft searched for each other and then locked on and communicated in a soundless digital exchange.

*   *   *

Four hours after Neil and I lifted off from the Sea of Tranquillity, we heard the capture latches clang shut above our heads. Mike had successfully docked with *Eagle*. I loosened the elastic cords and reached around to throw more switches. Soon Mike would unseal the tunnel so that Neil and I could pass the moon rocks through and then join Mike in *Columbia* for the long ride back.

I hadn't slept in almost 40 hours and there was a thickness to my voice and movements. Still I could feel a calmness rising inside me. A thruster fired on *Columbia*, sending a shiver through the two spacecraft.

Seven hours later, we were in our last lunar orbit, above the far side, just past the terminator into dawn. We had cast *Eagle*'s ascent stage loose into an orbit around the moon, where it would remain for hundreds of years. Maybe, I thought, astronauts will visit our flyweight locomotive sometime in the future. Mike rode the left couch for the trans-Earth injection burn. Our SPS engine simply had to work, or we'd be stranded. The burn would consume five tons of propellant in two and a half minutes, increasing our speed by 2,000 miles per hour, enough to break the bonds of the moon's gravity.

We waited, all three of us watching the DSKY. "Three, two, one," Mike said, almost whispering.

Ignition was right on the mark. I sank slowly into my couch. NASA's bold gamble with Lunar Orbit Rendezvous had paid off. Twenty minutes after the burn we rounded the moon's right-hand limb for the final time.

"Hello. *Apollo 11*, Houston," Charlie Duke called from Earth. "How did it go?"

Neil was smiling. "Tell them to open up the LRL doors, Charlie," he said, referring to our quarantine in the Lunar Receiving Laboratory.

"Roger," Charlie answered. "We got you coming home."

The moon's horizon tilted past my window. Earth hung in the dark universe, warm and welcoming.

Our first quarantine quarters were in a modified aluminum trailer parked on the hangar deck of the recovery ship, the aircraft carrier *Hornet*. In our first hour back on Earth I took what was the best shower of my life. Neil, Mike, and I dressed in comfortable blue flying suits and then went to a window of the quarantine trailer, where President Nixon officially welcomed us back. The hot television lights were right in our faces.

Nixon had a reputation for being cold and calculating, but on this morning in the western Pacific, he actually danced a little jig when he saw us. I was beginning to understand how historic our flight had been.

Twenty days later, we were released from quarantine in the large LRL facility in Houston. None of us had caught so much as a sniffle from the lunar dust.

On August 13, NASA sent us on a hectic one-day tour of New York, Chicago, and Los Angeles, before we began an even more frantic world tour. That morning in New York, Neil, Mike, and I rode in an open convertible up Broadway toward City Hall. The streets of lower Manhattan boomed with cheers and applause. The air was full of confetti and ticker tape. At one point the crowd surged past the police barriers and into the street, slowing our motorcade. A troop of Boy Scouts marched in place just ahead, each one holding an American flag.

America, I saw, had focused her pride on us, the young men who had planted her flag on the moon. I felt a sudden rush of pride for the country that had sent us on our bold mission.

EPILOGUE

VENTURING OUTWARD

1969 TO 2009

Kennedy Space Center, Cape Canaveral, 1989

Ten more Americans walked on the moon after July 1969, when Neil, Mike, and I splashed down in the Pacific beside the *Hornet*. The program's only in-flight emergency occurred during the *Apollo 13* mission in April 1970, when Jim Lovell, Jack Swigert, and Fred Haise were almost stranded in space after an oxygen tank exploded on their service module, halfway out to the moon. (They used their LM as a lifeboat for the free return loop around the moon and back to Earth.)

The Apollo moon landings were a great scientific and engineering achievement. By the time *Apollo 14* landed on the rolling hills of the Fra Mauro formation, the LM had been modified to permit surface stays of several days, and on the last three flights, the astronauts carried out geological surveys aboard the lunar rover, a lightweight, battery-powered "buggy" that greatly extended their range. The Apollo astronauts brought back over 1,000 pounds of lunar rock and soil, consisting of 2,000 separate samples taken from all of the moon's major types of geological formations.[1] In addition, they deployed sophisticated instruments to measure lunar seismic activity, lunar gravity, lunar magnetism, and solar radiation.

The Apollo astronauts proved themselves among the most skilled explorers in history. We helped unravel the mystery of the moon's origin, discovering that the moon is composed mainly of volcanic basalt-type rock dating to the birth of the solar system, about 4.6 billion years ago. Apollo surface samples also proved that the moon had been shaped by both volcanism and meteorite impacts.

The greatest technical achievement of Apollo probably was the development of a practical interplanetary exploration organization that combined the resources of NASA, the commercial sector, and our university laboratories. America answered John Kennedy's challenge and thus learned how to explore the solar system. Project Apollo matured remarkably during the four years that spanned the six landings. Neil and I landed four miles beyond our planned touchdown site on the Sea of Tranquillity, but NASA trajectory experts made sure that subsequent flights landed with pinpoint accuracy. For example, *Apollo 12* made an extraordinarily accurate touchdown only 600 feet from an unmanned Surveyor. Pete Conrad even recovered parts of the robot probe. And on the last moon landing, *Apollo 17*, Gene Cernan and Jack Schmitt landed in a narrow box canyon among the jumbled ridges of the Taurus Mountains, an area that is scientifically rich because of its varied geology. Earlier in the program this site would have been dismissed as too risky.

Project Apollo's success made its aftermath even more difficult to accept. As busy as Tom Paine and NASA leaders were during those first six months of 1969, they were also obliged to begin planning a post-Apollo manned spaceflight program. In February 1969, President Nixon reconstituted the Space Task Group to formalize this policymaking. Vice President Spiro Agnew was the titular head of this body, but Tom Paine, presidential science adviser Lee A. DuBridge, and Air Force secretary Robert Seamans, a former senior NASA official, were its most active leaders.

In the summer of 1969, the group presented their blueprint for America's future in space. The centerpiece was a bold initiative like Apollo: a Mars landing by American astronauts before the end of the century. The Space Task Group proposed three alternative ways of achieving this goal. The first was an all-out drive that would surpass even Apollo's intense effort and land on Mars by 1983. A slightly less intense (and considerably less expensive) effort called for the landing by the late 1980s. Finally, a slower, cheaper program would land Americans on Mars sometime in the 1990s.

They returned to Wernher von Braun's Mars project proposal of the 1940s, which involved assembling the interplanetary spacecraft at a permanently manned space station in low Earth orbit—a transportation depot perched halfway up Earth's gravity well. A fleet of large, completely reusable space shuttles would deliver crews and material to and from the space station. These vehicles would combine the best characteristics of large jet transports with the performance of powerful, expendable boosters.

The cost of this Mars program was staggering, even if Congress accepted the cheapest option. But in 1969 we were deeply involved in the Vietnam War. At the same time, the White House was dismembering the domestic initiatives of Lyndon Johnson's Great Society. Nixon's Republicans were in the White House, but the Democrats controlled Congress. It wasn't a good time for bold space challenges.

The projected Mars landing did not survive long, and the concept of a permanent orbiting spaceport was eventually abandoned. That left the space shuttle as a launcher without a valid mission. Unmanned expendable boosters—which we then had in great supply—could launch satellites and space probes more cheaply, without risking astronauts. But NASA's leaders couldn't bring themselves to accept the fact their spacefaring legs had been cut off.

The space shuttle would eventually be approved, but the program's budget virtually doomed it to failure years before it ever flew. Stripped of the goal of planetary exploration, NASA adapted its Apollo hardware to fly three separate, three-man crews aboard the *Skylab 1* space station, which had been adapted from a Saturn S-IVB upper stage. Even though Skylab was much less ambitious than the originally proposed orbiting spaceport, the facility was large and flexible, an ideal laboratory in which to test the physiological effects of spaceflight, to conduct space science experiments, and to expand the space manufacturing tests that had begun with Apollo. We discovered that the zero-G environment offered great promise for certain high-technology manufacturing processes: blending new alloys, purifying pharmaceuticals, and growing flawless crystals.

Skylab astronauts spent up to 84 days aboard *Skylab*, a world record at that time. The final Saturn-Apollo launch came in July 1975, with the Apollo-Soyuz Test Project (ASTP), an offshoot of the prevailing détente with the Soviet Union. Deke Slayton finally got his chance to fly in space. This flight gave NASA some insights into the Soviet space program, and provided the Soviets with no-risk detailed knowledge of our rendezvous and docking expertise and a most valuable observation of our quality and reliability program.

Developing the shuttle absorbed almost all of NASA's shrunken budget. *Skylab* was abandoned, marooned in orbit, supposedly waiting for the first space shuttle flights to bring crews to it. But the space shuttle's development dragged on, and *Skylab*'s orbit decayed. In 1979, the beautifully engineered orbital laboratory burned up in the atmosphere. Its reentry rained a billion-dollar cloud of debris on the western Australian desert.

Cost effectiveness was the driving factor in the design of the space shuttle. Because Congress had soured on bold exploration, NASA sold the shuttle as a versatile delivery vehicle that could move both cargoes and crews "routinely" to and from space at a fraction of what expendable boosters cost. Congress and the Nixon White House liked this idea.

But the shuttle NASA had first conceived and the one it got were vastly different. The original concept called for a *completely* reusable system: a large winged booster to be flown by astronauts that would carry a smaller winged orbiter, also manned by astronauts. The big booster would piggyback the orbiter from the launch pad to hypersonic speed above the atmosphere; then the booster would fly back to land at Cape Kennedy, while the orbiter would ignite an engine to kick itself the rest of the way into Earth orbit. This was a brilliant design. And NASA's best innovators, including Max Faget, the father of the Mercury and Apollo designs, contributed to it. But the concept would have required a large financial investment during the development phase, which would, however, result in relatively inexpensive operational costs.

The administration and Congress rebelled. NASA was given $6.5 billion and told it must build the shuttle for that. Further, NASA was pressured into promising that the shuttle would repay its development costs by routinely delivering cargo such as scientific, communications, and military satellites to space at a fraction of the cost of expendable boosters.

NASA produced a design for a *partially* reusable vehicle involving a delta-winged orbiter with a large cargo bay and its own cryogenic engines—strap-on solid rocket boosters (SRBs), which were ostensibly reusable—and a huge throwaway external tank. Fitting the heatproof tiles on to the curved surface of the orbiter turned out to be an almost impossible task. By January 1986, when the space shuttle *Challenger* exploded 50,000 feet above the Cape, killing its seven-member crew, the shuttle program had already demonstrated the failure of its compromised development process.

Since the *Challenger* accident, America has wisely returned to a mixed fleet of manned and unmanned launchers. The Atlas and Titan assembly lines are rolling again, just as they did during the days of Mercury and Gemini. From now on, the shuttle will launch only payloads that require the participation of astronauts. Expendable launch vehicles (ELVs) will launch weather satellites and military payloads without risking human crews. Fifteen years after the last Apollo moon landing, NASA is regaining some of our lost booster potential.

What has happened to manned spaceflight? During Apollo, American astronauts regularly flew the *240,000* miles out to the moon. In 27 space shuttle flights between 1981 and 1988, no American astronaut has flown higher than *240* miles above Earth.

In 1983, NASA resurrected the idea of a permanently manned space station. This large, low-Earth-orbit space station will be called *Freedom*. It is supposed to provide (in one convenient location) a materials research and a life sciences laboratory, as well as astronomy and manufacturing facilities. However, contrary to some people's belief, *Freedom* will not have the originally proposed function of a transportation depot (spaceport) for the assembly of manned interplanetary vehicles. In order to spread the cost and to promote Western technical cooperation, NASA has secured the participation of the Japanese, the Canadians, and the European Space Agency in the design and construction of *Freedom*.

NASA continues to believe in *Freedom*'s potential as a spaceport for planetary exploration, but the agency is faced with a by now familiar dilemma. Without bold leadership from the White House and Congress, our space policy is being shaped by the short-term, often conflicting goals of the disparate "aerospace community." Despite promises that *Freedom* will be all things to all members of this group, it will actually satisfy very few of them well.

For example, chemists and physicists investigating the properties of materials in microgravity are extremely concerned about the vibration and acceleration disturbances that *Freedom* will experience, since spaceborne astronomers would frequently be maneuvering their equipment to observe different phenomena. Likewise, orbital manufacturing specialists would have their needs, which often might involve "polluting" the local space environment with vented substances. Permanently manning the facility will require a dynamic life-support system, which in turn will interfere with space science and manufacturing processes.

Finally, we space exploration people will have an altogether different, and equally incompatible, set of requirements. A true space transportation depot entails a large tank farm of volatile propellants and an assembly hangar protected from radiation and space debris, as well as astronauts whizzing back and forth in space scooters and numerous remote, robotic manipulator units—all of which conflict with other space station requirements.[2]

While American space policy has floundered in the 20 years since the Apollo program, the Soviet Union has moved steadily ahead in space. We thought the race was over; they didn't. The Soviets tested their large G booster twice more after their July 1969 accident. In June 1971, the booster broke apart at an altitude of 40,000 feet. On November 24, 1972, a third G booster was launched, but was destroyed at the edge of the atmosphere after it became unstable.[3]

The Soviets' goals in space were permanent. While tens of thousands of technicians worked on their manned lunar program, other design bureaus were developing unmanned spacecraft of the Lunokhod series, for the return of lunar samples. These robot probes landed at several sites on the moon and brought back small but scientifically valuable samples of lunar rock and soil to the Soviet Union.[4] Moscow was then able to claim that it had never intended to "risk the lives" of cosmonauts by sending them to the moon.

Parallel to these efforts, the Soviets developed the *Salyut* space station. *Salyut* was relatively unsophisticated (when compared to *Skylab*), but had many innovations in its design, including automatic docking capabilities with Progress resupply freighters. The early *Salyut* tests had lots of problems, including the Soviets' worst space accident, when three cosmonauts died aboard *Soyuz 11* in June 1971 while returning from a three-week stay aboard the space station.[5]

This setback led to the redesign of the Soyuz spacecraft. The result was the improved T Model of the Soyuz, which is now one of the most adaptable space vehicles ever built. Again, the Soviets' technology was less sophisticated than the Americans', but it fit their needs. By the mid-1980s, the Soviets had launched their large new *Mir* ("peace") space station. *Mir* is the core of an expandable modular space station that will eventually include augmented living quarters, laboratories for astrophysics, astronomy, and space medicine, and space manufacturing facilities. Although the Soviets also face compatibility problems among these different laboratories and workshops, they have shown themselves to be quite innovative in solving them.

Above all, in the last two decades, the Soviets have become the world's manned spaceflight leaders, with men continuously in orbit since 1986. Two cosmonauts have spent up to a year aboard *Mir*; the Soviets have been resourceful in meeting the physiological challenges of prolonged zero-G flight, which can have disastrous effects on the human skeletal and cardiovascular systems. Through rigorous, disciplined daily exercise with special equipment that helps them partially compensate for the absence of gravity, cosmonauts have been able to avoid the debilitation that plagued their predecessors. It is now generally accepted in the West that these long-duration Soviet space station flights are test-beds for manned interplanetary missions, probably to Mars, and possibly for the establishment of lunar orbiting space stations as well.

The Soviet Union also took over world leadership in boosters when we abandoned Saturn. And this lead has grown dramatically. The Soviets rarely throw anything away, if it works. They're still flying the workhorse Semyorka, as well as an upgraded Proton, and they've recently made their huge Energia operational. This is the world's most powerful rocket, equal to the Saturn V. The Energia is the direct descendant of the G-1 moon booster that exploded 12 days before the launch of *Apollo 11*. Despite repeated test failures, the Soviets never abandoned the project, but instead worked patiently to combine basic kerosene-LOX propulsion and cryogenic technology. Their new booster is both robust and flexible; it's the launch vehicle for their space shuttle

254 MEN FROM EARTH

Buran, as well as for their massive space station modules. We threw away such capability with Saturn.

After years of studying Venus with unmanned probes, the Soviets have turned their attention to Mars, particularly its two moons, Phobos and Deimos. Their unmanned *Phobos 1* spacecraft, which was to have landed on the small Martian moon in the summer of 1989, malfunctioned en route, an indication of the Soviets' ongoing lack of sophisticated computers. But the backup probe (*Phobos 2*) will attempt to execute the mission.

It's obvious that the Soviet Union is in space to stay and is progressively expanding its capabilities. Space success has brought them great international prestige, despite the loss of the moon race. As *glasnost* has shown us, the Soviet Union is in many ways a vast Third World country. But their massive military forces, their nuclear arsenal, and their space program give them superpower status. Their space budget far exceeds that of the West. More important, the percentage of their gross national product that they spend on space is dramatically larger than that of the Western nations. The Soviet Union recognizes the value of a long-term investment in space exploration and exploitation.

Meanwhile, American space policy remains muddled. Our current concern with the federal budget deficit, with updating our outdated manufacturing base, and with solving the problems of our economic underclass has diverted national attention from space. Taxpayers can only hope NASA is looking after the country's best interests, and NASA moves from one budget crisis to the next behind a serene facade of traditional can-do competence.

NASA's future plans certainly give the impression of preserving the agency's heritage of ambitious innovation. Officially, the agency plans a practical balance of major initiatives: mission to planet Earth; exploration of the solar system; outpost on the moon; and humans to Mars. The planet Earth mission would use the space station and unmanned satellites to study Earth's oceans and continents and help solve our many ecological problems. Solar system exploration involves a variety of unmanned probes to the outer planets and the asteroid belt. The outpost on the moon would use the shuttle and space station to build spacecraft to eventually create a permanent human "home on the moon" for up to 30 people by the year 2010. Finally, NASA's humans-to-Mars missions involve "expeditions" including brief manned excursions to the planet's surface in the first decade of the twenty-first century.[6]

Like the original descriptions of the space shuttle and the space station, these projections seem balanced and appropriate. But they're just as unrealistic as NASA's plans for the shuttle and space station were in 1971 and 1983. NASA's budget simply does not provide for this scale of activity. Such fundamental technologies as automatic rendezvous and docking, orbital cryogenic propellant depots, aerobraking deceleration, artificial gravity, "closed ecology" food production, and in-space construction techniques will all take many years to develop.

One of the most important, but least understood, lessons of Apollo is that America had committed itself to developing expensive, innovative spaceflight technology—the Saturn, with its cryogenic upper stages, and the Apollo CSM—several years *before* Kennedy challenged America to land men on the moon by the end of the 1960s. It was actually this preliminary investment in innovation that made Kennedy's challenge possible.

The argument against making a similar investment today always comes back to the budget deficit and pressing domestic needs, but if the percentage of our steadily growing GNP we invest in space remains constant, a surprisingly small two-tenths of a percent, we should have more than ample funds for a bold program of outreach into the solar system, involving exploitation of the moon's resources as well as robotic and manned exploration of the nearby planets. The question is, however, whether we will have adequate technology to accomplish the mission.

By the middle of the next century, world population will have grown to the so-called "equilibrium" level of between eight and 10 billion.[7] Meeting the energy needs of this population using conventional technology will quickly exhaust our fossil fuel reserves and permanently poison the environment through the greenhouse effect, ozone layer depletion, desertification, and ocean pollution. But if this swollen population does not receive enough energy to modernize, a widespread social upheaval will probably rip apart human civilization. Energy consumption is at the center of our dilemma. But there is virtually limitless solar energy available just a few hundred miles above the planet's surface. Cislunar space is eternally radiant with sunlight. Unfortunately, constructing the immense solar power satellites necessary to convert this sunlight to microwaves and beam it down to Earth to meet the planet's energy needs is an enormously expensive challenge, primarily because of Earth-based launch costs—if we rely on construction materials from Earth. But as I stated in an editorial on the fifteenth anniversary of our lunar landing: "The Solar System's most desirable space station already has six flags on it. Let's use it."[8] It's called the moon.

Converting large areas of the moon's flat seas into a solar power station might seem like a pipe dream. But we should remember that America's technical experts laughed at Wernher von Braun in 1945 when he projected the landing of a man on the moon. We know from the rocks the Apollo astronauts returned to Earth that the lunar seas have a mineral composition suitable for the construction of solar collectors.[9]

Another exciting energy resource on the moon is receiving considerable attention in both the West and the Soviet Union. Lunar samples have revealed an ample supply of the isotope helium-3 (He-3), which is very rare on Earth but has been deposited on the lunar surface over billions of years by the solar wind. It is now estimated that at least a million tons of He-3 are readily recoverable from the regolith formations where lunar solar power stations would be practical. This He-3 offers a key to safe, practical nuclear fusion energy on Earth. Unlike the deuterium fusion reactors now being developed, nuclear fusion reactors powered by He-3 would be almost completely devoid of radioactivity, and the reactor vessel would not be bombarded with destructive neutrons.[10]

It is estimated that a single ton of He-3 delivered to Earth would be worth at least $1 billion. And much of Earth's future energy needs could be met by burning only 200 tons of He-3 a year in environmentally benign fusion reactors. From this point of view, the concept of a well-organized, large-scale return to the moon to exploit its resources becomes quite compelling.

America won the first moon race. But it is possible we will become a second-rate space power in the next century. Already the European Economic Community is looking toward the Soviet Union as its natural space partner. The Japanese are sitting on the fence, still impressed by our competence, but beginning to seriously question our resolve. These national rivalries pale in comparison to mounting global social, economic, and ecological problems. When I return to the Cape and walk across the pitted concrete apron of Launch Pad 39-A, I recall the urgency of the race between the Soviet Union and America for the moon. But I now know that neither great power can afford to waste its precious space resources on another "footprints and flagpoles" sprint expedition to Mars.

The alternative, proposed by some in the West, that we comply with *every* Soviet suggestion for peaceful space cooperation is equally unacceptable. Despite the euphoric post-*glasnost* atmosphere, our two countries are still deeply locked in a dangerous nuclear stalemate, both exploring military advantages to be gained by strategic defense systems. Complete cooperation with the Soviets in interplanetary spaceflight would entail giving them vital space defense technology, especially the computer software generally known as "artificial intelligence."

Carl Sagan and his supporters somehow manage to reject the obvious evidence that the Soviets have military ambitions in space. However, it seems to me that a new relationship with the Soviet Union in space could be a negotiated "nonrace." We could agree that our civil space programs, especially manned outreach into the solar system for scientific and commercial projects could be coordinated. The United States and the Soviet Union could share in the public relations achievement, thereby avoiding costly space races. This is a big agenda, but the payoff could be an enlightened era of peace and sharing in space exploration.

To begin, the two nations might examine a fundamental problem of interplanetary spaceflight: human endurance in zero gravity. The Soviets have more experience in this than we do, but because of our more advanced computer technology, our biophysical data are probably better. And both countries are novices when it comes to "spun-up" variable-gravity facilities: spacecraft sections, connected by a tether or a flexible boom, that spin around a gravitational center point and produce acceleration-type "gravity" at the habitation modules at one end.

Since our space station is at least six years from launch, and *Mir* is a going concern, why can't we agree to conduct a joint manned variable-gravity research project? When Soviet icebreakers came to Alaska to help free some icebound whales last fall, everyone gushed about superpower cooperation. Wouldn't it be more important to solve together the living problems of human beings "frozen" in the long trajectories of interplanetary spaceflight?

In 1995, about six months before the initial *Freedom* station launch sequence (which may take at least two years to complete), America could easily orbit some type of space station habitation modules near the Soviet *Mir* station. These modules with a multipurpose supporting structure—which I call *Grav-Star*—could be tethered to one of the space shuttle's empty external tanks or to the cargo-engine section of the new Shuttle-C and spun up to produce gravitylike forces. Space scientists and international space students, supervised by astronauts and cosmonauts, could commute between the two facilities. A year or two later we would not only have amassed a wealth of medical data about human performance in variable gravity, but would also have welded a solid bond of trust between our two countries' civil space programs. World interest in TV broadcasts would be enormous.

I feel confident that the United States and the Soviet Union will eventually establish a practical means of space cooperation. More to the point, both superpowers will be nudged in this direction by the emerging economic powers of Europe and the Pacific rim. Undoubtedly, the Soviets' robust Energia booster and Soyuz and *Buran*-type spacecraft capability will play a major role in the exploitation of the moon and cislunar space for its solar power potential, probably with an active financial investment from the energy-poor Japanese. Either the United States will become a major partner in this endeavor or we will sink to second-rate status.

As the economic exploitation of the solar system expands, we will begin to look farther afield, eventually toward Mars. But Mars is many times farther away from Earth than the moon is, both in terms of distance and in terms of the propellant and time needed for the trip. Traditional, Apollo-type modular spacecraft that shed their components along the way will be impractical for regular travel between the Earth-moon system and Mars and its moons. Therefore, permanent human outreach will no doubt involve reusable and cycling spaceships.

Over four years ago, Tom Paine, then chairman of the National Commission on Space, supported my development of trajectories for manned "rapid transit" cycling spaceships that would employ the principles of gravity assist ("slingshots") to take advantage of particular planetary encounters to oscillate repeatedly between Mars and Earth. This exciting innovation involves moderate energy use, with trajectories that loop in elliptical curves out beyond Mars and then toward Earth on the return trip. These cycling spaceships will be like miniature planets, just as the Apollo spacecraft was a microminiature biosphere. When Earth and Mars are in the right alignment, a cycling spaceship could accelerate away from Earth, loop outward, and then swing close to Mars about five months later.

While this is happening, a similar cycling spaceship would be returning toward Earth, also a five-month trip. This opportunity for sequences of high-speed flybys of both planets would recur at 26-month intervals, in tune with the geometric realignment of Mars, Earth, and the sun. But these cycling spaceships will not expend propellant to "burn" into a Mars orbit as we did to brake into lunar orbit during Apollo. Rather, the Mars-bound cycler will discharge several mutually supporting manned taxi vehicles destined for a Mars orbital station, where the crews will transfer for an eventual landing on the surface of Mars or on one of the Martian moons. The other, Earth-bound cycler, after its outward loop and during its close pass by Mars, would pick up taxis with returning crews from the Martian bases. These taxis, relatively small, four- to six-man vehicles, will employ shieldlike aerobrakes to decelerate in the planetary atmospheres of Mars and Earth. At the Earth's terminals, these small ferry craft could operate from the *Lunar Star Port* located at one of the "libration points," where the gravity wells of the Earth and the moon coalesce to form neutral spots. These islands provide a way station during trips between Earth, the moon, and Mars, taking advantage of the gravitational "trade winds" of the next great age of exploration.

The cycling spaceships would use the variable-gravity, spun-up architecture that I plan to help design in the next few years for testing first in Earth orbit (hopefully, with the Soviets) and then in the vicinity of the moon, to qualify the next generation of starcraft for interplanetary flight. The star cyclers will also have a closed-ecology artificial biosphere, so they could remain independent of any planet for years. Like ocean liners on regular trade routes, the cycling spaceships will glide perpetually along beautifully predictable trajectories—solar orbits— arriving and departing with clockwork regularity.

Certainly this concept is a quantum-leap improvement over wasteful, brute force, large chemical-propellant spacecraft that have to burn to accelerate and burn to brake at their destination. One of the problems I have encountered in promoting this exciting concept among space traditionalists, however, stems from its combination of beautiful simplicity and intricate celestial mechanics. But I have made converts in the aerospace community. After I proposed these Mars-Earth cycling concepts to Tom Paine, we had the Jet Propulsion Laboratory run the routes through their highly sophisticated computers. The experts at JPL verified that with appropriate navigation corrections, my cycling orbit concepts would work as I had claimed.

Trying to convince the current generation of NASA officials and contractor executives that America simply must begin now to invest in the development of such innovations if we are to retain our technological leadership has been frustrating. Like generals fighting the *last* war, not the next, proponents of the traditional "expedition" concept cannot think beyond Apollo-type hardware that sheds its used modules until all that's left is a reentry vehicle with a charred heat shield, suitable only for museum display.

A few years ago when I was in Moscow I spent hours explaining my ideas for the cycling Earth-Mars trajectories for manned missions. In the homeland of Tsiolkovsky, no one considers adventurous visions of spaceflight as impractical or too futuristic.

Riding the umbilical tower elevator to the top of Launch Pad 39-A at Cape Canaveral is bittersweet for me now. I stand there in the warm sea breeze, where I stood 20 years before. The space shuttle *Discovery* is on the next pad, grounded by yet another hardware problem. I look down the curve of Merritt Island toward the bend of the Cape, where Wernher von Braun's team launched the first V-2 after the war. A pale moon hangs in the Florida afternoon sky. I can just make out the Sea of Tranquillity above the terminator.

Acknowledgments

The authors are indebted to many for their help with this book. Twenty years after the hectic excitement of Project Apollo, peoples' memories of that time are still sharp.

But personal recollections were not sufficient to produce a history of this scope. Therefore, the authors depended on the talent and goodwill of professional historians. Lee D. Saegesser, archivist of the NASA History Office, was extremely helpful, as was the staff of the Smithsonian Institution Air and Space Museum Library. Professor John Logsdon of George Washington University provided valuable new insights about John Kennedy's lunar landing decision. Mrs. Eilene Galloway, a trustee of the International Academy of Astronautics, shared her rich experiences as a space adviser to President Lyndon Johnson.

NASA's Office of Public Affairs graciously provided the authors with mission videotapes, transcripts of "air-to-ground" exchanges, and photographs. NASA also allowed the authors to revisit Apollo flight hardware, including command and lunar modules. Gene Rocque of the Kennedy Space Center led the authors back to launch Pad 39-A.

Many key participants in Project Apollo were generous with their time and graciously agreed to repeated interviews. The authors wish to thank in particular Dr. Thomas O. Paine, Dr. George Mueller,

Dr. Robert Seamans, Chris Kraft, Deke Slayton, Gene Kranz, Max Faget, Steve Bales, Frank Borman, Jim Lovell, Charlie Duke, Bruce McCandless, and, of course, Mike Collins and Neil Armstrong.

Dr. Walter Haeussermann and Dr. Ernst Stuhlinger were very helpful in providing insights into the work of Wernher von Braun and his rocket team.

Former defense secretary Mel Laird, Lieutenant General Danny Graham, and other present and former senior US government and Pentagon officials provided the authors with important information on the Soviet space program. Nicholas Johnson of Teledyne Brown Engineering shared with the authors his wealth of information on Soviet spaceflight, as did Saunders B. Kramer. The authors are particularly indebted to Charles P. Vick for his insights, his advice, and the considerable quantity of information he generously provided on the Soviet manned lunar program. Vadim I. Vlasov and academician Vasily P. Mishin have also graciously cooperated.

Finally, senior editor Henry Ferris of Bantam Books worked tirelessly throughout this project; the authors greatly appreciate his editorial guidance.

References

BOOKS AND ARTICLES

"Adventure into Emptiness." *Time*, March 26, 1965, p. 85.

Apollo Accident: Hearings. Committee on Aeronautical and Space Sciences, US Senate, 90th Congress, First and Second Session. Washington, DC: US Government Printing Office, 1967.

Baker, David. *The Rocket: The History and Development of Rocket and Missile Technology.* New York: Crown, 1986.

Beard, Edmund. *Developing the ICBM: A Study in Bureaucratic Politics.* New York: Columbia University Press, 1976.

Bergaust, Eric. *Wernher von Braun.* Washington, DC: National Space Institute, 1976.

Borman, Frank, with Robert J. Serling. *Countdown: An Autobiography.* New York: Silver Arrow Books, 1988.

Broad, William J. "Space Sleuth Keeps Eye on Soviet Rockets." *The New York Times*, December 25, 1984, p. 33.

Burrows, William E. *Deep Black: Space Espionage and National Security.* New York: Random House, 1986.

Clark, Phillip S. *The Soviet Manned Space Program: An Illustrated History of the Men, the Missions, and the Spacecraft.* New York: Orion Books, 1988.

Clark, Phillip S. "Topics Connected with the Soviet Manned Lunar Programme." *Journal of the British Interplanetary Society,* Vol. 40, No. 6, pp. 235–240, 1987.

Collins, Michael. *Carrying the Fire.* New York: Farrar, Straus and Giroux, 1974.

Collins, Michael. *Liftoff: The Story of America's Adventure in Space.* New York: Grove Press, 1988.

Criswell, D.R., and R. D. Waldron. "Lunar-based Power Systems" (Paper IA-86-507, presented at the 37th Congress of the International Astronautical Federation, Innsbruck, Austria, October 4–11, 1986). *Journal of the International Academy of Astronautics (Special Issue, Future Lunar Base,* H. H. Koelle, ed.). Elmsford, New York: Pergamon Press, 1988, pp. 709–716.

"The Cruise of the *Vostok.*" *Time,* April 21, 1961, p. 46.

Cunningham, Walter, with Mickey Herskowitz. *The All American Boys.* New York: Macmillan, 1977.

Daniloff, Nicholas. *The Kremlin and the Cosmos.* New York: Knopf, 1972.

El-Baz, Farouk. "Apollo and the Scientific Harvest." In Hallion, *Apollo: Ten Years Since Tranquillity Base,* pp. 35–37 (see below).

Frankel, Max. "Russians Announce Firing Intercontinental Missile 'Huge Distance' to Target." *The New York Times,* August 27, 1957, p. 1.

Gibbons, R. F., and P. S. Clark. "The Evolution of the Vostok and Voskhod Programmes." *Journal of the British Interplanetary Society,* Vol. 38, No. 1, pp. 3–10, January 1985.

Hallion, Richard P., and Tom D. Crouch, eds. *Apollo: Ten Years Since Tranquillity Base.* Washington, DC: National Air and Space Museum, Smithsonian Institution Press, 1979.

Hart, Douglas. *The Encyclopedia of Soviet Spacecraft.* New York: Exeter Books, 1987.

Hewlett, R. G., and O. E. Anderson. *A History of the United States Atomic Energy Commission,* Vol. II, *Atomic Shield 1947/1952.* Washington, DC: US Atomic Energy Commission, 1969.

Hill, Broderick. "Air Operations by Air Defense of Great Britain and Fighter Command in Connection with the German Flying Bomb and Rocket Offensives, 1944–1945." HMG *London Gazette,* October 19, 1948.

Jane's All the World's Aircraft. New York: Jane's, 1964.

Johnson, Nicholas L. "Apollo and Zond—Race Around the Moon?" *Spaceflight,* Vol. 20, No. 12, pp. 403–412, December 1978.

Johnson, Nicholas L. *Handbook of Soviet Lunar and Planetary Exploration.* San Diego: Univelt, 1979.

Johnson, Nicholas L. *Handbook of Soviet Manned Space Flight.* San Diego: Univelt, 1988.

Kaszubowski, Martin J., and Kirk Ayers. "The Transportation Depot—An Orbiting Vehicle Support Facility" (Paper presented at the symposium Lunar Bases and Space Activities in the 21st Century, April 5–7, 1988). Available through the Smithsonian Air and Space Museum Library, Washington, DC.

Kefitz, N. *Population of the World and Its Regions, 1975–2050.* Laxenburg, Austria: International Institute for Applied Systems Analysis, 1977.

Khrushchev, Nikita S. *Khrushchev Remembers: The Last Testament.* trans. Strobe Talbott. Boston: Little, Brown, 1974.

Kulcinski, G. L., and H. H. Schmitt. "The Moon: An Abundant Source of Clean and Safe Fusion Fuel for the 21st Century" (Paper presented at the 11th International Scientific Forum on Fueling the 21st Century, Moscow, September 29 to October 6, 1987). Published by the Fusion Technology Institute, University of Wisconsin, Madison, August 1987.

Logsdon, John M. *The Decision to Go to the Moon: Project Apollo and the National Interest.* Cambridge, Massachusetts: MIT Press, 1970.

Low, George M. "Gemini Circumlunar Flight 'Feasible.'" *Missiles and Rockets,* May 18, 1964.

Mailer, Norman. *Of a Fire on the Moon.* Boston: Little, Brown, 1971.

McConnell, Malcolm. *Challenger: A Major Malfunction.* Garden City, New York: Doubleday, 1987.

McDougall, Walter A. *The Heavens and the Earth: A Political History of the Space Age.* New York: Basic Books, 1985.

Medvedev, Zhores A. *Soviet Science.* New York: Norton, 1976.

National Commission on Space, Thomas O. Paine, Chairman. *Pioneering the Space Frontier: An Exciting Vision of Our Next Fifty Years in Space.* New York: Bantam Books, 1986.

Oberg, James E. *Red Star in Orbit.* New York: Random House, 1981.

Oberg, James E. *Uncovering Soviet Disasters: Exploring the Limits of Glasnost.* New York: Random House, 1988.

Oberg, James E. "The Hidden History of the Soyuz Project." *Spaceflight,* Vol. 17, Nos. 8 and 9, pp. 282–289, August–September 1975.

Oberg, James E. "Russia Meant to Win the 'Moon Race.'" *Spaceflight,* Vol. 17, No. 5, pp. 163–171, November 1975.

Oberg, James E. "*Soyuz 1* Ten Years After: New Conclusions." *Spaceflight,* Vol. 19, No. 5, pp. 183–188, May 1977.

Ordway, Frederick I., III, and Mitchell R. Sharpe. *The Rocket Team.* Cambridge, Massachusetts: MIT Press, 1979.

Osman, Tony. *Space History.* New York: St. Martin's Press, 1983.

Penkovsky, Oleg. *The Penkovsky Papers.* Garden City, New York: Doubleday, 1965.

"The President's News Conference of September 17, 1959." In *Public Papers of the Presidents of the United States: Dwight D. Eisenhower*, January 1–December 31, 1959. Washington, DC: Library of Congress.

"President Speaks on U.S. Role in Struggle for Freedom, Space Tasks, Foreign Aid and Arms." *The New York Times*, May 26, 1961, pp. 11–13.

Reistrup, John V. "Soviet One Upsmanship May Have Slipped This Time." *The Washington Post*, July 13, 1969, p. E5.

"Rendezvous with Destiny." *Time*, April 20, 1959, pp. 17–24.

Riabchikov, Evgeny. *Russians in Space*, trans. Guy Daniels. Garden City, New York: Doubleday, 1971.

Schwartz, Harry. "Soviet Science Far Advanced in Many Fields." *The New York Times*, October 6, 1957, p. 2.

Sidey, High. *Kennedy, President.* New York: Atheneum, 1965.

Turnill, Reginald, ed. *Jane's Spaceflight Directory.* New York: Jane's, 1984.

Vick, Charles P. "The Soviet G-1-e Manned Lunar Landing Programme Booster." *Journal of the British Interplanetary Society.* Vol. 38, No. 1, pp. 11–18, January 1985.

Vick, Charles P. "The Soviet Super Boosters, Part 1." *Spaceflight*, Vol. 15, No. 12, pp. 452–470, December 1973.

Vladimirov, Leonid. *The Russian Space Bluff.* New York: Dial Press, 1973.

Von Braun, Wernher, Frederick I. Ordway III, and Dave Dooling. *Space Travel: A History*, 4th ed. New York: Harper & Row, 1985.

"Vostok RD-107." Illustrated technical pamphlet, Novosti News Service, 1967. Washington, DC: Smithsonian Air and Space Museum Library, Archive Folder Number 00150300.

Webb, James E. Testimony before the Committee on Aeronautical and Space Sciences. In *Apollo Accident: Hearings*, pp. 463–464.

Weidman, Deene J., William M. Cirillo, and Charles P. Llewellyn. "Study of the Use of the Space Station to Accommodate Lunar Base Missions" (Paper presented at the symposium Lunar Bases and Space Activities in the 21st Century, April 5-7, 1988). Available through the Smithsonian Air and Space Museum Library, Washington, DC.

Wilford, John Noble. "Apollo Crew Appears Calm 11 Days Before the Mission." *The New York Times*, July 6, 1969, p. 1.

Wilson, Andrew. *The Eagle Has Wings*. London: Unwin Bros., 1982.

Woods, D. R. "Lunar Mission Cosmos Satellites." *Spaceflight*, Vol. 19, No. 11, pp. 383–388, November 1977.

Yeviskov, Viktor. *Re-Entry Technology and the Soviet Space Program (Some Personal Observations)*. Falls Church, Virginia: Delphic Associates, 1982.

Young, Hugo, Bryan Silcock, and Peter Dunn. *Journey to Tranquility*. Garden City, New York: Doubleday, 1970.

DOCUMENTS FROM THE
NATIONAL AERONAUTICS AND SPACE ADMINISTRATION

Apollo Launch Complex 39. US Army Corps of Engineers, Merritt Island, Florida, 1967. Washington, DC: NASA History Office.

"*Apollo 10* (AS-505) Flight Summary." Houston, Texas: Manned Spacecraft Center, undated. Washington, DC: NASA History Office.

"*Apollo 11* Mission Commentary." Transcript, July 16–24, 1969. Houston, Texas: Johnson Space Center, Public Affairs Office.

"*Apollo 11* Mission Minutes, Mission Control, July 20, 1969." Videotape. Houston, Texas: Johnson Space Center.

Bilstein, Roger E. *Stages to Saturn*. Washington, DC: The NASA History Series, Scientific and Technical Information Branch, 1980.

Brooks, Courtney G., James M. Grimwood, and Loyd S. Swenson, Jr. *Chariots for Apollo*. Washington, DC: NASA History Office, 1979.

Ertel, Ivan D., and Roland W. Newkirk, with Courtney G. Brooks. *The Apollo Spacecraft: A Chronology*, Vol. IV, *January 21, 1966 to July 13, 1974*. Washington, DC: NASA History Office, 1978.

Geissler, Ernst D. "Project Apollo Vehicular Plans." Huntsville, Alabama: Marshall Space Flight Center Technical Archives, date not available.

"*Gemini VIII* Air-to-Ground Voice Transmission." Transcript, March 16, 1966. Washington, DC: NASA History Office.

"*Gemini XII* Flight Plan." Houston, Texas: Manned Spacecraft Center, Mission Operations Branch, Flight Crew Support Division, November 1, 1967.

"*Gemini XII* Mission Commentary." Transcript, November 13, 1966. Washington, DC: NASA History Office.

"Gemini Program." Houston, Texas: Manned Spacecraft Center, February 1965. NASA Fact Sheet No. 291. Washington, DC: NASA History Office.

"Gemini Program Summary." Houston, Texas: Manned Spacecraft Center, 1967.

Gilruth, Robert M. Memorandum to Nicholas E. Golovin, September 12, 1961. Washington, DC: NASA History Office.

Glenn, John H., Jr. "Summary Results of the First United States Manned Orbital Space Flight." In *Life Sciences and Space Research* (a session of the Third International Space Science Symposium, Amsterdam, April 30–May 9, 1962). Washington, DC: NASA History Office.

Grimwood, James M. *Project Mercury: A Chronology*. Manned Spacecraft Center Publication HR-1. NASA SP-4001. Washington, DC: NASA History Office, 1963.

Hacker, Barton C., and James M. Grimwood. *On the Shoulders of Titans: A History of Project Gemini*. NASA SP-4203. Washington, DC: National Aeronautics and Space Administration, 1977.

Houbolt, John C. Letter to Robert C. Seamans, Jr., November 15, 1961. Washington, DC: NASA History Office.

"Introduction of the Astronauts." NASA News Release 59-113, April 9, 1959. Washington, DC: NASA History Office.

Investigation into the Apollo 204 Accident: Hearings. House Committee on Science and Aeronautics, Subcommittee on NASA Oversight, 90th Congress, First Session, April 10–May 10, 1967. Washington, DC: NASA History Office.

Javits, Jacob. Memorandum to President Dwight D. Eisenhower, October 11, 1957. Washington, DC: NASA History Office.

Kraft, Christopher C., Jr. Memorandum to Donald K. Slayton, April 4, 1966. Washington, DC: NASA History Office, File of Colonel Edwin E. Aldrin.

Kraft, Christopher C., Jr. "Post-Launch Memorandum Report for MA-7," March 28, 1962. Washington, DC: NASA History Office, NASA Space Task Group Archives.

"LM Hardware Weight Reductions: Initial Submittal." Grumman Aircraft report, April 5, 1968. Houston, Texas: Johnson Space Center Archives.

Low, George M. "Gemini Missions." Memorandum to the associate administrator for manned spaceflight, November 27, 1963. Washington, DC: NASA History Office.

Low, George M. Memorandum to NASA administrator T. Keith Glennan, July 29, 1960. Washington, DC: NASA History Office, NASA Space Task Group Archives.

"News Briefing on *Apollo 8* Moon Orbital Flight" Transcript, November 12, 1968. Washington, DC: NASA History Office.

Phillips, Sam C. Memorandum to George E. Mueller, associate administrator for manned spaceflight, November 11, 1968. Washington, DC: NASA History Office.

"Preliminary Design of an Experimental World-Circling Spaceship." Douglas Aircraft Company, Report No. SM-11827, May 2, 1946. Washington, DC: NASA History Office.

Proceedings of a Conference on Results of the First U.S. Manned Suborbital Space Flight. NASA report, June 6, 1961. Washington, DC: NASA History Office.

"Report of the Apollo 204 Review Board to the Administrator, National Aeronautics and Space Administration," April 5, 1967. Washington, DC: NASA History Office.

Results of the Second U.S. Manned Suborbital Space Flight, July 21, 1961. Washington, DC: NASA History Office, NASA Space Task Group Archives.

Ride, Sally K. *Leadership and America's Future in Space*. Washington, DC: National Aeronautics and Space Administration, 1987.

Rosholt, Robert. *An Administrative History of NASA, 1958–1963*. Washington, DC: National Aeronautics and Space Administration, 1966.

Swenson, Loyd S., Jr., James M. Grimwood, and Charles C. Alexander. *This New Ocean: A History of Project Mercury*. The NASA Historical Series. Washington, DC: National Aeronautics and Space Administration, 1966.

Webb, James E. Letter to Vice Admiral William F. Raborn, Jr., USN-Retired, August 23, 1965. Washington, DC: NASA History Office.

Webb, James E. NASA memorandum, November 2, 1967. Washington, DC: NASA History Office.

Webb, James E. Testimony before the Subcommittee on Appropriations of the Committee on Aeronautical and Space Sciences, US Senate, July 26, 1967. NASA memorandum, November 2, 1967. Washington, DC: NASA History Office.

Notes

Full bibliographic information on the sources cited in these notes can be found in the preceding lists of references. The designation "(NASA)" means that the item is contained in the list "Documents from the National Aeronautics and Space Administration."

INTRODUCTION

1. Hallion and Crouch, *Apollo: Ten Years Since Tranquillity Base*, pp. 27–28. McDougall, *The Heavens and the Earth: A Political History of the Space Age*, p. 362.

2. Mailer, *Of a Fire on the Moon*, p. 436.

CHAPTER ONE

1. Bergaust, *Wernher von Braun*, pp. 81–82.

2. Hill, "Air Operations by Air Defence of Great Britain and Fighter

Command in Connection with the German Flying Bomb and Rocket Offensives, 1944-1945."

3. Bergaust, *Wernher von Braun*, p. 81.

4. Ordway, Sharpe, *The Rocket Team*, pp. 18–21.

5. Bergaust, *Wernher von Braun*, p. 64.

6. Ordway and Sharpe, *The Rocket Team*, chap. 5.

7. Von Braun, Ordway, and Dooling, *Space Travel: A History*, pp. 107–108. Von Braun's problems with the SS stemmed from his rejection of Heinrich Himmler's intrigues to gain control of the Peenemünde effort. There is good evidence that, later in the war, the SS in Bavaria planned to eliminate all the key members of the rocket team in a typical spasm of Nazi götterdämmerung. There is also reason to believe that von Braun's aristocratic background made him a special target of the SS.

8. Bergaust, *Wernher von Braun*, p. 87.

9. Ordway and Sharpe, *The Rocket Team*, pp. 254–270. Bergaust, *Wernher von Braun*, p. 96.

10. Authors' interview with Ernst Stuhlinger, July 22, 1988.

11. Osman, *Space History*, pp. 36–37.

12. Ordway and Sharpe, *The Rocket Team*, pp. 216–234.

13. Hewlett and Anderson, *A History of the United States Atomic Energy Commission*, Vol. II, *Atomic Shield 1947/1952*, p. 134.

14. Bilstein, *Stages to Saturn* (NASA), p. 8, pp. 129–130.

15. "Vostok RD-107."

16. Turnill, *Jane's Spaceflight Directory*, pp. 268–271.

17. Von Braun, Ordway, and Dooling, *Space Travel: A History*, p. 116.

18. *Jane's All the World's Aircraft*, pp. 223–225. The MiG-15 was designed by Artem Mikoyan and Mikhail Gurevich. In Russian, the acronym is formed with the first consonant and vowel of Mikoyan and the first consonant of Gurevich, hence "MiG," not all capital letters, as it is often presented in the popular press. It should be noted that the MiG-15 through MiG-21 series represents the cautious, evolutionary design development typical of Soviet aerospace technology. This successful pattern was repeated with the manned space boosters of the Vostok and Soyuz series.

19. Authors' interview with Colonel Glenn Nordin, USAF-retired, August 25, 1988. Colonel Nordin is the editor of *Daedalus Flyer*, a military aviation magazine, and a former commander of the 51st Tactical Fighter Wing.

20. Osman, *Space History*, pp. 36–40.

21. Beard, *Developing the ICBM: A Study in Bureaucratic Politics*, pp. 133–134.

22. Khrushchev, *Khrushchev Remembers: The Last Testament*, pp. 45–56.

23. "Preliminary Design of an Experimental World-Circling Spaceship" (NASA).

24. Bergaust, *Wernher von Braun*, pp. 518–520.

25. Young, Silcock, and Dunn, *Journey to Tranquility*, pp. 41–43.

26. Young, Silcock, and Dunn, *Journey to Tranquility*, p. 43.

27. Bergaust, *Wernher von Braun*, p. 243. Young, Silcock, and Dunn, *Journey to Tranquility*, pp. 45–46.

28. Bergaust, *Wernher von Braun*, p. 243.

29. Von Braun, Ordway, and Dooling, *Space Travel: A History*, p. 129.

30. McDougall, *The Heavens and the Earth: A Political History of the Space Age*, pp. 60–61.

31. Oberg, *Red Star in Orbit*, p. 27.

32. Frankel, "Russians Announce Firing Intercontinental Missile 'Huge Distance' to Target."

33. Riabchikov, *Russians in Space*, p. 146.

CHAPTER TWO

1. Schwartz, "Soviet Science Far Advanced in Many Fields," p. 2.

2. Javits, memorandum to President Dwight D. Eisenhower (NASA).

3. Authors' interview with Eilene Galloway, July 26, 1988. Ms. Galloway was Lyndon Johnson's leading space-policy expert in the Congressional Research Service in the late 1950s. She and Buzz Aldrin are long-time friends.

4. Young, Silcock, and Dunn, *Journey to Tranquility*, pp. 48–49.

5. McDougall, *The Heavens and the Earth: A Political History of the Space Age*, chap. 12. Vladimirov, *The Russian Space Bluff*, pp. 52–68.

6. Bergaust, *Wernher von Braun*, pp. 262–263.

7. Bergaust, *Wernher von Braun*, pp. 272–279. Authors' interviews with Ernst Stuhlinger and Walter Haeussermann, July 21, 1988.

8. Bergaust, *Wernher von Braun*, p. 278.

9. McDougall, *The Heavens and the Earth: A Political History of the Space Age*, pp. 169–170.

10. McDougall, *The Heavens and the Earth: A Political History of the Space Age*, p. 174.

11. McDougall, *The Heavens and the Earth: A Political History of the Space Age*, p. 175. *Jane's Spaceflight Directory*, pp. 60, 136, 198.

12. Wilson, *The Eagle Has Wings*, pp. 24–25.

CHAPTER THREE

1. Swenson, Grimwood, and Alexander, *This New Ocean: A History of Project Mercury* (NASA), p. 100.

2. Swenson, Grimwood, and Alexander, *This New Ocean: A History of Project Mercury* (NASA), p. 109.

3. Swenson, Grimwood, and Alexander, *This New Ocean: A History of Project Mercury* (NASA), pp. 133–148.

4. Collins, *Liftoff: The Story of America's Adventure in Space*, pp. 45–46.

5. Swenson, Grimwood, and Alexander, *This New Ocean: A History of Project Mercury* (NASA), pp. 160–161.

6. "Introduction of the Astronauts" (NASA).

7. Interview with Chuck Yeager, by Michael Jackson, on "The Michael Jackson Show", TalkNet Radio, September 28, 1988.

8. "Rendezvous with Destiny, " p. 24.

9. Swenson, Grimwood, and Alexander, *This New Ocean: A History of Project Mercury* (NASA), p. 148.

10. "Rendezvous with Destiny," p. 17.

11. "The President's News Conference of September 17, 1959," pp. 671–672.

12. Rosholt, *An Administrative History of NASA, 1958–1963* (NASA), p. 131.

13. Authors' interview with Walter Haeussermann and Ernst Stuhlinger, July 22, 1988.

14. Authors' interview with Walter Haeussermann and Ernst Stuhlinger, July 22, 1988.

15. Logsdon, *The Decision to Go to the Moon: Project Apollo and the National Interest*, p. 35.

16. Low, memorandum to NASA administrator T. Keith Glennan (NASA).

17. Logsdon, *The Decision to Go to the Moon: Project Apollo and the National Interest*, p. 65.

18. The best sources on the Nedelin disaster are Oberg, *Red Star in Orbit*, pp. 39–49; Oberg, *Uncovering Soviet Disasters: Exploring the Limits of Glasnost*, pp. 177–183; Penkovsky, *The Penkovsky Papers*, pp. 63–68; and Medvedev, *Soviet Science*, pp. 97–99. The quote from Khrushchev is from Khrushchev, *Khrushchev Remembers: The Last Testament*, p. 51.

19. Oberg, *Uncovering Soviet Disasters: Exploring the Limits of Glasnost*, p. 181.

CHAPTER FOUR

1. Authors' interview with Walter Haeussermann, July 21, 1988.

2. Swenson, Grimwood, and Alexander, *This New Ocean: A History of Project Mercury* (NASA), pp. 294–297.

3. Young, Silcock, and Dunn, *Journey to Tranquility*, p. 78.

4. For those interested in pursuing this subject, the authors recommend Riabchikov, *Russians in Space*; Vladimirov, *The Russian Space Bluff*; Oberg, *Red Star in Orbit*; Daniloff, *The Kremlin and the Cosmos*; and Gibbons and Clark, "The Evolution of the Vostok and Voskhod Programmes." The authors are indebted to James Oberg and Charles P. Vick, two of America's leading experts on the Soviet manned space program; they are diligent detectives and prolific writers. Together, they have answered many nagging questions about Soviet space history. Unless otherwise noted, the details of Sergei Korolev's effort to launch the first cosmonaut come from these sources, as well as from background briefings by senior Pentagon and other US government officials.

5. "The Cruise of the *Vostok*" p. 46.

6. Logsdon, *The Decision to Go to the Moon: Project Apollo and the National Interest*, p. 104.

7. Sidey, *Kennedy, President*, pp. 121–123.

8. Logsdon, *The Decision to Go to the Moon: Project Apollo and the National Interest*, p. 111.

9. Young, Silcock, and Dunn, *Journey to Tranquility*, p. 141.

10. For further details of Alan Shepard's MR-3 flight, see *Proceedings of a Conference on Results of the First U.S. Manned Suborbital Space Flight* (NASA), June 6, 1961.

11. Logsdon, *The Decision to Go to the Moon: Project Apollo and the National Interest*, pp. 125–126.

12. "President Speaks on U.S. Role in Struggle for Freedom, Space Tasks, Foreign Aid and Arms," pp. 11-13.

CHAPTER FIVE

1. Swenson, Grimwood, and Alexander, *This New Ocean: A History of Project Mercury* (NASA), pp. 365–368.

2. *Results of the Second U.S. Manned Suborbital Space Flight, July 21, 1961* (NASA), pp. 11–14.

3. Vladimirov, *The Russian Space Bluff*, pp. 108–109.

4. Vladimirov, *The Russian Space Bluff*, pp. 108–109.

5. Vladimirov, *The Russian Space Bluff*, pp. 110–111.

6. Vladimirov, *The Russian Space Bluff*, p. 109. McDougall, *The Heavens and the Earth: A Political History of the Space Age*, p. 249.

7. Riabchikov, *Russians in Space*, pp. 167–168.

8. Vladimirov, *The Russian Space Bluff*, pp. 109–110. Clark, *The Soviet Manned Space Program: An Illustrated History of the Men, the Missions, and the Spacecraft*, p. 21. Gibbons and Clark, "The Evolution of the Vostok and Voskhod Programmes," p. 3.

9. Bilstein, *Stages to Saturn* (NASA), p. 28.

10. Bilstein, *Stages to Saturn* (NASA), p. 45.

11. Authors' interviews with long-time Clear Lake residents, July 27–28, 1988. Authors' interview with Houston historian Robert B. Merrifield, January 9, 1989.

12. Swenson, Grimwood, and Alexander, *This New Ocean: A History of Project Mercury* (NASA), p. 391.

13. Glenn, "Summary Results of the First United States Manned Orbital Space Flight" (NASA), pp. 170–184.

14. Clark, *The Soviet Manned Space Program*, p. 23.

15. Wilson, *The Eagle Has Wings*, pp. 81–83.

16. Many details about the frantic competition between Sergei Korolev's design team and their American counterparts were provided to the authors during background briefings by senior Pentagon and US government officials during the summer and fall of 1988. For more background on this fascinating topic, see Clark, *The Soviet Manned Space Program*, chaps. 2, 4, and 5, and Appendix 4; Vladimirov, *The Russian Space Bluff*, pp. 110–119; Turnill, *Jane's Spaceflight Directory*, pp. 167–168; Oberg, *Red Star in Orbit*, pp. 75–76; and Osman, *Space History*, p. 52.

CHAPTER SIX

1. Young, Silcock, and Dunn, *Journey to Tranquility*, p. 106.

2. Young, Silcock, and Dunn, *Journey to Tranquility*, p. 107.

3. Gilruth, memorandum to Nicholas E. Golovin (NASA).

4. Bilstein, *Stages to Saturn* (NASA), pp. 62–63.

5. Houbolt, letter to Robert C. Seamans, Jr. (NASA).

6. Bilstein, *Stages to Saturn* (NASA), p. 66.

7. Bergaust, *Wernher von Braun*, p. 409. Bilstein, *Stages to Saturn* (NASA), pp. 67–68.

8. Kraft, "Post-Launch Memorandum Report for MA-7" (NASA).

9. Swenson, Grimwood, and Alexander, *This New Ocean: A History of Project Mercury* (NASA), p. 454.

10. Vladimirov, *The Russian Space Bluff*, pp. 111–119.

11. Turnill, *Jane's Spaceflight Directory*, p. 207.

12. Grimwood, *Project Mercury: A Chronology* (NASA), pp. 191–193.

13. Swenson, Grimwood, and Alexander, *This New Ocean: A History of Project Mercury* (NASA), p. 501.

14. Hacker and Grimwood, *On the Shoulders of Titans: A History of Project Gemini* (NASA), pp. 44–63, 75–80.

15. Geissler, "Project Apollo Vehicular Plans" (NASA), pp. 1–2.

16. Hallion and Crouch, *Apollo: Ten Years Since Tranquillity Base*, p. 136.

17. Oberg, *Red Star in Orbit*, p. 68.

18. Vladimirov, *The Russian Space Bluff*, p. 114.

19. Clark, *The Soviet Manned Space Program: An Illustrated History of the Men, the Missions, and the Spacecraft*, pp. 26–27.

20. Vladimirov, *The Russian Space Bluff*, pp. 125–127.

21. Turnill, *Jane's Spaceflight Directory*, p. 205.

CHAPTER SEVEN

1. Kraft, memorandum to Donald K. Slayton (NASA).

2. "Gemini Program" (NASA), p. 2.

3. Low, "Gemini Missions" (NASA). Low, "Gemini Circumlunar Flight 'Feasible.'" This proposed use of Gemini as a contingency lunar vehicle was eventually overruled by James Webb in mid-1964.

4. Hacker and Grimwood, *On the Shoulders of Titans: A History of Project Gemini* (NASA), p. 125.

5. Oberg, *Red Star in Orbit*, pp. 78–79.

6. Vladimirov, *The Russian Space Bluff*, pp. 139–140. Turnill, *Jane's Spaceflight Directory*, pp. 204–206. Osman, *Space History*, pp. 53–54.

7. Oberg, *Red Star in Orbit*, p. 85.

8. Vladimirov, *The Russian Space Bluff*, p. 141.

9. Gibbons and Clark, "The Evolution of the Vostok and Voskhod Programmes," p. 9.

10. Vladimirov, *The Russian Space Bluff*, p. 143. Oberg, *Red Star in Orbit*, pp. 80–81.

11. "Adventure into Emptiness," p. 85.

12. Hacker and Grimwood, *On the Shoulders of Titans: A History of Project Gemini* (NASA), p. 233.

13. Borman, with Serling, *Countdown: An Autobiography*, p. 132.

14. Collins, *Liftoff: The Story of America's Adventure in Space*, pp. 84–85.

15. Hacker and Grimwood, *On the Shoulders of Titans: A History of Project Gemini* (NASA), p. 241.

16. Hacker and Grimwood, *On the Shoulders of Titans: A History of Project Gemini* (NASA), p. 248.

17. Hacker and Grimwood, *On the Shoulders of Titans: A History of Project Gemini* (NASA), p. 269.

CHAPTER EIGHT

1. Vick, "The Soviet Super Boosters, Part 1." Oberg, "Russia Meant to Win the 'Moon Race,'" p. 167.

2. Johnson, *Handbook of Soviet Manned Space Flight*, p. 400.

3. Vick, "The Soviet G-1-e Manned Lunar Landing Programme Booster."

4. For more information on Korolev's death, see Oberg, *Red Star in Orbit*, pp. 87–90, and Vladimirov, *The Russian Space Bluff*, p. 146. Oberg and Vladimirov assembled the details of Korolev's death from a "samizdat" memoir of the chief designer's former colleague, G. A. Ozerov, which was eventually published in Yugoslavia. Also, Oberg confirmed this account with information from two Soviet émigrés, biologist Zhores Medvedev and surgeon Vladimir Golyakhovsky. As in every other case, when the authors independently verified this account with senior US government and Pentagon officials, Oberg's and Vladimirov's information was substantiated.

5. "*Gemini VIII* Air-to-Ground Voice Transmission" (NASA), pp. 70–71.

6. *Apollo Launch Complex 39* (NASA), pp. 1–47.

7. Brooks, Grimwood, and Swenson, *Chariots for Apollo* (NASA), p. 194.

8. Brooks, Grimwood, and Swenson, *Chariots for Apollo* (NASA), p. 130.

9. Brooks, Grimwood, and Swenson, *Chariots for Apollo* (NASA), p. 199.

10. Brooks, Grimwood, and Swenson, *Chariots for Apollo* (NASA), p. 201.

11. Hacker and Grimwood, *On the Shoulders of Titans: A History of Project Gemini* (NASA), p. 337.

12. "*Gemini XII* Flight Plan" (NASA), p. 35.

13. Hacker and Grimwood, *On the Shoulders of Titans: A History of Project Gemini* (NASA), p. 362.

14. Oberg, "Russia Meant to Win the 'Moon Race,'" p. 167. Oberg's principal source here is academician L. I. Sedov, quoted on Radio Moscow on August 13, 1965 at 9:00 PM Greenwich time, as transcribed by the Foreign Broadcast Information Service.

15. Daniloff, *The Kremlin and the Cosmos*, pp. 110–114.

16. Vick, "The Soviet Super Boosters, Part 1," p. 462.

17. Webb, letter to Vice Admiral William F. Raborn, Jr. (NASA).

18. Burrows, *Deep Black: Space Espionage and National Security*, p. 240. Authors' interview of William E. Burrows, December 6, 1988.

19. "Gemini Program Summary" (NASA), p. 6.

20. "*Gemini XII* Mission Commentary" (NASA), p. 5.

21. Clark, *The Soviet Manned Space Program*, p. 46. Oberg, "The Hidden History of the Soyuz Project," p. 284.

22. Oberg, "*Soyuz 1* Ten Years After: New Conclusions," p. 183.

CHAPTER NINE

1. Brooks, Grimwood, and Swenson, *Chariots For Apollo* (NASA), p. 209. "Report of the Apollo 204 Review Board to the Administrator, National Aeronautics and Space Administration" (NASA), p. 4–2.

2. Cunningham, with Herskowitz, *The All American Boys*, p. 14.

3. Cunningham, with Herskowitz, *The All American Boys*, p. 2.

4. The best sources on the *Apollo 1* fire are "Report of the Apollo 204 Review Board to the Administrator, National Aeronautics and Space Administration" (NASA); Ertel and Newkirk, with Brooks, *The Apollo Spacecraft: A Chronology* (NASA); and Young, Silcock, and Dunn, *Journey to Tranquility*, chap. 10.

5. "Report of the Apollo 204 Review Board to the Administrator, National Aeronautics and Space Administration" (NASA), pp. 5-8, 5-9. Former

astronaut Walter Cunningham, author of *The All American Boys*, was part of the accident investigation team reviewing the tapes of this last voice transmission; he verifies that the calls were from Chaffee and that the words, although sometimes hard to understand, were as given in the text.

6. Brooks, Grimwood, and Swenson, *Chariots for Apollo* (NASA), pp. 218, 460.

7. "Report of the Apollo 204 Review Board to the Administrator, National Aeronautics and Space Administration" (NASA), pp. 6-1 to 6-3.

8. *Investigation into Apollo 204 Accident: Hearings* (NASA), pp. 141–157.

9. Brooks, Grimwood, and Swenson, *Chariots for Apollo* (NASA), p. 221.

10. Borman, with Serling, *Countdown: an Autobiography*, pp. 211–212. McConnell, *Challenger: A Major Malfunction*, p. 69.

11. Brooks, Grimwood, and Swenson, *Chariots for Apollo* (NASA), p. 227.

12. Clark, *The Soviet Manned Space Program: An Illustrated History of the Men, the Missions, and the Spacecraft*, p. 48.

13. Yeviskov, *Re-Entry Technology and the Soviet Space Program (Some Personal Observations)*, pp. 1, 59–60 (as cited in Clark, *The Soviet Manned Space Program: An Illustrated History of the Men, the Missions, and the Spacecraft*).

14. Oberg, "*Soyuz 1* Ten Years After: New Conclusions," p. 186.

15. Clark, *The Manned Soviet Space Program: An Illustrated History of the Men, the Missions, and the Spacecraft*, p. 47.

CHAPTER TEN

1. Webb, Testimony before the Subcommittee on Appropriations of the Committee on Aeronautical and Space Sciences (NASA).

2. Brooks, Grimwood, and Swenson, *Chariots for Apollo* (NASA), pp. 234–235.

3. Bilstein, *Stages to Saturn*, p. 357.

4. Brooks, Grimwood, and Swenson, *Chariots for Apollo* (NASA), p. 244.

5. Brooks, Grimwood, and Swenson, *Chariots for Apollo* (NASA), pp. 154–155, 200–201, 244–245.

6. "LM Hardware Weight Reductions: Initial Submittal" (NASA).

7. Webb, Testimony before the Committee on Aeronautical and Space Sciences.

8. See Clark, *The Soviet Manned Space Program: An Illustrated History of the Men, the Missions, and the Spacecraft*, chap. 4; Oberg, *Red Star in Orbit*, chap. 7; Daniloff, *The Kremlin and the Cosmos;* and Hart, *The Encyclopedia of Soviet Spacecraft*, pp. 145–156. For more detailed confirmation of the Soviet manned lunar landing program see Oberg, "Russia Meant to Win the 'Moon Race'"; Clark, "Topics Connected with the Soviet Manned Lunar Programme"; and Vick, "The Soviet G-1-e Manned Lunar Landing Programme Booster."

9. Robert Hotz, former editor of *Aviation Week & Space Technology*, told the authors in an interview on December 12, 1988, that Soviet cosmonauts complained about this helicopter training for the lunar landing mission to their American colleagues at the Paris Air Show in 1968.

10. Clark, *The Soviet Manned Space Program: An Illustrated History of the Men, the Missions, and the Spacecraft*, p. 38. Turnill, *Jane's Spaceflight Directory*, p. 207. Johnson, "Apollo and Zond—Race Around the Moon?" p. 404–405.

11. Clark, *The Soviet Manned Space Program: An Illustrated History of the Men, the Missions, and the Spacecraft*, pp. 38–39.

12. Vick, "The Soviet G-1-e Manned Lunar Landing Programme Booster," pp. 12–13. Baker, *The Rocket: The History and Development of Rocket and Missile Technology*, p. 225. Authors' interview with Charles P. Vick, December 17, 1988. Vick is recognized as the undisputed Western expert on the Soviet G booster. He has devoted 20 years to the study of this rocket and its lunar mission. For more on Vick's background see Broad, "Space Sleuth Keeps Eye on Soviet Rockets."

13. Authors' interviews with Saunders B. Kramer, December 16 and December 24, 1988. Kramer, a scientist with the Department of Transportation, was a project scientist with the Lockheed Space and Missile Company in the 1960s; one of his responsibilities was to monitor the progress of the Soviet space program. In that capacity, he had access to top-secret US reconnaissance satellite images of Tyuratam. Unless otherwise cited, the physical descriptions of the G-1 booster are derived from either Vick's work or the Kramer interviews.

14. Burrows, *Deep Black: Space Espionage and National Security*, pp. 240–241.

15. Authors' interview with Robert C. Seamans, Jr., former deputy administrator of NASA, December 13, 1988.

16. Bilstein, *Stages to Saturn* (NASA), p. 361.

17. Young, Silcock, and Dunn, *Journey to Tranquility*, p. 227.

CHAPTER ELEVEN

1. Ertel and Newkirk, with Brooks, *The Apollo Spacecraft: A Chronology* (NASA), pp. 237–239.

2. Authors' interview with Ernst Stuhlinger, January 15, 1989.

3. Borman, with Serling, *Countdown: An Autobiography*, p. 189. Authors' interview with Colonel Frank Borman, January 16, 1989.

4. Authors interview with Donald K. Slayton, January 10, 1989.

5. Authors' interview with George E. Mueller, January 13, 1989.

6. Authors' interviews with Christopher C. Kraft, Jr., and Eugene Krantz, July 22, 1988. Both men denied that Soviet pressure was a major factor in the *Apollo 8* decision; however, Kraft conceded that overall competition between the Soviet and American manned space programs was one of NASA's key concerns.

7. Brooks, Grimwood, and Swenson, *Chariots for Apollo* (NASA), p. 259.

8. Ertel and Newkirk, with Brooks, *The Apollo Spacecraft: A Chronology* (NASA), p. 240.

9. Clark, *The Soviet Manned Space Program: An Illustrated History of the Men, the Missions, and the Spacecraft*, pp. 36–39. Turnill, *Jane's Spaceflight Directory*, pp. 207–208. Johnson, "Apollo and Zond—Race Around the Moon?" pp. 39–40.

10. Johnson, *Handbook of Soviet Manned Space Flight*, p. 150.

11. Clark, *The Soviet Manned Space Program: An Illustrated History of the Men, the Missions, and the Spacecraft*, p. 50.

12. Phillips, memorandum to George E. Mueller, associate administrator for manned spaceflight, November 11, 1968 (NASA), p. 5.

13. Brooks, Grimwood, and Swenson, *Chariots for Apollo* (NASA), pp. 273–274.

14. Turnill, *Jane's Spaceflight Directory*, p. 208. Johnson, *Handbook of Soviet Lunar and Planetary Exploration*, p. 117.

15. "News Briefing on *Apollo 8* Moon Orbital Flight" (NASA), pp. 1–44.

16. Johnson, *Handbook of Soviet Lunar and Planetary Exploration*, p. 115.

17. Borman, with Serling, *Countdown: An Autobiography*, p. 197.

18. Brooks, Grimwood, and Swenson, *Chariots for Apollo* (NASA), p. 276.

19. Borman, with Serling, *Countdown: An Autobiography*, p. 203.

20. Brooks, Grimwood, and Swenson, *Chariots for Apollo* (NASA), p. 281.

CHAPTER TWELVE

1. Authors' interview with George E. Mueller, January 13, 1989.

2. Johnson, *Handbook of Soviet Lunar and Planetary Exploration*, p. 118.

3. Clark, *The Soviet Manned Space Program: An Illustrated History of the Men, the Missions, and the Spacecraft*, p. 42.

4. Authors' interview with Thomas O. Paine, December 17, 1988.

5. Johnson, "Apollo and Zond—Race Around the Moon?" p. 407.

6. Collins, *Carrying the Fire*, p. 280.

7. The authors have extensively reviewed all the pertinent material in Western technical journals, have been briefed on the subject by NATO intelligence officers, and have consulted present and former senior US government and Pentagon officials. Even with *glasnost* we may never be certain of the details, but the authors are confident they have uncovered the essence of the Soviet manned lunar program.

8. Clark, *The Soviet Manned Space Program: An Illustrated History of the Men, the Missions, and the Spacecraft*, pp. 42–43. In this excellent recent book, Clark skillfully combines the evidence amassed by all the leading Western experts on the subject.

9. For more details see Vick, "The Soviet G-1-e Manned Lunar Landing Programme Booster"; Woods, "Lunar Mission Cosmos Satellites"; and Oberg, "Russia Meant to Win the 'Moon Race,'" pp. 168–169.

10. Clark, *The Soviet Manned Space Program: An Illustrated History of the Men, the Missions, and the Spacecraft*, pp. 51–52.

11. Johnson, *Handbook of Soviet Manned Space Flight*, pp. 151–159.

12. Authors' interview with Charles P. Vick, January 23, 1989.

13. Brooks, Grimwood, and Swenson, *Chariots for Apollo* (NASA), pp. 293–294.

14. For a full examination of the decisions regarding the lunar EVA sequence and *Apollo 11* experiments, see Brooks, Grimwood, and Swenson, *Chariots for Apollo* (NASA), pp. 319–326.

15. Brooks, Grimwood, and Swenson, *Chariots for Apollo* (NASA), p. 303.

16. "Apollo 10 (AS-505) Flight Summary" (NASA), p. 11.

17. Collins, *Liftoff: The Story of America's Adventure in Space*, p. 149.

18. To gain a good sense of the intensity of this period, see Ertel and Newkirk, with Brooks, *The Apollo Spacecraft: A Chronology*, pp. 298–309.

19. Authors' interviews with senior US government and Pentagon officials. Vick, "The Soviet G-1-e Manned Lunar Landing Programme Booster," p. 17. Burrows, *Deep Black: Space Espionage and National Security*, p. 240.

20. Authors' interview with Saunders B. Kramer, December 24, 1988.

21. Reistrup, "Soviet One Upsmanship May Have Slipped This Time," p. E5.

CHAPTER THIRTEEN

1. All conversations between the spacecraft and Mission Control have been taken from the official transcript, *"Apollo 11* Mission Commentary" (NASA).

2. *"Apollo 11* Mission Minutes, Mission Control, July 20, 1969." Authors' interviews with Stephen G. Bales, July 23, 1988, and February 2, 1989.

EPILOGUE

1. El-Baz, "Apollo and the Scientific Harvest," pp. 35–37.

2. For the best recent analysis of this dilemma, see Kaszubowski and Ayers, "The Transportation Depot—An Orbiting Vehicle Support Facility," and Weidman, Cirillo, and Llewellyn, "Study of the Use of the Space Station to Accommodate Lunar Base Missions."

3. Vick, "The Soviet G-1-e Manned Lunar Landing Programme Booster," p. 17. Clark, *The Soviet Manned Space Program: An Illustrated History of the Men, the Missions, and the Spacecraft*, pp. 43–45, 174.

4. Johnson, *Handbook of Soviet Lunar and Planetary Exploration*, pp. 50–52, 169.

5. For the best description of the Salyut program, see Clark, *The Soviet Manned Space Program: An Illustrated History of the Men, the Missions, and the Spacecraft*, chaps. 6–8.

6. Ride, *Leadership and America's Future in Space*, pp. 21–35.

7. Kefitz, *Population of the World and Its Regions, 1975–2050*, pp. 11–24.

8. *Los Angeles Times*, July 22, 1984, Part IV, p. 7.

9. Criswell and Waldron, "Lunar-based Power Systems."

10. Kulcinski and Schmitt, "The Moon: An Abundant Source of Clean and Safe Fusion Fuel for the 21st Century."

Index

A-4 missile, 1, 3–4
A-12 booster, 5
Ablation, 37
ABMA (Army Ballistic Missile
    Agency), 22, 23, 45
Accidents
    Apollo 1 fire, xxi, 161–169
    Bassett and See: T–38
    crash, 138
    bombing of Mexico, 12
    Dolgov's death, 58
    Liberty Bell 7, 72–75
    LLRV crash, 187
    lunar probe explosion, 48
    MA-1 explosion, 47
    Mars I explosion, 48–50
    Soviet G booster explosion,
        223–224
    Soyuz 11, 253
    Soyuz 1 crash, 170–172
    Vostok reentry burning, 57
Acquisition of signal. *See* AOS

ADI. *See* Attitude direction
    indicator
Aerodynamic pressure, maximum.
    See Max Q
Aero Medical Laboratory, 38
Agena spacecraft, 118, 131, 139,
    146–147, 154
Aggregate-4. *See* A-4 missile
Agnew, Spiro, 248
Air and Space Museum, xx
AiResearch, 143
Air Force (US)
    Aldrin's decision to join, 8
    astronauts from, 40, 64
    Atlas missile, 12, 19, 21, 27,
        33–34
    Blue Gemini program, 115, 118
    early spaceflight program, 31–32
    interservice rivalry, 12, 23, 30, 115
    manned spaceflight program, 35,
        46, 51
    postwar missiles, 20–21

Air Medal, 42
Airplanes
    cargo, for booster transport, 105
    long-range bombers, 9
    robot, 1
    spy, 22
    see also specific type, e.g., Sabre
        jet
Alcohol (fuel), 1
Aldrin, Joan Archer, 19, 103, 138,
    150–151, 206, 207
Aldrin, Marion Moon, 7
Aldrin, Mike, 18
Aldrin, Edwin E., Jr. (Buzz)
    Apollo 8 backup, 199
    Apollo 11, xiii–xvii, 206–207,
        214–216, 220–223, 225–246
    awards and honors, 8, 17
    Borman, conflict with, 179–180
    career decision, 8
    on Gemini IX backup crew,
        144–146
    early work on Project Gemini,
        116–119
    EVA, 146, 148, 155–158
    Gemini XII, 150–159
    helicopter training, 186
    Korean War, xx, 13–18, 158
    mission planning, 116–117, 186
    MIT, xx, 69–71
    moon walk, 240–243
    on NATO forces, 18, 31
    requests spaceflight, 130–131
    selection as astronaut, 102–103
    West Point, xx, 6–8, 13
Aldrin, Edwin E., Sr., xx, 7–8
AMU (Astronaut Maneuvering
    Unit), 118–119, 145, 148
Anders, Bill, 178, 185, 198–203, 225
Animals in space
    chimpanzees, 55, 63, 66, 69, 81
    dogs, 28, 48, 55, 57, 58
Annapolis (U.S. Naval Academy),
    7, 40, 115

Antwerp (Belgium), 2
AOS (acquisition of signal), 201
Apollo. See Project Apollo;
    individual spacecraft names
Apollo 1 (spacecraft), xxi, 161–169,
    222
Apollo 4 (spacecraft), 175
Apollo 5 (spacecraft), 177–178
Apollo 6 (spacecraft), 184–185
Apollo 7(spacecraft), 175, 178, 189,
    193–194
Apollo 8 (spacecraft), 178, 185,
    189–191, 196, 197, 198–203, 205
Apollo 9 (spacecraft), 178, 205,
    211–214
    see also Gumdrop
Apollo 10 (spacecraft), 205–206,
    217–220
Apollo 11 (spacecraft), xiii–xvii,
    205–207, 214–216, 220–223,
    224–246
Apollo 12 (spacecraft), 248
Apollo 13 (spacecraft), 247
Apollo 14 (spacecraft), 247
Apollo 17 (spacecraft), 248
Apollo 204 mission. See Apollo 1
Apollo-Soyuz Test Project. See
    ASTP
Archer, Joan. See Aldrin, Joan
    Archer
Armed forces. See Air Force (US);
    Army (US); Defense,
    Department of (US); Navy (US)
Arms race, 19–20
Armstrong, Neil
    Apollo 8, 179
    Apollo 11, xiii–xvii, xix, xxi, 205,
        206–207, 214–216, 221–222,
        225–246
    flying mishaps, 187
    Gemini VIII, 139–141
    Korean War, 17–18, 187
    photographer of flag on moon,
        129

selection as astronaut, 103
Army (US)
    Aldrin Sr.'s opinion of, 7–8
    early rocketry research, 11–13
    interservice rivalry, 23, 30
    Jupiter missile, 22–23, 28–30
    Project Adam, 35–36
    Redstone missile, 21
    von Braun's surrender to, 5–6
    see also West Point
Army Ballistic Missile Agency. See
    ABMA
ASTP (Apollo-Soyuz Test Project),
    250
Astronaut Maneuvering Unit. See
    AMU
Astronauts
    chief astronaut, 114
    coining of word, 37
    competition among, 113–114
    idolization of, 39, 41, 115
    language of, 71–72
    medical examinations, 38, 41
    psychological tests, 38
    qualifications of, 37, 69–70
    selection of, 37–43, 102–103
    see also Cosmonauts; individual
        names
ATDA (Augmented Target Docking
    Adapter), 144, 145
Atlas-Able booster, 48
Atlas missile
    Air Force research project, 12
    conflict with satellite program, 21
    development program, 27, 33–34
    first US ICBM, 19
    reliability, 75
    weight limits, 36
    see also Mercury-Atlas system
Atmosphere system, cabin,
    162–163, 167, 174, 193
Atomic bomb, 6, 9, 13
Attitude direction indicator (ADI),
    73

Atwood, Leland, 196
Augmented Target Docking
    Adapter. See ATDA
Aurora 7 flight, 95–97

Babbitt, Donald, 161, 164, 165
Bales, Steve, 235, 236–237
Ballistic missiles. See Missiles,
    ballistic
Bassett, Charlie, 137–139
Bassett, Jeannie, 138–139
Battin, Dick, 69
Bay of Pigs, 57, 62
BECO (booster engine cutoff), 73
Belka (dog), 48
Bell, David, 61
Belyayev, Pavel, 121
Beregovoi, Georgy, 194–195
Bergen, William, 168, 174
Berlin Wall, 77–78
Bland, Bill, 84
Blue Gemini program, 115, 118
Bolt, Jack, 15
Bombers, long-range, 9
Booster engine cutoff. See BECO
Boosters
    early developments, 4–5
    for moon flights, 62–63, 78–80
    pogo effect of, 184–185, 190
    Soviet superiority, 54, 253–254
    strap-on, 11, 250
    see also specific booster name
Boost protective cover. See BPC
Borman, Frank
    Aldrin, conflict with, 179–180
    Apollo 1 disaster review board,
        167, 168–169
    Apollo 8, 178, 190–191, 196, 197,
        198–203
    Gemini cabin, comment on, 126
    Gemini VII, 131–132
    selection as astronaut, 103
    West Point, 8, 40

BPC (boost protective cover), 162,
    164
Breakfast, preflight, 64, 151
Brezhnev, Leonid, 120
Brucker, Wilbur, 29
Buran (space shuttle), 253–254,
    258
Bureaucracy, 90–95, 114
Burke, Walter, 131
Buzz bomb. *See* V-1
Bykovsky, Valery, 108, 170

Canada, 251
Capcom, 63
Cape Canaveral
    Atlas launch, 34
    Aurora 7 flight, 95–97
    first American in space, launch
        of, xvii, 63–67
    Friendship 7 flight, 82–85
    Jupiter-C launch, 23
    Liberty Bell 7 launch, 72–75
    NASA takeover, 32
    Project Mercury preliminaries,
        46, 51–53, 55
    renaming of, 119, 257
    Saturn I booster test, 79–80
    Sigma 7 mission, 99
    vehicle assembly building, 105
    see also Kennedy Space Center
Cape Kennedy. *See* Cape Canaveral
Capsule, space, 36
    see also CM; individual
        spacecraft names, e.g.,
        Columbia
Carpenter, Malcolm Scott, 39, 64,
    81, 95–97
Central Intelligence Agency. *See*
    CIA
Cernan, Gene, 138, 139, 144,
    145–146, 205, 217–220, 248
Chaffee, Roger, 161–165, 169
Chaika (call sign), 109
Challenger (spacecraft), 251

Chamberlain, Jim, 101
Charlesworth, Cliff, 200
Charlie Brown (command-service
    module), 218–220
Chelomei, Vladimir N., 56, 77,
    110, 135–136, 148–150, 160, 170
Chimpanzee, 55, 63, 66, 69, 81
China, 13, 14
Chiswick, England, 1–2
Churchill, Sir Winston, 7
CIA (Central Intelligence Agency),
    57, 62, 150, 191
Cislunar space, 230, 255, 258
Ciudad Juárez, Mexico, 12
Clark, Phillip, 170, 195, 208
Clear Lake, Texas. *See* Manned
    Spacecraft Center
CM (command module), 91, 105,
    143, 162
    see also CSM
Coastal Sentry (ship), 140, 154
Cold War, 7, 18, 67
Collins, Mike
    Apollo 8, 178, 200
    Apollo 11, xiii, xix, 205, 206, 207,
        220–221, 222, 225–246
    Gemini X, 131, 146–147
    surgery, 185
    West Point, 8, 40
Columbia (spacecraft), xiii, xiv, xv,
    226, 244
Command module. *See* CM
Communications from space
    acquisition of signal, 201
    loss of signal, 201
    radio signals, 107
    satellites, 109, 119, 128
    TV transmissions, 98, 99, 194,
        195, 210, 230–231, 240
Communism, *See* Cold War; Soviet
    Union
Computers, 19, 118, 130, 219, 212,
    237
Concentric orbit flight plan, 116

Congress (US)
  Glenn's address to, 89
  Johnson's relations with, 53, 68, 81
  Kennedy's address on moon race,
    67–68
  Mars program cost, 249
  Project Apollo support, 119, 124,
    133, 150, 173–174, 183
  reaction to Soviet manned
    spaceflight, 61
  space shuttle program, 250
  unauthorized food in spacecraft,
    126, 127
Conrad, Pete, 129, 130, 147–148,
  152, 153, 248
Contractors, problems with,
  142–144, 166
Controls. See Computers;
    Instruments; Thrusters
Convair company, 34, 46, 51, 100
Cooper, Leroy Gordon (Gordo)
  Air Force, 40, 64
  Gemini V flight, 129–130
  Mercury flights, 63, 65, 83,
    100–101, 114
Cosmonauts
  command over, 56, 60
  first woman in space, 108–109, 124
  residential and training complex,
    180
  selection of, 58–59
  see also individual names
Cosmos flights, 121–122, 160,
  169–170
Crashes. See Accidents
Crawler transporter, 141, 142
Cronkite, Walter, 175
Cryogenics, 44, 78, 79, 143, 182
CSM (combined command and
    service module), 91, 106, 193,
    196, 197
Cuba, 57, 62, 99–100, 108
Cunningham, Walt, 137, 175, 178,
  193, 194

Daily Mail (London), 62
Daniloff, Nicholas, 149
Debus, Kurt, 29, 52, 65, 79, 123,
  142, 161
Deceleration, xiv, 55, 106–107
Defense, Department of (US)
  astronaut candidate list, 37
  creation of, 12
  JPL transferred to NASA, 45
  NASA as separate entity, 32, 33
  Project SCORE, 34
  satellite program responsibility,
    21
  spy satellites, 22
Descent orbit insertion. See DOI
Design, spacecraft, 55–56, 104, 135
Dinner, in space, 154–155, 230
Direct-Ascent moon landing, 90,
  92, 93
Display-keyboard. See DSKY
Distinguished Flying Cross, 17, 42
Docking. See Orbital rendezvous
Dogfights, 16–17, 31
Dogs, 28, 48, 55, 57, 58
DOI (descent orbit insertion),
  234–235
Dolgov, Pyotr, 58
Dora concentration camp, 4
Dornberger, Walter, 3, 4, 5, 6
Douglas Aircraft Company, 20, 105
Dramamine, 211
Dryden, Hugh, 36, 61, 67, 127
DSKY (display-keyboard), 219, 233,
  234, 237, 240, 244
DuBridge, Lee, 248
Duke, Charlie, xiii–xvii, 231,
  235–237, 239, 245
Dyna-Soar space glider, 36, 40, 115

Eagle (lunar module), xiii–xvii, 106,
  226, 234–239, 244–245
Early Bird (satellite), 128
Earth
  Earthshine, 232

Earth *(continued)*
  escape velocity from, 200
  satellite projects, 20–24
  view from space, 155–156, 201,
    243
Earth Orbit Rendezvous. *See* EOR
Edwards Air Force Base
    (California), 32, 63
EEC (European Economic
    Community), 256
Eisele, Donn, 175, 178, 193
Eisenhower, Dwight
  manned spacecraft programs,
    35–36, 45–46, 52
  Marshall Space Flight Center
    dedicated to, 45
  NASA, formation of, 32–33
  space race, 21, 22, 27, 30–31,
    33–34, 43
  World War II, 2
Ejection systems. *See* Escape
    devices
Electricity, 101, 106
ELVs (expendable launch vehicles),
    251
Energia booster, 253–254, 258
Energy needs, future world
    population, 255–256
Engines, rocket
  clustered, 78–79
  hypergolic service propulsion,
    106
  liquid-fuel, 21
  multiple vertical stages, 10–11
  pogo effect of, 184–185, 190
  solid-fuel, 21
  see also specific name
England, 1–2
Enos (chimp), 81
EOR (Earth Orbit Rendezvous)
  moon landing, 90–91, 92, 93, 94
Escape devices, 37, 58, 72, 117
Espionage. *See* Reconnaissance
    satellites

Essex (aircraft carrier), 17, 194
European Economic Community.
    See EEC
European Space Agency, 251
EVA (Extra-Vehicular Activity)
  Aldrin's 155–158, 240–243
  crew transfer via, 209, 210
  lunar rover, 247
  moon walk, 216, 240–243
  problems during, 120–123,
    145–146, 147–148
  as rehearsal for moon walk, 107,
    118–119
  repairs to spacecraft during, 145
  early successes of, 128–129, 147,
    155–158
  training for, 146, 148, 210
Expendable launch vehicles. *See*
    ELVs
Experiments in space
  gravity gradient, 158
  ton moon, 216, 241–242, 243,
    247
  radiation and, 126
  space stations, 249, 251–252
  weightlessness and, 126
*Exploration of Cosmic Space with
    Reactive Devices* (Tsiolkovsky),
    10
Explorer I (satellite), 28–30
Explorer II (satellite), 33
Explorer III (satellite), 33
Explosions. *See* Accidents
Extra-Vehicular Activity. *See* EVA

F-1 engine, 44, 184
F-86 Sabre, 14–17
F-100
Super Sabre, 18
Faget, Max, 36, 65, 84, 117, 167,
    250
Fail-safe plan, 126
Faith 7 mission, 100–101

Fédération Aéronautique
    Internationale, 60
Feoktistov, Konstantin, 109, 110
FIDO (flight dynamics officer),
    220, 235
Filipchenko, Anatoly, 223
"Fireflies," 83, 95–96, 101
Fires. *See* Accidents
Flag (US), 129, 222, 242
Flight dynamics officer. *See* FIDO
Food
    preflight breakfast, 66, 151
    rehydration of, 230
    space meals, 154–155, 230
    space snacks, 95
    unauthorized, 126, 127
Fort Bliss, Texas, 6, 11
Freedom 7 flight, 63–67
Freedom space station, 251–252,
    258
Friendship 7 flight, 81–85
"Frostflies." *See* "Fireflies"
Fuel. *See* Propellants; specific fuel
Fuel cells, 101, 106, 117
Fulton, James, 61

G-1 booster, 135, 149, 150, 181–183,
    223–224, 252
Gagarin, Yuri, xx–xxi, 58–60, 66,
    227
Gasoline, 3
GE (General Electric), 86
Gemini. *See* Project Gemini;
    individual spacecraft names
Gemini 3 (spacecraft), 119, 125–127
Gemini IV (spacecraft), 127–129
Gemini V (spacecraft), 129–130
Gemini VI (spacecraft), 131–132
Gemini VII (spacecraft), 131–132
Gemini VIII (spacecraft), 139–141,
    146–147
Gemini IX (spacecraft), 139,
    144–146
Gemini X (spacecraft), 139, 146–148

Gemini XI (spacecraft), 147–148
Gemini XII (spacecraft), 139, 148,
    150–159
General Electric. *See* GE
Germany
    Berlin Wall, 77–78
    World War II missiles, 1–6
Gestapo. *See* SS
GET (ground elapsed time), 152,
    231
G forces, 66, 96, 125, 129, 148, 152
Gilruth, Robert
    Apollo 8 mission change, 190, 191
    Apollo 11, 236
    chain of command, position in,
        115, 124
    on EVA repair of spacecraft, 145
    lunar landing modes, debate
        over, 89–95
    MA-1 test flight, 46, 47
    MR-1 launch, 52
    selection of first man in space, 63
    selection of Glenn for manned
        orbital flight, 81
    Space Task Group, 36, 38
Glenn, John
    addresses Congress, 89
    Friendship 7, 81–85
    Korean War, 17, 39
    media, relations with, 41, 42
    Project Mercury role, 63, 64
    retirement, 114
Glennan, T. Keith, 33, 36, 37,
    38–39, 41, 45
Glider, space, 36, 40, 115
Goddard, Robert, xx, 21, 44
Goddard Space Flight Center, 33
Goebbels, Joseph, 1
Goering, Hermann, 3
Gold, Thomas, 159, 222
Gordon, Dick, 147–148
Gorodomlya Island, Russia, 8–11
Gravity
    cislunar space, 230

Gravity *(continued)*
  Earth's, speed needed to escape,
    200
  gradient, 158
  lunar, 233, 240, 241, 245
  variable, facilities for studying,
    257–258
  see also G forces; Weightlessness
Grav-Star modules, 258
Great Britain. *See* England
Grissom, Gus
  Air Force training, 40, 64
  Apollo 1 fire, 161–165, 169
  Gemini 3, 119, 125–127
  Korean War, 17, 40
  public relations, 41, 72
  suborbital mission, 63, 72–75
Gröttrup, Helmut, 5, 8, 9
Ground elapsed time. *See* GET
Grumman Corporation, 106–107,
    143–144, 176
GUIDO (guidance officer), 235
Gumdrop (Apollo 9 command
    module), 213–214

Haeussermann, Walter, 29, 184
Haise, Fred, 185, 247
Ham (chimp), 55, 63, 66
Hammarskjöld, Dag, 48
Harter, Alan, 165
Healy, John, 168
Heat shield, 36–37, 53, 56, 84, 160
Helicopters, 180–181, 186, 208
Helium. *See* He-3
Hello, Bastian, 168
He-3, 256
Himmler, Heinrich, 4
Hitler, Adolf, 1, 4
Hornet (aircraft carrier), 245
Houbolt, John C., 91–93, 219, 236
House of Representatives. *See*
    Congress (US)
Houston. *See* Manned Spacecraft
    Center

Huntsville, Alabama, 11–13, 20–23,
    28–31, 43–46, 104–105
  see also Marshall Space Flight
    Center
Hydrazine, 106, 118, 177
Hydrogen, liquid, 44, 78, 101, 106,
    117, 143, 182, 228
Hydrogen bomb, 19
Hypergolic fuel, xiv, 106, 118, 136

ICBM (Intercontinental ballistic
    missile), 8, 12, 19–20, 24, 55
IGY. *See* International Geophysical
    Year
Instruments
  automatic flight control, 56, 60,
    64
  for manned orbital rendezvous,
    70–71
  manual flight control, 64
  see also Computers; Thrusters
Intercontinental ballistic missile.
    See ICBM
International Geophysical Year
    (IGY), 20, 30
Interplanetary flight, 91–92, 248,
    249, 253
Intrepid (aircraft carrier), 97

J-2 engines, 184–185, 190
Japan, 251, 256
Jargon. *See* Language, astronauts';
    specific word or phrase, e.g.,
    Launch window; Mach 1
JATO systems (jet assisted takeoff), 21
Javits, Jacob, 26–27
Jenkins, Morris, 186
Jet assisted takeoff. *See* JATO
    systems
Jet planes. *See* specific type, e.g.,
    Sabre jet
Jet Propulsion Laboratory. *See* JPL
Johnson, Lyndon B.
  Big Space alliance, 54

comments on *Sputnik*, 27
lunar landing mode, debate over, 94
renaming of Apollo launch site, 119
space program under Kennedy, 53–54, 61–63, 67–68
space race, 32
support of manned space program, 108
Johnson, Nicholas, 208
Johnson, Sam, 158
Johnson Space Center, xx
JPL (Jet Propulsion Laboratory), 23, 28–30, 33, 45, 260
Jupiter missile, 22–23, 28–30

Kammler, Hans, 4
Kapustin Yar (Soviet Union), 9
Kearsarge (aircraft carrier), 99, 101
Kelly, Fred, 165
Kennedy, John F.
   Apollo launch complex named for, 119
   assassination of, 107–108
   Bay of Pigs, 57, 62
   Cuban missile crisis, 99–100, 108
   Glenn, congratulations to, 85
   lunar landing mode, debate over, 94–95
   space challenge presented by, xix, xx, 26, 47–48, 53
   space program, 59, 60–63, 67–68
Kennedy, Robert, 62
Kennedy Space Center
   Apollo 1 fire at, xix, 161–166
   Gemini flights from, 124–129, 131–133, 139–141, 144–148, 150–159
   launch facilities at, 141–142
   naming of, 119
   see also individual Apollo spaceflights

Kerimov, Kerim, 207
Kerosene (fuel), 10, 44, 182
Kerr, Robert, 53–54
Key Hole (spy satellites), 150, 180, 223–224
Khrunov, Yevgeny, 170, 210
Khrushchev, Nikita
   "City Buster" missile, 136
   Cuban missile crisis, 100, 108
   deposition of, 111
   ICBM development under, 20, 24
   International Geophysical Year, 20
   manned space flight, 56–60
   mockery of US satellites, 33
   politics and space program under, 75–78, 97, 108–111, 120
   space race under, 43, 48, 49, 57, 75–78, 97–98
   Sputnik, 27
Komarov, Vladimir, 110, 170–172, 227
Korabl-Sputniks, 48, 55, 57–58
Korean War, xx, 13–18, 39, 158, 187
Korolev, Sergei
   circumlunar flyby planned by, 149
   death of, 136
   design bureau, 56, 62
   early research, 9–11
   ICBM development, 19–20, 24
   illness of, 120–121
   Mars 1 explosion, 48–50
   Soyuz spacecraft, 86–87, 108, 111, 135–136
   Sputnik launch, 27
   Voskhod flights, 110–111, 119, 120–124
   Vostok spacecraft, 56–58, 75–78, 85–86, 98, 108–109, 159
Kosygin, Aleksey, 120
Kraft, Chris, 84, 95, 116–117, 145, 189–190, 200, 205, 236

Kramer, Saunders, 182
Kranz, Gene, 139, 140, 177,
    235–237
Kremlin and the Cosmos, The
    (Daniloff), 149
Kubasov, Valery, 223

Laika (dog), 28
Lake Champlain (aircraft carrier),
    66, 129
Landing spacecraft
  computer guidance system, 118,
    130
  deadman's zone, 238
  deceleration of, xiv, 55
  on moon, alternative methods,
    89–95, 181–182
  parachute system, 126
  paraglider, 118
  powered descent, xiii, 106–107
  Soviet method, 56, 60
  see also Reentry
Language, astronauts', 71–72
  see also specific word or phrase,
    e.g., Launch window;
    Mach 1
Launch window, 48
Lenin-class booster. *See* G-1
    booster
Leonov, Aleksey, 121–123
Lewis, Jim, 74
Liberty Bell 7 (spacecraft), 72–75
Life (magazine), 15, 115
Liquid oxygen. *See* LOX
Little Joe (booster rocket), 51
LLRV (lunar landing research
    vehicle), 187
LM (lunar module)
  conception of, 91, 106–107
  development difficulties of,
    143–144, 175–178, 189–190
  docking mechanism difficulties
    of, 218–219
  initial testing of, 212–213

lightweight construction of, 144,
    212, 232
  thrusters on, 107, 177
  see also LLRV; module names,
    e.g., *Eagle*
LOI (lunar orbit insertion), 201
Loki rockets, 21
LOR (Lunar Orbit Rendezvous)
  moon landing, 91–95, 118, 144,
    154, 176, 186, 219–220
LOS (loss of signal), 201
Lovelace Clinic, 38
Lovell, Jim, 131, 144, 145, 166, 179
  Apollo 8, 198–203
  Apollo 13, 247
  Gemini XII, 150–159, 185
Low, George, 45, 52, 168, 176
  Apollo 8 mission, 189–190, 191,
    198
  Apollo 11 flight, 215, 216, 219,
    236
  space program recommendations
    of, 43–44, 93
LOX (liquid oxygen), 1–2, 3, 10,
    44, 65, 78, 182
Luna 12 (spacecraft), 159
Luna 15 (spacecraft), 231
Luna probe, 43
Lunar landing research vehicle. *See*
    LLRV
Lunar missions. *See* Moon
Lunar module. *See* LM
Lunar orbit insertion. *See* LOI
Lunar Orbit Rendezvous. *See* LOR
Lunar probes, 159, 231, 252
Lunar Receiving Laboratory, 222,
    246
Lunar rover, 247
Lunar Star Port, 259
Lunney, Glynn, 154, 217

MA-1, 46–47
Mach 1, 16, 65, 152
Mailer, Norman, xxi–xxii

Manhattan Project, 9
Manned Orbiting Laboratory, 115
Manned Spacecraft Center. *See*
    MSC
Manned spaceflights
    Air Force, 35, 46, 51
    cost of, xxi, 46, 68
    early program proposals for, 35–36
    first, 59–60
    first orbital, 81–85
    future programs for, 251–252
    orbital rendezvous, research into,
        69, 70–71
    Soviet endeavors in, 35, 48
    value questioned, 54
    see also project names; spacecraft
        names, e.g., Project
        Mercury; *Friendship 7*
Marine Corps (US), 39, 65, 81–82,
    115
Mark II project. *See* Mercury Mark
    II; Project Gemini
Mars, 13, 48, 248–249, 253, 254,
    258–260
Mars I (spacecraft), 48
Marshall, George C., 45
Marshall Space Flight Center, 45,
    78–79, 92, 93, 94, 184–185
Mars Project, 13
Mason (ship), 140
Massachusetts Institute of
    Technology. *See* MIT
Mathews, Chuck, 115, 124
Max Q (maximum aerodynamic
    pressure), 47, 64, 83, 152
Maynard, Owen, 174
McCandless, Bruce, 228, 233, 240
McDivitt, Jim, 17, 127, 128, 179,
    205, 211–214
McDonnell Aircraft Corporation, 54
    astronauts' crash into, 138
    Gemini spacecraft, 117, 125, 127,
        131–132
    "golden slippers" for EVA, 151

Mercury program, 37, 46, 64, 72
McDougall, Walter, 24, 32
McElroy, Neil, 28
McNamara, Robert, 62, 67
Meals in space. *See* Food
Medaris, John, 22, 23, 28, 29, 30,
    35–36
Media. *See* Press relations
Mercury. *See* Project Mercury
Mercury-Atlas system
    MA-1, 46–47
    Mercury-Atlas 5, 81
    Mercury-Atlas 7, 95–97
Mercury Mark II, 101–102
    see also Project Gemini
Mercury-Redstone system (MR-1),
    51–53
Merritt Island. *See* Kennedy Space
    Center
Meyer, André, 128
Mexico, 12
Michoud Test Facility, 141
MiG Alley, 14
MiG fighters, xx, 14–17, 39
Mikoyan, Anastas, 111
Mir (space station), 253, 258
Mishin, Vasily Pavlovich, 136–137,
    149, 159, 160, 169, 170
Missiles, ballistic
    first, 4
    military vs. civil programs, 55
    nuclear, 13, 100, 108
    Soviet, in Cuba, 100, 108
    winged cruise, 20–21
    see also ICBM; specific missile
        name
Mission control. *See* MSC
Mission planning, 116–117
    see also MPAD; specific project
Mission Planning and Analysis
    Division. *See* MPAD
MIT (Massachusetts Institute of
    Technology), xx, 43, 69–71, 80,
    186

Mitchell, Billy, 7
Mittelwerk factory. *See* Nordhausen
Modules, spacecraft, 91
    see also CM; CSM; LM
Molly Brown (spacecraft), 125–126
Moon, Marion. *See* Aldrin, Marion
    Moon
Moon
    atmosphere, lack of, 241
    choosing first man to walk on,
        214–216
    circumlunar mission around,
        43–44, 118, 135, 197
    as described by astronauts, 202,
        219, 233, 239
    items to be left by *Apollo 11*
        crew on, 222, 227, 242, 243
    landing, alternative modes, 89–95
    Luna crash, 43
    lunar probes, 159, 231, 252
    maneuvering on, 241–242
    samples from, 222, 242, 247
    soft landing, first, 159
    as solar power station, 256
    surface, composition of, 159, 222,
        240, 256
    translunar injection, 104
    see also Project Apollo; Space
        race
Moon race. *See* under Space race
Moon walk, 240–243
MPAD (Mission Planning and
    Analysis Division), 179, 186
Mrazek, Willy, 29
MR-1, 51–53
MR-2, 55
MSC (Manned Spacecraft Center)
    Aldrin's early exposure to, 102,
        113
    chain of command, 114–115
    establishment of, 80–81
    Gilruth, head of, 89–90
    Lunar Receiving Laboratory, 222
    mission control begun at, 127

Muchka (dog), 57
Mueller, George E., 124, 132, 143,
    166, 191–192, 196, 227

NACA. *See* National Advisory
    Council on Aeronautics
Name That Tune (TV quiz show),
    42
NASA (National Aeronautics and
    Space Administration)
    Astronaut Office, 103, 114–115,
        119
    circumlunar mission proposed
        by, 43–44
    creation of, 32–33
    future programs at, 251–252,
        254–255
    JPL transferred to, 45
    logo of, 39
    space shuttle program at,
        250–251
    Space Task Group, 36, 38, 80,
        101, 248
    von Braun transferred to, 45
    Webb to administer, 53–54
    see also Astronauts; MSC;
        individual projects, e.g.,
        Project Mercury
National Advisory Council on
    Aeronautics (NACA), 32
National Aeronautics and Space
    Act, 32
National Aeronautics and Space
    Administration. *See* NASA
National Space Council, 53
NATO (North Atlantic Treaty
    Organization), 18, 31
Navigation, 233–234, 248
Navy (US)
    astronauts from, 39–40
    blockade of Cuba, 100
    interservice rivalry, 12, 23, 30,
        115
    manned spaceflight program, 35

Project Vanguard, 22–23
Viking rocket, 21
see also Annapolis
Nedelin, Mitrofan, 49
New York Times, The, 25, 26
Nikolayev, Andrian, 98, 109
Nitrogen tetroxide, 106, 118
Nixon, Richard, 242, 245–246, 248
NKVD. *See* Secret police (Soviet)
Noa (ship), 85
Nordhausen (Germany), 4, 6, 8, 12
North American Aviation
  Apollo 1 disaster, 161, 162, 166,
    167–169
  delivery problems, 142–143, 168
  Downey plant, 168–169, 178
  management changes at, 168
  revisions to Apollo, 174
  Rocketdyne division, 104, 143,
    185
North Atlantic Treaty Organization.
  See NATO
Nova booster, 44, 79, 90
Nuclear weapons, 9, 12, 13, 19, 100,
  108
OAMS (orbit attitude and
  maneuvering system)
  thrusters, 125
Oberg, James, 49, 110, 148–149,
  208
Oberjoch, Germany, 5
Oberth, Hermann, 2, 44
Of a Fire on the Moon (Mailer),
  xxi–xxii
Operation Paper Clip, 6
Orbital flight
  defined, 35
  fail-safe maneuver, 126
  first true maneuver, 125
  gravity gradient, 158
  heaviest object launched into,
    200, 211
  perilune, xiii, 219
  see also LOR; Orbital rendezvous

Orbital paradox, 70, 128
Orbital rendezvous
  first US, 129, 132, 139–141
  Gemini IX, 145
  mechanics of, 70, 102, 116–117
  procedures for, 153–154
  Soviet missions, 98
  see also LOR
Orbit attitude and maneuvering
  system. *See* OAMS
Orbiter. *See* Project Orbiter
Orel spacecraft, 77
Oscillations, pogo. *See* Pogo effect
Oxygen, breathing in spacecraft,
  162–163, 167, 174, 193
Oxygen, liquid. *See* LOX

Paine, Tom
  Apollo 8 mission change, 190,
    191, 192, 196, 197
  Apollo 11, 209, 224, 226
  Mars, cycling spaceships to,
    258, 259
  Space Task Group reorganized
    by, 248
Peenemünde (Germany), 3–5, 6
PDI (powered descent initiation),
  235
Pentagon. *See* Defense,
  Department of (US)
Perilune, xiii, 219
Petrone, Rocco, 226, 227
Petrovsky, Boris, 136
Phillips, Sam, 143, 163, 166, 185,
  192, 196, 197, 227, 236
Phobos spacecraft, 254
Pickering, William, 30
PLSS (portable life support
  system), 213, 216, 240
Pogo effect, 128, 184–185, 190, 211,
  217
Popovich, Pavel, 98
Portable life support system. *See*
  PLSS

Powered descent initiation. *See*
    PDI
Powers, Gary, 22, 97
Powers, John (Shorty), 71, 81, 97
Pravda (Soviet newspaper), 110–111,
    136, 210
Press relations
    astronauts', 39, 41, 72, 206–207
    candidness in, 71, 101
    regarding moon landing mission,
        222
    NASA, 47, 52, 81, 109
    see also specific publication
Project Adam, 35–36
Project Apollo
    announced, 47
    Apollo 1, xxi, 161–169, 222
    Apollo 4, 175
    Apollo 5, 177–178
    Apollo 6, 184–185
    Apollo 7, 175, 178, 189, 193–194
    Apollo 8, 178, 185, 189–191, 196,
        197, 198–203, 205
    Apollo 9, 178, 205, 211–214
    Apollo 10, 205–206, 217–220
    Apollo 11, xiii–xvii, 205–207,
        214–216, 220–223, 224–246
    Apollo 12, 248
    Apollo 13, 247
    Apollo 14, 247
    Apollo 17, 248
    choosing first man on moon,
        214–216
    contractors, difficulties with,
        142–144, 166
    design phase, 104–107
    launch complex, 119, 141–142
    lunar landing modes debated,
        89–95
    lunar module flaws, 175–178,
        189–190
    naming of, 45
    navigation and guidance system
        contract, 80

    orbital rendezvous techniques,
        102
    sequence of missions, 174
    spacecraft design, 86
Project Gemini
    astronaut selection, 114
    cabin size, 126
    Gemini 3, 119, 125–127
    Gemini IV, 127–129
    Gemini V, 129–130
    Gemini VI, 131–132
    Gemini VII, 131–132
    Gemini VIII, 139–141, 146–147
    Gemini IX, 139, 144–146
    Gemini X, 139, 146–148
    Gemini XI, 147–148
    Gemini XII, 139, 148, 150–159
    importance to Apollo project,
        107, 118–119
    naming of, 75, 102
    spacecraft design, 117
Project Mercury
    astronaut selection, 37–43
    Aurora 7 flight, 95–97
    first test flight, 46–47
    Faith 7 mission, 100–101
    Freedom 7 flight, 63–67
    Friendship 7 flight, 82–85
    Liberty Bell 7, 72–75
    Mercury-Redstone test flights,
        51–53, 55
    program established, 36–37
    Sigma 7 flight, 99
Project Orbiter, 21–22
Project SCORE (Signal
        Communications by Orbiting
        Relay Equipment), 34
Project Vanguard, 22–23
Propellants
    advanced technology, 44–45
    hypergolic, xiv, 106, 118, 136
    liquid vs. solid, 76
    lunar landing, requirements for,
        90, 177

see also specific fuel
Propst, Gary, 164
Proton booster, 135, 136, 148–149, 159–160, 181, 253
Psholka (dog), 57
Public relations. *See* Press relations

Quarantine, 222, 245–246

R-7 missile, 24, 27, 48
Raborn, William F., 150
Radar, 153–154
Radiation, tests in space, 126
Radiation belts, 33
Radio, 107
Randall, Clarence, 27
RAND Corporation, 20
Randolph (aircraft carrier), 74
Rathman, Jim, 193
Rayburn, Sam, 68, 81
RCA Communications Company, 164
RCS (reaction control system) thrusters, 70, 83, 95, 177
RD-107 engine, 10, 11, 57
RD-108 engine, 11
Reconnaissance satellites, 22, 97, 100, 150, 180, 223–224
Recovery ships, 74, 85, 97, 99, 101, 129, 140, 158, 194, 205, 245
Red Star in Orbit (Oberg), 110
Redstone Arsenal, 13
Redstone missile, 21, 27, 29, 51, 55
Reentry
    early technology, 23, 36–37, 56–57
    emergency during, 171–172
    G forces, 64–65, 96, 129
    heat shield for, 36–37, 53, 56, 84, 160
    from moon, 198
    skip maneuver of Soviets, 198, 207
Reistrup, John, 224

Rendezvous, orbital. *See* Orbital rendezvous
Rice University, 81
Riedel, Klaus, 5
Right Stuff, The (Wolfe), 42, 65
Rocketdyne, 104, 143, 185
Rockets
    Army (US) early research, 11–13
    German V-1 and V-2, 1–2, 4, 6, 8, 12, 21
    Goddard's early studies, xx, 21
    von Braun's pioneer work, 2–6
    see also Boosters; Missiles; specific names
Rosen, Milton, 93
Ruff, George, 72
Russia. *See* Soviet Union

Sabre jet, 14–17, 18
Sagan, Carl, 257
Salinger, Pierre, 59, 61
Salyut (space station), 145, 252–253
Satellites
    communications, 109, 119, 128
    Earth, 20–24
    and manned spacecraft, 54
    sizes of, 33–34
    spy, 22, 97, 150, 180, 223–224
    weather, 119
    see also satellite names
Saturn-class boosters
    advantages, 90–91, 104
    propellant, 44–45
    Saturn I, 78–80
    Saturn V, xix, 104–105, 141–143, 149, 175, 184, 196, 211, 253
Saunders, William, 84
Scheer, Julian, 222
Schirra, Wally, 39, 63, 64, 95, 114
    Apollo 7, 175, 178, 193–194
    Gemini VI, 131–132
    Korean War, 17
    Sigma 7 flight, 99
Schmitt, Jack, 248

Schmitt, Joe W., 64, 225, 226
Schneikert, Fred, 6
Schwartz, Harry, 26
Schweickart, Rusty, 179, 205,
    211–214
Scientific Advisory Committee, 93,
    94
Scissors maneuver, 16
Scobee, Dick, 97
Scott, Dave
    Apollo 9, 179, 205, 211–214
    Gemini VIII, 139, 146–147
    West Point, 8, 40
Seamans, Robert, Jr., 93, 166, 248
Sea of Tranquillity, 129, 217, 219
Secret police (Soviet), 10
See, Elliot, 138
Seismometer, passive, 243
Semyorka booster, 24, 98, 108, 149,
    253
Senate. See Congress (US)
Sergeant rockets, 23, 30
Service module, 91, 105–106
    see also CSM
Service propulsion system engine.
    See SPS engine
Shatalov, Vladimir A., 209–210
Shea, Joe, 168
Shepard, Alan, xix, 39–40, 63–67,
    99, 114–115
Shonin, Georgy, 223
Sigma 7 mission, 99
Silverstein, Abe, 36, 43, 44–45, 67,
    78, 104
Simulators, 187, 220–221
Skylab space stations, 145, 249, 250
Slayton, Donald K. (Deke), 63,
    114–115, 116
    Air Force, 40, 64
    and Aldrin, 130–131
    and Aldrin's selection as
        astronaut, 103
    and Aldrin's suggestion for
        repairs during EVA, 145

Apollo 1 disaster, 165
Apollo 8 mission change, 190,
    191, 198
Apollo 11, 225, 237
Apollo crew assignments by,
    178–179
and decision on first man on
    moon, 215–216
mission sequence changes,
    205–206
space flight, 250
Snacks, space, 95
Snoopy (lunar module), 218–220
Solar energy, 255–256
Solar wind collector, 242
Sonic boom, 2
Soviet Manned Space Program, The
    (Clark), 170
Soviet Union
    Apollo-Soyuz Test Project, 249
    atomic bomb, 13
    Berlin Wall, 77–78
    Cuban missile crisis, 100
    design bureaus, 55–56, 135
    early missile development, 8–11
    International Geophysical Year, 20
    joint projects with US,
        possibilities for, 257–258
    Korean War, 13, 14
    lunar mission configuration,
        probable, 208–209
    Mars I explosion, 48–50
    nuclear weapons, 13, 19–20

    secrecy of space program, 75–78,
        97–98, 180, 209–211
    Sputnik launch, 24
    technological superiority of, xxi,
        14–15, 20, 54
    Vostok spacecraft, xxi, 55–59
    see also Arms race; Cold War;
        Cosmonauts; Space race;
        Tyuratam, Kazakhstan;
        spacecraft names

Soyuz spacecraft
  booster needed for, 149–150,
    181–183
  Cosmos flights, 160, 169–170
  delays in development, 108, 111,
    135–136, 149–150
  design of, 86–87
  first successful manned flight,
    194–195
  lunar mission configuration,
    probable, 208–209
  naming of, 87
  redesign of, 253
  Soyuz 1 crash, 170–172
  Soyuz 2, 171, 172, 194–195
  Soyuz 4, 209, 210
  Soyuz 5, 210
  Soyuz 11, 253
  Zond flights, 181, 192, 196–197,
    198, 207
Space capsule, 36
  see also CM; individual spacecraft
    names, e.g., Columbia
Spacecraft
  cabin atmosphere, 162–163, 167,
    174, 193
  cycling to Mars, 258–260
  design of, 104
  first three-man, 109–111
  last named, 125
  module types, 91
  see also Landing spacecraft;
    spacecraft names; specific
    components, e.g.,
    Propellants
Spaceflight record, 60
"Spaceport USA." See Kennedy
  Space Center
Space race
  as alternative to war, xxi
  Eisenhower's role in, 21, 22, 27,
    30–31, 33–34, 43
  Kennedy's program, 59, 60–63,
    67–68

Khrushchev's role in, 43, 48, 49,
    57, 75–78, 97–98
  to moon, 67–68, 85–87, 120–124,
    133, 137, 148–150, 160,
    180–181,190–191, 197–198,
    208, 224
  recent developments in, 252–254
  Sputnik, 25–28
Space shuttle, 249, 250, 253–254
Space sickness, 77, 82–83, 98, 109,
  200–201, 211, 212
Space stations, 249, 251, 252–253,
  258
Spacesuits, 107, 122, 129, 199
Space Task Group, 36, 38, 80, 101,
  248
Space walks. See EVA
Spider (lunar module), 213–214
SPS (service propulsion system)
  engine, 193, 196, 197, 201
Sputnik satellite, 24, 25–28
Spy satellites, 22, 97, 100, 150, 180,
  223–224
SS (Nazi Germany), 4, 5
Stafford, Tom, 131–132, 138, 139,
  144, 145, 205, 217–220
Staging, 152, 228
Stalin, Josef, 8
Star Port, lunar. See Lunar Star
  Port
Stars, in orbit, 156
Steering. See Navigation; Thrusters
Storms, Harrison, 168
Strelka (dog), 48
Stuhlinger, Ernst, 29
Suborbital flight, definition of, 35
Sunday Times (London), 64
Sunshine, effect in space, 229–230
Surveyor I, 159
Swigert, Jack, 247

T-38 jet trainer, 138
TASS (Soviet news agency), 76, 194
Teague, Olin (Tiger), 81

Technology
  capsule design, 36
  EVA, 121
  future needs, 255–256
  lunar module, 176–177
  multiple vertical stages, 10
  propellant, 44–45
  reentry, 23, 36–37, 56–57
  Soviet superiority, xxi, 15, 20, 54
Television. *See* TV
Teller, Edward, 19
Tereshkova, Valentina V., 108–109,
  124
Testing of astronauts, 37–38
Thermonuclear weapon. *See*
  Hydrogen bomb
Theta sub N calculation, 130, 132
Thomas, Albert, 80
Thompson, Floyd, 167
Thor missile, 27
Thrusters
  hand-held for EVA, 128
  lunar module, 107, 177
  orbital attitude and maneuvering
    system, 125
  reaction control system, 70, 83,
    95
Time (magazine), 42, 47, 123–124
Tindall, Bill, 179, 186
Titan II booster, 101, 117–118, 125,
  132
Titov, Gherman, 58–59, 77
TLI (translunar injection), 104, 181,
  196, 200, 218, 228–229
Toftoy, Holger, 6, 11–12
Tracking ships, 140, 154
Training
  for EVA, 146, 148, 210
  helicopter flying, 180–181, 186,
    208
  LM, 187, 221
Tranquillity Base, xvii, 238
  see also Sea of Tranquillity
Translation, 70

Translunar injection. *See* TLI
Transporter. *See* Crawler
  transporter
Treaty of Versailles, 3
Truman, Harry, 8, 19
Tsiolkovsky, Konstantin, 10, 25, 44
Tupolev, A. N., 10
TV, transmissions from space, 98,
  99, 194, 195, 210, 230–231, 240
Tyuratam, Kazakhstan
  G booster, 149, 223–224
  ICBM development, 19–20, 24
  Mars I explosion, 48–50
  Soyuz development, 75–76
  Sputnik launch, 24
  see also Soyuz spacecraft; Vostok
    spacecraft

U-2 reconnaissance plane, 22, 97,
  100
United States Military Academy.
  See West Point
United States Naval Academy. *See*
  Annapolis
Unsymmetrical dimethyl
  hydrazine. *See* Hydrazine
US 1, 219
USSR. *See* Soviet Union

V-1 and V-2 (German vengeance
  weapons), 1–2, 4, 5, 6, 8, 12
VAB (vehicle assembly building),
  105, 141, 142
van Allen, James, 33
Van Bockel, John, 221
Vanguard I (satellite), 33
Vehicle assembly building. *See*
  VAB Velocity, escape, 200
Vergeltungswaffe. *See* V-1 and V-2
Versailles, Treaty of, 3
VfR (Verein für Raumschiffahrt), 3
Vick, Charles, 149, 208, 211
Vietnam War, 115, 119, 133, 158,
  183, 215

Viking booster, 21, 28, 29
  see also Project Vanguard
Vladimirov, Leonid, 97–98
Volynov, Boris, 210
Vomit comet, 148
von Brauchitsch, Walther, 3
von Braun, Magnus, 5
von Braun, Wernher
  Apollo 8 mission change, 190, 191
  Apollo 11 launch, 227
  early research in U.S., 11–13
  Explorer mission, 28–30
  Freedom 7 modifications, 65
  lunar landing modes debated,
    89–95
  satellite booster development,
    21–23, 44, 51–52, 55,
    62–63, 78–80
  Saturn V booster, 104–105, 184
  as scientist for Germany, 2–5
  surrender to US, 5–6
  transfer to NASA, 45
  use of Goddard's patents, 21
Voskhod flights, 110–111, 119,
    120–124
Voskresensky, Leonid
    Aleksandrovich, 86, 120–121
Vostok spacecraft, xxi, 55–59,
    75–78, 85–86, 97–98, 100,
    108–111

Washington Post, The, 224
Wasp (aircraft carrier), 159
Water, 106, 117
Weapons, nuclear. See Nuclear
    weapons
Webb, James
  Apollo 1 disaster, 166
  Apollo 8 mission change, 191–192
  congressional support for space
    program, 127, 133, 150,
    173–174
  Gemini management team, 124

lunar landing method, debate
    over, 90, 94
Manned Spacecraft Center
    established by, 80
  named NASA head, 53–54
  resignation of, 196
  space race recommendations by,
    61, 62, 67, 183
  space walk advocate, 128
  veto of Gemini lunar flyby, 118
Webster Presbyterian Church, 239
West Point (US Military Academy)
  Aldrin's career, xx, 6–8, 13
  astronaut graduates, 8, 40, 103,
    115
Weightlessness, 101, 126, 131, 146,
    152, 253, 257
Wendt, Gunter, 64, 125, 151, 199,
    226
White, Ed
  Apollo 1 fire, xxi, 161–165, 169
  Gemini IV, 127, 128–129
  NATO forces, 18
  selection as astronaut, 103
  spaceflight program, 31–32, 42,
    69
  West Point, 8, 40, 115
White room, 64, 151, 164
White Sands Proving Ground, 6, 12
Wiesner, Jerome
  Johnson's snub of, 63
  and Kennedy's knowledge of
    manned Soviet flight, 59
  on Kennedy's role in space race,
    62
  lunar landing methods, debate
    over, 90, 93–94, 219
  negative views on space
    program, 54, 61, 67, 81
Williams, Walt, 84
Wilson, Charles, 23
Wolfe, Tom, 42, 65
Woman cosmonaut, 108–109, 124
Woodruff, Dean, 239–240

World War II, 1–6
Wright, Bobby, 103
X-15 spaceplane, 36, 103, 187

Yangel, Mikhail K., 56
Yardley, John, 65, 131
Yeager, Chuck, 40–41, 63, 81
Yegorov, Boris, 86, 110
Yeliseyev, Aleksey, 170, 210

Yorktown (aircraft carrier), 205
Young, Hugo, 64
Young, John, 119, 125–127, 131, 146,
    205, 217–220

Zero-G. *See* Weightlessness
Zond flights, 181, 192, 196–197,
    198, 207
Zvezdni Gorodok, 180

About the Author

Buzz Aldrin was raised in Montclair, New Jersey, the son of Marion Moon, daughter of an Army chaplain, and Edwin Eugene Aldrin, aviation pioneer, student of rocket developer Robert Goddard, and aide to the immortal General Billy Mitchell. Educated at West Point, Aldrin graduated in 1951, number three in his class. As a USAF jet fighter pilot in the Korean War he shot down two MiG-15s. He earned a doctorate in astronautics from the Massachusetts Institute of Technology in the area of manned space rendezvous. The space rendezvous techniques he devised were used on all US rendezvous missions, including the space docking with Soviet cosmonauts.

Following his historic *Apollo 11* moon walk, Aldrin was presented with the Presidential Medal of Freedom, the highest among his numerous distinguished medals and awards.

In a 1974 autobiography, *Return to Earth*, Aldrin described his difficult midlife transition, from having reached the pinnacle in human exploration of space to dealing with a profession that was being "shelved until further notice." One effect of this difficult transition was his struggle with and recovery from alcoholism. Today he lends his active support to combating substance abuse and is a highly visible example, having enjoyed more than 10 years of total sobriety.

Since retiring from NASA, the Air Force, and his position as commander of the Test Pilot School, Aldrin has remained at the forefront of efforts to ensure a continued leading role for America in manned space exploration. To advance his lifelong commitment to venturing outward in space, he is creating a master plan of evolving missions for sustained exploration utilizing his concepts of perpetual cycling orbits and a segmented tetrahedron design for "starcraft" and "starports." In addition he lectures throughout the world giving his unique perspective on America's future in space.

On Valentine's Day in 1988, Buzz Aldrin married Lois Driggs Cannon of Phoenix, Arizona. She is a Stanford University graduate and an active community leader in Southern California, where they reside. Their combined family comprises six grown children and one grandson. Their leisure time is spent exploring the deep-sea world of scuba diving and skiing the mountaintops of Sun Valley, Idaho. Buzz Aldrin's life today is filled with happiness as he wrestles with the challenges of being of service to his country and to humanity.